'AN POLITICS AND SOCIETY

AMERICAN POLITICS AND SOCIETY
FOURTH EDITION

DAVID MCKAY

First published 1997

2 4 6 8 10 9 7 5 3 1

Blackwell Publishers Ltd
108 Cowley Road
Oxford OX4 1JF
UK

British Library Cataloguing in Publication Data

A CIP catalogue record for this book is available from the British Library.

ISBN 0–631–20257–9

Commissioning Editor: Jill Landeryou
Desk Editor: Neil Curtis
Production Controller and Text Designer: Emma Gotch
Picture Researcher: Leanda Shrimpton

Typeset in 11 on 13 pt Plantin
by Wearset, Boldon, Tyne and Wear.
Printed in Great Britain by T.J. International, Padstow, Cornwall

This book is printed on acid-free paper

CONTENTS

PLATES

PREFACE TO THE FOURTH EDITION

This fourth revision of *American Politics and Society* is the most comprehensive thus far. There are a number of reasons for this. First, the pace of change in America and the world seems to be gathering pace. Textbooks rapidly date, therefore, and to keep up with events something more than a superficial revision is needed. Second, the early and mid 1990s witnessed a dramatic change in the nature of American government not seen since the 1930s. In two successive congressional elections, the Republicans won control of the national legislature. This had not happened since the 1920s. Indeed, if there was a fixed point in American politics it was the apparently permanent tenure of the Democrats in the House of Representatives. Dozens of books and articles were written explaining the phenomenon. Today, however, the Republicans are in control which has led many observers to conclude that there has been a realignment of the electorate towards the GOP. Claims of a 1932-style realignment may be premature, however, given that the Democrats have won the last two presidential elections. What prevails in the late 1990s, therefore, is the precise opposite of the 1980s when this book first appeared: a Democratic presidency and a Republican Congress. Americans still have to live with divided government, therefore, but it is a very different – and unexpected – variety of divided government compared with the 1980s. Few expect this change to make the US any easier to govern.

In addition there has been what can only be called a transformation in world politics since the 1980s. With the demise of Communism in Europe and the rise of a new world order, America's foreign policy role is now fundamentally different from the Reagan years. Some would argue that it is now much more complex and controversial, even if the terrible dangers of the Cold War years have all but passed.

The new edition reflects all these changes. The book has also been expanded with separate chapters now devoted to beliefs and values, social, economic and foreign policy. I would like to thank Michael Smith of the University of Essex who personally scanned the last edition to make it machine readable, and the Department of Government at the University of Essex for continuing to provide such a stimulating intellectual environment.

David McKay
Manningtree, Essex

1

INTRODUCTION

'What do you think of our institutions?' is the question addressed to the European traveller in the United States by every chance acquaintance. The traveller finds the question natural, for if he be an observant man his own mind is full of these institutions. But he asks himself why it should be in America only that he is so interrogated. In England one does not inquire from foreigners, nor even from Americans, their views on the English laws and government; nor does the Englishman on the Continent find Frenchmen or Germans or Italians anxious to have his judgement on their politics.

James Bryce, *The American Commonwealth*

The Study of American Politics

Although Bryce's observation on the relative interest shown by different nationalities in their political institutions is no longer entirely true – many Europeans are now deeply immersed in self-analysis and self-criticism – it remains the case that Americans are truly obsessed with the functioning and even viability of their political system. To the student of American politics this is a problem, for literally thousands of books on American politics exist, many of which have something important or interesting to say about the United States. Even at the level of undergraduate textbooks the choice is formidable, and almost every teacher of American politics begins his or her course with an apology for having to recommend books which provide only a particular perspective or cover only some of the ground.

Non-Americans suffer from the additional problem that the vast majority of books have been written by Americans for Americans. They therefore tend to assume a certain prior knowledge or they are tailored to the specific needs of the US educational system. The present volume was written for both a non-American and an American audience. Its approach is traditional in the sense that it covers all the main political institutions and processes of American national government. But no text on American politics can claim to be truly comprehensive; the subject is simply too vast to be covered by a single volume. This book narrows the area by concentrating on national as opposed to state and local politics (although intergovernmental relations are given special attention) and by providing extensive references to the major research findings in individual subject areas.

Perhaps the most difficult decisions facing authors of textbooks concern the relationship between factual presentation and more general comment and criticism. A book which confined itself simply to describing institutional and political processes would be dull in the extreme, while a book devoted to comment would more resemble a reflective essay than a text. The compromise reached in this volume will not please everyone but it will, I hope, make each chapter more than a mere descriptive account. Most chapters have, in fact, a central argument or arguments around which basic facts and figures are organized. Most of these arguments relate to current controversies in the literature or ones currently debated in the broader society and polity. Naturally these controversies change as the political agenda and the central concerns of academics change. Moreover, no book could cover all of current debate; to be coherent and effective it has to select a particular approach based on certain normative judgements. Whether wittingly or not, all texts on American government do just this notwithstanding that most also aim to present the reader with factual information. A good way to justify the present book's stance is to review the main objectives and orientations which other texts have taken over the last 40 years.

Three main approaches can be identified: the self-congratulatory, the critical and the functional. Let us deal with each of these in turn. Perhaps predictably, self-congratulatory texts were most influential during the 1950s and early 1960s. At that time America's dominant position in world economic and foreign affairs, together with relative domestic tranquillity, encouraged optimistic interpretations of American politics. Some political scientists, worried about continuing inequality in American society and the apparent failure of the political parties to provide coherent platforms for social change, were less sanguine, but the general tone of the literature was optimistic.[1] The system appeared to work, albeit imperfectly. Most Americans were

---

[1] The most eloquent of the dissenting voices in this period was that of E. E. Schattsneider in his book, *The Semi Sovereign People*, (New York, Holt, Rinehart and Winston, 1960).

prosperous as never before, recent presidents were of an acceptably high quality and, the problem of Southern racial segregation apart, few issues appeared to divide the country.

By the late 1960s all had changed. Poverty was 're-discovered' and the often serious inequalities in wealth and income in American society became increasingly obvious. The 'revolution' in civil rights was followed by racial unrest in America's cities; crime and social pathology generally were rising rapidly, and between 1963 and 1968 three of the nation's most prominent public figures were assassinated (President John Kennedy, presidential candidate Robert Kennedy and civil rights leader Martin Luther King). Above all, the war in Vietnam had inspired fierce domestic opposition and had helped to alienate large sections of American youth from political authority. The institutional response to these events was widely perceived as inadequate. Presidents could apparently wield power in foreign affairs with relative impunity. Congressional control of the executive was hampered by fragmented decision-making. The political parties, and particularly the Democrats, were internally divided, organizationally weak and often corrupt.

The subsequent events of Watergate and the Nixon presidency generally seemed to confirm the worst fears of many observers. If presidents could break the law so easily and be discovered only by the chance apprehension of paid criminals in the act of breaking in to the opposition party's headquarters, then how could citizens expect to hold political authority in high regard? In response to these events and to the traumas of the 1960s, American textbooks on politics began to take on a quite different look. During the 1950s, titles referring to 'American democracy' or 'government by the people' were considered adequate. By the early 1970s the emphasis had shifted to 'democracy under pressure', or 'a critical introduction'. Even those books that had established themselves as standard texts felt obliged to add chapters on race, foreign policy or political protest. This reappraisal was motivated not only by the functional question of how the system could be improved and institutions reformed. Many of the new texts made fundamental criticisms of American government. Some employed perspectives informed by radically different value positions. In particular, the late 1960s and early 1970s saw a new concern with the distribution of power in the United States and the consequences of this for patterns of wealth, income and racial equality. So, one of the most influential of these new books was entitled *American Politics: Policies, Power, and Change*[2] and contained chapters on the 'power structure' and the role of ideology in moulding the political behaviour of elites

[2] Kenneth M. Dolbeare and Murray J. Edelman, (New York, D.C. Heath, First Edition, 1971).

and non-elites. Interest in power was not, of course, new. More than ten years earlier pluralist political scientists had joined battle with power elite sociologists in academic debate on 'who rules America?' or in many instances 'who rules particular cities or communities?'[3] The debate was never resolved because the two schools were asking similar questions inspired by quite different value perspectives on the very concept of power. What this and the later debates provoked by the troubled 1960s and 1970s did produce, however, was a much greater sensitivity to questions of equality and the distribution of power. Scholars still disagreed, but they generally became more careful in their use of language when referring to the consequences for different social groups of America's particular political and institutional arrangements. And of course no one now disputes the facts of unequal power resources, the existence of elites and masses, leaders and followers, the wealthy and the poor. Where controversy continues to rage is over the responsiveness of existing institutions to these inequalities, and over the *trade-offs* which exist between the pursuit of greater equality and other values, notably economic efficiency and individual freedom.

This brings us to the third and current emphasis of texts on American politics. During the 1980s and 1990s the political agenda changed again, the new focus being on economic issues and the apparently intractable problem of how to achieve low rates of inflation and unemployment and high rates of growth and a balanced budget all at the same time. Blame for poor economic performance was, at first, placed on the enormous oil-price hikes of the 1970s. Later, economists and politicians began to question whether the system of public benefits which the welfare state and Keynesian economics had brought was compatible with an efficient economy. Government had, so the argument ran, become too big; too many social groups depended on public largesse; inflation was encouraged by excessive government borrowing. At the same time, all those social problems which the programmes and policies of the 1960s and 1970s had sought to solve were still very much there. Small wonder then that public and politicians began to question a system that had encouraged high spending but had produced few results. Of course, antipathy to an intrusive state role is nothing new in American history; it has been a recurrent theme, as later chapters will show. The difference by the 1980s was that government expenditure had reached a high level, and, although many observers were concerned at the economic consequences of this, few could provide realistic suggestions on how,

---

[3] For an extensive summary and discussion of this debate, *see* Kenneth Prewitt and Alan Stone, *The Ruling Elites: Elite Theory, Power and American Democracy*, (New York, Harper and Row, 1973).

exactly, the state *could* disengage from society. Through access to Congress and political institutions at all levels, industry receives aid, old people pensions, the poor welfare benefits, farmers subsidies, the military weapons systems, and so it goes on. By the late 1980s the Iran-Contra arms deal and other cases of the abuse of power again raised the question of government accountability. The Iran-Contra affair also highlighted the extent to which the exercise of American power abroad had become an increasingly difficult and complex business.

During the 1970s and 1980s the public policy agenda changed in other ways. In particular a number of new issues came on to the agenda including environmental and consumer protection, affirmative action, the rights of sexual and other cultural minorities and the 'family values' questions – abortion, prayers in public schools and the role of women in society. In terms of the position of individual citizens, these issues often cut across the older distributional questions such as welfare and social security, producing a much more complex and confusing policy agenda. Increasingly the public was losing confidence in the ability of politics, including the political parties, to accommodate these issues by producing coherent and workable programmes. By the 1990s, there was talk of 'gridlock' in Washington as presidents of one party and Congresses of another repeatedly failed to reach agreement on major policies such as the annual federal government budget and health care reform.

After 1994 President Bill Clinton faced a further problem as the Republicans recaptured Congress and presented a right-wing programme for radical change as an alternative to the president's policies.

Texts on American politics now reflect these problems. They have, in other words, become more concerned with the functioning of government and the policy process and how institutions might be reformed to reconcile as well as possible the conflict between efficiency and equality or between effectiveness and accountability. As a result, they are both less optimistic and less passionate than earlier generations of texts. Neither the enthusiasm for democracy prevalent in the 1950s nor the moral fervour of the 1960s is appropriate today. Instead, students are advised to counsel caution when assessing plans for institutional reform or social change.

The present volume is written in much the same spirit. It emphasizes the limitations of political institutions and of recent attempts to reform them. An essentially functionalist perspective is adopted, therefore – although other values are not ignored – and a particular effort is made to explain the persistence of political and social inequalities in a society so enthused with an ideology of egalitarianism and opportunity. In one quite fundamental respect, however, this book does differ from its American counterparts: it puts the American

experience in comparative perspective. In other words, the criteria by
which US political institutions and processes are assessed are not
derived exclusively from American history or peculiarly American values. How the United States looks in terms of British and European
values and perspectives is also involved. Naturally, this entails making
judgements and drawing conclusions which can differ from those that
American scholars might make. It is to be hoped that the result will
be an analysis that adds new insights into the workings of American
politics to add to those already provided by the vast and often impressive output of American political science.

Finally, when discussing institutions and processes, the book
adopts at least a partly interdisciplinary approach. It is not unique in
this, of course. Almost all of the more influential American texts recognize that to understand the budgetary process or social policy it is
necessary to have some grasp of economics, sociology and history.
Non-American texts on US politics, however, have tended to take a
rather narrow institutional approach to the subject, which this book
consciously avoids.

The Chapters to Come

As suggested earlier the book follows a conventional format, although
the balance between different subjects and areas reflects recent developments in American society and politics. Chapter 2 is very much a
background introduction which presents basic statistical information
on demography, society and economy. Chapter 3 is devoted to a discussion of the role of beliefs and values in American politics, and
places a special emphasis on the role of political culture and ideology
in the United States. Chapters 4 to 13 cover the main institutions and
processes of American government with each designed to present
basic information and to discuss the significance of historical trends as
well as the relevance of recent research findings in political science.
Special attention is paid to the role of bureaucracy and organized
interests – two areas often neglected at least by non-American students of the subject. Chapters 14 to 16 inclusive are designed to add
substance and perspective to earlier chapters by looking at the policy
process in three currently crucial areas – social policy, economic policy and foreign policy. Chapter 17 addresses some of the more influential critiques of American political arrangements which recent
economic and social difficulties have inspired. The general orientation
of this and earlier chapters reflects my conviction that the study of
political institutions can be productive only when placed in the
broader social, political and economic environment. Such an

approach can have costs – references to recent developments and events may lead to hasty judgements which can render a book painfully obsolete very quickly. But the cost of failing to put institutional relationships in broader context is even higher. For then the reader is condemned to an uninspired descriptive account, which fate I would not want to impose on any student of what should be one of the most interesting subjects in social science.

2

SOCIETY, ECONOMY AND COMMUNICATIONS

The Growth of the USA:
Immigration and Demographic Change

Until the mid-nineteenth century the United States was an 'imperialist' continental power, constantly expanding its territory by treaty, annexation and conquest. It was expansionist both in the sense that it dominated the other continental powers – Mexico, Britain, France and Spain – and in the sense that numerous native American tribes were overwhelmed by a technologically more advanced and populous society. It was, above all, America's economic might that enabled it to swallow up huge tracts of territory during this period (map 2.1). Population increases were also very considerable and did not fall below 20 per cent per decade until 1920 (table 2.1). Ever since then, the population has continued to grow rapidly and the rate remains at around 10 per cent increase a decade – a remarkably high figure for an advanced industrial country with a small agrarian population. Both high natural increases and immigration account for this population growth although, since 1971, there has been a natural *decrease* for the white population.[1]

The United States was virtually built on an ideology of immigration, with successive generations of Americans promoting the country as a land of freedom and opportunity. The appeal was simple. Free from the corruption and oppression of Europe and rich in land and natural resources, the United States could and did absorb vast numbers of immigrants, first mainly from Britain, then from Germany,

---

[1] Deaths and abortions have exceeded live births; *see Statistical Abstract of the USA 1991*, US Department of Commerce, Bureau of the Census, 1991, table 86.

Map 2.1 The territorial expansion of the USA.
Note: Dates under state names denote year of statehood.
Source: Statistical Abstract of the USA 1981, figure 7.2, p. 208.

Ireland, southern and eastern Europe, and most recently from Asia, Mexico, Cuba, the Caribbean and other American countries. As table 2.2 shows, a high level of immigration continues even today with almost 6 million new Americans arriving in the 1981–89 period.

In comparative context this is a high figure; for no other industrial country allows such an influx. During periods of labour shortage or political emergency, many European countries have encouraged some (often temporary) immigration, but none permits a continuing high level of immigration that persists even during periods of high unemployment and low rates of economic growth.[2] Not that mass immigration has gone unopposed. During and following the truly massive waves of immigration from southern and eastern Europe which occurred in the 1880–1910 period, opposition to what for

___

[2] Other immigrant societies – Canada, Australia, New Zealand – have also encouraged immigration, but have generally been more selective in their policies towards newcomers, especially in recent years.

Society, Economy and Communications

Table 2.1 Population and area, 1790–1900

| Census date | Resident population | | | | Area (square miles) | | |
| | Number | Per square mile of land area | Increase over preceding census | | Gross | Land | Water |
			Number	Per cent			
Conterminous US[1]							
1790 (2 August)	3,929,214	4.5	n.a.	n.a.	888,811	864,746	24,065
1800 (4 August)	5,308,483	6.1	1,379,269	35.1	888,822	864,746	24,065
1810 (6 August)	7,239,881	4.3	1,931,398	36.4	1,716,003	1,681,828	34,175
1820 (7 August)	9,638,453	5.5	2,398,572	33.1	1,788,006	1,749,462	38,544
1830 (1 June)	12,866,020	7.4	3,227,567	32.5	1,788,006	1,749,462	38,544
1840 (1 June)	17,069,453	9.8	4,203,433	32.7	1,788,006	1,749,462	38,544
1850 (1 June)	23,191,876	7.9	6,122,423	35.9	2,992,747	2,940,042	52,705
1860 (1 June)	31,443,321	10.6	8,251,445	35.6	3,022,387	2,969,640	52,747
1870 (1 June)	39,818,449	13.4	8,375,128	26.6	3,022,387	2,969,640	52,747
1880 (1 June)	50,155,783	16.9	10,337,334	26.0	3,022,387	2,969,640	52,747
1890 (1 June)	62,947,714	21.2	12,791,931	25.5	3,022,387	2,969,640	52,747
1900 (1 June)	75,994,575	25.6	13,046,861	20.7	3,022,387	2,969,834	52,533
1910 (15 April)	91,972,266	31.0	15,977,691	21.0	3,022,387	2,969,565	52,822
1920 (1 January)	105,710,620	35.6	13,738,354	14.9	3,022,387	2,969,451	52,936
1930 (1 April)	122,755,046	41.2	17,064,426	16.1	3,022,387	2,977,128	45,259
1940 (1 April)	131,669,275	44.2	8,894,229	7.2	3,022,387	2,977,128	45,259
1950 (1 April)	150,697,361	50.7	19,028,066	14.5	3,022,387	2,974,726	47,661
1960 (1 April)	178,464,236	60.1	27,766,875	18.4	3,022,261	2,966,054	54,207
United States							
1950 (1 April)	151,325,796	42.6	19,161,299	14.5	3,615,211	3,552,206	63,005
1960 (1 April)	179,323,175	50.6	27,997,377	18.5	3,615,123	3,540,911	74,212
1970 (1 April)	203,211,926	57.4	23,888,751	13.3	3,618,467	3,540,023	78,444
1980 (1 April)	226,545,805	64.0	23,243,774	11.4	3,618,770	3,539,289	79,481
1990 (1 April)	248,709,873	70.3	22,164,068	9.8	3,787,425	3,536,342	251,083
1995 (1 April)	263,034,000	n.a.	n.a.	n.a.	n.a.	n.a.	n.a.

[1] Excludes Alaska and Hawaii.
[2] Rounded to nearest 1000.
Source: Statistical Abstract of the USA, 1996, tables 1 and 2.

Table 2.2 Immigration, 1820–1989

Period	Total No. (1000s)	Rate[1]	Period or Year	Total No. (1000s)	Rate[1]	Year	Total No. (1000s)	Rate[1]
1820–1989	55,458	3.4	1951–1960	2,515	1.5	1976	399	1.9
			1961–1970	3,322	1.7	1977	462	2.1
1820–1830[2]	152	1.2	1971–1980[6]	4,493	2.1	1978	601	2.8
1831–1840[3]	599	3.9	1981–1986	3,466	2.4	1979	460	2.1
1841–1850[4]	1,713	8.4	1965	297	1.5	1980	531	2.3
1851–1860[4]	2,596	9.3	1966	323	1.6	1986	602	2.5
1861–1870[5]	2,315	6.4	1967	362	1.8	1987	602	2.5
1871–1880	2,812	6.2	1968	454	2.3	1988	643	2.6
1881–1890	5,247	9.2	1969	359	1.8	1989	1091	4.4[7]
1891–1900	3,688	5.3	1970	373	1.8	1990	1536	6.1
1901–1910	8,795	10.4	1971	370	1.8	1991	1827	7.2
1911–1920	5,736	5.7	1972	385	1.8	1992	974	3.8
1921–1930	4,107	3.5	1973	400	1.9	1993	904	3.5
1931–1940	1,528	0.4	1974	395	1.9	1994	804	3.1
1941–1950	1,035	0.7	1975	386	1.8			

[1] Annual rate per 1000 US population. Rate computed by dividing sum of annual immigration totals by sum of annual US population totals for same number of years.
[2] 1 Oct. 1819–30 Sept. 1830.
[3] 1 Oct. 1830–1 Dec. 1840.
[4] Calendar years.
[5] 1 Jan. 1861–30 June 1870.
[6] Includes transition quarter, 1 July to 30 Sept. 1976.
[7] Includes persons granted residence under the 'amnesty' programme of the 1986 Immigration Reform and Control Act.
Source: Statistical Abstract of the USA, 1996, table 5.

many Americans represented an 'invasion' by alien cultures was fierce and finally culminated in the 1924 Immigration Act. This law specifically discriminated against southern and eastern Europe by fixing national immigration quotas favouring immigrants from Britain and Canada. Immigration fell dramatically during the 1930s and 1940s as depression and war took their toll on economic opportunity and on freedom of movement.

With immigration increasing once more after 1950, criticism of the patent biases in immigration law intensified, and in 1965 a new law was adopted with fairer, more balanced quotas. Nonetheless, following amendments in 1965 and 1980, a total annual maximum of 270,000 (excluding dependants of US citizens) was set which, together with a permitted total of up to 50,000 refugees, is still a relatively high figure.

Since about 1970 the immigration controversy has been fuelled anew by substantial illegal immigration, mainly from Mexico, and by

Plate 2.1 Immigrants leaving Ellis Island, waiting for ferry to New York *c.* 1900.

the social tensions that large numbers of Cuban, Haitian and central American newcomers have brought, particularly to California and Florida. Illegal immigration has accelerated as poorer Mexicans have sought employment across a long and poorly policed border. Estimates of the numbers involved vary widely, but are at least in the low millions. In 1994 voters in California approved an initiative (Proposition 187) which denied welfare and other state benefits to illegal immigrants. Very generally Republican politicians take a hard line on illegal immigration while Democrats, although they condemn it, are more prepared to accept that the government has some responsibility towards supporting the families of illegal immigrants.

In spite of these differences, very few politicians are openly anti-immigrant, and America's comparatively liberal attitude to immigration and the continuing belief that, at least for some, the USA should remain the land of opportunity and freedom, still strike many non-Americans as remarkable.

As the country and economy have grown, so both the composition and spatial distribution of the population have changed. Obviously with mass immigration during the nineteenth and early twentieth centuries the country became more ethnically diverse, and although these

earlier immigrants are now generally assimilated into American society, many retain some national, ethnic or religious identity that has its
origins in Europe. More recently, immigration and high relative birth
rates have led to substantial increases in the Afro-American (Black)
and Hispanic populations. By 1995 some 26.8 millions (10.2 per
cent) of Americans were Hispanic (mainly Mexican, Puerto Rican
and Cuban) and 33.1 million (12.6 per cent) were Black. In the case
of the Hispanic population, a linguistic as well as ethnic dimension is
involved, for Spanish is the mother tongue for many, and in some
areas, notably California and the South-west, demands for an official
bilingualism grow stronger from year to year.

America today is a highly urban society, with more than 75 per cent
of the population living in cities with populations over 2500 in 1995.
A more meaningful measure of urbanism is, perhaps, the number of
people living in metropolitan areas, and in 1992 no less than 79.7 per
cent of the population was classified thus.[3] One interesting post-1970

Table 2.3 Population change in the nation's 20 largest metropolitan areas, 1970–90

*Metropolitan statistical area****	*1970 population (1000s)*	*1980 population (1000s)*	*1990 population (1000s)*	*1970 rank*	*1990 rank*	*% change*	
						1970– 80	*1980– 90*
New York	18,193	17,540	18,087	1	1	−3.6	3.1
Los Angeles	9,981	11,498	14,532	2	2	15.2	26.4
Chicago	7,779	7,937	8,006	3	3	2.0	1.6
San Francisco	4,754	5,368	6,253	5	4	12.9	16.5
Philadelphia	5,749	5,681	5,889	4	5	−1.2	3.9
Detroit	4,788	4,753	4,665	6	6	−0.7	−1.8
Boston	3,939	3,972	4,172	7	7	0.8	5.0
Washington DC	3,040	3,251	3,924	8	8	6.9	20.7
Dallas	2,352	2,931	3,885	10	9	24.6	32.6
Houston	2,169	3,100	3,711	9	10	42.9	19.7
Miami	1,888	2,644	3,193	12	11	40.0	20.8
Atlanta	1,684	2,138	2,834	16	12	27.0	32.5
Cleveland	3,000	2,834	2,760	11	13	−5.5	−2.6
Seattle	1,837	2,093	2,559	18	14	14.0	22.3
San Diego	1,358	1,862	2,498	19	15	37.1	34.2
Minneapolis	1,982	2,137	2,464	17	16	7.8	15.3
St Louis	2,429	2,377	2,444	14	17	−2.2	2.8
Baltimore	2,089	2,199	2,382	15	18	5.3	8.3
Pittsburgh	2,556	2,423	2,243	13	19	−5.2	−7.4
Phoenix	971	1,509	2,122	24	20	55.4	40.6

* These cities cover metropolitan areas, not just central cities, so 'New York' refers to the New
York/New Jersey/Long Island area.
Source: Statistical Abstract of the USA, 1991, table 36.

[3]   According to the census categories Metropolitan Statistical Area and Consolidated
Metropolitan Statistical Area. Such areas do contain some 'small' communities
because jurisdictional fragmentation ensures that large conurbations contain numerous governmental units.

trend has been an increase in the non-farming rural population. In the last census period (1980 to 1990) non-metropolitan areas grew by 18.2 per cent while metropolitan areas grew by just 11 per cent. These new rural dwellers are not, in the main, farmers, but people seeking a new lifestyle away from the crowded cities and suburbs. Indeed, the growth of smaller towns and rural areas is a general phenomenon in advanced industrial societies.

Nonetheless, urban areas are still growing, although not in a uniform or even manner. The inner or central areas of the older industrial cities continue to decline, although during the 1980s a number of these cities experienced a revival of their downtown areas. As table 2.3 shows, there have been some quite dramatic changes in the distribution of population among the largest metropolitan areas. Two broad trends can be discerned. First, the very rapid growth of the Southern and Western cities and the relative decline of the Northern cities. This is, of course, part of the 'Sunbelt/Snowbelt' divide much talked of in the 1970s. Second, since 1990 there are clear signs of revival among some of the older metropolitan areas, with the Chicago, Detroit and Cleveland areas showing renewed growth. At the same time, some of the Sunbelt cities' growth rates began to slow – although admittedly from a very high level. These figures should, however, be treated with some caution. The metropolitan census areas cover large urban agglomerations which contain within them many variations. Within the Detroit region, for example, the central part of the city of Detroit continues to decline while many of the surrounding suburbs, towns and cities are growing quite rapidly.

By the late 1980s some commentators were characterizing the United States as having a 'bi-coastal' economy with booming East and West coasts and a relatively depressed Midwest. Such labels were premature, however. By 1997, some parts of the coastal economies – for instance the Boston area – were in minor relative decline, while the economy of the Midwest experienced something of a renaissance. What we can say is that there is a continuing drift of population to the South and to the West. At the same time, local and regional economies are vulnerable to the vagaries of economic change with those areas that are most dependent on a single industry (agriculture, oil, steel) being the most likely to be the victims of a boom/bust cycle.

Americans are also getting older. The percentage of over 65-year-olds in the population has increased dramatically over the last 60 years as medical care has improved and the birth rate has fallen. In 1920 only 4.7 per cent of the population was over 65, but by 1995 this figure had risen to 12.7 per cent. Both the size of the Sunbelt and the 'ageing of America' have important political consequences which later chapters will catalogue.

From very humble beginnings the American economy had grown to the world's largest by the end of the nineteenth century, and by 1945 the United States had established an effective global hegemony in economic affairs. America's per capita income was easily the highest in the world for a large country, and the economy had achieved a remarkable degree of self-sufficiency. By 1996 the economy had grown to a staggering 7 trillion dollars and per capita income exceeded $25,000. As the economy has grown so there has been a shift, first out of agricultural employment to manufacturing and, most recently, out of manufacturing into service industries. By 1996 less than 3 per cent of the labour-force was employed in agriculture – even though the USA is the world's largest food producer. Of the non-agricultural labour-force, those employed in goods-related jobs (mining, construction and manufacturing) fell from 37.7 per cent in 1960 to 23 per cent in 1994 while service-sector jobs increased to over 70 per cent of the total. With most Americans working in the service sector, talk of a post-industrial society is not entirely misplaced[4] – although it is only through great productivity advances in agriculture and manufacturing that the economy is able to sustain such a diversity of service-sector jobs.

In spite of these advances, the American economy began to experience difficulties in the early 1970s. Some of these derived from world economic problems, but others were a result of peculiarly American circumstances. Very generally, US productivity increases did not keep pace with those of major competing countries. Concern at the apparent 'deindustrialization' of the US increased perceptibly during the early 1980s as unemployment rose and industrial output fell. Between 1982 and 1989, however, the economy recovered well, with unemployment and inflation falling rapidly (table 2.4), and US productivity rates improving in relation to those of other countries, with the notable exception of Japan. But much of this new growth was in the service sector, which generated mainly low-paid skilled jobs.

By the early 1990s the economy had slowed once again with unemployment rising to 7.4 per cent (table 2.4). There was general acceptance that the recession of the early 1990s resulted in part from excessive borrowing (by the government and individuals) during the 1980s. Indeed, by 1992 there was an emerging consensus that the boom of the 1980s had been built on very shaky foundations. US investment levels had remained relatively low, and few American families had seen their real incomes rise during the decade. Indeed, the

---

[4]   *See* Daniel Bell, *The Coming of Post Industrial Society*, (London, Heinemann, 1974) for a discussion of this theme.

Table 2.4 US unemployment and inflation, 1960–96

	Annual percentage change in the consumer price index	Unemployment (percentage of total civilian work-force)
1960	1.6	5.5
1965	1.7	4.5
1970	5.9	5.0
1975	9.1	8.3
1980	13.5	7.2
1982	6.1	9.7
1984	4.3	7.5
1986	2.0	7.0
1988	4.4	5.5
1989	4.6	5.3
1990	6.1	5.5
1991	3.1	6.7
1992	2.9	7.4
1993	3.0	6.8
1994	2.7	6.1
1995	2.7	5.8
1996	3.0	5.3

Source: Economic Report of the President, 1995, The Economist, 9 November 1996 (for 1996).

poorest 20 per cent of families saw their incomes decline (figure 2.1). This fact, above all, led to a major reappraisal of the role of government in the economy during the 1990s. A new consensus emerged on the need for fiscal rectitude – an imperative that happily coincided with a long and steady economic recovery between 1993 and 1997. Unemployment fell (table 2.4) although the long-term decline in real wages was arrested, if not reversed.

As we will discover in later chapters, governments have become increasingly involved in the economy both by attempting to pull broad levers of macro-economic management and through more detailed micro-intervention into the activities of individual sectors, regions and corporations. By 1995, 35 per cent of GNP was accounted for by public spending – a very high figure in historical perspective, although a lower figure than for most comparable countries. So, although government now plays a more intrusive role, the United States remains a country where, in comparative terms, the market and large corporations continue to play the major part in the distribution of resources. In the US, however, defence spending takes a high percentage of GNP. We will return to these themes in later chapters.

One final point on the economy is that, with the relative decline of American hegemony, the United States has become more interdependent with the economies of other countries. Over 18 per cent of GNP is now accounted for by exports and imports, up from only 10 per cent in 1960. No administration can afford, therefore, to ignore the

Figure 2.1 Changes in family-income growth by percentile, 1947–89

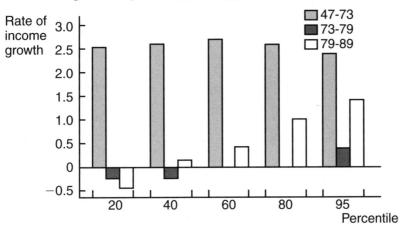

Source: Paul Krugman, *Peddling Prosperity: Economic Sense and Nonsense in the Age of Diminished Expectations* (New York, Norton, 1994), p. 131.

rest of the world. American governments and corporations have a direct interest in maintaining a stable and prosperous international trading environment. Indeed, the relative decline of American economic power has put new pressures on US domestic institutional arrangements. Later chapters will examine this problem in some detail.

Social Structure

One of the most fundamental questions in social science is the relationship between social structure and political activity. In most countries social class, religion, language or region are important determinants of how people think and behave in relation to political authority. The purpose of this section is, therefore, to provide some background on American society as a prelude to our later analysis of political attitudes and behaviour.

Income and wealth

The study of social class in the USA is often influenced by the absence of a coherent working-class or socialist political movement. Americans are supposed to be essentially middle class eschewing both the working-class and aristocratic values associated with many European countries. By many objective indicators the United States should, indeed, have a predominantly middle-class culture. In 1993 more than 45 per cent of all workers were in professional, technical, managerial or administrative jobs. Only 30 per cent of all workers were in blue-collar jobs, with a further 22 per cent in service jobs and 3 per cent in farm employment.[5] Americans are also highly educated and enjoy a very high level of home ownership, two indicators commonly employed to measure social class. In 1993 80 per cent of all 18-year-olds had achieved a high school certificate, and of these approximately 30 per cent went on to complete of four-year undergraduate degree, a very high percentage in cross-national context. As notable are the housing figures, over 60 per cent of all housing units being owner occupied. Another measure of the middle-class nature of American society is the high level of stock (share) ownership in corporations. No less than one in five American families owns stock, dramatically more than in most developed countries, although most stock holders own less than $15,000's worth of equity.

Yet some sociologists have questioned these 'objective' indicators, arguing that the relationship between employed and employer is little different for white- and blue-collar workers.[6] Moreover, these figures tell us nothing about the distribution of wealth and income, or about the continuing existence of many truly poor Americans. In fact, most measures place the United States at or near the bottom end of income and wealth inequalities, when comparisons across countries are made. There has also been a trend towards increasing inequality of incomes in the US over the last 15 years. As fig. 2.1 graphically illustrates, the poorest 20 per cent of the population have suffered falls in income in the decade to 1989 while the richest 20 per cent experienced increased income.

These figures do not always translate into increased levels of poverty. In fact, measuring the number of poor people in the USA is difficult. Poverty is a relative concept and it is extraordinarily hard to measure accurately. There is in fact an *official* poverty measure and there is a broad acceptance that families living below 125 per cent of this level are effectively living in poverty. This translates into an income of around $17,000 for a family of four in 1992. As can be seen from table 2.5 the incidence of poverty has remained roughly at around 15 to 17 per cent of the population since 1980. The biggest single drop in recent years occurred between 1960 and 1966 when many of today's social programmes were first enacted.

No matter which way it is measured one thing is certain: America does have a large population of poor people; not perhaps poor in the

[5] This is a narrower category than that implied by service *sector*, and includes workers in catering and domestic service.

[6] For a discussion of this point *see* Ira Katznelson and Mark Kesselman, *The Politics of Power*, (New York, Harcourt Brace Jovanovich, 1987).

Table 2.5 Families below poverty level and below 125 per cent of poverty level: 1960–92

| Year | Number below poverty level (1000) | | | | Per cent below poverty level | | | | Below 125 per cent of poverty level | |
	All races[1]	White	Black	His- panic[2]	All races[1]	White	Black	His- panic[2]	Number (1000)	Per cent
1960	8,243	6,115	n.a.	n.a.	18.1	14.9	n.a.	n.a.	11,525	25.4
1970	5,260	3,708	1,481	n.a.	10.1	8.0	29.5	n.a.	7,516	14.4
1974	4,922	3,352	1,479	526	8.8	6.8	26.9	21.2	7,195	12.9
1975	5,450	3,838	1,513	627	9.7	7.7	27.1	25.1	7,974	14.2
1976	5,311	3,560	1,617	598	9.4	7.1	27.9	23.1	7,647	13.5
1977	5,311	3,540	1,637	591	9.3	7.0	28.2	21.4	7,713	13.5
1978	5,280	3,523	1,622	559	9.1	6.9	27.5	20.4	7,417	12.8
1979	5,461	3,581	1,722	614	9.2	6.9	27.8	20.3	7,784	13.1
1980	6,217	4,195	1,826	751	10.3	8.0	28.9	23.2	8,764	14.5
1981	6,851	4,670	1,972	792	11.2	8.8	30.8	24.0	9,568	15.7
1982	7,512	5,118	2,458	916	12.2	9.6	33.0	27.2	10,279	16.7
1983	7,647	5,220	2,161	981	12.3	9.7	32.3	25.9	10,358	16.7
1984	7,277	4,925	2,094	991	11.6	9.1	30.9	25.2	9,901	15.8
1985	7,223	4,983	1,983	1,074	11.4	9.1	28.7	25.5	9,753	15.3
1986	7,023	4,811	1,987	1,085	10.9	8.6	28.0	24.7	9,476	14.7
1987	7,005	4,567	2,117	1,168	10.7	8.1	29.4	25.5	9,338	14.3
1988	6,874	4,471	2,089	1,141	10.4	7.9	28.2	23.7	9,284	14.1
1989	6,784	4,409	2,077	1,133	10.3	7.8	27.8	23.4	9,267	14.0
1990	7,098	4,622	2,193	1,244	10.7	8.1	29.3	25.0	9,564	14.4
1991	7,712	5,022	2,343	1,372	11.5	8.8	30.4	26.5	10,244	15.3
1992	8,144	5,255	2,484	1,529	11.9	9.1	31.1	26.7	10,859	16.1
1993	8,393	5,452	2,499	1,625	12.3	9.4	31.1	27.3	11,203	16.4
1994	8,053	5,312	2,212	1,724	11.6	9.9	27.3	27.8	10,721	15.5

n.a. Not available.
[1] Includes other races not shown separately.
[2] Persons of Hispanic origin may be of any race.
Source: Statistical Abstract of the United States, 1994, Washington DC 1995, table 735.

sense of living below subsistence level, but certainly poor in the sense of having little hope of full-time, secure employment and access to good housing and an acceptable living environment.

Of course poverty is not randomly scattered throughout the country. Its incidence is highest in the Southern states and in rural and inner-city areas. Blacks and one-parent families headed by women are also greatly overrepresented among the poor (table 2.6). We will return to this point later.

In spite of these inequalities, most of which have been characteristics of American society for many generations, class has not emerged as a major social cleavage in American politics. True, there have been occasions when at least the embryo of a national working-class or populist movement could be identified. And in particular geographical areas, class-based parties have achieved some considerable success. But their impact has been limited. Compared with the effects of radical movements on the national politics of other countries, it has

Table 2.6 Social and economic characteristics of the white and Black populations: 1980–93

| | Number (1,000) | | | | | | Percentage distribution | | | |
| | White | | | Black | | | White | | Black | |
Characteristic	1980	1990	1993	1980	1990	1993	1980	1993	1980	1993
Total persons	**191,908**	**206,983**	**211,955**	**26,033**	**30,392**	**32,036**	**100.0**	**100.0**	**100.0**	**100.0**
Under 5 years old	13,307	15,161	15,611	2,444	2,932	3,262	6.9	7.4	9.4	10.2
5 to 14 years old	28,828	28,405	29,543	5,190	5,546	5,837	15.0	13.9	19.9	18.2
15 to 44 years old	88,570	96,656	96,423	12,247	14,660	15,180	46.2	45.5	47.0	47.4
45 to 64 years old	39,302	40,282	42,876	4,112	4,766	5,088	20.5	20.2	15.8	15.9
65 years old and over	21,898	26,479	27,501	2,040	2,487	2,880	11.4	13.0	7.8	8.3
Years of school completed										
Persons 25 years old and over	**114,763**	**134,687**	**139,019**	**12,927**	**16,751**	**17,796**	**100.0**	**100.0**	**100.0**	**100.0**
Elementary: 0 to 8 years	18,738	14,131	12,189	3,559	2,701	2,183	16.3	8.8	27.5	12.3
High school: 1 to 3 years	15,064	14,080	13,479	2,748	2,969	3,079	13.1	9.7	21.3	17.3
4 years	43,148	52,449	49,538	3,980	6,239	6,451	37.6	35.6	30.8	36.3
College: 1 to 3 years	17,350	24,350	32,428	1,618	2,952	3,908	15.1	23.3	12.5	22.0
4 years or more	20,460	29,677	31,385	1,024	1,890	2,164	17.8	22.6	7.9	12.2
Labour-force status										
Civilians 16 years old and over	**146,122**	**160,415**	**163,921**	**17,824**	**21,300**	**22,329**	**100.0**	**100.0**	**100.0**	**100.0**
Civilian labour-force	93,600	107,177	109,358	10,865	13,493	13,943	64.1	66.7	61.0	62.4
Employed	87,715	102,087	102,812	9,313	11,966	12,146	60.0	62.7	52.2	54.4
Unemployed	5,884	5,091	6,547	1,553	1,527	1,796	4.0	4.0	8.7	8.0
Unemployment rate	6.3	4.7	6.0	14.3	11.3	12.9	(X)	(X)	(X)	(X)
Not in labour-force	52,523	53,237	54,562	6,959	7,808	8,396	35.9	33.3	39.0	37.6

Family type

	Number						Percent			
Total families	**52,243**	**56,590**	**57,858**	**6,184**	**7,470**	**7,858**	**100.0**	**100.0**	**100.0**	**100.0**
With own children	26,474	26,718	27,334	3,820	4,378	4,580	50.7	47.2	61.8	57.8
Married couple	44,751	46,981	47,601	3,433	3,750	3,743	85.7	82.3	55.5	47.5
With own children	22,415	21,579	21,684	1,927	1,972	1,945	42.9	37.5	31.2	24.7
Female householder, no spouse present	6,052	7,306	7,543	2,495	3,275	3,680	11.6	13.0	40.3	46.7
With own children	3,558	4,199	4,552	1,793	2,232	2,434	6.8	7.9	29.0	30.9
Male householder, no spouse present	1,441	2,303	2,409	256	446	450	2.8	4.2	4.1	5.8
With own children	500	939	1,096	99	173	182	1.0	1.9	1.6	2.3

Family income in previous year in constant (1992) dollars

	Number						Percent			
Total families	**52,243**	**56,590**	**57,858**	**6,184**	**7,470**	**7,888**	**100.0**	**100.0**	**100.0**	**100.0**
Less than $5000	952	1,240	1,547	424	691	893	1.8	2.7	6.9	11.3
$5000 to $9999	2,213	2,370	2,608	899	968	1,186	4.2	4.5	14.5	15.0
$10,000 to $14,999	3,239	3,567	3,542	803	968	933	6.2	6.6	13.0	11.8
$15,000 to $24,999	8,223	8,145	8,780	1,356	1,383	1,480	15.7	15.2	21.9	18.8
$25,000 to $34,999	8,416	8,377	8,525	861	1,021	1,023	16.1	15.3	13.9	13.0
$35,000 to $49,999	12,189	11,590	11,571	956	1,110	1,104	23.4	20.0	15.5	14.0
$50,000 or more	17,002	21,303	20,685	886	1,329	1,263	32.5	35.8	14.3	16.1
Median income (dol.)	38,751	40,704	38,909	21,944	22,866	21,161	(X)	(X)	(X)	(X)
Families below poverty level	3,581	4,409	5,160	1,722	2,077	2,435	6.9	8.9	27.8	30.9
Persons below poverty level	17,214	20,785	24,523	8,050	9,302	10,613	9.0	11.6	31.0	33.3

Housing tenure

	Number						Percent			
Total occupied units	**70,768**	**80,163**	**82,063**	**8,586**	**10,486**	**11,190**	**100.0**	**100.0**	**100.0**	**100.0**
Owner-occupied	49,913	54,094	55,915	4,173	4,445	4,726	70.5	68.1	48.6	42.2
Renter-occupied	19,581	24,685	24,765	4,257	5,862	6,235	27.7	30.2	49.6	55.7
No cash rent	1,272	1,384	1,383	156	178	229	1.8	1.7	1.8	2.0

X Not applicable.

Source: Statistical Abstract of the United States, 1994, Washington DC, 1995, table 49.

been slight. Scholars have pondered long and hard as to why this should be so. As later chapters will show, institutional arrangements, particularly federalism and the electoral system, militate against minority and radical political parties. Probably more important is the absence of a feudal and aristocratic past, with all the deeply rooted social cleavages that such arrangements imply. Related is what has been called a dominant ideology of equality and liberty, with its promise of unlimited opportunity and social mobility.[7] Certainly the United States has in the main been a remarkably successful country economically. Even by the mid-nineteenth century the American standard of living exceeded that of Britain, then one of the most affluent of the old European powers. Combined with bountiful and cheap land, this must constitute at least part of the explanation for the failure of socialism.

Nonetheless, rapid urbanization and industrialization had their social costs, just as they did in other countries,[8] and the economy has by no means always performed well. During the Great Depression, for example, the level of social distress among working- and middle-class people was very high. Given this, many historians and social scientists are obliged to fall back on the explanations based on beliefs, values and ideology when accounting for the absence of a powerful socialist party, which is a subject we will return to later.

Some scholars have argued that a repressive state (mainly at the state and local levels) in co-operation with repressive private (corporate) power prevented the emergence of a radical trade-union and socialist movement during the late nineteenth and early twentieth centuries. But comparisons with equivalent events in Europe appear seriously to weaken this argument. There certainly was repression in the USA, but its character was essentially fragmented, erratic and unco-ordinated, compared with what were often quite Draconian and highly centralized measures employed by some European governments.

Race and ethnicity

As noted, the United States is highly diverse in its ethnic and racial make-up. Within the white population it is increasingly difficult to

---

[7]   The classic statement of this position is Louis Hartz, *The Liberal Tradition in America*, (New York, Harcourt Brace Jovanovich, 1955). *See also* Seymour Martin Lipset, *The First New Nation*, (London, Heinemann, 1964).

[8]   For a graphic account of conditions in Chicago at the turn of the century *see* Upton Sinclair, *The Jungle*, (New York, New American Library, 1964).

find distinctive characteristics based on ethnicity. To be sure, many Americans still describe themselves as Italian Americans or Irish Americans, but these labels have less meaning than they used to as groups are assimilated into the broader American culture. Not surprisingly, this is less true of more recently arrived immigrant groups, most of whom are Hispanic or Asian. 'Hispanic American' is a very broad category and embraces people of Mexican origin who have been in the US for many generations (some in the South Western states since before the founding of the Republic) as well as immigrants from Mexico, Central and South America and some parts of the Caribbean. Chinese, Vietnamese and Japanese make up the majority of the Asian population, although there is an increasing number of arrivals from other parts of Asia including the Indian subcontinent. Finally, there are around 1.8 million native Americans living (often in abject poverty) mainly in the West and South West.

As can be seen from table 2.7 the numbers of Hispanic and Asian Americans have been increasing particularly rapidly in recent years, reflecting high birth rates and immigration. With the partial exception of some Asian groups, these minorities are generally poorer and less well educated than the white population (for Black/white differences, *see* table 2.6). While some improvement in the status of Blacks and Hispanics has occurred over the last 30 years, by many measures the position of Blacks in particular has actually deteriorated. There are good historical reasons for the disadvantaged status of African Americans. Until the 1960s they suffered from what was effectively an apartheid system in the Southern states. Over the last 20 years, the continuing collapse of the Black family unit is cited by many commentators as a major cause of the cycle of poverty and disadvantage that affects so many American Blacks, especially those living in inner-city areas.

One particular problem for African Americans is that because they are greatly overrepresented among blue-collar and low-paid jobs they are more vulnerable to fluctuations in the economy than are other social groups. This has become particularly serious as the labour market has become more flexible and unions weaker. An official acknowledgement of this situation was made in the 1995 *Economic Report of the President* which pointed to the deterioration in the earnings of many Black workers during the 1990s.[9] Better-educated and professional African Americans, by way of contrast, have continued to improve their position in society.

Although the political behaviour of the Black population is distinctive (as Chapter 6 will show), Black separatist or nationalist

---

[9] *The Economic Report of the President, 1995,* (Washington, DC, 1995), p. 179.

Table 2.7 Resident population, by ethnic-origin status, 1980–92, and projections, 1993–2050 [in thousands, except as indicated]

				Not of Hispanic origin		
Year	Total	Hispanic origin	White	Black	American Indian, Eskimo Aleut	Asian, Pacific Islander
1980 (April)[1]	226,546	14,609	180,906	26,142	1,326	3,583
1980	227,225	14,869	181,140	26,215	1,336	3,665
1981	229,466	15,560	181,974	26,532	1,377	4,032
1982	231,664	16,240	183,782	26,856	1,420	4,357
1983	233,792	16,935	183,561	27,159	1,466	4,671
1984	235,825	17,640	184,243	27,444	1,512	4,986
1985	237,924	18,368	184,945	27,738	1,538	5,315
1986	240,133	19,154	185,678	28,040	1,606	5,855
1987	242,289	19,946	186,353	28,351	1,654	5,985
1988	244,499	20,786	187,012	28,669	1,703	6,329
1989	246,819	21,648	187,713	29,005	1,755	6,696
1990 (April)	248,710	22,354	186,300	29,273	1,796	6,966
1990	249,391	22,553	186,580	29,370	1,801	7,087
1991	252,180	23,379	189,674	29,820	1,826	7,451
1992	255,082	24,238	190,802	30,316	1,850	7,876

Projections

Middle series:

1993	257,927	25,085	191,899	30,768	1,876	8,296
1994	260,711	25,939	192,932	31,212	1,902	8,727
1995	263,434	26,796	193,900	31,648	1,927	9,161
2000	276,241	31,166	197,872	33,741	2,055	11,407
2005	268,285	35,702	200,842	35,793	2,190	13,759
2010	300,431	40,525	203,441	37,930	2,336	16,199
2020	325,942	51,217	206,260	42,459	2,541	21,345
2030	349,993	62,810	210,480	46,934	2,960	28,810
2040	371,505	75,130	209,148	51,489	3,314	32,424
2050	392,031	88,071	206,849	56,346	3,701	38,054

Percentage distribution

Middle series:

1995	100.0	10.2	73.6	12.0	0.7	3.5
2000	100.0	11.3	71.6	12.2	0.7	4.1
2005	100.0	12.4	69.7	12.4	0.8	4.8
2010	100.0	13.5	67.7	12.6	0.8	5.4
2020	100.0	15.7	63.9	13.0	0.8	6.5
2030	100.0	17.9	60.1	13.4	0.8	7.7
2040	100.0	20.2	56.3	13.9	0.9	8.7
2050	100.0	22.5	52.5	14.4	0.9	9.7

Percentage change (middle series)

1993–2000	7.1	24.2	3.1	9.7	9.5	37.5
2000–2010	8.8	30.0	2.8	12.4	13.7	42.0
2010–2020	8.5	26.4	2.4	11.9	13.1	31.8
2020–2030	7.4	22.6	1.1	10.5	12.1	25.6
2030–2040	6.1	19.6	−0.6	9.7	12.0	20.9
2040–2050	5.5	17.2	−1.6	9.4	11.7	17.4

[1] Persons of Hispanic origin may be of any race.

Source: Statistical Abstract of the United States, 1994, Washington DC, 1995, table 18.

movements have never achieved any significant success. Along with other ethnic minorities, African Americans have tended to mobilize politically within the context of established institutions and political parties. This is not to deny the importance of an ethnic dimension to politics; within the Democratic party, for example, and at the level of local politics, ethnicity has been and continues to be a significant voting and organizational cue. But the United States has never nurtured an ethnic politics based on separatism or a complete rejection of the dominant 'American' values and political institutions.

In one key area Blacks have made considerable advances: they now hold more important political offices than at any time in their history. However, an inverse relationship between the status of the office and the number of African Americans represented exists. By 1997, 8.5 per cent of members of the House of Representatives were Black (compared with 12 per cent represented in the population as a whole). Only one of the incumbents in the more prestigious US Senate was Black, however. At the state and local levels their advance is equally patchy. For, while in 1992, 25 of the nation's largest cities had Black mayors, including Detroit, Atlanta, Chicago, New York and Los Angeles, in the same year only 1.5 per cent of all elected officials in the US were African Americans.

Gender

One of the most important developments in American society over the last 30 years has been the changing attitude towards the status of women. In almost every area of social life, gender is now an important issue. Most objective indicators point to some improvement in the position of women.[10] This said, women continue to earn less than

Table 2.8 Median weekly earnings by sex, 1983 to 1993 ($)

	1983	Earnings as a percentage of all males	1993	Earnings as a percentage of all males
Males	378		514	
16 to 24 year-olds	223	59	289	56
25 and older	406	107	559	109
Female	252	66.6	395	76.8
16 to 24 year-olds	197	52	274	53.3
25 and older	267	70.6	416	80.1

Source: Statistical Abstract of the United States, 1994, Washington DC, 1995, computed from table 665.

[10] *See* Paula Ries and Anne J. Stone, *The American Woman, 1992–93 Status Report,* (New York, Norton, 1992).

men (table 2.7), although the relative improvement in the ten years to
1993 was considerable. Note also how younger women made very little relative progress in this period. Few women occupy the very top
positions in society, whether in the professions, government or industry and commerce. In one crucial area, child care, the US lags behind
comparable countries. Government-provided or subsidized preschool
places are few and far between, and child care has become an important political issue during the 1990s. In 1993 a Clinton Administra-
tion-sponsored family-leave bill was passed by Congress which gave
workers in all larger companies the right to take time off work for
pregnancy and family emergencies.

One reason why the status of women has changed relates to the flat
or declining real hourly earnings of American workers (fig. 2.1). As
earnings have declined, so more women have entered the labour-force
to maintain the real value of family incomes. They have often found
lower-paid jobs in the service sector, while the number of higher-paid
traditionally 'male' jobs in the manufacturing sector has declined.
Indeed, by the late 1990s the unemployment rate for men was actually higher than for women – although women's rate of participation
in the labour-force was lower – and this is a trend likely to accelerate
during the rest of the decade.

Given these developments, it is not surprising that women have
mobilized politically to elevate a range of issues from child care to
abortion and family leave to the top of the political agenda.

Women have also become more active in politics generally and are
increasingly regarded as politicians in their own right irrespective of
their positions on 'women's' issues. As can be seen from table 2.9,
however, they still have a long way to go.

Table 2.9 Women in elective office, selected years, 1975–91

		Percentage women			*Number of women*
Elected office-holders	*1975*	*1981*	*1987*	*1991*[1]	*1991*[1]
Members of Congress[2]	4	4	5	6	31
State-wide elected officials[3]	10	11	15	18	58
State legislators	8	12	16	18	1,359

[1] As of 18 February, 1991.
[2] Includes the US House of Representatives and the US Senate. Includes one non-voting
delegate to the House from the District of Columbia elected in 1990.
[3] Does not include officials in appointed state cabinet-level positions, officials elected to
executive posts by state legislatures, members of the judicial branch or elected members of
university boards of trustees or boards of education.
Source: Official statistics reproduced from Paula Ries and Anne J. Stone, *The American Woman,
1992–93 Status Report*, (New York, Norton, 1992).

Religion

Americans are a highly religious people – more so indeed than the populations of most comparable countries (table 2.10). There is also a multiplicity of religions, sects and denominations, and some commentators have argued that religion has been a prime source of the 'creedal passion' associated with various reform movements in American history.[11] Yet, in spite of this and the clear links between religion and politics, religion has not constituted a major social division in American society equivalent to the role played by denomination in Ireland, the Netherlands, Belgium or even Germany. Like ethnicity, religious differences are important in the United States but they have, more often than not, been subsumed under a dominant set of peculiarly *American* beliefs, values and institutions.

This accepted, the fundamentalist or Christian right has asserted itself in national politics over the last 20 years as the Supreme Court and Congress have increasingly set national (and usually liberal) standards on such issues as abortion, religious prayers in schools, gay rights and women's rights in employment. It would be wrong,

Table 2.10 Religious commitments in the 1970s, selected countries (per cent)

	Religious beliefs very important[1]	Believe in God[2]	Believe in life after death[3]
United States	58	94	71
Canada	36	89	54
Italy	36	88	46
Benelux	26	78	48
Australia	25	80	48
United Kingdom	23	76	43
France	22	72	39
West Germany	17	72	33
Scandinavia	17	65	35
Japan	14	44	18

[1] Question asked: 'How important are your religious beliefs – very important, fairly important, not too important, or not at all important?'
[2] Question asked: 'Do you believe in God or a universal spirit?'
[3] Question asked: 'Do you believe in life after death? Do you believe that there is life after death?'
Source: Surveys in 1974–75 by Gallup International Research Institute for non-US countries and in 1978 by the American Institute of Public Opinion (Gallup), Princeton Religion Research Center, and the Gallup Organization, Inc., for the United States. Reported in *Public Opinion 2* (March/May 1979), pp. 38–9. Reproduced from Huntington, *American Politics: The Promise of Disharmony*, Cambridge, Mass., Harvard University Press, 1981, p. 156. Reprinted by permission.

[11] For a good discussion, *see* Samuel P. Huntington, *American Politics: The Promise of Disharmony*, (Cambridge, Mass., Harvard University Press, 1981), chapters 1, 2, 5 and 6.

however, to argue that Americans are becoming more religious. As Andrew Greeley has shown, in terms of the most commonly used indicators – belief in God and the afterlife, and church attendance – religious attitudes have remained remarkably constant over the last 30 years.[12]. And while the preferred party political candidates of the religious right have been on the ascendant during this period, only on relatively rare occasions have they been successful in national elections. Indeed, all the evidence indicates that the support of the religious right may as often hurt rather than help presidential candidates, as the examples of George Bush in 1992 and Bob Dole in 1996 demonstrate.

Region

Region has played a somewhat different role in American history. From the very beginning the South was culturally and economically separate from the rest of the United States, and, although a rising sense of national identity strengthened North–South linkages during the 1820–50 period, this was shattered by the Civil War and its aftermath. Only very slowly, between 1865 and 1960, was the South reincorporated into the mainstream of American society. The South's distinctiveness was, of course, based on its slave and later segregationist economy which produced a system of social stratification with no parallel in the rest of the country.[13] It was also a one-party region dominated by racist and often corrupt local and state Democratic parties. But the South was different in other ways. Until the post-1945 period it was predominantly rural and poor. Immigrants avoided the region; industrial and infrastructure investment was sparse; change came only slowly. Not until what had effectively become an economic and social backwater was jolted by the rapid economic growth of the 1950s and 1960s and by an increasingly strident civil rights movement, did Southern society begin to change. Since 1960, in fact, many Southern states have been transformed by migration, urbanization and economic growth. To the casual visitor many parts of the South are today indistinguishable from the rest of the country. Democratic party hegemony has broken down although, the Black population apart, the region remains essentially conservative. But old-style Southern society has by no means disappeared, especially in the poorer, less-developed states (notably Arkansas, Mississippi and

[12]   Andrew M. Greeley, 'The Religious Phenomenon,' in Byron E. Shafer (ed.), *Is America Different?*, (Oxford, Oxford University Press, 1991), pp. 94–115.

[13]   The best characterization of Southern society remains W. J. Cash, *The Mind of the South*, (Harmondsworth, Middlesex, Penguin, 1973), p. 19.

Alabama). Racism still exists, as does a peculiarly 'un-American' resistance to change. But the South can no longer lay claim to the very special and separate status which for so long distinguished it from the rest of the country.

No other region has the distinctiveness of the South, but they are no less complex and diverse for that. Perhaps the most remarkable feature of these other states and regions is that they have not been the springboard for successful separatist or even third-party movements – a fact which speaks volumes for the strength of universally held *American* values and beliefs.

Communications

It is not always easy for Europeans to grasp just how vast the United States is. To put it in perspective, the USA has about five times the population of the United Kingdom, yet the US population per square mile in 1994 was 74 compared with 623 for the UK. From the very beginning of the Republic, communications have assumed a central place in American life. While today modern air transport has shrunk the size of the country considerably, intra-US business still has to be conducted in four time zones (six including Alaska and Hawaii).

Until the advent of radio in the 1920s and 1930s almost all news in America was locally generated. Even today virtually every one of the over 1500 newspapers in the US has a local base (the major exceptions being *USA Today* and *The Christian Science Monitor*). The vast majority of the more than 3000 television and radio stations are also locally based.

It would be misleading to claim that most *news* is local, however, or that Americans do not have a consciousness of national affairs and events. On the contrary, most Americans are reading, listening to or viewing the same national news most of the time. There is a number of reasons for this. First, most newspapers carry syndicated national columns put out by news services or by the more prominent regional papers such as *The New York Times* and *Washington Post*. Second, and more important, most local stations subscribe to one of the three major national networks: CBS (Central Broadcasting System), ABC (American Broadcasting Corporation) and NBC (National Broadcasting Corporation). Each puts out a nightly national news which receives very high viewing figures. Indeed the anchor persons for these shows have become national celebrities. In addition, CNN (Cable News Network) broadcasts national and international news around the clock.

The three national networks are available to all television viewers but over 60 per cent of the population subscribe to cable television which provides access to dozens of additional channels. Most radio stations

Figure 2.2 Media usage, 1984–97

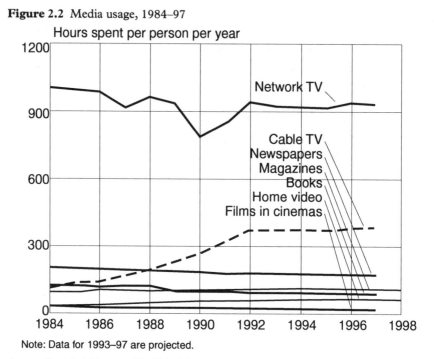

Note: Data for 1993–97 are projected.

Source: Statistical Abstract of the United States (Washington D.C., 1995), figure 18.1.

broadcast music. 'Talk radio' as Americans call it, is limited mainly to news and religious programmes, some of them broadcast nationally. For all these reasons, information dissemination in the US has a strong national dimension – stronger, for example, than in Canada. This is not to say that local news is unimportant or disregarded. It is, rather, to claim that Americans have a strong sense both of national and of local events. *International* events tend to come a distant third in terms of people's consciousness. Only international events with a clear American dimension, for example, the Gulf War or fighting drug barons in Columbia, receive full attention from the media.

As fig. 2.2 shows, the viewing of network television has declined slightly over the last ten years while cable TV viewing has increased. Note the flat or declining usage of other media outlets over this period. Fig. 2.2 does not include internet usage on which there is little information. What we do know is that there are over 30 million internet subscribers in the US (as of 1996) – more than in the whole of the rest of the world. It seems likely that this particular medium will grow further in importance over the next few years.

All of the recent technological changes in communications have had or will have an important impact on American politics. As later chapters will show, the role of the media in political life is a source of considerable controversy.

3

BELIEFS AND VALUES: DOMINANT IDEOLOGY OR POLITICAL CULTURE?

It has been our fate as a nation, not to have ideologies but to be one.

Richard Hofstadter

So powerful is the dominant ideology in this country that existing economic and political arrangements frequently appear not merely as the best possible arrangements, but as the only possible ones.

Ira Katznelson and Mark Kesselman

One of the most enduring debates in social science concerns the relationship between the public's beliefs and values and political authority. Liberal scholars label these beliefs 'political culture', or 'a historical system of widespread, fundamental, behavioural, political values actually held by system members (the public)'.[1] Political culture therefore embraces the dominant pattern of beliefs and values, which are acquired and modify and change as a result of a complex process of socialization and feedback from the political system. In other words, individual citizens acquire attitudes towards politics through learning from parents and their environments (socialization), and these adapt and change as political authorities produce particular responses or policies over time (feedback). Political culture is made up of the sum of individual beliefs and values and, crucially, it is essentially *independent* of political authority. In some systems it may be incompatible with prevailing political institutions – as in pre-Revolutionary Mexico or Weimar Germany – in which case regime change occurs. In other systems, ethnic, religious, racial, cultural or linguistic divisions may be so great that no single political culture and

[1] Donald J. Devine, *The Political Culture of the United States*, (Boston, Little, Brown, 1972) p. 17.

institutional structure can accommodate these differences. In such cases civil war may ensue or the country may break up. The break-up of the former Soviet Union and Yugoslavia and Czechoslovakia could be explained in this way. In other cases again, the political culture supports and succours the political system. Liberal scholars invariably label the American system thus. Politics and political culture may change in the USA, but they tend to be mutually supportive. Regime change is extremely unlikely in such a situation.

Advocates of the 'dominant ideology' position take a quite different stance. To them public beliefs and values are imposed from above by those in positions of power. Beliefs constitute an *ideology*, therefore, the function of which is to legitimate the prevailing system of political authority and economic organization. This radical, often Marxist, perspective identifies the United States as a country where the dominant ideology is particularly powerful:

> The dominant ideology is more powerful in the United States than in any other capitalist democracy. Most political debates in the United States take place within the framework of this ideology, a situation related to the absence of a broadly based working class movement pressing for fundamental change. So powerful is the dominant ideology in this country that existing economic and political arrangements frequently appear not merely as the best possible arrangements but as the only possible ones.[2]

These two apparently incompatible positions are not as far apart as they may seem, for when American beliefs are examined, both liberals and radicals accept the importance of similar public attitudes and values. Samuel Huntington has summed these up as 'liberty, equality, individualism, democracy and the rule of law under a constitution'.[3] Unfortunately we do not have the space in this chapter to do complete justice to what exactly these values mean in the American context, but we can summarize what is a very large body of research below.

Liberty

Survey research from the 1950s and early 1960s found a high level of support among Americans in favour of *general* statements of free speech and opinion (for example, 'people who hate our way of life should still have a chance to talk and be heard'), but much lower sup-

[2]   Katznelson and Kesselman, *The Politics of Power*, p. 29.
[3]   Huntington, *American Politics*, p. 14.

Plate 3.1 Statue of Liberty.

Table 3.1 Public opinion on civil liberties, 1940–91 (per cent)

Issue/year	Allow[1]	Don't forbid[2]
Public speeches against democracy		
1940	25	46
1974	56	72
1976a	55	80
1976b	52	79

Issue/year	Allow to speak	Allow to teach college	Keep book in library
Atheist[3]			
1954	37	12	35
1964[4]	—	—	61
1972	65	40	61
1973a	65	41	61
1973b	62	39	57
1974	62	42	60
1976	64	41	60
1977	62	39	59
1978	63	—	60
1980	66	45	62
1982	64	46	61
1984	68	46	64
1985	65	45	61
1987	69	47	66
1988	70	45	64
1989	72	51	67
1990	73	50	67
1991	72	52	69
Admitted communist[3]			
1954	27	6	27
1972	52	32	53
1973a	60	39	58
1973b	53	30	54
1974	58	42	59
1976	55	41	56
1977	55	39	55
1978	60	—	61
1980	55	41	57
1982	56	43	57
1984	59	46	60
1985	57	44	57
1987	60	46	61
1988	60	48	59
1989	64	50	62
1990	64	52	64
1991	67	54	67
Racist[3]			
1943[5]	17	—	—
1976	61	41	60
1977	59	41	61
1978	62	—	65
1980	62	43	64

Table 3.1 Continued

Issue/year	Allow to speak	Allow to teach college	Keep book in library
1982	59	43	60
1984	57	41	63
1985	55	42	60
1987	61	44	64
1988	61	42	62
1989	62	46	65
1990	63	45	64
1991	62	42	66

Note: — indicates not available.

[1] Question: 'Do you think the United States should allow public speeches against democracy?'

[2] Question: 'Do you think the United States should forbid public speeches against democracy?'

[3] Question: 'There are always some people whose ideas are considered bad or dangerous by other people. For instance, somebody who (is against all churches and religion/admits he is a communist/believes that blacks are genetically inferior). If such a person wanted to make a speech in your (city/town/community), should he be allowed to speak or not? Should such a person be allowed to teach in a college or university, or not? If some people in your community suggested that a book he wrote (against churches and religion/promoting communism/which said blacks are inferior) should be taken out of your public library, would you favor removing this book or not?' (Slight variations in wording across groups.)

[4] In 1964 the question was as follows: 'Suppose a man admitted in public that he did not believe in God. Do you think a book he wrote should be removed from a public library?'

[5] In 1943 the question was as follows: 'In peacetime, do you think anyone in the United States should be allowed to make speeches against certain races in this country?'

Source: Harold W. Stanley and Richard G. Niemi, *Vital Statistics on American Politics*, Congressional Quarterly Press, Washington DC, 1994, table 1.9.

port for *specific* statements (for example, 'a book that contains wrong political views cannot be a good book and does not deserve to be published').[4] Moreover, the level of support for specific freedoms was much higher among elites (political influentials) than among the mass public. This disjunction between general and specific support is not exclusively American; citizens of many countries would answer positively to general statements advocating freedom. Clearly freedom of expression is not an absolute value, and there have been times in American history when public tolerance of 'un-American' values has been very low. The red-baiting periods following World Wars I and II demonstrated just how limited freedom could be in the United States.[5] And, until the mid-1960s, the attitude of white Americans in the South towards the Black population was the very antithesis of libertarian.

[4] More than 80 per cent of respondents to a 1962 survey agreed with the first question, and just 50 per cent with the second. Herbert McClosky, 'Consensus and ideology in American politics', *American Political Science Review*, vol. 8 (1964), tables 2 and 3. This article also contains a good summary of the literature on this subject.

[5] *See* Seymour Martin Lipset and Earl Raab, *The Politics of Unreason: Right Wing Extremism in America, 1790–1970*, (Chicago, University of Chicago Press, 1978).

Since the 1960s, however, there is evidence of some important changes. Social tolerance has generally improved, and attitudes towards 'un-American' beliefs (communism, atheism) have become more liberal (table 3.1).

In spite of these changes, antipathy to 'non-American' values clearly remains, so it would be quite misleading to characterize the United States as a country where 'freedom of expression' or 'liberty' is assigned an inviolate status.

Three final qualifications need to be added to this conclusion, which should serve as a warning against simple overgeneralizations in this area. First, as later chapters will show, there have been quite dramatic advances in the legal protection of all individual rights, and especially freedom of expression over the last 40 years. Not all these advances have been simply procedural; objectively American citizens, newspapers and other media enjoy much more freedom than they used to. As this development can often cause governments and officials serious difficulty and embarrassment, it seems to contradict the more reductionist of the 'dominant ideology' positions. Second, the American political system is uncommonly fragmented and devolved. Some of the worst examples of the infringement of individual freedom have occurred within *local* jurisdictions with the open acquiescence of local populations. This applies particularly to racial questions and criminal procedural rights. As society has become nationalized, so such activity has become more difficult to get away with. Although this development could be interpreted as part of the advance of a 'dominant ideology', it is difficult to make the connection between less repressive local polities and the particular interests of national political authorities or corporations. Third, if we expand liberty or freedom to include economic individualism or the freedom to accumulate wealth, then there is no doubting that the United States is a free country. We will return to this theme later.

Equality

Early foreign observers of the American scene, from de Tocqueville to Dickens and Bryce, noted the remarkable absence of deference to position or status in the United States. 'Equality of estimation' is what Bryce called it, or the tendency of Americans to treat each other as equals, whatever their education, occupation or social class. This remains broadly true – although, of course, European countries have been moving in the same direction. 'Equality' was one of the earliest rallying cries of Revolutionary America but, from the very beginning, it implied an equality of opportunity rather than equality of condition.

The argument ran something like this: provide equal status for all citizens (except slaves, of course) under the law and every individual would be capable of achieving self-fulfilment. As the country developed, so it became accepted that the precondition for equality of opportunity was a certain standard of education. Consequently, education achieved – and retains – a very special status in American social policy. Almost alone among the major social services, there is a broad consensus that education should be provided out of public rather than private funds.

Supporters of the dominant ideology position claim that the constant stress on equality of opportunity helps legitimize what is a very unequal society. Originally, the emphasis was on the frontier and unlimited land. More recently, the appeal has shifted to education and all the benefits this can bring. By constantly reassuring the population that everyone can succeed given personal effort and a good educational base, the citizenry is, so the argument runs, being duped into accepting the system. No doubt there is something to this – certainly Americans have traditionally believed that their economic position (or the position of their children) would improve[6] – but such a perspective fails to distinguish between equality before the law and the material or economic benefits that equality of opportunity can bring. The former, which is close to equality of dignity or esteem, is highly developed in the United States and recognized as an important element in citizenship. Legislation designed to prevent unfair or unequal treatment by private persons and public authorities is far-reaching and, compared with similar laws in other countries, is quite rigidly enforced. In recent years discrimination against women and racial minorities has been the main focus of these laws, but the idea that all citizens, irrespective of background, should be treated equally is deeply entrenched.

Clearly such laws can be implemented in such a way that they conflict with notions of individualism. As the next section will highlight, by placing the interests of the group above those of the individual's worth, affirmative action can cause serious tensions between equality and individualism.

Individualism

Nothing more accurately seems to represent Americanism than a stress on individual, rather than collective, action. Trade union membership is low in the USA, collectivist political parties of the left (and

---

[6] Although by the 1990s falling or flat, real family incomes led many Americans to doubt that their living standards would continue to rise. This fact helped secure Democrat Bill Clinton's victory in 1992.

Table 3.2 Attitudes toward various forms of government activity (per cent)

Agree government should . . .	United States	West Germany	Britain	Austria	Italy
Control wages by legislation	23	28	32	58	72
Reduce working week to create more jobs	27	51	49	36	68
Control prices	19	20	48	—	67
Provide health care	40	57	85	—	67
Finance job-creation projects	70	73	83	—	84
Spend more on old age pensions	47	53	81	—	80
Reduce differences in income between those with high and low income	38	66	65	70	80
Agree/strongly agree that . . .					
Wearing seat-belts should be required by law	49	82	80	81	81
Smoking in public places should be prohibited by law	46	49	51	58	89

Source: Various, summarized by Seymour Martin Lipset, *American Exceptionalism: A Double Edged Sword*, New York, Norton, 1996, table 2.3).

also of the right) have failed to win mass support, and the society is infused with a degree of self-reliance which is rarely found in other countries. This spirit of self-reliance has its roots in the Puritanism which flourished in colonial and in post-colonial America, and it remains a potent force as public antipathy to 'welfare scroungers' as a surprisingly wide acceptance of job insecurity shows. For general indicators of American self-reliance in comparative context, *see* table 3.2

So, as far as the distribution of resources is concerned, Americans prefer private to public institutions. Indeed, the 'state' as such is held in quite low esteem compared with its status in other countries. Unfortunately, social surveys have tended not to ask more sophisticated questions in cross-national context, so one must be wary of inferring that Americans are always antipathetic to state-provided goods and services. If anything, the evidence suggests that, when the question is couched in general terms, Americans show antipathy to government provision, but when asked about specific programmes, such as social security, health care or education, they show a higher level of support.[7] Perhaps this is unsurprising given the much more visible role that governments, and especially the federal government, now play in economy and society.

America's anti-statist tradition has a number of roots, and there is no time for an extensive discussion here. We should note, however, that this liberal tradition has at least in part depended on the continuing success of capitalism. From beginnings where self-reliance and

[7] *See* the General Social Surveys, 1972–90, Cumulative Codebook, National Research Center, University of Chicago, 1990.

economic individualism were the very essence of the new society, capitalism flourished as in no other country, and not until the 1930s did
it need sustained support from government. Industrialization, infrastructure development and urbanization were predominantly market
phenomena. Of course, government played a role, but mainly in
response to the needs of capitalism, not as a leader and director of
investment and resources. Even today, when government intrudes
into almost every aspect of society, it is treated with suspicion by
many Americans. Again, it is very difficult to separate out the extent
to which economic individualism has been 'imposed' on the American
people by the needs of capitalism, from broader historical/cultural
forces such as the absence of a feudal tradition and the fact that many
Americans have benefited from economic development.

Two further points on individualism. First, observers make the mis-
take of inferring a general *cultural* individualism when noting the
undoubted prevalence of *economic* individualism in the United States.
Yet, as our discussion of freedom and references to religion suggest,
Americans are often influenced by collectivist thinking. Whether it be
McCarthyism, fundamentalist Christianity or a sometimes violent
rejection of outsiders from carefully protected local communities,
there is no shortage of examples of Americans moving, sometimes
blindly, in masses. By this measure the society is almost certainly less
individualist than British or French society.

Second, and related, is the fact that laws designed to provide equality of opportunity often conflict with notions of individualism. Positive discrimination in favour of ethnic minorities, women or the
disabled can mean the application of rules and standards intended to
benefit whole social *groups*. In such instances, the merits of *individuals*
are sometimes subordinated to those of the group. Hence racial or
gender quotas applied to employment or admission to college give
preference to particular groups at the expense of 'advantaged' individuals who are not members of these groups (usually white males or
Asians). This tension between equality and individualism has become
an important issue in American politics. Very generally, the right and
the Republican party favour laws that respect individual merit while
the left and the Democratic party favour laws that respect the interests
of disadvantaged groups. In 1996 voters in California passed a law
that outlawed affirmative action, but it is doubtful that the courts
would unambiguously endorse a total ban on all positive-discrimina-
tion programmes.

What is interesting about this question is the intensity of feelings
that it arouses. For, while affirmative action is an issue in many countries, only in the USA does it provoke such passionate debate. This is,
perhaps, because equality and individualism are so central to the

American creed, and conflicts between them have long been recurring themes in American history.[8]

Democracy and the Rule of Law

If democracy is defined in terms of a simple devotion to *majoritarianism* then there is no doubting that Americans believe in it. Majority opinion carries a weight and independent value in the US which is unusual elsewhere. This translates not only into a broad acceptance of the legitimacy of elections and, at the state and local levels, referendums, it also means that, on occasion, ill-judged policies and programmes have been adopted following a surge of (often populist) moral fervour. Such was the case with prohibition and, arguably, some of the tax-cutting measures of the 1978–81 period when citizens in a number of states voted to reduce property taxes to levels insufficient to provide for local services. More recently, politicians have scrambled to be among the first supporting 'quick-fix' solutions to America's crime problems. Hence, in the 1990s many states passed laws designed to ensure that repeat offenders were sent to prison for good. These 'three strikes and you're out' laws (named after the baseball rule for the batter at the crease) led to all sorts of absurdities, including the imposition of life sentences for minor offenders and the release of long-term violent offenders to make room for such unfortunates.

As far as general political arrangements are concerned, American attitudes present us with something of a paradox, for they combine strong support for the Constitution and the system as such with considerable disillusionment with particular processes and institutions. One of the first and most impressive of the political culture studies discovered that, compared with other countries, Americans were overwhelmingly supportive of the political system and Constitution.[9] True, this survey dates from the early 1960s when people were generally more optimistic about society, but there is still evidence that Americans believe their system to be basically sound (few want to

---

[8]   For a good discussion of this point, *see* Aaron Wildavsky, 'Resolved, that Individualism and Egalitarianism be made Compatible in America: Political–Cultural Roots of Exceptionalism', in Byron E. Shafer (ed.), *Is America Different: A New Look at American Exceptionalism*, (Oxford, Oxford University Press, 1991), pp. 116–37.

[9]   82 per cent of respondents said they were proud of their constitution and governmental system, compared with 46 per cent of the British, 7 per cent of West Germans and 3 per cent of Italians. Gabriel A. Almond and Sidney Verba, *The Civic Culture: Political Attitudes and Democracy in Five Nations*, (Boston, Little, Brown, 1965), table 1, p. 102.

Figure 3.1 Individual confidence in government, 1952–92

Percentage difference index

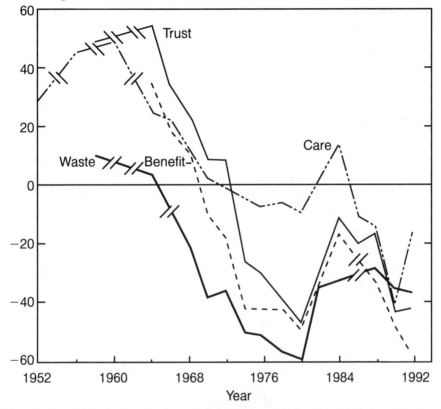

Note: Broken line indicates question not asked that year in the biennial National Election Study. Questions: (Care) 'I don't think public officials care much about what people like me think'. (Trust) 'How much of the time do you think you can trust the government in Washington to do what is right – just about always, most of the time, or only some of the time?'. (Benefit) 'Would you say the government is pretty much run by a few big interests looking out for themselves or that it is run for the benefit of all people?'. (Waste) 'Do you think that people in the government waste a lot of money we pay in taxes, waste some of it, or don't waste very much of it?'. The percentage difference index is calculated by subtracting the percentage giving a trusting response from the percentage giving a cynical response.

Source: Vital Statistics on American Politics, Table 5.9.

emigrate, most greatly admire the Constitutional framework). Since the mid-1960s, however, increasing numbers of people have become disillusioned with the party system, the presidency, Congress and the federal bureaucracy.

Confidence in government reached a low by 1980 following the events of Vietnam, Watergate and the Iranian hostage crisis. With the Reagan presidency, some confidence returned – but not to the levels of the 1960s (fig. 3.1).

But too much can be read into these shifting sentiments. Citizens

Plate 3.2 Registration day, 25 May 1918. Mrs Anne J. Curry, the first woman to sign her name on the register sheets.

may be disillusioned with particular institutions, governments or politicians, but they are not *alienated* from the system in a way that threatens the regime.[10] The institutions and processes that succour American democracy and the rule of law are highly respected. If anything, recent evidence of declining trust in government reflects an increasing sophistication among voters who are now making more conscious connections between what parties and politicians promise and how they perform. Chapter 6 will deal with this point in some detail.

Claims that the system is essentially stable appear to be supported by the relative absence of regime-challenging parties and protest movements in American history. The Civil War apart, most protest activity has been inspired by single issues (civil rights, the Vietnam War), or has been accommodated within existing parties and institutions.[11] Radical critics are quick to point out that this is because truly revolutionary movements have been nipped in the bud by an unholy alliance of corporations and government. But much more repressive tactics have been employed in other countries to no avail. Why should much less extensive measures have been so successful in America?

More convincing, perhaps, is the claim that, unable to mobilize politically against the dominant ideology, increasing numbers of Americans have turned to anomic violence and antisocial behaviour. There can be no doubting that America is a violent society (more than 23,000 people were murdered in 1994 alone) but it is extraordinarily difficult to make clear causal connections between this sort of pathology and political values and institutions. Violence and crime have always been a part of what was, for many generations, a frontier society. What we can conclude is that until the 1960s (and possibly beyond), violence and intimidation in the South were part of a Southern social structure built on racism and exploitation. Obviously this was as much a political as social or economic phenomenon. As significant is the increasing incidence of random violence and serious crime among the racial and ethnic minorities of America's inner cities. It seems absurd to argue that these people are not politically excluded, isolated and socially alienated. If the dominant ideology thesis carries any conviction, it does so with respect to the inner-city poor. For them, the optimism, materialism and egalitarianism which continue to dominate political discourse and which are encouraged by the highly commercial media, must seem either an irrelevance or must serve as a diversion from their plight.

We can conclude that both the dominant ideology and political culture perspectives carry some conviction. But the dominant ideology

[10]   *See* Jack Citrin, 'The political relevance of trust in government', *American Political Science Review*, vol. 68, September 1974, for a discussion of this point.
[11]   *See* Alec Barbrook and Christine Bolt, *Power and Protest in American Life*, (Oxford, Martin Robinson, 1980).

view is, with the possible exception of its effects on the new poor of America's cities, difficult to demonstrate as valid, while the political culture approach tends to understate the extent to which those in positions of political power can manipulate the mass public. Few dispute, however, that there is such a thing as the 'American creed' or 'American ideology', and that it has been uniquely effective in overpowering other systems of beliefs and values. Samuel Huntington has made this point well:

> It is possible to speak of a body of political ideas that constitutes 'Americanism' in a sense which one can never speak of 'Britishism', 'Frenchism', 'Germanism' or 'Japanesism'. Americanism in this sense is comparable to other ideologies or religions. 'Americanism is to the American', Leon Samson has said, 'not a tradition or a territory, not what France is to a Frenchman or England to an Englishman, but a doctrine – what socialism is to a socialist'. To reject the central ideas of that doctrine is to be un-American. There is no British Creed or French Creed; the Académie Française worries about the purity of the French language, not about the purity of French political ideas. What indeed would be an 'un-French' political idea? But pre-occupation with 'un-American' political ideas and behavior has been a recurring theme in American life. 'It has been our fate as a nation', Richard Hofstadter succinctly observed, 'not to have ideologies but to be one'.[12]

What is interesting about this ideological consensus is how it is adhered to by apparently antagonistic individuals and groups. As Michael Foley notes, 'Americans fight each other in their efforts to expand the American creed'.[13] Even citizens from as close a country (geographically and culturally) as Canada find this phenomenon startling. What follows is a description of a Canadian's first encounter with the USA in the 1960s:

> My first encounter with American consensus was in the late sixties, when I crossed the border into the United States and found myself inside the myth of America. Not of North America, for the myth stopped short of the Canadian and Mexican borders, but of a country that despite its arbitrary frontiers, despite its bewildering mix of race and creed, could believe in something called the True America, 'and could invest that patent fiction with all the moral and emotional appeal of a religious symbol . . . Here was the Jewish anarchist Paul Goodman berating the Midwest for abandoning the promise; here the descendant of American slaves, Martin Luther King, denouncing injustice as a

---

[12]   Huntington, *American Politics*, p. 25.
[13]   Michael Foley, *American Political Ideas: Traditions and Usages*, (Manchester University Press, 1991), p. 44.

violation of the American way; here an endless debate about national destiny. . . . conservatives scavenging for un-Americans, New left historians recalling the country to its sacred mission.

Nothing in my Canadian background had prepared me for this spectacle . . . It gave me something of an anthropologist's sense of wonder at the symbol of the tribe. . . . to a Canadian skeptic, a gentile in God's country [here was] a pluralistic, pragmatic people bound together by an ideological consensus. Let me repeat that mundane phrase: *ideological consensus*. For it wasn't the idea of exceptionalism that I discovered in '68 . . . It was a hundred sects and factions, each apparently different form the others, yet all celebrating the same mission.[14]

Further Reading

For a truly comprehensive statistical background, *see* the annual *Statistical Abstract of the United States*, US Department of Commerce, Bureau of the Census. A good summary of the dominant ideological position is presented in Ira Katznelson and Mark Kesselman, *The Politics of Power*, (New York, Harcourt Brace Jovanovich), 4th edition, 1987. For a political culture perspective *see* Donald J. Devine, *The Political Culture of the United States*, (Boston, Little, Brown, 1972). The classic statement of the liberal view is Louis Hartz, *The Liberal Tradition in America*, (New York, Harcourt Brace, 1955). On exceptionalism, *see* Byron Shafer (ed.), *Is America Different?*, (Oxford and New York, Oxford University Press, 1991). For an overview of American political ideas *see* Michael Foley, *American Political Ideas: Traditions and Usages*, (Manchester, Manchester University Press, 1991). For an up-to-date account of exceptionalism, *see* Seymour Martin Lipset, *American Exceptionalism: A Double Edged Sword*, (New York, Norton, 1996).

---

[14] Quoted in Foley, *American Political Ideas*, p. 44.

4

CONSTITUTIONAL GOVERNMENT

The American Constitution is the most wonderful work ever struck off
at a given time by the brain and purpose of man.

W. E. Gladstone

Good government should be sufficiently neutral between the different
interests and factions to control one part of the society from invading
the rights of another, and at the same time sufficiently controlled itself,
from setting up an interest adverse to that of the whole society.

James Madison

Almost all governments pay formal allegiance to a written or (more
rarely) unwritten constitution, but in few countries is the constitution
a real and continuing constraint on the exercise of power. Even more
rarely do constitutions survive political and social changes, invasions
and wars. The American Constitution is unusual, both because it has
remained almost unaltered since its ratification in 1789, and because
it continues as a major source of authority in the political system.
Indeed, even the most cursory examination of America's basic political institutions – Congress, presidency, federalism, the electoral system – instantly shows the influence of the Constitution. To the
foreign observer, the apparent resilience of the Constitution and constitutionalism is one of the most remarkable features of American
politics, and one which requires some explanation. Among the most
important questions raised by this phenomenon are: Why has the
Constitution been amended so little through history? Has it been a
major contributor to political and social stability? What real influence
does it have today? In particular, does it remain an independent
source of political power, or has it simply been interpreted in a way
that reflects a pattern of political and economic power which would in

any case have prevailed? Before we tackle these questions it is necessary to approach the crucial issue of why the Constitution took the shape that it did.

Origins

Most dramatic regime changes following a revolution or war are quite easy to explain. France in 1789 was seething with discontent at a corrupt and insensitive monarchy. Russia in 1917 was long overdue for a revolution to sweep away an archaic, semi-feudal order. And the numerous colonial wars of independence in the post-1945 period were predictable, given the rapid political and economic changes which World War II and its aftermath had precipitated. The American Revolution fails to fit any of these neat stereotypes, however. In fact, by some definitions it was not a revolution at all. Many of the citizens of the 13 colonies considered themselves 'true born Englishmen' who, being increasingly denied the rights which they thought all free English deserved to enjoy, were entitled to challenge the 'illegitimate' exercise of power by George III. They saw their task, therefore, as one of asserting independence from a regime that had betrayed its own principles. Moreover, unlike most revolutionary wars, the War of Independence and the eventual emergence of a new constitutional system had few immediate consequences for the distribution of wealth, power and status. If anything, it reinforced trends already underway. It was essentially a conservative revolution which, in marked contrast to parallel events in France, did not lead to new class divisions in society. This is not to say that radical or revolutionary elements were absent. They were very much present, but the real power remained in the hands of a solid middle-class and professional property-owning elite.

The unusual nature of these events stems from the unique characteristics of American colonial society. From the very beginning, the British Americans had displayed a marked degree of independence and self-sufficiency. In the 13 colonies, and especially in New England, the local community became virtually the only meaningful level of government – and even then government is far too strong and modern a label to attach to what were remarkably successful self-governing entities. Sam Bass Warner has captured the spirit of these seventeenth-century communities very well:

> For a generation or two, medieval English village traditions fused with a religious ideology to create a consensus concerning the religious, social, economic and political framework for a good life. Each of several

hundred villages repeated a basic pattern. No Royal statute, no master-plan, no strong legislative controls, no central administrative officers, no sheriffs or justices of the peace, no synods or prelates, none of the apparatus typical of government then or now.[1]

Although such communities were partly transformed by economic development and population increases during the eighteenth century, the essential independence of the colonies continued to be expressed through local governments and, later, colonial assemblies whose activities were largely tolerated by Crown-appointed governors. Admittedly, considerable variation existed between different colonies – and particularly between the plantation and slave economy of the South, and the more diverse agrarian and mercantilist economy of the North – but each colony respected the independence of the other.

This description implies a colonial rule which was essentially distant and benign, and such indeed was the case until the 1760s when the English, acting under a monarch determined to assert his power over increasingly corrupt and strident Whig interests at home, decided to exercise much greater control over the colonists. All goods imported to the colonies had to pass through British ports, a tax (stamp duty) was imposed on all legal documents and newspapers, a revenue tax was levied, and colonial assemblies were prohibited from issuing their own paper currency. These economic restrictions were viewed by the colonial elites as an outrageous infringement of basic rights. During the eighteenth century the idea that men possessed certain inalienable rights spread rapidly under the influence of the social contract theorists (Locke, Rousseau) and pamphleteers (Thomas Paine), and became particularly popular in a colonial America infused with a spirit of liberty and independence. Life, liberty and property were rights that governments were obliged to protect through the representation of the people in parliaments and assemblies. And should those assemblies fail to fulfil their contractual obligations to the people, then elections would ensure the incumbency of new representatives charged with carrying out the people's wishes. A monarch exercising executive power outside any representative mechanism was clearly not legitimate.

While this rather sophisticated view of events was probably held only by educated elites, the smallholders and artisans who made up the bulk of the population did have some notion of individual rights and were, by any European standard, highly independent and assertive. Indeed, for more than 100 years up to the Revolution, acts

---

[1] Sam Bass Warner, *The Urban Wilderness: A History of the American City*, (New York, Harper and Row, 1972), p. 8.

of political (usually mob) violence were quite common, as they were in England. Most people with some stake in society – a farm or other property, or a valuable manual or intellectual skill – were quite used to resorting to extra-legal methods should their grievances be ignored by established political channels. Given this tradition, a growing sense of being independent colonists which economic growth and better communications had brought, and the sudden change in English policy, outbreaks of armed resistance were almost to be expected. In 1774 the colonial assemblies sent delegates to a national Continental Congress – the first real assertion of national independence by the colonists. By 1775 fighting had broken out in Massachusetts, and in 1776 the Continental Congress adopted the Declaration of

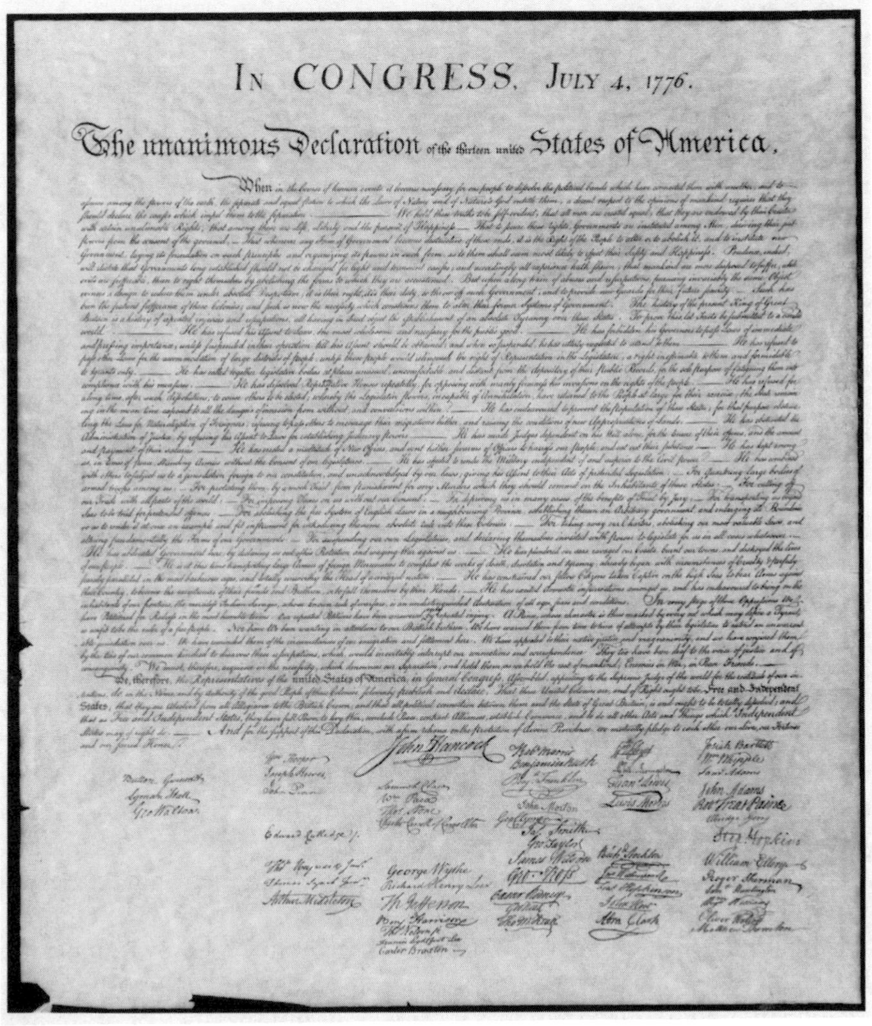
IN CONGRESS, JULY 4, 1776.

The unanimous Declaration of the thirteen united States of America,

Plate 4.1 Declaration of Independence, 4 July 1776.

Independence which, with stirring rhetoric, marked the true beginnings of the United States:

> We hold these truths to be self-evident, that all men are created equal,
> that they are endowed by their Creator with certain unalienable rights,
> that among these are life, liberty, and the pursuit of happiness; that to
> secure these rights, governments are instituted among men, deriving
> their just powers from the consent of the governed; that whenever any
> form of government becomes destructive of these ends, it is the right of
> the people to alter or to abolish it, and to institute new government,
> laying its foundation on such principles, and organizing its powers in
> such form, as to them shall seem most likely to effect their safety and
> happiness.

For the next five years, the colonists successfully fought their revolutionary war against the British and, in 1781, established a new system of government under the Articles of Confederation. In effect, this
– the first American Constitution – was little more than a formal
recognition of the Continental Congress. A congress was created, but
no executive or judiciary. The new government was very much a confederation: individual states retained considerable autonomy giving to
the Congress only limited powers – namely to declare wars, establish
treaties, regulate weights and measures, oversee Indian affairs, run a
post office and establish an army and navy. Crucially, no mandatory
power to raise taxes was established. Instead, Congress had to rely on
voluntary subventions from the state legislatures. Also, each state
could issue its own paper money and generally regulate commerce
within its boundaries.

Such a weak, leaderless system of government could not last long,
especially in the face of a number of very urgent problems confronting
the new nation. Revenue needed to be raised nationally to provide a
common defence. Some central control of the currency and the
enforcement of contracts needed to be created, and a common external tariff was needed to protect American goods from cheap British
imports. Moreover, the war had widened the gulf between the better-
off, who had lent money to finance the fighting, and a growing debtor
class who had mortgaged small farms and houses to raise incomes in
the face of economic dislocation. In 1786 a small rebellion had broken out in Massachusetts, a state where the law on debtors was particularly harsh, when Daniel Shays led over 1000 men to block the
proceedings of the state's high court.

Although quickly put down, Shays's rebellion served to remind the
better-off that the new Congress was ill-equipped to provide some
degree of national economic security and uniformity. Prior to the
rebellion a number of attempts had been made to strengthen Con-

gress, and a convention to discuss trade problems had met at Annapolis, Maryland, in 1786. Although only five states attended, a resolution to meet in Philadelphia with the more ambitious aim of constitutional revision had been agreed at the convention. Shays made such a meeting that much more imperative, and during the summer of 1787, 55 delegates assembled in Philadelphia charged with the momentous task of producing new constitutional arrangements for the United States.

The American Constitution

While the 55 delegates – the Founding Fathers – were obviously not operating in the absence of political and economic constraints, they were able genuinely to combine normative judgements on what best would make for a good system, with provisions imposed on them by political necessity. They were not, in other words, engaged in the exercise of naked political power. Nor were they obsessed with retributive measures against past masters. And, unlike many twentieth-century harbingers of regime-change, their actions were not informed by a single, closed ideology. Instead, they could afford to compromise, to show pragmatism and to draw on a number of political theories and constitutional arrangements at that time commonly discussed by the educated and liberal minded.

The Founding Fathers were certainly educated, about one-half having college degrees – a very high proportion for that time. They were also established (and comparatively young) men of property and status – merchants, lawyers, planters, doctors, intellectuals. George Washington presided over the meetings, although he played virtually no role in the proceedings. Inviting Washington – who came only reluctantly – was a clever ploy, as he was the one figure almost universally respected in the new nation. The real driving forces behind the convention and its proceedings were James Madison of Virginia, a brilliant young politician who had helped to write Virginia's constitution, and Alexander Hamilton from New York, one-time aide to Washington during the war, who had helped set up the Annapolis convention.

As delegates from the state legislatures, the Founding Fathers were not directly elected by the people – indeed one state, Rhode Island, was not even represented, dominated as it was by a disgruntled debtor class. In one curious respect, this lack of a universal popular mandate gave them some extra freedom, for, meeting in secret, they could eventually produce a document as a *fait accompli* and then lobby hard for its acceptance by the states. As we will see, this in effect is precisely what they did.

What were the main influences on the framers? Four main ideas stand out: social contract theory, representation, the separation of powers and federalism. We have already mentioned the idea of the social contract, with its provision of obligation on both governed and governors. Although central to the thinking of Hobbes and Rousseau, it was Locke's vision of the social contract which most influenced the founders. To Hobbes, the contract was a very one-sided affair where the people traded their freedom for the security which a strong state would bring. Rousseau's contract was far more idealized, involving as it did the identification and implementation of the general will of the people. Locke, in contrast, made *representation* the central canon of his ideal society. Citizens, or those with a stake in society, men of property, were entitled to a government that would champion their natural rights. Through representative institutions – free elections and assemblies – the people could hold the rulers accountable for their actions. Obedience to the law (the people's side of the contract) was, therefore, conditional on the government fulfilling its side of the contract – the guarantee of life, liberty and property.

Representative government carries with it other notions, notably majority rule and the implication that there are clear limits to democracy. Both were accepted by the Founding Fathers, and their limits on democracy were, by modern standards, quite severe. Only the lower house of the legislature, the House of Representatives, was to be elected directly by the people (Article 1, Section 2).[2] Senators were to be nominated by the state legislatures (Article 1, Section 3), and the president was to be elected by an electoral college, the members of which were to be appointed by the state legislatures (Article 2, Section 1). The framers' very limited acceptance of democracy reflected their fear of unbridled majority rule. If the people could vote for all the main officers directly, it raised the spectre of an insensitive – and possibly tyrannical – permanent majority capable of riding roughshod over the minority. As Thomas Jefferson had noted some years before the convention, 'an elective despotism was not the government we fought for'.[3] Note also that the electoral qualifications of those who could vote for the House of Representatives were to be determined by the state legislatures (Article 1, Section 2). In most cases this meant a very limited suffrage consisting of white property-owning males. None of this was incompatible with popular sovereignty or a republican form of government. Sovereignty resided in the people (albeit a minority of them) not in a monarch or emperor. And this, together

---

[2]   The full text of the Constitution is given in Appendix 1, pp. 337–57.
[3]   Quoted in T. Mason (ed.), *Free Government in the Making*, (New York, Oxford University Press, 3rd edn, 1965), p. 165.

with the majoritarian provisions in the Constitution, guaranteed a republican system.

The framers were not only worried about the possibility of tyranny by the majority; they were also aware of the dangers of concentrating too much power in any one institution. A powerful executive suggested monarchal or despotic leadership. A powerful legislature carried with it the possibility of rule by an insensitive majority. A device existed to overcome these dangers – the separation of powers. Borrowing in part from the ideas of the French philosopher Baron de Montesquieu, who greatly admired what he thought was a division of powers in the English system, the framers went about a deliberate separation of authority between legislature, executive and judiciary. Congress was accordingly given a separate power base (or constituency) from the presidency, and although the judiciary was not given the quite awesome power of judicial review it was later to assume, Supreme Court and other federal judges were to be appointed by the president. The precise jurisdiction of the courts, however, as well as the final say on the appointment of judges, were accorded to Congress (Article 3).

To ensure a division of power between the major institutions, a system of *checks and balances* was introduced. So both houses of the legislature had to approve a bill, but the president could exercise a veto over it. The Senate and House of Representatives could, in turn, override a veto if two-thirds of the members present in both houses voted for it (Article 1, Section 7). Congress was also given some control over executive appointments, which had to be filled with the 'advice and consent' of the Senate (Article 2, Section 2). These checks and balances should not imply an *equality* of power and authority between the institutions. There is no doubt that the framers intended the Congress, and in particular the House of Representatives, to be the key *source* of policy. This is clear from Article 1, Section 8, which enumerates the powers of Congress. Because these included fiscal, monetary and regulatory powers, as well as the authority to raise armies and declare war, they were, in contemporary terms, quite comprehensive. Significantly, the directly elected chamber, the House of Representatives, was given special responsibility for revenue bills (Article 1, Section 7) thus reflecting the popular demand ('no taxation without representation') that the 'people's branch' should be directly accountable to the voters on taxation matters. (*See* fig. 4.1.)

Executive and judicial branches were, in contrast, given few specific powers, although the dictum that the 'executive power shall be vested in a president' (Article 2, Section 1) leaves open the question of where executive power begins and ends. Congress was, then, expected to be the source of most legislation, but its power would be checked

Figure 4.1 The separation of powers and the law-making process

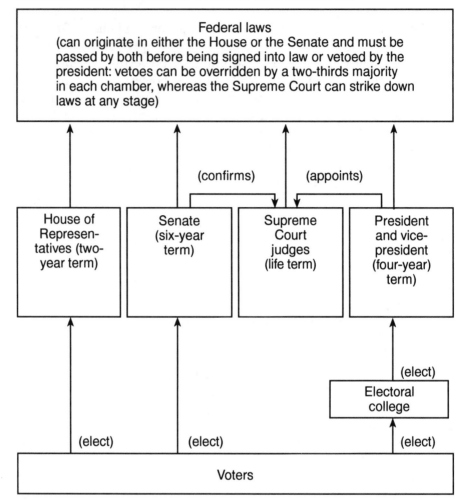

both internally (via bicameralism) and by the president. These checks are essentially negative in nature, suggesting that the framers had a greater fear of the abuse of power than of an inability to exercise it. We have already mentioned the fear of democracy, majority rule and a despotic executive. In addition, some of the framers were deeply suspicious of the machinations of groups, parties or 'factions'. James Madison, in particular, feared that government might become the creature of some class or special interest. He eloquently outlined his position in *The Federalist*:[4]

---

[4] The *Federalist* papers written mainly by Madison and Hamilton were published after the convention as a tract to persuade some of the states to accept the Constitution. They comprise a remarkable collection of essays which reflect some of the most crucial debates of the convention.

Among the numerous advantages promised by a well constructed Union, none deserves to be more accurately developed than its tendency to break and control the violence of faction . . . By a faction, I understand a number of citizens, whether amounting to a majority or minority of the whole, who are united and actuated by some common impulse of passion, or of interest, adverse to the rights of other citizens, or to the permanent and aggregate interests of the community. There are two methods of curing the mischief of faction: the one, by removing its causes; the other by controlling its effects. There are again two methods of removing the causes of faction: the one, by destroying the liberty which is essential to its existence; the other by giving to every citizen the same opinions, the same passions and the same interests.[5]

Madison is in no doubt that the only solution is to control the effects of faction. Liberty is essential and where it exists factions will exist, and giving an equal voice to every citizen can be achieved only in a pure democracy; pure democracy is impractical and dangerous except in very small communities. This leaves the control of faction to a republican form of government, or the sort of representative system with a limited suffrage, some indirect elections, a separation of powers and the operation of checks and balances, which was eventually adopted.

The convention was by no means united on basic constitutional arrangements. Alexander Hamilton feared that without a strong executive, few of the nation's pressing problems would be solved. Madison, in contrast, feared both a strong executive and an overbearing legislature. More generally, the larger states (Virginia, Massachusetts, Pennsylvania) favoured a strong central government (whether dominated by Congress or not) while the smaller states, fearing an encroachment by the more populous areas, favoured more decentralized arrangements. In fact, debates on federalism and the delineation of powers between centre and periphery were among the most acrimonious at the convention. For, in addition to the small/large state dichotomy, there was the thorny problem of the very different interests represented by the Southern, as opposed to the Northern, states. Following intense debate between those wanting a strong federal government (the so-called Virginia Plan) and those demanding decentralized power (the New Jersey plan), a compromise was reached by giving the Senate a representative base founded on territory rather than on population (two Senators from each state, Article 1, Section 3). The House was to be elected on a population basis and (a further compromise) given special powers over federal revenues.

---

[5] *The Federalist*, no. 10, in *The Federalist Papers*, (New York, Mentor Books, 1961), pp. 77–8.

The distinctive economy and culture of the South posed a potentially even greater problem and was eventually resolved only by the unsavoury expedient of counting slaves as three-fifths of a free person for the purpose of representation in the House and in distributing federal taxes. Of course, this did not mean that slaves played any part in the political process. They did not. Many Northern delegates disliked this compromise, but accepted it knowing that the South would not tolerate any serious incursion into its slave-based economy. The South was also an exporter of cotton and other agricultural produce and had much less interest in the protectionist (barriers against free international trade) policies which Northern politicians favoured. To safeguard their position, Southerners demanded that a two-thirds majority be required to ratify treaties in the Senate. In this way, it was hoped that trade agreements favouring the North would be avoided.

These controversies over the status of the South and large versus small states should not obscure the fact that the framers were obliged to create some sort of federal system. After all, the convention was made up of representatives of the states, and the war had been waged against a strong central government. A unitary system in the style of England was completely unacceptable to most delegates. What eventually transpired was a highly flexible federalism. Indeed, reading the Constitution it is not at all clear where federal power begins and ends, which gives at least great potential power to the centre.

The genius of the Constitution was that although it was the first written constitution ever to be adopted by a country, and although it propounded the virtues of a republican form of government – a radical idea, indeed, in the late eighteenth century – it remained intrinsically *conservative* in content and implication. The Founders, and particularly the most influential and able of them, Madison and Hamilton, were hardly social visionaries. Instead their hopes for the New Country were tinged with caution and not a little pessimism about human greed and selfishness. As Madison put it:

> As there is a degree of depravity in mankind which requires a certain degree of circumspection and distrust, so there are other qualities in human nature which justify a certain portion of esteem and confidence.[6]

As with most educated eighteenth-century men, the essentially inegalitarian view that there are worthy and unworthy, talented and talentless, wise and stupid men in the populace, prevailed. The president was to be elected by an electoral college made up, it was

---

[6]   *The Federalist*, no. 55, p. 346.

hoped, of wise, educated and established citizens, free from the rabble-rousing and instant judgements which democratic processes inspired. Senators, too, were expected to be elder statesmen elected by their peers for a leisurely six years and able, therefore, to hold in line a potentially capricious and unruly lower house. What the framers hoped for, therefore, was firm, cautious and responsible government. The Constitution was designed to provide the basic framework for such a system of stable and limited political power. It was also intended to stand the test of time – an objective which was greatly aided by a cumbersome amendment process. Amendments have to be proposed by a two-thirds vote in both houses of Congress and then ratified by three-quarters of the state legislatures or by a ratifying con- vention in two-thirds of the states. Alternatively a national convention at the behest of two-thirds of the state legislatures can propose an amendment which in turn can be ratified by Congress or by a ratifying convention (Article 5). The first method (Congress proposing, the state legislatures ratifying) has become the normal amending mecha- nism, and it is testimony both to the flexibility of the Constitution and to the difficulties inherent in the amending process that, between 1791 and 1992, there have been only 17 amendments. [*See* tables 4.1 and 4.2]

Reflecting on the personal interest which the framers had in a suc- cessful economy and on the pressing economic problems that the Articles of Confederation had patently failed to solve, some commen- tators have claimed that the whole exercise in Philadelphia was moti- vated by economic interest rather than by the higher ideals of liberty, republicanism and civic virtue.[7] While there is certainly something to this, it seems odd that the fundamental disagreements on major questions which did occur involved delegates with an equal stake in economic success. Virtually *all* the delegates were men of property, so the more simplistic of the economic theories of the Constitution should predict no real disagreement on basic principles. Yet those who voted against the Constitution had just as much of a stake in prosperity and stability as those who voted for it.[8] A more persuasive way to characterize the framers' motivations is to accept that they were indeed troubled by economic dislocation and the ever-present threat of uncontrolled democracy, but differed markedly on which system would best overcome these problems. Crucially these differ- ences were not only instrumental and pragmatic. Delegates also dif- fered *intellectually* and represented more than one political philosophy

[7] The classic statement of this view is Charles Beard's *Economic Interpretation of the Constitution of the United States,* [New York, Macmillan, 1913 (paperback, 1961)].
[8] As established by Forrest McDonald, *We the People – The Economic Origins of the Constitution,* (Chicago, University of Chicago Press, 1958).

and conception of human nature. What they all undoubtedly did agree on was the need for a stronger central government to ensure that the fragile new Republic at least had a reasonable chance of survival.

Ratification

Fearful of failure, the framers wrote into the Constitution the requirement that ratification could be achieved by just nine of the 13 states, and then by special state conventions rather than by the (often untrustworthy) state legislatures. The framers also labelled themselves *Federalists*, thus imposing on opposition groups the unattractive sobriquet 'Anti-Federalist'. Opposition was, in fact, fragmented, coming as it did mainly from the more remote rural areas. There was a geographical split, but not a North/South one. Instead, it was the commercial interests of the coastal areas, the larger towns and cities and the big landowners of the South who supported ratification. The Anti-Federalists were concentrated in 'the part most remote from commercial centres, with interests consequently predominantly agricultural. It included fractious Rhode Island, the Shays regions of Massachusetts and the centre of a similar movement in New Hampshire'[9] (see map 4.1).

Federalist lobbying in favour of the Constitution was intense and inspired the first truly national political debate in the United States. Very generally, the Anti-Federalists complained that the Constitution was insufficiently democratic and that it implied a strong and domineering central government. Complaints that individual rights were not specifically guaranteed by the Constitution were also common, and to ensure ratification in some states, the Federalists accepted that a Bill of Rights would be added as soon as the first federal government was established. Between 1787 and 1789, state conventions, one after the other, voted for ratification. Success was assured when the New York convention eventually ratified by a margin of three votes. The Federalists won because they were better organized, had all the leading politicians and statesmen behind them, and because the Anti-Federalists were obliged to fight a negative campaign, the Articles of Confederation being their only immediate alternative to the Constitution. To appease the remaining Anti-Federalists the first Congress quickly voted for ten amendments, which, once ratified by the states in 1791, became the Bill of Rights. Interestingly, a number of additional

[9]   O. G. Libby, quoted in J. C. Clark Archer and Peter J. Taylor, *Section and Party*, (Chichester, John Wiley, 1981), p. 49.

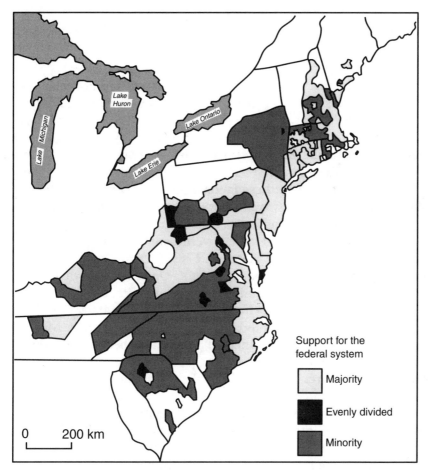

Map 4.1 The geography of ratification.
Source: O. G. Libby, as reproduced in J. C. Clark Archer and Peter J. Taylor, *Section and Party* (Chichester, John Wiley, 1981), p. 50.
Reprinted by permission of John Wiley & Sons Ltd.

amendments failed in Congress or during ratification, almost all of which would have made the system more democratic. One proposed that the electorate should issue binding instructions to their members of Congress, thus turning them into delegates. Another suggested that there should never be less than one member of Congress for every 50,000 inhabitants. The mind boggles at the consequences for American politics if either or both of these proposals had been adopted.

The Adaptive Constitution

Change by amendment

No constitution can elaborate the precise relationship between institutions and political forces. If it attempts to do so it runs the danger of being ignored. Successful constitutions must, therefore, be flexible and open to varying interpretations. In some ways, the shorter and vaguer the document the better. Completely unambiguous statements lead to rigidity and can render a constitution unworkable. The US Constitution is free of all these faults. It does, of course, lay down certain guidelines and rules, but it says remarkably little about the precise powers of the main institutions, or about how authority should be shared between federal and state governments. When a comparison is made between the United States of 1789 (3.5 million people, agrarian, confined to the east coast) and the United States of the 1990s (263 million people, highly industrial, a continental and world power) the true success of the Constitution can be appreciated. For virtually the same document applies today as applied 220 years ago. Moreover, if we examine the 17 Amendments[10] which have been accepted in this period, their significance is almost certainly not as great as the changes in interpretation to which the Constitution has been subjected.

Of the 17 Amendments, some are relatively trivial, two were devoted to the adoption and subsequent rejection of prohibition and the remainder are devoted either to electoral questions or to limiting and expanding the role of the federal government.

Amendments affecting elections and office-holders

The first important amendment here was the 12th which was adopted in 1804 to simplify the election of the electoral college, which in turn elects the president. As mentioned earlier, the Founding Fathers hoped that a group of elder statesmen (the electoral college) would choose the president but, with the emergence of competing political parties, it soon became obvious that the college had become highly partisan. In 1800 the vote in the college was a tie between Thomas Jefferson and Aaron Burr. When the vote was referred to the House of Representatives it took numerous ballots to decide the eventual winner (Jefferson). The 12th Amendment ensured that any election in which a candidate received less than a majority of the electoral college would then be decided in a run-off election in the House of Represen-

[10]   Excluding the first ten Amendments (The Bill of Rights).

tatives. Votes for president and vice-president were combined. Previously the college had elected the two officers separately. Gradually between 1800 and 1832 the state legislatures voted to provide for the direct popular election of members of the electoral college. Surprisingly, this system persists. Americans still do not vote directly for a presidential candidate, but for members of the college. Moreover, it is a *winner-take-all* mechanism, so that the candidate who gets a majority of votes in a particular state wins *all* that state's electoral college votes. What determines the number of electoral college votes in a state? Each state simply has one vote for each representative and senator which means that the votes are distributed roughly in proportion to population (the number of representatives in any state changes regularly in accordance with population shifts (*see* chapter 7), and because there are only two senators per state this introduces a very small bias in favour of low-population states). The major criticism of this system is that it is possible for a candidate to win the electoral college vote, but receive fewer popular votes than another candidate. Just this happened in 1824, 1876 and 1888, although it has not occurred since. Another criticism focuses on the danger of electoral college members failing to vote for the candidate mandated by the electorate. Again, this has happened on rare occasions, but it has never been critical.

Clearly the electoral college system favours the larger states. If a candidate wins just seven states: New York, California, Texas, Pennsylvania, Illinois, Florida and Ohio, he or she amasses 210 votes even if he/she wins by only a narrow margin in each of these states. And only 270 electoral college votes are needed for victory. Talk of reforming the system is never far from the surface in the United States, and the mechanism probably persists because there are only two main parties,[11] and some bias in favour of big population centres does compensate for other biases in the system in favour of smaller states and rural areas.

Almost all the other amendments affecting elections have been designed to expand the electorate or to hold elected officials more accountable or responsive to the public (table 4.1). These changes, together with the abolition of property qualifications for voting at the state level during the first part of the nineteenth century have, in total, greatly increased the democratic element in the Constitution. None is

---

[11] Should no candidate receive a majority in the college – a likelihood if the USA had a multi-party system – then the House of Representatives chooses the president on the basis of *one vote* per state delegation. This massive bias in favour of the small states would not be tolerated for long were the system put to the test (although it did occur twice in the nineteenth century). In recent years the USA has only rarely produced a serious third-party candidate, and few have accumulated electoral college votes.

Table 4.1 Constitutional amendments affecting elections and office-holders

Amendment	Purpose	Proposed	Adopted
12	Reform of electoral college	1803	1804
15	Voting rights extended to all races	1869	1870
17	Direct election of senators	1912	1913
19	Voting rights extended to women	1919	1920
20	'Lame duck' session of Congress abolished[1]	1932	1933
22	Presidents limited to two terms	1947	1951
23	Voting rights extended to residents of District of Columbia	1960	1961
24	Voting rights democratized – abolition of poll tax	1962	1964
25	Reform of presidential succession in case of disability	1965	1967
26	Voting age lowered to 18	1971	1971
27	Prohibition on members of Congress to raise their salaries before the next election	1990	1992

[1] This changed the date of new congressional sessions from March to January to shorten the period during which the old Congress could act.

controversial except the 22nd limiting presidential terms to no more than two. Although never tested, it is conceivable that a popular and successful president may be denied a third term by the amendment.

Amendments affecting the powers of the federal government

In one sense, changes in electoral qualifications were to be expected as the democratizing trends of the nineteenth and twentieth centuries took hold. If this is so, it would also be unsurprising if the Constitution had been frequently amended to expand the powers of the federal government. Yet as table 4.2 shows, only three amendments have had this purpose, the 13th to assert federal power over those states practising slavery, the 14th imposing the Bill of Rights on the states and the 16th establishing the power to introduce a national income tax. And of these three, the 14th Amendment was not, in fact, applied to the states until the twentieth century.

Evidence of just how difficult it is to ratify an amendment is provided by the experience of the Equal Rights Amendment (ERA). This amendment, which reads 'Equality of rights under the law shall not be denied or abridged by the United States or any state on account of sex', has, in fact, been before Congress since 1923. In 1972 Congress voted for the amendment by large majorities and within a year 25 states had voted for it. It then ran into trouble, however, as some state legislators began to fear that in its implementation women might, for example, be required to take up combat positions in battle. Eventually, the amendment died three short of formal ratification.

Table 4.2 Amendments affecting the powers of the federal government

Amendment	Purpose	Proposed	Adopted
11	Limited federal courts' jurisdiction over suits involving the states	1794	1798
13	Abolished slavery	1865	1865
14	Extended due process of Bill of Rights to the states	1866	1868
16	Established power to introduce a national income tax	1909	1913

The other major attempt to amend the Constitution in recent years also failed. By the late 1980s, 33 states had passed the Balanced Budget Amendment requiring the federal government to balance its annual budget. By the early 1990s most commentators doubted that the amendment would win the approval of any more state legislatures. With the election of a Republican Congress in 1994, however, and again in 1996, and given Republican advances in state politics, the Balanced Budget Amendment is set to return to the centre of the political stage.

Change by interpretation

Much more important have been changes in Constitutional interpretation which owe more to the development of American society and economy than to the wording of the Constitution as such. We can identify four such changes:

1 the assertion of federal over state power;
2 the assertion of executive over legislative power;
3 the emergence of the Supreme Court as the final arbiter of the Constitution;
4 the growing protection of individual rights under the federal government.

Each of these four will be dealt with in detail in later chapters. For now it is enough to point out the first two were certainly not intended or envisaged by the framers, the third probably was, and the fourth has developed in a way which could not possibly have been predicted in 1787.

Although the Constitution is ambiguous on the question of federal/state relations, there can be no doubt that the relationship which had developed by the 1990s was light-years away from anything the framers could have intended. Today the federal government intrudes into almost every facet of economic and social life, leaving to the states very little that *constitutionally* they can call their own except perhaps their territorial integrity. In 1791 it was broadly expected that the 10th Amendment's dictum: 'The powers not delegated to the United States by the Constitution, nor prohibited by it to the States, are reserved to the States respectively, or to the people', would leave the states unequivocally in charge of a number of governmental functions. As the next chapter will demonstrate, this was not to be.

Similarly, Congress was expected to be the major source of legislative initiative, while the president implemented laws with prudence and efficiency. The late twentieth-century reality is very different. For while Congress does play a greater role in policy initiation than most national legislatures, and is indisputably a powerful and independent institution, it has largely forfeited the lion's share of the legislative function to the president and to an awesomely large and complex executive branch.

The reasons why government has become larger, more centralized and concentrated in executive rather than legislature will be addressed in detail in later chapters. But these trends have occurred in almost all countries with rapid economic and social development, the mobilization of populations by parties and groups and the corresponding increase in demands placed on all governments, particularly those with the greatest potential for resource distribution and regulation – central governments.

In 1803 the Supreme Court asserted the power of judicial review, or the right to declare any act of Congress or action by the executive branch as incompatible with the Constitution and therefore illegal. Actions by states can also be struck down by the Supreme Court. Although used sparingly at first, this power has been utilized with increasing frequency, and as we will see in chapter 13, has had profound consequences for the working of the political system. Although some of the Founders may have envisaged the Court playing the role of final arbiter of the Constitution, none could have foreseen the intimate involvement of the nation's highest court in such questions as abortion, electronic bugging and political party campaign finance.

Finally, citizens' right to free speech, assembly, religion and privacy, and to 'due process' and the equal protection of the laws have slowly been extended to apply to the states. This is crucial, for slavery was an institution protected by state governments and constitutions. Following the Civil War, the 13th and 14th Amendments swept away slavery and, in theory, discrimination. The Supreme Court failed to enforce the 14th Amendment in the South until after World War II, however, so allowing the perpetuation of segregation and the worst sort of racial discrimination. Deference to states' rights extended to other areas such as standards of occupational safety, employment conditions and criminal justice. So for many Americans, civil rights and liberties were anything but 'God given rights'. Only under federal legislation did they exist, and, until the twentieth century, the federal government played only a small role in the lives of individual citizens. Beginning in the 1930s and accelerating between 1945 and 1970, this anomalous situation was slowly corrected, with the Supreme Court insisting in case after case that the Bill of Rights and 14th Amendment apply to all American governments, whatever their status. So in cases involving national security, privacy, racial, religious and sex discrimination, and the administration of justice, the Supreme Court has insisted that all authorities have an obligation to heed constitutionally defined rights. Of course, this does not mean to say that the Court has always favoured the individual rather than government – although in recent years more often than not it has. Changes in official attitudes to civil rights and liberties parallel the growth of government noted earlier. As governments at all levels have increasingly intruded into the lives of individuals, so the need for protection from arbitrary governmental authority has grown. As we will discover in chapter 12, governments – and especially federal governments – have also been active in controlling the abuse of individual rights by *private* bodies, in particular by corporations. It seems highly unlikely that the framers could have foreseen that the question of individual rights would have become part of a complex web of interaction between myriad private and public institutions and individuals.

Assessing the Constitution

Some of the most dramatic changes in American government and society over the last 200 years have involved institutions and political processes not even referred to in the Constitution. Parties emerged during the early years of the nineteenth century as the major agents of political mobilization. Interest groups have grown in number and influence until today some commentators seriously argue that they are the true sources of political power and influence. Similarly the nationally organized media equipped with formidable electronic resources can play a critical role in swaying political opinion. Does this mean that the Constitution is of relatively little importance? Not at all, for all these changes have had to be accommodated within certain institutional limits which the Constitution imposes. Political and economic changes have indisputably altered the relationships between institutions and the broader society, but they have not been transformed in such a way that the document has ceased to have meaning. Congress remains separated from the presidency. Interest groups, presidents, individual citizens, the media – even foreign governments- – have to accept that the independent power of Congress can and frequently does thwart presidents. The courts are also independent and have shown, especially in the last 40 years, that president and Congress must sometimes tread warily when exercising their powers. States, too, remain important political units – although, as we will discover in the next chapter, their relationship with the federal government is now more one of interdependence than autonomy.

Criticisms of the modern Constitution usually concentrate either on the continuing political hiatus between executive and legislature, or on the progressive weakening of the states in relation to the federal government. The first of these will become a constant theme in later chapters, and there is little doubt that American presidents are, in comparison with chief executives in most industrial countries, uncommonly constrained by the essentially negative power of Congress. But as we will see, American government is not only fragmented by the separation of powers. Getting policy efficiently formulated and implemented is also affected by the complexity of the executive branch and, simply, by the many competing interests in American society which have created and nurtured so many access points to those with political power. It seems reasonable to infer that this would have happened whatever the precise constitutional arrangements in force.

Arguments suggesting that the decline of the states' legal autonomy is in part attributable to the Constitution's failure to define precisely where state sovereignty begins and ends are less persuasive. Such a strict delineation of powers would have been inflexible and ultimately unworkable, and in any case the states were admirably independent until this century. The gradual erosion of their legal powers is not, therefore, a matter so much of constitutional failure as it is a consequence of the states' inability to deal with the pressing social and economic problems that industrialization and other changes brought.

Any assessment of the Constitution has to recognize that, as with any constitution, its continuing influence is ultimately dependent on those in positions of political power accepting its legitimacy. Had its provisions proved a major threat to power-holders, it would have been ignored or radically amended. No doubt the Founding Fathers recognized this and, anticipating problems, deliberately opted for a short and rather vague document that would stand the test of time. But this would hardly have been enough had America been torn by fundamental divisions based on class, ethnicity, language or religion. The framers knew that good government was all about the business of reconciling differences between competing groups and interests in society, and no doubt they were aware that the United States would experience social and political conflict of varying intensity. But the conflict between North and South apart – and this very nearly put paid to the Union – the United States has been remarkably unaffected by fundamental political divisions. Free from a feudal past and lacking deeply rooted religious, ethnic, linguistic and, at least in recent decades, regional divides, the country was able to accommodate quite extraordinary economic and demographic changes within a single, almost unchanging, constitutional structure. Above all it is this relative consensus on political fundamentals amid rapid change that has allowed what is in any case a brilliantly adaptive Constitution to survive.

This does not mean to say that the Constitution will continue for ever, of course. And there are more than enough critics who claim that the basic division of power between legislature and executive is inappropriate for the sort of efficient policy-making needed to run an economically powerful world power at the millennium's end. Whether this is true, later chapters will reveal. But whatever the charges, the Constitution is under no imminent threat either from domestic political conflict or from radical amendment. According to the simple measure of its ability to survive, therefore, it must be deemed a success.

Further Reading

On the revolutionary period, *see* Bernard Bailyn, *Faces of Revolution: Personalities and Themes in the Struggle for American Independence*, (New York, Knopf, 1990). *See also* his *Ideological Origins of the American Revolution*, (Cambridge MA, Harvard University Press, 1967). Two classic accounts of the making of the Constitution and the early years of the Republic are Samuel H. Beer, *To Make a Nation: The Rediscovery of American Federalism*, (Cambridge, MA, Harvard University Press, 1993) and Stanley Elkins and Eric McKitrick, *The Age of Federalism: The Early American Republic, 1788–1800*, (New York and Oxford, Oxford University Press, 1993).

5

EIGHTY–THOUSAND GOVERNMENTS: FEDERALISM AND INTERGOVERNMENTAL RELATIONS

> The problem which all federalized nations have to solve is how to secure an efficient central government and preserve national unity, while allowing free scope for the diversities, and free play to the members of the federation. It is . . . to keep the centrifugal and centripetal forces in equilibrium, so that neither the planet States shall fly off into space nor the sun of the Central government draw them into its consuming fires.
>
> Lord James Bryce, *American Commonwealth*

> This Nation has never fully debated the fact that over the past 40 years, federalism – one of the most essential and underlying principles of our Constitution – has nearly disappeared as a guiding force in American politics and government. My administration intends to initiate such a debate . . .
>
> Ronald Reagan

To the European student of American government, the practice of federalism presents itself as something of a conundrum. On the one hand is the extraordinary variety of contrasting public policies displayed by the states. Most states levy an income tax, but ten do not; most have capital punishment, but 12 do not; state-mandated land-use planning is light-years away from the policy agenda in Texas – a state which prides itself on its free market in land – but in Oregon and Hawaii state planning is a fact of life. In Louisiana laws governing the sale of intoxicating liquors are lax, while Utah is close to being a 'dry' state with drink available only in private clubs. On the other hand, American observers repeatedly tell us that federalism is dying – or is even dead; that the federal government has effectively usurped the powers of the states and now plays the dominant role in American government. Federalism, so we are told, has been transformed from a system of shared sovereignty, with each level of government supreme in its own sphere, and converted into a complex web of intergovernmental relations where political and economic forces, not constitutional imperatives, are the key variables.[1] A major purpose of this chapter is to explain the apparent paradox of continuing state variety and increasing federal power. To achieve this, special attention will be paid to what has been called 'fiscal federalism' or the financial relations between different levels of government. As will be shown, such an approach focuses attention not only on federal-state relationships, but also on *local-federal* links. Finally, some reference will be made to recent attempts to revive the institution of federalism.

Federalism in Theory and Practice

It was not so long ago that Europeans viewed the federal arrangements of the United States with a combination of distanced interest and condescension. A constitutional division of powers between centre and periphery might, so the argument ran, suit such large and diverse countries as the United States, but they were clearly inappropriate for homogeneous countries like Britain and France, with their centralized metropolitan political cultures based on dominant capital cities. For social reformers, federalism was viewed with particular scepticism. How, after all, could resources be distributed from rich to poor areas and from the haves to have-nots of society in the absence of a powerful central government operating unhindered by 'regressive' state governments? Critics pointed to the stark inequalities of American society which seemed so often to correlate with state boundaries – abject poverty in Mississippi and Alabama, and easy affluence in Connecticut and Oregon.

In recent years, however, the institution of federalism has experienced something of a revival. Centralized governments have been criticized as spendthrift and insensitive, and federalism has been cited as a compromise solution to the claims for more autonomy by increasing numbers of regions and ethnic minorities in a variety of countries. To the critic of the over-centralized state, federalism's advantages seem obvious. Local and regional cultural, political and economic characteristics can be preserved; government can be brought 'closer to the people'; and central power can be limited by ensuring that the administration of a whole range of domestic policies is conducted at the

---

[1] *See* Joseph P. Zimmerman, *Contemporary American Federalism: The Growth of National Power*, (Leicester University Press, 1992).

state and local level. Federalism is, of course, much more than the mere devolution of powers which, to a greater or lesser extent, exists in all states, unitary and federal. *Dual sovereignty* is the central theoretical condition for federalism. This involves not just the sharing of policy responsibilities between different levels of government, it additionally *guarantees* constitutional integrity to state governments. No federal government can abolish its constituent states as a British government can, theoretically at least, abolish all its local governments. Naturally, the crucial question is: Which powers should reside in the state governments and which in the federal government? Historically under 'classic' or 'dual' federalism,[2] defence and foreign affairs, together with some aspects of financial or macro-economic management, have been considered federal government responsibilities, while most domestic policies – education, roads, welfare, the administration of justice – have been allocated to state and local governments.

Few constitutions, however, specify precisely which policy areas should be the responsibility of different levels of government. Article 1, Section 8 of the US Constitution, for example, does enumerate the powers of Congress, but it does not do so in a way that unambiguously defines the federal role. Congress is given the power to regulate interstate commerce, but what does this mean: the regulation of interstate transport? the movement of manufactured goods across state boundaries? the regulation of banking across state lines? the regulation of those aspects of *intra*state commerce that are affected by *inter*state transactions? Or what? Clearly what Congress does here and *what* remains a *state* responsibility is left undefined by the Constitution.

In reality the delineation of the federal and state roles has been left to judicial interpretation and to the ways in which the courts have reacted to shifting political and economic environments. As was pointed out in chapter 4, workable constitutions have to be flexible and open to new interpretation, and any attempt to lay down in a permanent fashion the limits to federal or state powers would be doomed to failure. As we shall see, for federalism the cost of flexibility has been the gradual and steady erosion of the states' powers by the federal government.

In strict constitutional terms, the states are guaranteed just four things: equal representation in the Senate (Article 1, Section 3); the right to jurisdictional integrity (Article 4, Section 3); the right to a republican form of government (Article 4, Section 4); and protection against invasion and domestic violence (Article 4, Section 4). What in

---

[2] For a discussion of the operation of dual federalism *see* Morton Grodzins, *The American System*, (Chicago, Rand McNally, 1966).

Table 5.1 Types of government, USA, 1967–87

Type of government	1987	1977	1967
Total	83,217	79,913	81,299
US government	1	1	1
State governments	50	50	50
Local governments	83,166	79,862	81,248
County	3,042	3,042	3,049
Municipal	19,205	18,862	18,048
Township	16,691	16,822	17,105
School district	14,741	15,174	21,782
Special district	29,487	25,962	21,264

Source: 1987 Census of Governments, Preliminary Report, Bureau of the Census, 1987, table A, p. 1.

reality they have retained in addition to this has varied with the historical period and a whole range of economic, social and political forces. They remain an important level of government, not just for constitutional reasons, but also because they are a convenient jurisdictional base for a range of powerful actors and interests in contemporary America. Political parties, for example, are organized on a state, rather than a national, basis – a fact that gives the states a key role in nominating presidents and in electing members of Congress and senators. We will elaborate on this point later but, for now, it is important to stress that local, as well as state, governments are important power bases in the American system. Localism is as strong in the USA as in any country and this in spite of the weak constitutional position of local governments (in theory, they are constitutionally subordinate to state governments). The power of local governments is reflected in their resilience. In spite of the many pressures to consolidate into larger units – pressures which exist in all industrial countries – the number of local units in the USA remains high (table 5.1).

Note also the variety of local units that derives from variations in state law. Twenty states, for example, have townships which generally have the powers of municipalities but which, unlike municipalities, cover areas irrespective of population concentrations. Special districts, which continue to increase in number, have been created to perform a specific local function such as fire protection, soil conservation, water supply or sewerage. They are legally separate from, although almost always linked politically to, municipal and county governments.

In recognition of the weakness of classic or dual federalism, and of the strength of local governments, some commentators have argued that, rather than become involved in arcane discussions on the constitutional status of federalism, it is now more appropriate to talk of *intergovernmental relations* (IGR).[3] Such a focus obliges the student to examine the political and economic relationships between different levels of government – a focus largely adopted by this chapter.

To understand why the federal role has increased so rapidly and why, as a constitutional concept, federalism has changed so much over time, it is necessary to examine the historical evolution of IGR in the USA.

The Evolution of American Federalism

Opting for a federal rather than a unitary or confederal system of government in 1787 was understandable. Government under the Articles of Confederation had been minimal. A weak Congress (there was no executive branch) was obliged to rely on the co-operation of 13 near-independent states. In economic affairs this proved almost impossible, and internal tariff barriers, together with the absence of a common currency, rendered the new Republic almost impotent against the economic might of Britain. If a confederal system, relying on the co-operation of constituent states, was unworkable, the other most tried alternative, unitary government, was inappropriate for historical and political reasons. It was, after all, the centralized and highly insensitive power of England that had prompted the revolt of the colonies. Each colony had, in addition, its own traditions and history which might have been threatened by a centralized system. Finally, unitary government was associated with a strong executive – not a feature likely to endear the system either to the artisans and smallholders who made up the bulk of the American population or to those sections of the elite who supported Madison's notion of limited government.

A federal system involving the sharing of authority between central authority and constituent states was a natural compromise. Hence, the Constitution gave to the federal government authority to raise armies, to tax, and to regulate interstate commerce – powers that were notably absent under the Articles of Confederation – while the individual traditions of the states were protected by the checks and balances imposed on the central institutions of Congress and presidency and by the 10th Amendment.[4] The fundamental problem that federalism attempts to solve – the tension between central authority and

---

[3]   This abbreviation is taken from Deil S. Wright, *Understanding Intergovernmental Relations*, (North Scituate, Mass., Duxbury, 1978).
[4]   'The powers not delegated to the United States by the Constitution, nor prohibited by it to the States, are reserved to the States respectively, or to the people.'

local autonomy – is still very much with us today. In the late eighteenth century, however, this tension took on a very different form from that presently at work in the United States. Then, a strong federal government was needed for two purposes: to defend the young republic against a hostile outside world and to provide an open and orderly market for the free exchange of goods and services within the borders of the new nation state. At all levels government's role was limited and, although some conflict between state and federal governments existed, it rarely reached the point where it intruded greatly into citizens' lives. In an agrarian and small-town society characterized by poor communications and a strong tradition of localism, the federal government was a remote and, in terms of people's everyday dealings, a relatively minor authority. Today, in contrast, federal, state and local governments intrude into almost all areas of social life through a bewildering array of policies and programmes. It is not surprising, therefore, that federal-state-local relations today are very different from those of late eighteenth-century America. Initially, debate was concentrated on the *regulatory* powers of the federal government – and especially the extent to which federal law was *supreme* in the regulation and promotion of commerce. By the mid-nineteenth century, with the emergence of slavery as a national issue, the role of the federal government in protecting the rights of citizens was added to the policy agenda. These issues remain an important part of current debate on federalism, but they have been transformed by the vastly enhanced spending power of the federal government.

An examination of the more celebrated Supreme Court cases on federal-state relations confirms these shifts in emphasis. Prior to the Civil War, the most significant cases concerned such things as the right of the federal government to establish a national bank (*McCulloch v. Maryland*, 1819) and to run ferries between New York and New Jersey (*Gibbons v. Ogden*, 1824). Later the Court led by Chief Justice Taney resolutely defended the right of the states to permit slavery – a right promptly removed by the War and the subsequent 13th and 14th Amendments. Between 1870 and 1938, the Court resisted attempts by the federal government to regulate industrial and commercial life – although anti-monopoly laws were upheld and a graduated federal income tax (one where the more you earn the more tax you pay) was eventually approved through constitutional amendment (16th Amendment, 1913). With the exception of the income tax question, which did inspire a vociferous debate on the role of the federal government, the period up to 1933 was characterized by a general agreement that the states were the proper level of government for most domestic policy formulation and implementation. Federal government power was on the increase, but presidents and congresses generally accepted that *direct* intervention by the government in the economic and social life of the nation was undesirable.

All changed with the depression of the 1930s and the advent of the New Deal. From 1933 the federal government began to legislate in a variety of new areas, from social security to public works. In reaction to what it saw as an unlawful interpretation of the Commerce Clause and Necessary and Proper Clause, the Court struck down much of this new legislation in the name of the states' rights. Had the decisions in such cases as *Schechter Corporation v. the USA* (1935) and *Carter v. Carter Coal Company* (1936) prevailed, Roosevelt's New Deal would have been in serious trouble, and only a last-minute change in Court opinion prevented a constitutional crisis. (*see* chapter 13 pp. 291–2).

Since this famous turnabout, the executive and judicial branches have been in approximate agreement over the *economic* role of the federal government in American society. Conflict has not disappeared from debate on federalism, however. The civil rights issue, in particular, inspired intense dispute between the states and all branches of the federal government during the 1950s and the 1960s. While state (and more recently local) resistance to federal civil rights laws and judicial decisions should not be underestimated, scholars have probably been right in emphasizing that conflict as such is not now the main characteristic of American federalism. Morton Grodzins was the first to recognize the co-operative nature of federalism in the 1940s and 1950s.

Using the metaphors of layer cake and marble cake to characterize conflictual and co-operative federalism, Grodzins identified the crucial transition of federalism from the intergovernmental antagonisms of the nineteenth century to the mutual interest and collaboration typical of the late 1930s to the late 1950s period.[5] Economic distress and external threat combined to transform the role of the federal government during this period. Lower-level governments responded to national emergency not with antagonism but in a spirit of co-operation and consensus. Since the 1960s, however, federalism has developed further, and co-operation is certainly not the main characteristic of intergovernmental relations today. Now, with the proliferation of programmes and policies at all levels of government, a much more confused and fragmented situation exists.

There are two main aspects to the complex picture that makes up federalism today: fiscal federalism and the continuing debate over whether national standards in public policy should prevail as opposed to standards set by state governments. As we will see, these two areas have been the source of intense passions in modern America.

---

5   Grodzins, *The American System.*

Fiscal Federalism: the Rise and Decline of the Federal Role

The reasons why the federal role increased over time are complex. Most relate to the close connection between administrative and political centralization and what has been called the nationalization of economic and social life.[6] It is easy to be overdeterministic in this area – certainly the causal lines run in many directions. The evolution of mass-based political parties nominating presidents with national appeals was no doubt both an effect and a cause of the increasingly nationalized nature of economic life during the late nineteenth and early twentieth centuries. As corporations began to organize on national lines, so the need for national standards and regulations grew. Demands for minimum standards of (say) food processing or for fair competition required the sort of political mobilization which could come only from mass-based political parties. As these strengthened, so the need for better and more centralized organization on the part of commerce and industry to combat (or co-operate with) the federal government emerged. The growth of news dissemination inevitably aided this process, especially after the introduction of radio and television.

While all these forces were important, the main impetus to the growth of federal power came from two rather different sources – economic depression and war. As we noted earlier, it was the programmes of the New Deal and the massive military spending on World War II which transformed the federal role. Public spending as a percentage of GNP increased from just 10 per cent in 1929 to 23 per cent in 1949 and the federal share of this expenditure increased from 2.6 per cent to 16 per cent – much of it after 1939 as a result of increased defence spending.

A major spur to increased federal spending and to producing qualitative changes in intergovernmental relations was the growth of federal grants in aid to state and local governments. There are two distinctions within any intergovernmental transfer system which must be drawn if the system is to be understood. First, it is necessary to distinguish between grants and payments which are paid *directly* to the population by the federal government and those which are paid to lower-level governments. The former – in the USA such things as social security,[7] Medicare, agricultural subsidies[8] – do constitute a

---

[6] *See* the collection of essays edited by Theodore Lowi and Alan Stone, *Nationalizing Government: Public Policies in America*, (Beverly Hills, Sage, 1978).

[7] In the USA, social security applies specifically to *contributory* benefits such as unemployment, old age and disability allowance. *Welfare* applies to non-contributory maintenance benefits.

[8] Medicare is the national health allowance scheme for the old introduced in 1965. It is mainly contributory, whereas Medicaid, a similar scheme for the poor, is not.

major part of federal spending. Grants to states and localities include both aid which goes directly to individuals through state and local governments – welfare is the most important item here – and aid for programmes such as highways and law enforcement where the state or local government constitutes the final stage in the transfer transaction. Table 5.2 makes some of these distinctions by breaking down federal budget outlays for the 1970–96 period. Note the rapid rise in grants to state and local government between 1970 and 1980, and their subsequent decline after 1980. The 'payments for individuals' category includes social security, medical and welfare payments. As we will see, however, the levelling-off in this category between 1980 and 1985 is mainly accounted for by cuts in welfare (which is channelled through the states) rather than cuts in social security and other benefits which go directly to individuals. Finally, note that government expenditure has continued to rise because of sizeable increases first in defence expenditure and more recently in payments to individuals (almost entirely social security, Medicare and Medicaid). Note also the increasing burden of interest payments since 1980. A clue to the rapid rise in grants of aid to lower-level governments during the 1970–80 period is the increase in general-purpose block grants after 1972; Indeed, the second crucial distinction in IGR is between block grants, which are general appropriations given to states and localities, and *categorical* grants, which are given for specific programmes and policies and which often have strings attached. For example, the Urban Renewal Programme introduced in 1949 was categorical: it allocated monies to local governments specifically for the financing of downtown renewal. From 1954 until 1974, this money was available only if recipient governments abided by a 'workable programme' or general plan of how new development would fit in with existing housing and other facilities.[9] In 1974, however, Urban Renewal, along with a number of related programmes, was replaced by Community Development Block Grants which carried considerably fewer restricting regulations. The Community Development Block Grant was just one of a series of block grants introduced by the Nixon and Ford administrations between 1970 and 1976. President Nixon was the architect of the main block grant scheme, General Revenue Sharing, introduced in 1972.

The 1960s as well as the 1970s were periods of rapidly rising federal expenditure. Many of the programmes through which this money was spent were associated with Lyndon Johnson's Great Society:

---

[9]   For a history of the Urban Renewal Programme *see* the collection of essays edited by Jewell Bellush and Murray Hausnecht, *Urban Renewal: People, Politics and Planning*, (New York, Anchor, 1967).

Table 5.2 Percentage distribution of federal budget outlays, 1970–96

Year	Amount in 1982 dollars (billions)	Total %	Defence	Payments to individuals	Net interest	Aid to state and local governments	Other
1970	509.4	100	44.3	29.9	6.8	12.0	7.0
1975	586.0	100	27.3	45.4	6.9	14.8	6.6
1980	699.1	100	23.5	46.4	8.9	15.1	7.1
1985	849.6	100	27.1	44.7	13.7	11.1	3.1
1990	912.2	100	26.4	46.8	14.6	10.7	1.5
1996*	1612	100	16.3	55.1	15.9	10.8	1.8

* estimate

Source: Statistical Abstract of the United States, 1995, table 5.14

Model Cities (1966) to reinvigorate inner-city areas; mass transit (1966) to provide cities with more efficient public transport; subsidized housing for 'moderate' and lower-income families (1968); Medicare and Medicaid (1965), and a whole host of smaller social welfare and other policies. In addition, the Great Society period witnessed an expansion of *existing* programmes[10] – Urban Renewal, public housing, welfare, social security. Many of these programmes – and especially the newer ones – had two features which, although not new, became much more pronounced during the 1960s. There was, first, the tendency for them to bypass the states and transfer monies directly to local governments. The states had long been identified as 'regressive' or 'backward' participants in the social reform process.[11] Dominated by rural conservatives, state legislatures tended not to favour social reform measures. Given this, the Great Society's focus on aid to local governments was understandable. Second, it was within the jurisdictions of local, not state, governments that the social problems which inspired increased federal aid existed. Urban problems – racial conflict, inner-city decay, crime, poor housing, poverty – began to dominate the policy agenda during these years.

By the mid-1970s, therefore, through a broad range of categorical and block grant programmes, the federal government was providing

[10] The 1960s saw a particularly rapid increase in welfare spending. For a discussion of the causes of this, see Frances Fox Piven and Richard Cloward, *Regulating the Poor*, (New York, Pantheon, 1971).

[11] A reputation which was reinforced by the depression of the 1930s which exposed the inadequacy of existing state welfare provision. *See* Walter I. Trattner, *From Poor Law to Welfare State*, (New York, Free Press, 2nd edn, 1979). Even after the passage of the 1935 Social Security Act, provisions in the law requiring welfare funds to be distributed on a matching basis, with the federal government agreeing to match whatever states were willing to put up, resulted in massive discrepancies in welfare assistance. In 1994, for example, per capita expenditure on welfare in Mississippi was $123, whereas in New York State it was $543.

help for most local governments as well as increasing numbers of individuals. A slightly more analytical way of putting this is that the federal government was increasingly perceived as a provider for both
redistributive and *developmental* policies. The former redistributes
income, usually through individuals, from better-off to poorer citizens. Developmental policies are those designed to improve the infrastructure – water and utility supplies, roads, mass transit, education
and law enforcement. Redistributive policy had, since its inception in
the 1930s, always been viewed as a federal responsibility although
welfare benefits were channelled through the states. Developmental
policy had traditionally been considered a state and local government
function.[12]

Small wonder that these new emphases, together with burgeoning
civil rights legislation, bothered both fiscal conservatives and defenders of classic federalism. By-passing the states was bad enough, but
when this was combined with huge increases in government expenditure in areas where the federal government had traditionally played
little or no role, it appeared to many that not only federalism but
America's free enterprise tradition was withering away.

The 1970s: the high water mark of federal aid

Both Reagan and Ford faced a solidly Democratic Congress throughout their tenure in office, and federal aid to state and local governments increased rapidly during these years. As can be seen from table
5.3, by 1977 no less than $125 billion or 3.1 per cent of America's
gross national product was devoted to this purpose and both developmental and redistributive aid were growing fast. Although, during the
second term of the Nixon administration, efforts were made to cut
many of these programmes, they came to little. Not only was Congress deeply hostile to this project, the administration was itself weakened by the unfolding drama of the Watergate scandal. President
Ford was even more hemmed in than was his predecessor, for, in
1974, the Democrats won a landslide victory in the mid-term elections. The so-called 'Watergate Congress' was intent on a further
expansion of the federal role, and federal aid to state and local
government increased more rapidly during the mid-1970s than at any
time since World War II.[13]

---

[12]   These distinctions are taken from Paul E. Peterson, *The Price of Federalism*,
(Washington DC, Brookings Institution, 1995).
[13]   For an account of the pressures for increased spending during this era *see* David
McKay, *Domestic Policy and Ideology: Presidents and the American State, 1964–1987*,
(Cambridge, Cambridge University Press, 1989), chapter 4.

Table 5.3 Developmental and redistributive federal grants to state–local governments, by category, selected years, 1957–90

Function and category	Percentage of GNP							Amount (billions of 1990 dollars)						
	1957	1962	1967	1972	1977	1982	1990	1957	1962	1967	1972	1977	1982	1990
Developmental														
Transport	0.2	0.5	0.5	0.4	0.3	0.3	0.3	4.3	11.6	15.4	14.7	12.7	11.6	15.5
Natural resources	0.0	0.0	0.0	0.1	0.0	0.0	0.0	0.6	0.6	0.9	1.8	1.9	1.3	2.2
Safety	0.0	0.0	0.0	0.0	0.2	0.2	0.1	0.2	0.3	0.6	1.7	1.0	1.7	2.8
Education	0.1	0.3	0.5	0.6	0.6	0.5	0.4	2.7	4.9	14.6	20.7	22.1	19.6	23.2
Utilities	0.0	0.0	0.0	0.0	0.0	0.0	0.0	0.0	0.0	0.0	0.0	0.0	0.0	0.0
Miscellaneous	0.1	0.1	0.2	0.1	0.7	0.5	0.3	1.6	3.0	6.0	4.7	36.8	25.2	16.4
Total[1]	**0.4**	**0.9**	**1.2**	**1.2**	**1.8**	**1.5**	**1.1**	**9.4**	**20.4**	**37.5**	**43.6**	**74.5**	**59.4**	**60.1**
Redistributive														
Pensions/medical insurance	0.0	0.1	0.0	0.1	0.1	0.1	0.1	0.0	1.9	0.0	2.2	3.0	2.8	2.8
Welfare	0.4	0.4	0.5	1.1	0.9	1.0	1.1	7.0	10.2	15.8	37.9	37.0	41.8	60.0
Health and hospitals	0.0	0.0	0.0	0.1	0.1	0.1	0.1	0.5	0.7	1.5	3.8	3.5	3.8	5.9
Housing	0.0	0.1	0.1	0.1	0.2	0.2	0.2	0.5	1.5	2.5	4.4	7.1	9.8	10.8
Total[1]	**0.4**	**0.6**	**0.7**	**1.3**	**1.3**	**1.3**	**1.4**	**8.0**	**14.3**	**19.8**	**48.3**	**50.6**	**58.2**	**79.5**
Total domestic expenditure[1]	**0.8**	**1.4**	**1.9**	**2.7**	**3.1**	**2.8**	**2.5**	**17.4**	**34.7**	**57.3**	**91.9**	**125.1**	**117.6**	**139.6**

[1] Totals may not add because of rounding.
Source: Paul E. Peterson, *The Price of Federalism* (Washington DC, Brookings Institution, 1995), table 3.5.

The election of Jimmy Carter led many commentators to conclude that the federal role would receive a further impetus. Carter was, of course, a Democrat and at that time the influence of the 'urban lobby' – supporters of grants, affirmative action, housing subsidies and welfare – in the Democratic Party remained strong. Paradoxically, however, it was during the Carter years that federal aid to state and local governments peaked. Very broadly there were three reasons for this. First, unlike Kennedy and Johnson, Carter had no clear vision of what the federal government's role in relation to state and local governments should be. Above all the believed in fiscal rectitude or the idea that the first responsibility of the national government was to balance the budget. What this meant in effect was holding back that part of federal spending that was considered 'controllable'. In practice this translated into attempts to limit aid to state and local governments. Other items on the budget were much less easy to cut. Defence spending had been reduced during the 1970s but the latter half of the decade saw increased East–West tensions which required greater defence expenditures. The other major budget item – social security – involved the distribution of *automatic* payments to old age pensioners, widows and the disabled, so could not be touched. Carter did attempt to reform the federal welfare role and he even tried to forge a 'national urban policy', but lacking a clear commitment to specific reforms in these areas, his plans came to nothing.

A second reason for the decline in support for federal aid in the late 1970s was an increasing awareness that many of the new programmes of the Johnson/Nixon era were inefficient, corrupt or both. In many instances state and local governments, strapped for cash, simply diverted money from programmes designed for particular purposes into general funds which were used to pay salaries and the like. This was an especially serious problem when federal money went directly to local governments or to the private sector. Housing and urban-development programmes were particularly prone to this sort of abuse. Awareness of this general problem relates to the third reason for the decline in federal grants. Put simply, intellectual and political opinion was turning against the view that big government was the answer to all of society's problems. For, in spite of all the new programmes and policies, no discernible improvement in crime, education, and urban conditions generally was evident. At the same time, the economic dislocations of the 1970s led many to believe that excessive government spending was a cause of inflation and recession. An obvious step towards correcting these problems would be a reduction in federal government aid to state and local governments. As we will see, it was left to the Reagan administration to implement these changes.

The Reagan administration: federalism revived?

In his campaign speeches and his 1981 inaugural address, Ronald Reagan made the revival of federalism a central part of his programme to rekindle traditional American values. The federal government had become inefficient, insensitive and cumbersome and, so the argument ran, should be reduced radically in size. One way to achieve this was to revive Richard Nixon's original idea and consolidate myriad categorical grants-in-aid programmes into a number of block grants. In this way, the states would be returned to their 'rightful' position as the main source of domestic policies and programmes. Accordingly, during 1981, the administration proposed consolidating 83 categorical programmes into six human-services block grants (health services, preventive health services, social services, energy and emergency assistance, local education services and state education services). The total amount of federal money involved here was $11 billion. At the same time the 1981 Budget Reconciliation Act reduced federal spending in a wide range of programmes. Some intergovernmental programmes were eliminated altogether, while others were subject to substantial real cuts.

Later, in 1982, the administration presented an even more radical plan for a 'New Federalism' involving a 'swap' of the three main welfare programmes funded by the states and federal government on a matching basis. Welfare and food stamps would be taken over by the states while the federal government assumed responsibility for Medicaid (medical care for the poor). This plan was combined with a massive 'turnback' to the states of most other grant-in-aid programmes which, initially at least, would be funded by a special trust fund. In just five years, however, the fund would be wound up leaving the states in glorious isolation. In the meantime, an immediate 25 per cent cut in funding would be imposed.

The plan was greeted with almost unanimous opposition from the states, Congress and even from within the Office of Management and Budget – Medicaid was the most rapidly growing item in the federal budget. Within months the 'swap' plan was dropped as was the grandiose scheme for a near complete devolution of programmes to the states. In the event, Congress accepted some of the consolidations into block grants and some of the cuts. During the rest of the Reagan years this became the general pattern. Generally, transport, education and capital-spending programmes suffered most. As can be seen from table 5.3, these 'developmental' programmes had been reduced considerably by 1990.

Although the grand strategy of the New Federalism had to be abandoned, Ronald Reagan had succeeded in reversing the historical trend towards ever-increasing federal aid for developmental purposes. As we will see, this change in the policy agenda continued during the Bush and Clinton years.

Bush and Clinton: a permanent change in the federal role?

In his 1989 inaugural address, George Bush mentioned federalism and the states not once. And although the president did later pledge that he would continue the Reagan agenda of devolving power to the states, he lacked the political and emotional commitment to the idea.

During the Bush years a Democratic Congress found itself under increasing pressure to resume higher levels of intergovernmental aid. By 1989/90 a number of states and cities were beginning to experience fiscal stress as economic recession eroded tax bases, but politicians were unwilling or unable to increase taxes. Federal programmes were, once again, viewed by states and localities as possible saviours. In 1992, first the Los Angeles riots and then the Miami hurricane demonstrated that, like it or not, federal governments are expected to come up with major aid programmes following local or regional disasters. In both cases the Bush administration produced emergency aid packages. In spite of these events, the Bush years saw no major reversal of the trends established during the Reagan years.

During his first campaign for the presidency, Bill Clinton gave the strong impression that he would resume the old-style fiscal federalism of the 1960s and 1970s. He proposed an immediate $19.5 billion economic development package to stimulate the economy. He was politically close to a group of economists who believed that the federal government should play an enhanced role in the provision of infrastructure, and in particular transport and communications, to facilitate faster economic growth. What this would mean in practice would be greatly increased developmental aid to state and local governments. Once elected, he appointed one of these economists, Robert Reich, as his Secretary of Labour and, during the first two months of his administration, a revival of fiscal federalism looked imminent.

By the end of Clinton's first term, however, the political agenda had changed to such an extent that the administration's position on federalism looked more like that of President Reagan's than President Johnson's. What accounts for this transformation? For one thing, President Clinton's ambitious economic stimulus programme immediately ran into trouble in Congress. Republican Senators managed to block the legislation and, by the summer of 1993, many Democrats had become sceptical of the need for such an ambitious programme. For another thing, the economy recovered fast, and any new federal expenditure looked incompatible with the need to reduce the budget deficit. Within the administration, the influence of the fiscal conservatives increased while that of the proponents of an enhanced federal role declined. In the event, the only important measure passed that enhanced the federal role was a crime bill which provided new federal resources for local police enforcement.

The agenda changed again after the election of the Republican 104th Congress in 1994. Thereafter, proposed changes involved a *reduction* rather than an increase in federal aid to state and local governments. In particular, the new Congress wanted to change the *redistributive* as well as the *developmental* role of the federal government. Federal welfare programmes, especially, were seen to encourage dependency and discourage work. 'Workfare' rather than welfare became the slogan of the 1990s, and the states were to be allocated a major role in a reformed welfare system. We will return to this subject in chapter 14.

As of 1997 the outcome of these proposed changes is uncertain. What is for sure, however, is that it is now broadly accepted that the federal government should play only a limited role in developmental policy. Such matters as transportation, public safety and economic development are now accepted as primarily state and local responsibilities. Most experts agree that the federal government should play the major part in redistributive policy[14] – mainly because many of the poorer states do not have the tax capacity to provide adequate welfare programmes for the needy. This is broadly the position of the Clinton administration although, as indicated, some concessions to the Republican Congress have been made. Even liberal Democrats are now sensitive to the fact that the public's regard for the federal government has declined while its faith in state government has increased. This represents a sea change for the 1930s and the 1940s when public opinion took precisely the opposite direction (fig. 5.1).

The Pressure for National Standards

President Clinton's relations with the states are being tested not only by the problems associated with fiscal federalism. For, since the 1960s and accelerating during the 1980s, Congress began to employ a number of devices to achieve national standards in social and economic life. The most important of these are federal (or Congressional) pre-emption and cross-over sanctions.

Federal pre-emption, which can be statutory or attached to a condition of aid, is a legal requirement that states or local governments

---

14 *See* Peterson, *The Price of Federalism*, chapter 8.

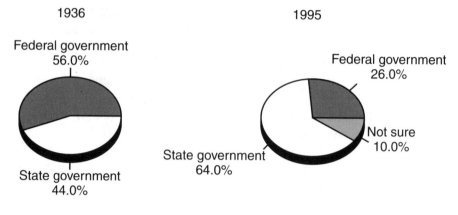

Figure 5.1 Public regard for federal and state governments, 1936 and 1995

Question asked: 'Which do you favor – concentration of power in the
federal government or in state government?'

Source: Gallup (1936) and Hart and Teeter Research Companies (1995) as presented by
Richard P. Nathan in 'Overview Essay on Federalism and Social Policy', unpublished, University of Princeton, 1996.

meet minimum standards or provide particular services. States cannot
now, for example, establish a minimum retirement age or regulate air-
line, bus or truck companies. In other areas, such as environmental
protection, states have to conform to national mandates or standards
and pay to do so. Some pre-emption statutes do provide some compensation towards the cost of implementation, but these rarely cover
the full costs.

Cross-over sanctions require states to comply with a law or lose
monies authorized earlier under other federal laws. In health care and
transport, threats of such sanctions are increasingly common. Perhaps
the most famous was the Reagan administration's insistence that all
states increase their minimum drinking age to 21 or lose federal highway funds. By 1987 all had complied. Cross-over sanctions can
involve the states and localities in expensive new policies.

Clearly, insistence on minimum or national standards introduces a
further element of conflict in US intergovernmental relations. Many
of the Reagan/Bush measures were aimed at freeing the market from
what were considered restrictive state laws or involved the application
of minimum penalties for such things as motoring offences. Clinton
has been more inclined to support minimum standards in environmental protection, civil rights, consumer protection and occupational
safety and health. These are more expensive to implement and are,
therefore, potentially more conflictual.

The Future of American Federalism

Most observers would agree that classical federalism, with state and federal governments each sovereign and separate in their own designated area, is very much dead – indeed, there is serious doubt that it ever applied in the United States. Co-operative federalism, which dominated intergovernmental relations from the 1930s to the 1970s, is also inappropriate as a description of the 1980s and 1990s. Competitive interdependence is a much more accurate label; but it describes federal, state and local relations not just federal-state interactions. If this is so, what is left of federalism? In strictly constitutional terms, not very much. Given the encroachment of federal powers and the relative independence of local governments, it is highly misleading to talk of shared sovereignty in the USA today. The states do remain important administrative and political units, however. As we noted at the beginning of the chapter, the states preserve variety – each continues to have its own separate legal and political system, and travelling from state to state, the observer is aware of distinctive political cultures. Certainly, the states preserve a degree of local or regional political autonomy which is quite unfamiliar in unitary systems. The states are now also much more *efficient* and professional as policy-makers than ever before. As state government has increased in size and status, it has attracted more able personnel. Governors are of higher quality, and corruption, although still very much a part of some states' political cultures, is less prevalent than it used to be. Finally, as suggested earlier, states now do a great deal more than they used to, not only in administering federal programmes but in running their own. But this resilience and growth derive not so much from constitutional imperatives as from traditions, custom and the fact that the states remain *convenient* jurisdictions for the representation of a variety of interests.

The weak constitutional position of the states was confirmed in a landmark 1985 Supreme Court decision, *Garcia v. San Antonio Metropolitan Transit Authority*, which permitted the federal government to regulate the wages of San Antonio bus workers. What was significant about the decision (arrived at by a five to four majority) was the rejection by the Court of any constitutional basis for this exercise of federal power. Instead the Court argued that limits to federal power 'inhered principally in the workings of the national government itself'.

While this decision is of great legal or constitutional import, the limits of federal power are as much set by political as by constitutional imperatives. For, irrespective of the legal position, the states will remain important administrative and political units. State law remains pre-eminent in many areas of economic and social life including industrial relations, insurance and all aspects of family law. At the same time, state and local taxes are the main source of revenue for a range of distinctive state and locally provided services including transport, education and law enforcement. If anything, the role of the states has increased as federal governments have required them to participate in the implementation of federally funded or partly funded programmes. By the late 1990s, there was an emerging consensus that the states should take on some of the tasks hitherto performed by the federal government. American society may be becoming more nationalized as federal standards increasingly apply. The constitutional position of the states may also be weak, but they remain highly convenient political and administrative units for the implementation of a broad range of federal and state programmes. As later chapters will show, federalism is at the very heart of some of the most important issues in American politics. The right to abortion, for example, is mandated by federal law. Anti-abortion or pro-choice activists want to return decisions on the subject to state legislatures many of which would abolish the right to abortion. In contrast, during the 1970s, the Supreme Court returned to the states the final say on capital punishment.

While federalism has been utilized by localist and anti-statist interests to inhibit the co-ordinating and planning role of the federal government, social reformers should be wary of criticizing the institution of federalism as such. They would be better advised to study those political and economic forces which have used federalism so successfully. The great paradox of the 1990s is that the main critics of federal power often have strong links with states and localities which are now locked into an interdependent relationship with the federal government.

Further Reading

The best general account of recent changes in American fiscal federalism is Paul E. Peterson, *The Price of Federalism*, (Washington DC, Brookings Institution, 1995). For the traditional view of the transition from conflictual to co-operative federalism, *see* Morton Grodzins's *The American System*, (Chicago, Rand McNally, 1966). Michael Reagan's *The New Federalism*, (New York, Oxford University Press, 1972), 2nd edition with John G. Sanzone, (1981), is a well-written account of changes in IGR during the 1960s and 1970s. For an account of the evolution of federalism from Johnson to Reagan, *see* David McKay, *Domestic Policy and Ideology: Presidents and the American State, 1964–1988*, (Cambridge, Cambridge University Press, 1989). An up-to-date account of the rise of federal power is Joseph P. Zimmerman's *Contemporary American Federalism: The Growth of National Power*, (Leicester University Press, 1992).

6

AMERICAN POLITICAL PARTIES IN TRANSITION

A democratic society has to provide a mode of consistent representation of relatively stable alignments or modes of compromise, in its polity. The mechanism of the American polity has been the two party system. If the party system, with its enforced mode of compromise, gives way, and 'issue politics' begin to polarize groups, then we have the classic recipe for what political scientists call 'a crisis of the regime', if not a crisis of disintegration and revolution.

Daniel Bell, *The Public Interest*

The American political party system is not an insoluble puzzle. But it does have more than its share of mysteries. The main one, arguably, is how it has survived for so long, or perhaps, how it survived at all, in a difficult and complicated environment.

William J. Keefe, *Parties, Politics and Public Policy in America*

To the outside observer, the American party system conjures up almost a caricature picture of American politics. Parties appear non-ideological, organizationally weak and in a constant state of crisis. In contrast, most European political parties have quite vivid public images based on class, regional, religious, linguistic, ethnic or ideological divisions. And when new parties emerge claiming support based on social consensus rather than cleavage (as did the British Social Democratic Party during the early 1980s) their 'pragmatism' or even 'opportunism' is viewed with distrust and suspicion.

While this is an oversimplified characterization of the two types of party system, it remains broadly true that American parties cover a much narrower band of the ideological spectrum than do their European counterparts. They are also much less *programmatic*, offering their supporters very general and diffuse policy options rather than the more structured and specific policy programmes associated with European parties. What is true of almost all party systems is that they are constantly developing and adapting to rapid social and economic changes – a fact which leads so many commentators to attach the label 'crisis' to the most recent development or electoral event. The remarkable thing about the American system is that it has always had just two major parties – although not always the same two parties – competing for major offices at any one time. Moreover, these parties have been largely non-ideological in style and policy substance, and this in a country constantly being buffeted by the very major social changes which immigration, industrialization and urbanization have brought.

A large part of this chapter will be devoted to explaining why the American party system has taken this particular shape. As we shall see, however, although this system has retained its two-party, largely non-ideological status through history, it has by no means been static or unchanging. In organization and function the parties have changed quite dramatically over the last 200 years – and indeed have even changed considerably over the last 30 years. To understand these changes it is first necessary to discuss the functions that political parties normally play in political systems.

The Functions of Parties

Although often abused by politicians and publics alike, political parties do perform vital functions in every political system, and in countries with democratic traditions they are an indisputably necessary part of the democratic process. In the American context parties perform at least five major functions.[1]

Aggregation of demands

In any society, social groups with particular interests to promote or defend need some means whereby their demands can be aggregated and articulated in government. Traditionally, political parties have performed this function – hence the association of party with particular social groups, regions or religions. In the USA, parties have acquired just such associations, although to a rather lesser extent than in some other countries. Hence, the Democrats became the party of

---

[1]   This list of functions – although not the discussion of them – is taken from Gerald M. Pomper, 'Party functions and party failures', in Gerald M. Pomper et al., *The Performance of American Government: Checks and Minuses*, (New York, Free Press, 1972), pp. 46–63.

Southern interests quite early in history although, by the 1930s, the Democrats had also become the party of the Northern industrial working class. The Republicans emerged from the Civil War as the party of national unity and later became identified as the party most interested in defending free enterprise and corporate power, an identification which remains today. But generally, parties in the United States have not been exclusively identified with one social group or class or one geographical region. Instead they tend to be coalitions of interests, aggregating demands on behalf of a number of social groups and regional interests. Given the relatively low level of ideological division and conflict in the USA (*see* chapter 3), this is, perhaps, unsurprising.

Conciliation of groups in society

Even in the most divided society some conciliation between competing or conflicting interests has to occur if government is to operate efficiently. Political parties often help this conciliation process by providing united platforms for the articulation of diverse interests. Indeed, in the USA there has hardly been a major political party that has not performed this function. In recent history, the Democrats have attempted (and until 1964 largely succeeded) in reconciling a rural segregationist South with the interests of the urban industrial North. In specific elections, the particular coalition of support established is uniquely determined by contemporary issues and candidates. So, in 1960, Democratic presidential candidate John F. Kennedy managed to appeal to the Catholic voters of the North (Kennedy was himself a Catholic) and Southern Protestants. In 1968 and 1972, the law-and-order issue cut across regions and classes and helped bring victory to Richard M. Nixon, the Republican candidate. By 1980 the Republicans had forged a new coalition consisting of a regional component (the West and the South), a religious/moral component (the fundamentalist Christian right) and an economic/ideological component (the middle classes and supporters of a 'return' to free enterprise). By conciliating such diverse groups and offering a common programme, Republican candidate Ronald Reagan was assured victory. In 1988 George Bush managed to retain the loyalty of sufficient numbers of these same groups to ensure victory. In 1992 Bill Clinton was successful in reviving at least parts of the old New Deal coalition by appealing to industrial workers, minorities, women and many middle-class voters on the issue of economic revival. His appeal in 1996 was slightly different based as it was on a vote for the status quo. As in 1992, however, Clinton managed to form a complex coalition of support based on gender, ethnicity and region (the West and the industrial North).

Clearly, political parties have to appeal to a number of competing and potentially conflicting interests if they are to succeed in a country as diverse and complex as the United States. As a result, parties have tended to move towards the middle of the ideological spectrum, avoiding those more extreme positions which are likely to alienate potential supporters. Noting this tendency towards moderation, political theorists have produced a more general model of party behaviour which assumes that if parties are rational and really want to win elections they will *always* move towards the centre. For, only in this way can they ensure majority electoral support.[2] Whatever its merits in other countries, this theory seems particularly apt in the United States where, with rather few exceptions (of which more later), parties have remained remarkably moderate.

Staffing the government

In a modern, complex society parties are a necessary link in the relationship between government and people. According to social-contract theory, governments must be held accountable for their actions. If they are perceived to be failing, then the people can always replace them at election time. Unfortunately, accountability and responsiveness can never be continuous or complete except in very small societies or communities. Given this, parties provide the public with a focus for accountability. Once elected, a president appoints government officials to fill the major posts in the new administration. Not only departmental chiefs (members of the cabinet) but also the top civil service positions are filled in the main through party linkages (*see* chapter 11). When judging the performance of the government, therefore, the public can look to the record of an administration united by a common party label and, presumably, a common set of policies. As the party is rooted in society via democratic party organization, staffing the government through party helps to ensure an intimate link between the implementation of policies and public preference. This at least is the theory of how party should operate in government. As we will discover later the practice is rather different. One serious practical problem occurs when party organization, rather than reflecting the interests of social groups or regions, is instead merely the vehicle for the promotion and election of a particular *candidate*. Another problem, to which we will now turn, occurs when different branches of government have different constituencies and therefore distinct party organizations.

---

[2]   Anthony Downs, *An Economic Theory of Democracy*, (New York, Harper and Row, 1957).

Co-ordination of government institutions

As has already been noted several times in this book, American government is uncommonly fragmented. National legislature is separated from executive. Federalism adds further fragmenting influence by giving state (and through the states, local) governments considerable independence from the federal authorities. In centralized systems with cabinet government, parties actually dominate institutions. In Britain, for example, powerful political party organizations nominate candidates, fight elections, and, if successful, form the government out of a majority in the House of Commons. By exercising control over the party organization, governments (or oppositions) can usually ensure the obedience of individual Members of Parliament. In this sense party is hardly needed as a co-ordinating influence, because a system of party government prevails. In marked contrast, America's separated powers and federal arrangements greatly aggravate problems of co-ordination, and, as numerous American political scientists have pointed out, party is the main means whereby disparate institutions can co-ordinate the formulation and implementation of policy.[3]

So, even if state and local government, Congress and president have different constituencies, a common party label can provide a means of communication and co-ordination. In fact, Democratic governors, mayors and members of Congress normally do have more in common with Democratic presidents than with Republican presidents – although we will discover later they often do not. Moreover, there have been periods in American history when relations between Congress and president have been greatly aided by political party ties. During the Jeffersonian period, for example, something approaching party government prevailed. More recently, Presidents Franklin Roosevelt and Lyndon Johnson (both Democrats) used party ties greatly to enhance their relations with Congress and thus erect major new social programmes. During the 1969–77 and 1981–93 periods, Republican presidents faced a Congress dominated by Democrats although the Republicans held the Senate between 1981 and 1987. Divided government of a very different sort prevailed after 1994 when the Republicans controlled Congress and the Democrats the presidency. As we will see, government co-ordination became particularly difficult during these years.

At the state and local levels, the co-ordinating function of party has taken a rather different form. In the decades immediately following

---

[3] Hence the pleas for a system of 'responsible party government' in the USA. For a summary of this literature, *see* Austin Ranney, *Curing the Mischiefs of Faction: Party Reform in America*, (Berkeley, University of California Press, 1975).

the Civil War, municipal and, to a lesser extent, state governments proved less than adequate in dealing with successive waves of immigrants from Europe. Hopelessly divided and fragmented institutionally and politically, local governments could do little to improve transport, housing and other urban facilities, or even to ensure a reasonable degree of public order. Political parties filled this void through the creation of the political machine – an informal 'government' based on patronage, bribery and corruption.[4] Machines depended on tightly knit grass-roots organization with the party providing ordinary citizens with direct access to the political authorities. Officials in the legitimate government gained through patronage and bribes and the party was given a guarantee of political power in return. Although hardly welfare organizations, the urban machines of the late nineteenth and early twentieth centuries did at least keep government going in the great cities by providing an essential buffer between the immigrant masses and a hostile economic and political environment.

Promotion of political stability

Parties do not always promote political stability. In many countries parties mobilize movements against existing regimes and are a major force in bringing regime change. Moreover, if *governmental* (as opposed to regime) stability is the measure, it is clear that the multi-party systems of Western Europe do anything but promote stability, as the Danish, Dutch and Italian systems testify. In 'mature' democracies, however, parties do help socialize citizens into an acceptance of the regime, if only by legitimizing national parliaments and assemblies and facilitating the peaceful transferral of power from one government to another.

For reasons which we will discuss later, America's two-party system has proved remarkably resilient, with the result that the country has never suffered the problems associated with a proliferation of organized parties. Although the causal lines are blurred, it does seem reasonable to argue that American political parties have helped promote political stability. Quite frequently, for example, political movements outside the mainstream of American political life have had their policies pre-empted by one of the leading parties. This happened to the Populists during the 1890s when much of their programme was adopted by the Democrats, and to a number of left-wing parties and movements during the early New Deal period. Moreover, the two

---

[4]   The classic account of the machine is by Harold F. Gosnell, *Machine Politics: Chicago Model*, (Chicago, University of Chicago Press, 1937).

most significant third parties of the twentieth century, the Progressives and the American Independent Party, grew out of existing parties and were eventually reincorporated into them. In both cases the breakaway was led by a single charismatic figure – Theodore Roosevelt in the case of the Progressives and George Wallace in the case of the American Independent Party. In fact, George Wallace effectively *was* the party and without him it simply disappeared. But the crucial point is that the issues that inspired both movements – disputes over the federal government's role in economy and society and the racial integration of the South – and which the existing parties could not accommodate – did *not* lead to a permanent split in the party movement. Instead, either the Democrats and Republicans adapted to the new demands or the movements themselves were reincorporated into the mainstream once the protest had been made. In a rather different context, Ross Perot's strong showing as a third candidate in 1992 (19 per cent of the vote) showed disillusionment among voters with the Republican and Democratic party candidates. Significantly, however, it did not lead in any way to the emergence of a third party. Indeed Perot's second challenge to the two-party system in 1996 proved much less effective, when he managed just 8 per cent of the vote.

The constantly impressive ability of American political parties to

Plate 6.1 Jefferson Davis. Undated political cartoon.

Table 6.1 The development of American political parties

Period	Majority party	Minority party
1789–1800	*Federalist:* A coalition of Mercentile and Northern land-owning interests led by Alexander Hamilton, George Washington and John Adams.	*Republican* (the first Republican party): A coalition of farmers and planters based in the central and Southern states and led by Thomas Jefferson.
1800–56	*Democratic–Republican:* The original Republican coalition was consolidated in this period under James Madison. Later, under the leadership of Andrew Jackson and Martin Van Buren, the party broadened its mass appeal and was renamed the Democratic Party.	*Federalist* then *Whig:* Federalists, Whigs and a number of smaller parties failed to challenge the Democratic–Republican ascendancy. Victories by the conservative Whigs in 1840 and 1848 were temporary exceptions and led to the rather inauspicious presidencies of William Harrison and Zachary Taylor, both of whom died in office.
1856–1932	*Republican:* The Civil War produced a second Republican Party championing the Unionist cause under Abraham Lincoln. Following the War, a coalition of industrialists, bankers, Northern and Western farmers and some industrial workers proved formidable. Apart from Abraham Lincoln, only Theodore Roosevelt (1901–9) proved a memorable president. The era of strong local and state party organizations and machine politics.	*Democratic:* Democratic strength remained firmly rooted in the South where poor whites and larger landowners supported the party (those Blacks briefly enfranchised after the War supported the Republicans). The four Democratic victories of 1884, 1892, 1912 and 1916 were greatly aided by splits in the Republican ranks.
1932–64	*Democratic:* The era of the New Deal coalition, with the South, the unions, the big cities, ethnic groups and intellectuals providing a near-permanent majority in the House and the Senate. Franklin Roosevelt, Harry Truman, John Kennedy and Lyndon Johnson are all notable presidents.	*Republican:* Relegated to minority status, the Republican victories in 1952 and 1956 are attributable to the charismatic appeal of Dwight Eisenhower. Main Republican support comes from rural areas, big business, middle-class suburbanites, the West and New England.
1964–80	*Democratic:* Period of the breakdown of the New Deal Coalition. The South first votes for segregationist candidate George Wallace and then increasingly for Republican candidates. Vietnam and social issues split the traditional blue-collar, industrial-worker Democratic vote, some of which defects to the Republicans. The Democrats remain the majority party in Congress and in state and local government, but manage only one presidential election victory in 1976.	*Republican:* With victories by Richard Nixon in 1968 and 1972, the Republicans exploit divisions in the Democratic Party. They also make major inroads into the South. Their association with the Watergate scandal (1973–77), however, leads to an overwhelmingly Democratic Congress in 1974 and indirectly helps the defeat of President Ford in 1976.

Table 6.1 Continued

Period	*no clear majority party*	
1980–	*Democratic:* Although the Democrats win the 1992 and 1996 presidential elections, their support is gradually eroded during these years. They lose the Senate, 1981 to 1987 and both houses of Congress after 1994. Generally their support collapses in the South, and they are no longer the dominant party at the state and local levels. Their appeal remains high among women, minorities and in the North-East of the country, however.	*Republican:* With three presidential election victories and success in Congress after 1994, there is much talk of a Republican realignment. While this is true of the South, the West and the North and East remain highly competitive at the state, local and national levels. The Republicans do, however, redefine themselves as the party of fiscal rectitude, moral or family values and a transfer of power from the federal to state governments. Generally, public identification with the two parties declines which shows itself in declining electoral turn-out and increasing disillusionment with political institutions.

absorb potentially destabilizing social movements has no doubt contributed to the stability of the system, although the more enquiring mind could note that the two major parties have been able to perform this function only because there have been so few deep ideological divisions in American society. A more divided society could not possibly sustain such a monopoly of power shared by two such amorphous and adaptable parties.

Crisis and Change in the American Party System

At least since the early 1950s, political scientists have bemoaned the decline of American political parties. The 'crisis' has been identified mainly in terms of a constant erosion of the five functions listed above. In what is already a highly fragmented political system, the decline of these functions has, so the argument runs, led to highly inefficient government ridden with indecision and confusion.

To understand this critique it is necessary to be familiar with the development of American political parties. Table 6.1 provides a schematic outline of their history by identifying five distinct stages of development. Such a brief summary of the parties' growth must oversimplify somewhat. In particular the outline implies that the parties have mobilized different regions and social groups in a coherent way throughout history. But this has never been the case. With the notable exception of the Civil War period, the parties have always represented broad coalitions, and they have almost always eschewed appeals to those class-based ideologies that exploit social divisions in society.

Until the early years of the nineteenth century, parties were considered useful only as temporary expedients, or as 'factions' necessary to mobilize political power in response to particular crises. As was emphasized in chapter 3, the Constitution and the political culture generally in the New Republic were deeply suspicious of political parties and their implied threat of government by factions, tyrannical majorities and mass political action. Significantly, when, under the guidance of Andrew Jackson and Martin Van Buren, mass parties did develop, they did so in a way that largely avoided the dangers foreseen by the Founding Fathers. The new Democratic Party appealed to broad principles of political equality (at least for white males) rather than to narrow class and sectional interests. It also transformed the party into a highly *instrumental* organization. For the first time the idea that working for the party could bring specific rewards for the individual became influential. So party membership and loyalty brought with it rewards or political 'spoils' of which patronage was the most important. Clearly, delivering the vote and distributing patronage required organization, and it was during this period that local and state parties acquired permanent organizations, as Michael Wallace and others have documented.[5] What united these new party organizations was a simple belief in equal opportunity for white males (and a concomitant opposition to aristocratic political values) and in the party as a distributor of spoils. Beyond this the party represented little that was tangible. Great local and regional variety was encouraged rather than tolerated.

A party based on equality and democracy (achieved mainly through the extension of the franchise) and which adopted a new instrumentalism in organization was hardly likely to undermine the republicanism and constitutionalism which the Founding Fathers so feared would be threatened by mass parties. From the very beginning, therefore, mass political parties in the United States built their electoral competition not on appeals to class, ethnic or religious division, but rather by adapting their programmes to what was always a broad base of support for individualism and democracy. In this context the parties were also able to aid the presidential nomination process by limiting competition and providing truly national constituencies.

As we know, this new party system was far from being completely successful. Southern Democrats were determined to champion their exclusive sectional interests, and the Civil War effectively destroyed

[5]   Michael L. Wallace, 'Changing concepts of party in the United States: New York, 1815–28', *American Historical Review* 74, 1968, pp. 453–91.

the first mass party system. As table 6.1 shows, what emerged after the War was a dominant Republican Party, again depending on a broad coalition of support. It was also during the latter half of the nineteenth century that parties became associated with corruption and the growth of the large urban political machine. Much has been written about the machine, although nobody quite captured the spirit of the period as did George Washington Plunkitt, the notorious boss of New York's Tammany Hall. His comment that 'you can't keep an organization together without patronage. Men ain't in politics for nothin'. They want to get somethin' out of it'[6] gives some of the flavour of the time. Milton Rakove has characterized the machine in slightly more academic terms: 'An effective political party needs five things: offices, jobs, money, workers, and votes. Offices beget jobs and money; jobs and money beget workers; workers beget votes; and votes beget offices.'[7] It follows that if one party controls all the offices, it effectively controls the politics in that jurisdiction. Just such a pattern emerged in numerous nineteenth-century towns and cities (and in a modified form in some states). Scholars have cited a number of reasons for the spread of machine politics, the most important being the growing need for an institution capable of integrating a diverse and ever-increasing number of urban immigrants into American society. With state and local authorities unwilling or unable to provide immigrants with good government, political machines stepped in to fill the gap.

The new Americans, confused, intimidated or exploited by employers, landlords or the police, could turn to party precinct captains or ward bosses for help. In return the machine demanded electoral loyalty.

Machine politics permeated party systems from the lowest ward and precinct level up to city and, in some cases, state committees. Fig. 6.1 shows the basic party organizational structure which emerged during this period and which still holds true in most states today. As will be developed later, this structure used to be very much a 'bottom up' affair with the committees at county level and below as the key organizational units.

In spite of the emergence of a largely middle-class reform movement intent on cleansing the cities of machine politics, the machine remained an important part of the American scene until well after World War II. But some of the reforms introduced in the late nine-

---

[6]   William Riordan, *Plunkitt of Tammany Hall*, (New York, E. P. Dutton, 1963), p. 63.
[7]   Milton Rakove, *Don't Make No Waves, Don't Back No Losers*, (Bloomington, Indiana University Press, 1975), p. 42.

Figure 6.1 Party organizational structure

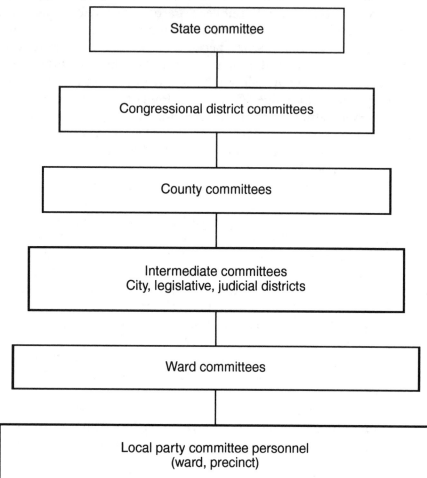

teenth and early twentieth centuries did have a significant and lasting
effect on American politics. A major concern of the reformers was to
remove the partisan element from the electoral process. Accordingly,
most of the proposed changes involved weakening the link between
parties and electors. Party labels were removed from voting lists;
elected mayors were sometimes replaced by city managers appointed
by the local assembly; candidates were elected 'at large' or from a list
covering the whole city rather than on a ward-by-ward basis; and,
most significant, *primaries* were introduced to deny the party machines
control over nominations for office. Instead, voters were given a direct
say in who was to be nominated through an intra-party primary election. These and other reforms hardly transformed the American party
system. At best they had a limited effect in certain areas and regions,

particularly in the more populist Mountain and Western states. *Local party machines* were, in any case, the main target of the reformers for it was in the burgeoning industrial cities that the most corrupt regimes had developed.

Primary elections, however, soon affected national parties as an increasing number of states adopted them for presidential elections. By 1916 no less than 20 states required the parties to go direct to the voters to decide the selection of delegates to the national nominating convention (*see* table 6.2)[8] rather than rely on party machines with party bosses deciding among themselves who should go to the convention pledged to a particular candidate.

In fact, between the 1920s and the 1960s, this democratizing trend in American political parties received little fresh impetus. On the contrary, this period witnessed something of a return to old-fashioned party politics. Presidential primaries declined (to a mere 16 or 17 in 1968), as the nominating power reverted to the state party caucuses. And at the local level parties often found ways of bypassing the institutional obstacles to party hegemony.[9] It would be misleading, however, to characterize these trends simply as a return to the old model. In many ways they were profoundly different from the late nineteenth century. Above all, after 1932 the Democratic Party emerged as the 'majority' party constructed around a seemingly invincible coalition consisting of the South, Northern industrial workers, ethnic minorities and an increasingly insecure middle class. Local, state and even national Democratic Party organizations were greatly strengthened by this enduring coalition which scored victory after victory at every level of politics. But, unlike the nineteenth century, these party organizations did not primarily function as intermediaries between the authorities and urban masses. By the 1930s, welfare and social security reforms reduced the dependence of the poor on party workers, and government officials themselves became increasingly professional and less susceptible to bribery and corruption. Instead, parties developed into modern organizations performing, albeit imperfectly, many of the functions described above. The parties also became markedly more ideological, with the Democrats clearly emerging as the party of the left and the Republicans as the party of the right. Indeed almost all the major social and economic reforms in the 1933 to 1968 period

---

[8] Nominating conventions are the party conferences held during the summer preceding presidential elections to choose presidential and vice-presidential candidates. For a fuller discussion, *see* chapter 9.

[9] Chicago, for example, was 'reformed', but the mayor retained his position as 'boss' through control over the Cook County Democratic Party which contains the city of Chicago. See Mike Royko, *Boss. Mayor Richard J. Daley of Chicago*, (New York, E. P. Dutton, 1971).

were initiated by Democratic administrations. While hardly socialist in conception or outcome, these have resulted in a much enhanced role for the federal movement in society.

But, even by the 1940s, there were signs that the New Deal coalition was not completely secure. The South, in particular, found what were very hesitant steps taken by the Truman administration on civil rights unpalatable and, by the 1968 election, the Democratic-led integration of the South resulted in open revolt, with George Wallace leading a breakaway Southern party intent on preserving racial segregation. As important, the considerable – and very 'un-American' – ideological cohesion of the Democratic Party began to crumble as suburbanization, affluence and a changing occupational structure slowly transformed the political agenda. We will discuss the relationship between these changes and voting in some detail in chapter 7, but for now it is important to explain their effects on political parties.

It obvious that if parties are to perform their functions competently they must have some internal cohesion. Within Congress a party label must mean something more than mere nomenclature. If a common party is the major means whereby Congress and president can liaise, then president and legislators must have at least some shared policies and perspectives. When a president staffs the executive branch, he or she must assume that his/her appointees broadly share the same philosophy of government as he/she does. Such party cohesion must have roots in the broader society; in effect, some form of party organization must exist to facilitate the exchange of ideas, and to mobilize electoral support and nominate candidates. It was the apparent erosion of cohesion and party organization from the mid-1960s that worried so many commentators. Three major questions are raised here: what was the nature of party decline? what explains it; and, more controversially, does it really matter – especially given recent evidence of revival in the state and national parties?

Party Decline

There is a number of ways of measuring party decline, the most common of which are: membership, party identification, organization and control over candidate nominations, ideological cohesion and, of course, voting patterns including electoral turn-out. By all these measures parties have been in decline, although party membership is not a meaningful measure in the USA as it is equivalent to the simple act of registering (usually as a Democrat or Republican) to vote in most states. In other words, people do not *join* and pay dues in the European manner. Party identification, or the psychological attachment that individual voters have to particular parties has been weakening steadily over the last 40 years, with the number of Independents[10] clearly on the rise – at least until the late 1970s. (*See* fig. 6.2.)

Weaker party identification produces a much more fickle electorate prone to sudden shifts in loyalty, to ticket splitting and to voting for individual candidates or issues rather than according to traditional party ties. Measuring changes in party organization is rather more difficult. Certainly the party machine model no longer applies. Recent research has shown that, even in an archetypal machine city, elected officials no longer expect party loyalty and service in return for the patronage they dispense.[11] But the typical party organization described earlier still applies even if individual activist's motivations have changed.

Party organization has always been loose in the United States, and it remains the case that the higher the level of committee the looser it becomes. Much of the essential work of fund-raising and campaigning occurs at the precinct level, with the counties also playing a major role in some states. State parties vary in organizational strength. In some states (mainly in the West) state parties are quite powerful in such areas as fund-raising and slating state-wide candidates. Unfortunately, there is no consistent pattern; much depends on the history and tradition of individual states.[12]

Until the 1970s it was normal to characterize the national party committees as little more than very loose *ad hoc* organizations which emerged every four years to help arrange the national conventions. They are very much more than this today, however. The Republican National Committee (RNC), in particular, has acquired a range of new resources and powers since the 1970s, including a capacity to run direct-mailing campaigns on behalf of candidates at the national and the state levels. The RNC also provides staff and technical services (polling, breakdowns of local and regional voting patterns) for candidates. Much of the impetus for this new role came from RNC Chairman William E. (Bill) Brock (1977–81) who realized the potential for a national role in what had become a much more ideologically unified Republican Party. Although stronger than it used to be, the Democratic National Committee (DNC) has not assumed a similar role – probably because the Democratic Party is more fragmented than the Republican, and the ideological unity between different candidates

---

[10]   The concept of 'independent' voter, virtually unknown in most European countries, well established in America. *See* chapter 7, pp. 128–9.

[11]   For a general discussion, *see* Martin P. Wattenberg, *The Decline of American Political Parties, 1952–1988*, (Cambridge, Mass., Harvard University Press, 1990).

[12]   For a discussion, *see* John F. Bibby et al., 'Assessing party organizational strength', *American Journal of Political Science*, vol. 27, 1983, pp. 193–222.

Figure 6.2 Democrats, Republicans, and Independents in the United States, 1952–90

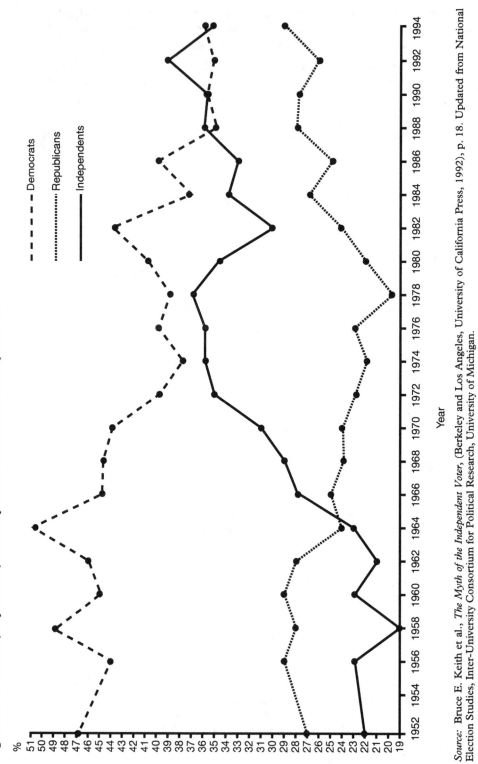

Source: Bruce E. Keith et al., *The Myth of the Independent Voter*, (Berkeley and Los Angeles, University of California Press, 1992), p. 18. Updated from National Election Studies, Inter-University Consortium for Political Research, University of Michigan.

and local parties is lower. The staff of the RNC grew from just 30 in 1972 to 600 in 1984 and had acquired a budget of over $100 million. In addition, the Republican committees responsible for helping House and Senate candidates also grew in strength and influence. Under the leadership of Bill Paxon of New York the national Republican Party played a key role in the famous mid-term Congressional victories in 1994.

Generally, the Democratic national committees, although much more active than they were during the 1960s, have employed fewer staff and raised less money than the Republican total. This said, in 1992 under the guidance of Democratic Chairperson Ron Brown, the DNC was successful in raising money for Bill Clinton and Al Gore. Even so, they received most of their funds from direct contributions.

What the DNC has initiated, however, is a series of enquiries into the presidential nominating process, including how the party chooses delegates to the national convention. The first of these, the McGovern–Fraser Commission (1969), recommended that state parties change their rules so as to allow greater participation by minorities, women and the young at the convention. Two subsequent enquiries, the Mikulski Commission (1972–73) and the Winograd Commission (1975–78), further refined these rule-changes. Most recently, the Hunt Commission (1981–82) and the Fairness Commission (1984–85) have moved the party in a quite different direction, requiring as they did increased representation of party regulars and elected officials (the so-called super-delegates). The background to these changes will be discussed below.

What of the party activists themselves? Only about 2 per cent of the adult population are active participants in party organizations, almost all of which are locally based. Generally, over the last few years, these activists have become more candidate- and issue-oriented, one of their main motivations being to promote a particular candidate or to fight for just one special issue. Critics argue that these trends have weakened party organization and coherence even further.

One area where the role of party organization can be accurately measured is control over nominations. At the presidential level, at least, the trend here was, until 1980, unequivocal. As table 6.2 shows, primaries spread to the point where, in 1980, around 75 per cent of Democratic and Republican delegates to the national conventions were chosen or bound by primary elections. In quite dramatic fashion, therefore, the intra-party means of choosing delegates (party caucuses and conventions the use of which actually increased between 1916 and 1968) were rejected, leaving this key decision to the mass of voters themselves. After 1980 concern in the Democratic Party, in particular, that it was losing control of nominations led to a partial return to

Table 6.2 Number of presidential primaries and percentage of convention delegates from primary states, by party, 1912–96

Year	*Democratic*[2]		*Republican*	
	Number of primaries	*Percentage of delegates from primary states*[1]	*Number of primaries*	*Percentage of delegates*
1912	12	32.9	13	41.7
1916	20	53.5	20	58.9
1920	16	44.6	20	57.8
1924	14	35.5	17	45.3
1928	17	42.2	16	44.9
1932	16	40.0	14	37.7
1936	14	36.5	12	37.5
1940	13	35.8	13	38.8
1944	14	36.7	13	38.7
1948	14	36.3	12	36.0
1952	15	38.7	13	39.0
1956	19	42.7	19	44.8
1960	16	38.3	15	38.6
1964	17	45.7	17	45.6
1968	17	37.5	16	34.3
1972	23	60.5	22	52.7
1976	29[1]	72.6	28[1]	67.9
1980	31[1]	74.7	35[1]	74.3
1984	26	62.9	30	68.2
1988	34	66.6	35	76.9
1992	39	78.8	38	80.4
1996[3]	37	83.5	41	85.9

[1] Does not include Vermont, which holds non-binding presidential preference votes but chooses delegates in state caucuses and conventions.
[2] Includes party leaders and elected officials chosen from primary states.
[3] Based on preliminary primary and caucus schedules as of April 1995.
Source: Stephen J. Wayne, *The Road to the White House, 1996,* (New York, St Martin's Press, 1996), table 6.2.

the caucus method (table 6.2). Even these, however, are more open to popular pressure than 'old-style' party meetings. In fact, by 1988, the trend towards the use of primaries was re-established and, by 1996, more than 83 per cent of delegates to the conventions were chosen by this route. As we will discuss later, these particular changes have had particularly significant consequences for the state of the modern presidency.

The evidence on intra-party cohesion is also quite unequivocal. A host of surveys has shown how, since the mid-1960s, the issues which bound the New Deal coalition together – and which provided a convenient target for the Republicans – have either receded in importance or have been diluted by the emergence of other, less class-based issues. Until the mid-1970s, the major change involved the decline of economic issues in relation to 'social' issues. In 1975 Walter Dean Burnham characterized this shift in the terms shown in fig. 6.3.

Figure 6.3 Cross-cutting issues in the late 1960s and early 1970s

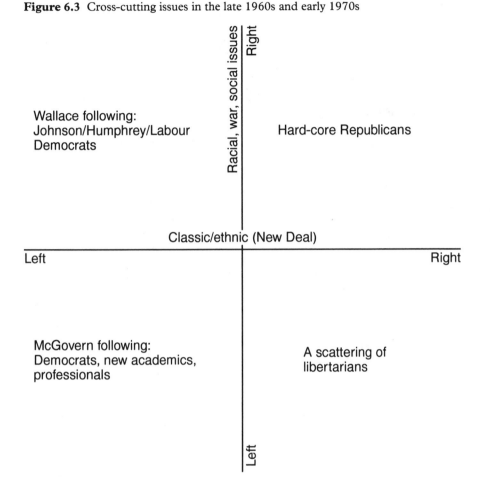

Source: Adapted from *The American Party Systems: Stages of Political Development*, 2nd edn, edited by William Nisbet Chambers and Walter Dean Burnham, © 1975 Oxford University Press Inc. p. 340. Reprinted by permission.

What Burnham was describing here was what social scientists call 'cross-cutting cleavages' or the fact that individuals and social groups often lack ideological coherence across all issues. Hence, in the late 1960s, many industrial workers and trade unionists remained left wing on economic or class issues, while finding themselves on the right of the political spectrum over racial questions and the Vietnam War. While fig. 6.3 is now out of date, the phenomenon of cross-cutting cleavages is still very much with us. Fig. 6.4 attempts to characterize the divisions of the early-1980s. Although not shown by these figures, which give no indication of the *distribution* of support for these issues, the major shift from the earlier period is the emergence of a much more ideologically coherent right, organized around the presidency of Ronald Reagan. In the early 1970s, the majority party, the

Figure 6.4 Cross-cutting issues in the early 1980s

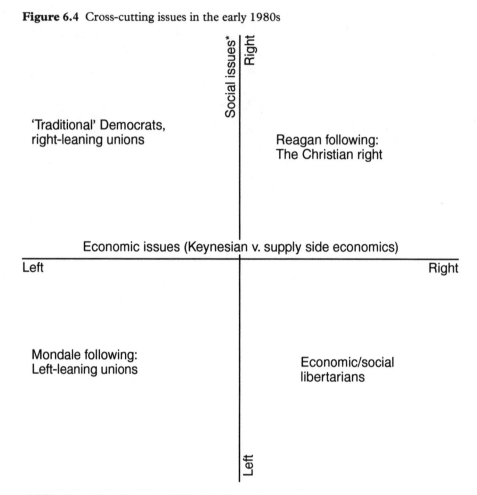

'Traditional' Democrats, right-leaning unions

Reagan following: The Christian right

Economic issues (Keynesian v. supply side economics)

Mondale following: Left-leaning unions

Economic/social libertarians

* Affirmative action, abortion, civil liberties, the environment.

Democrats, was in disarray, its support being split between the two left-hand segments of fig. 6.3. By the early 1980s this division continued to affect the Democrats, and a number of commentators were claiming that the Republican right was fast assuming the status of majority party. But the Reagan victories were not to be repeated at the Congressional or state levels, and by 1988 Democratic presidential prospects improved, even though George Bush was the eventual winner.

Clearly this recovery was related to the personalities of the respective candidates, but it was also related to issues. As fig. 6.5 shows, by the late 1990s, it was possible to make distinctions according to the public's and candidates' association with economic/welfare state issues and social policy issues. The former refer to such questions as the budget deficit, job security (providing a minimum notice of dismissal for laid-off workers), education, training, relief for economically distressed regions and health care and welfare reform. The latter refer to the conscience and gender issues (abortion, civil liberties, prayers in public schools), affirmative action (civil rights enforcement), the environment, consumer protection, occupational safety and child care. Note that by 1996 the three presidential candidates were closer together on the economic/welfare dimension than was the case in the 1970s and 1980s. Today, social issues are the main source of division between the parties, or at least between politicians.

Indeed, as the electorate has become more volatile and a politics of personalities rather than issues has developed, so it has become increasingly difficult to characterize the parties in terms even of a loose ideological profile. Ever more complex cross-cutting issues are leading the system further and further away from the relative ideological cohesion associated with the New Deal. Such an analysis helps

Figure 6.5 Cross-cutting issues in the late 1990s

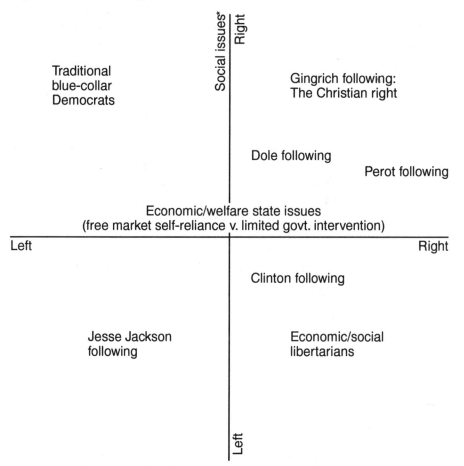

* Affirmative action, abortion, child care, civil liberties, the environment.

explain the success of Ross Perot in 1992, an independent candidate who stood as a protest candidate in opposition to traditional party politics.[13] The rise of split-ticket voting provides additional evidence of a public less committed to one party or another. As we will discuss in later chapters, split-ticket voting and the consequent phenomenon of divided government have become the rule rather than the exception in American government.

Explaining Party Change

Reference has already been made to the social and economic changes usually invoked to explain party decline. Affluence, increasing levels of education and suburbanization have produced less 'solidaristic' communities, as the sociologists put it. In other words, a political life based on an individual's place of work or neighbourhood has become increasingly irrelevant as the mobile service-sector worker living in a sprawling suburb or semi-rural area, replaces the blue-collar inner-city industrial worker as the 'norm' in American society. This new, essentially middle-class citizen has acquired a political life defined not just in terms of occupation or geographical location, but also in terms of his or her individual characteristics, preferences, prejudices and particular interests. In response to this much more complex and less categorizable voter, the parties have themselves changed, becoming even less programmatic and ideological. But, in trying to be all things to all citizens, parties have become progressively less appealing. It stands to reason that an ideology- or class- (or region-, or religion-) based party can have instant attraction to voters whose lifestyles and occupational interests coincide closely with those represented by party policies. A more amorphous, non-ideological party is rarely as appealing and always runs the risk of alienating a particular section of society should it commit itself to a specific policy. Should one of the parties decide to commit itself to a single position or grouping – much as did George McGovern on the left in 1972 and, to a lesser degree, George Bush with his wooing of the Republican right in 1992 – then electoral defeat is almost certainly going to follow.

But we should counsel caution in accepting this sociological analysis. Many groups – and particularly ethnic and racial minorities – remain 'solidaristic', concentrated as they are in ghettos and in lower-paid manual jobs. At the other end of the political spectrum,

---

[13]   For a discussion of Perot in the 1992 election *see* Gerald M. Pomper, 'The Presidential Election,' in Gerald M. Pomper et al., *The Election of 1992: Reports and Interpretations*, (Chatham N. J., Chatham House, 1993).

the Republican right has shown an impressive ideological cohesion on a range of issues. More importantly, this analysis suggests some simple past when American political parties represented 'left' and 'right' in society with reasonable coherence. But, as repeatedly pointed out in this chapter, this has never been the case. Parties have always been essentially non-ideological, and even the New Deal Democratic Party was marked by a degree of internal dissension and compromise over policies which would be unusual in European class-based parties.

A related explanation for the decline of parties concentrates less on societal changes and more on the performance of government itself. Hence the 'overload' thesis argues that the increasing democratization of American society has placed an excessive load on what is in any case a complex decision-making system. Unable to cope with the array of competing demands placed on them, institutions have increasingly come under fire from a disenchanted public. Indeed, during the early 1970s a burgeoning literature on declining trust in government hinted that public disillusionment with political institutions posed a threat to democracy itself.[14] Although this particular argument is now largely discredited, it remains the case that parties continue to take much of the blame for public disenchantment with politics. For to repeat the point, it has been the failure of parties to provide coherent programmes, to staff the government, to help smooth relations between Congress and president which, so the criticism goes, accounts for the failure of successive administrations to solve America's problems.

Paradoxically, attempts within the parties to improve their performance may actually have aggravated the situation. By the mid-1960s activists in both parties, but particularly from within the ranks of the Democrats, became increasingly disillusioned with the undemocratic nature of intra-party decision-making. Both parties were dominated by age cohorts recruited during the New Deal period – male, white, middle aged and middle income (upper middle income in the case of the Republicans). The new activists, most of whom were strongly committed to the 'new' issues of the 1960s – social reform in the case of the Democrats, economic liberalism with the Republicans – slowly but surely began to take over local and state party organizations. In doing so they insisted on more open decision-making structures and better access by underrepresented groups – within the Democratic Party, Blacks, women, the poor and younger people. It was this quite virulent intra-party reform movement that paved the way for the

[14] For a discussion of this literature, *see* David McKay, 'The United States in crisis: a review of the political literature', *Government and Opposition*, vol. 14, no. 3, summer 1979.

spread of primary elections and for new rules at nominating conventions favouring delegates from underrepresented groups (as recommended by the 1969 McGovern-Fraser Commission). As we have mentioned, the spread of primaries actually weakened both parties as the crucial power of control over nominations passed directly to the voters. And more open conventions led, in the case of the Democrats, to party opinions and policies seriously out of tune with those supported by the 'typical' Democratic voter. Hence, the now famous 1972 Democratic convention was dominated by new 'social issue' delegates (*see* bottom left quadrant of fig. 6.3) who nominated a candidate, George McGovern, with very little support from traditional 'economic issue' Democrats.[15] Since 1972 the Democrats have modified the party rules so as to permit a less rigid selection of delegates and to ensure some representation of party regulars and elected officials (the so-called super-delegates) but, in one important sense, the change was permanent, for the events of the late 1960s and early 1970s reduced the influence of regular activists in myriad state and local parties. In their stead, a new breed of party volunteers had taken over many party organizations. Paradoxically, this new type of activist was *more* middle class than the people they replaced, in spite of the fact that the changes were themselves inspired by calls for equal opportunity and greater representation of the poor and minorities. The explanation here is simple: people who *volunteer* their services and who care about issues are usually educated, competent and well informed. Many of the old-style party workers were recipients of party patronage or had become active during the 1930s and 1940s when there was a clearer relationship between party and class. As a result, the old-style Democratic activists, although white, male and middle aged, were decidedly less well educated and generally of lower socio-economic status than the new-style party workers who replaced them.

Unravelling cause and effect when explaining party decline is difficult. The rise of the social issue during the 1960s resulted in large part from changes in American society, although also from the way in which the Vietnam War was being conducted. Parties and political institutions were profoundly affected by these changes and, once affected, in turn influenced the public's perception of the performance of government. This complex interaction of institutions and society is, of course, a continuous process and it may well be that, not only in the USA but in other mature democracies, the age of the highly organized and effective political party is over. A crucial question is raised

---

[15]   See Jeane Kirkpatrick, *The New Presidential Elite*, (Russell Sage, Twentieth Century Fund, 1976).

by this prospect: can liberal democracy function properly without strong political parties?

Towards the Millennium: a New Role for Political Parties

To the more pessimistic observers, the fact of party decline is incontrovertible. Pointing to the indicators discussed above, they reluctantly accept the demise of the parties, warn of the deleterious consequences and plead, somewhat forlornly, for party revival, or more 'consensual' institutions.[16] In essence, weak parties erode the vital five functions discussed earlier. Presidential/Congressional liaison becomes difficult; presidents have few cues to guide them when appointing officials; a presidential nominating process outside the control of party boosts 'media-created' candidates who may be skilful at campaigning and winning primaries but rarely make good presidents. Above all, political competition based on special interests or causes, rather than on broadly contrasting party programmes, results in a politics of confusion and waste. Certainly, examples – and sometimes dramatic examples – of all these maladies can easily be found in recent American politics.

Before we accept the critique in full, however, we should note the following. First, amid all the furore over disintegrating parties, not a single third party has emerged with even the semblance of electoral strength. Third-party *candidates* have sometimes done well, but they represent more of a protest vote than some discernible social movement. Such was certainly the case with John Anderson in 1980 and Ross Perot in 1992 and 1996. The institutional obstacles in the way of third parties in the USA are well known[17] and continue to apply. But a much more significant obstacle is the continuing distaste among the American electorate for parties based on class, region, religion, ethnicity or a single ideology. Second, it may be that the parties have *not* declined in the sense that they have ceased to be important *in government* or to be an indicator of electoral behaviour. Instead they have *changed*, and today perform rather different functions or perform

[16] Two eloquent essays on this theme are Samuel P. Huntington, *American Politics: The Promise of Disharmony*, (Cambridge, Mass., Harvard University Press, 1981), and Ranney, *Curing the Mischiefs of Faction*.
[17] The US electoral system puts additional burdens on third parties, for all states require a minimum number of registered voters to sign a petition before a party can field a candidate. Also, acquiring strength in one state or region – the usual pattern for American third parties – is rarely enough to ensure national impact. Victory in a presidential election is achievable only via mass national support, and without at least the prospect of winning at this level, third parties cannot hope to be taken seriously.

traditional functions in a different manner. Indeed, recent research shows that state and national party organizations have in some respects been strengthened in recent years.[18] In addition, the influence of party in Congress has undoubtedly increased since the 1980s. We will return to this point in chapter 9.

The very same forces which precipitated the reforms of the early 1970s also set in motion a period of soul searching which is still very much with us. As noted earlier, the Democrats have launched a series of enquiries into the presidential nominating process, and, as will be elaborated in chapter 7, disquiet with the ways in which Democratic candidates are selected remains. National parties are now stronger, but their authority in part depends on the support of incumbent presidents. This is one reason why the Republican National Committee was able to achieve so much during the 1980s compared with its Democratic counterpart. With Bill Clinton as president the Democratic National Committee has experienced a revival during the 1990s.

Recent party revival is not equivalent to the party strength associated with smoke-filled rooms and party machines, but more, not fewer, people are now actively involved in party organizations. Party activists may be motivated more by issues or candidates than by party loyalty, in any case, nothing new in American politics – but the label 'Democrat' or 'Republican' continues to mean something to most Americans. That this is so is amply demonstrated by the continuing importance of party label in congressional elections – very few candidates dare to call themselves independent. Research has also revealed that the electorate, rather than being *alienated* from the parties, increasingly view them neutrally. They continue to see important differences between them but, crucially, find it difficult to link these differences to the policies of particular candidates.[19] So rather than the parties disintegrating into a 'shambles', they have become even looser coalitions of diverse interests. In some ways they have gained organizational strength, particularly at the national level. But their control over candidates and nominations has weakened.

All this implies that, should politics again crystallize around a few central issues, the parties are poised to resume the role they played during the New Deal period. They are not about to disappear. On the contrary, they continue to function in the erratic, confusing and often inefficient manner which is the hallmark of the American system.

---

[18]   On this theme *see* John H. Aldrich, *Why Parties? the Origin and Transformation of Political Parties in America*, (Chicago, University of Chicago Press, 1995), chapter 8.
[19]   Martin P. Wattenberg, 'The decline of political partisanship in the United States: negativity or neutrality?', *American Political Science Review*, vol. 75, 1981. *See also* his *The Rise of Candidate Centred Politics*, (Cambridge Mass., Harvard, 1991).

Further Reading

An excellent account of the origins and changes in the party system is provided by John H. Aldrich, *Why Parties? The Origin and Transformation of Political Parties in America*, (Chicago, Chicago University Press, 1995). The best historical (but analytical) account of American parties is William Nisbet Chambers and Walter Dean Burnham (eds), *The American Party Systems: Stages of Political Development*, (New York, Oxford University Press, 1975). *See also* David R. Mayhew, *Placing Parties in American Politics*, (Princeton, New Jersey, Princeton University Press, 1986). Critiques of the reforms of the early 1970s include Austin Ranney, *Curing the Mischiefs of Faction: Party Reform in America*, (Berkeley, University of California Press, 1975). A good recent account of party decline is Martin P. Wattenberg's *The Decline of American Political Parties, 1952–1988*, (Cambridge, Mass., Harvard University Press, 1990). One of the better textbook treatments of parties is William J. Keefe, *Parties, Politics and Public Policy in America*, (Washington DC, Congressional Quarterly Press, 5th edition, 1988).

7

POLITICAL PARTICIPATION AND ELECTORAL BEHAVIOUR

Elections commit the people to a sense of responsibility for their own betterment . . . It seems clear that they are essential to us as props of the sentiment of legitimacy and the sentiment of participation.

W. J. M. Mackenzie, *Political Studies*

There is currently a widespread sense, shown by public opinion surveys and complaints by informed observers, that the American electoral system is in trouble. Some believe that this trouble is minor and can be dealt with through moderate reforms; others think it goes deep and requires extensive political surgery, perhaps accompanied by sweeping changes in the larger social order.

A. James Reichley, *Elections, American Style*

America's claim to status as a democratic country depends almost entirely on the nature and extent of public participation in political life, and from the earliest years of the Republic there has been dispute and controversy over what, precisely, participation means. To the educated eighteenth-century man, 'democracy' was equivalent to a republican form of government which limited electoral participation to those with an established stake in society – white men of property. Any further extension of participation raised the spectre of rule by the mob and the eventual breakdown of civil society. In contrast, many artisans and small farmers, especially in the North East, were imbued with a more egalitarian brand of democracy which implied participation by a much wider electorate. Slowly, during the nineteenth and twentieth centuries, this egalitarian spirit gained ascendancy over the more elitist views of the Founding Fathers.

Today, the degree of electoral participation would truly shock eighteenth-century man. Measured in terms of the number of public

Plate 7.1 Campaign buttons for Bob Dole, 1996, San Diego, California

offices open to electoral choice, the United States is the most democratic of countries; in total some 530,000 posts are elected, from the humblest local officials to local and state judges, mayors, councillors, governors and legislators to the vice-president, president and members of the US Congress. In addition, many Americans vote in primary elections to nominate which party candidates will stand in the election proper. Many states and localities have also introduced a number of devices associated with populism or direct democracy. Hence, some citizens vote in referendums, or in initiative and recall elections, all of which are designed to give the voter a direct say in policy making.[1] Further, there are no formal barriers to the participation of any particular social group. Property and tax-paying restrictions were abolished by the 1830s, effectively enfranchising all adult white males. Women won the right to vote in national elections following the adoption of the 19th Amendment in 1920. Formal restrictions on Southern Blacks' electoral participation were swept away by the 1965 Voting Rights Act and by a number of Supreme Court decisions. Finally, the 26th Amendment, ratified in 1971, reduced the minimum voting age to 18.

By the simple measure of electoral access, therefore, there is no

[1]   Recalls enable the electorate on presentation of a minimum number of signatures to hold a special election to recall an official from office. Initiatives are similar devices enabling the electorate by petition to vote directly on a proposal (such as tax change) rather than go through the local or state legislature. Initiatives are, in fact, a type of referendum and are often referred to as such.

doubting the democratic nature of the American system. Yet, as our discussion of political parties revealed, there is very much more to participation than mere access to elections. More important are questions of *choice* and *control* over government policy. Many people ask whether the United States can be 'truly' democratic when electoral turn-out is so low and when the choice offered by elections is so narrow. Others probe further and claim that, in modern complex societies, elections must, by their very nature, be but limited means of control over governments and bureaucracies. The remainder of this chapter will be devoted to these and related questions. The first section will concentrate on electoral behaviour – why Americans vote as they do, what sort of choice they are offered by the electoral process and how patterns of behaviour have changed over time. The second section will introduce a discussion of non-electoral participation which will be continued in later chapters.

Patterns of American Electoral Behaviour

Basic questions

Observers of voting behaviour usually first ask the simplest and most obvious question, 'Who has voted for which party?'. So we are used to reading opinion-poll findings which indicate that support for a particular party has risen or fallen or that some region, ethnic or social group has shifted its allegiance away from or towards a party. Survey or poll data can be an invaluable aid when answering these questions, and have helped to establish some very general norms or expectations about people's voting behaviour. So, table 7.1, showing the distribution of votes by social group in the 1996 presidential election, confirms tendencies that apply in most democratic countries: higher socio-economic-status, white voters tend to be more conservative (i.e. vote for Dole) than younger, lower-status, ethnic-minority voters. Table 7.1 also reveals patterns that may be peculiarly American: the South of the USA appears markedly more conservative than the East; women are much more prone to vote Democratic than are men. But even these general trends provoke a number of deeper questions. What, precisely, is meant by 'conservative' and 'liberal' in the American context? To what extent does the *party*, as opposed to candidates and issues, determine voting behaviour? It must be that the balance of influence shifts quite markedly between the three, for some candidates manage to overcome party ties and attract voters from the other party. Hence the phenomenon of the 'Reagan Democrats' during the 1980s when many traditional Democratic voters switched their allegiance to

Table 7.1 Percentage distribution of the 1996 presidential vote by social group and issues

	Clinton	Dole	Perot	Total
Sex and race				
Men	44	44	10	48
Women	54	37	7	52
White men	39	48	11	48
White women	49	42	8	52
White	44	45	9	83
Black	83	12	4	10
Hispanic	72	21	5	4
Age				
18–29	53	34	11	16
30–44	49	40	9	32
45–59	48	41	9	26
60 plus	49	43	7	25
Income				
<$30,000	56	33	10	35
30–49,000	48	40	10	28
50–74,999	46	45	7	21
>75,000	42	50	6	18
Region				
East	55	34	9	22
Mid-West	48	40	10	26
South	47	46	7	30
West	49	39	8	22
Political ideology				
Liberal	78	11	7	20
Moderate	57	32	9	47
Conservative	20	71	8	33
Condition of the economy				
Excellent/good	64	30	5	56
Not so good/poor	32	52	14	42
Most important issues and qualities				
Medicare and social security	67	26	6	15
Taxes	18	73	7	11
Economy and jobs	61	27	10	21
Federal deficit	28	51	19	12
Shares my view of government	42	45	10	20
Is honest and trustworthy	9	84	7	20
Has vision of the future	77	12	9	16

Source: Washington Post Exit Poll as reported in *The Washington Post*, 6 November 1996, p. A 5.

the Republicans. Other questions arise. Why are African Americans so overwhelmingly Democratic in their loyalties? What accounts for the regional variations in voting behaviour? We will return to these questions in detail later but, for now, it should be noted that American voting behaviour seems considerably more complex than electoral participation in other countries. In many European countries, for example, class, regional, ethnic or religious divisions are quite clearly defined and can function as accurate predictors of voting intentions. In the USA, however, the political parties are loose coalitions, and ideological and other social cleavages are relatively weak, so analysing who votes and why can be that much more difficult.

We can broadly categorize the Democrats as the liberal or even 'left' party and Republicans as the conservative or 'right' party but, when the whole range of candidates in each of these parties is examined, there are numerous exceptions even to this generalization. To complicate matters further, federalism and the separation of powers have spawned myriad elections and distinctive levels of government, each with a different constituency. At the national level this shows itself most graphically in the relationship between presidential and congressional elections. Individual members of Congress are beholden to their own constituents whose interests may be quite separate from those of the national electorate responsible for electing the president. It used to be the case that the successful party at the presidential election would also at least be partly successful at the congressional level but, in recent years, voters have increasingly split their tickets and voted for one party at the congressional level and the other at the presidential level. In 1972, for example, the near landslide victory of a Republican president, Richard Nixon, was not accompanied by any significant inroads by his party into the Democratic majorities in both Houses of Congress. The pattern was similar in 1984, 1988 and 1992 and 1996. In 1996, Bill Clinton won the presidency for the Democrats but the Republicans retained control of both houses of Congress.

A second question raised in any simple description of voting behaviour is: who actually votes? A wealth of social-science and professional opinion-poll research enables us to make quite accurate assessments of electoral participation patterns. Very generally people of higher socio-economic status (a combination of income, occupation and education) vote and participate in other political activities to a much greater extent than people of lower socio-economic status.[2] The relationship between voting and age is a little more complex, with participation rising from a low at 18 to a peak during middle age and then declining gently in later middle and old age. Until the late 1960s one of the most dramatic differences in participation was between Black and white Americans. Until the civil rights legislation of the mid-1960s, very few Southern Blacks were able to register to vote (for example, in 1964 a mere 7 per cent in Mississippi) and, among those registered, actual

[2]   *See* in particular Sidney Verba and Norman H. Nie, *Participation in America: Political Democracy and Social Equality*, (New York, Harper and Row, 1972).

turn-out was low. Since the 1965 Voting Rights Act, however, registration has steadily increased, and by 1990 the percentage of Blacks registered to vote was only 8 per cent below the figure for whites. Black turn-out remains generally lower than that of whites, but mainly because a disproportionate number of Blacks are of low socio-economic status. Finally, turn-out among women is slightly higher than for men. The gap is small (around 2 per cent), however, and, compared with differences based on socio-economic status and age, voter participation rates between men and women are quite close.

A third basic question is: how many of the people actually vote? In

Table 7.2 Turn-out in presidential and House elections, 1930–92 (percentage of voting-age population)

Year	Presidential elections	House elections
1930	—	33.7
1932	52.4	49.7
1934	—	41.4
1936	56.9	53.5
1938	—	44.0
1940	58.9	55.4
1942	—	32.5
1944	56.0	52.7
1946	—	37.1
1948	51.1	48.1
1950	—	41.1
1952	61.6	57.6
1954	—	41.7
1956	59.3	55.9
1958	—	43.0
1960	62.6	58.5
1962	—	45.4
1964	61.9	57.8
1966	—	45.4
1968	60.9	55.1
1970	—	43.5
1972	55.4	50.9
1974	—	36.1
1976	54.4	49.5
1978	—	35.1
1980	53.4	48.1
1982	—	37.7
1984	53.3	47.4
1986	—	33.4
1988	50.1	44.7
1990	—	33.0
1992	55.2	50.8
1994	—	38.0
1996	48.8	n.a.

Source: Norman J. Ornstein, Thomas E. Mann, Michael J. Malbin, Allen Schick and John F. Bibby, *Vital Statistics on Congress*, 1991–92 edition, Washington DC, American Enterprise Institute, table 2.1. Data for 1992 from *The New York Times*, 5 November 1992, p. B9. Updated from the *New York Times*, 6 November 1996, p. B13.

the USA turn-out is notoriously low for all elections. Even the contest perceived by most people as the most significant – electing the president – hardly inspires a high level of mass participation. Since 1960 turn-out has been declining, and now rarely exceeds 55 per cent for presidential elections and 50 per cent for Congressional contests (table 7.2).

In 1996, turn-out sank to 48.8 per cent – the lowest for a presidential election since 1924. At the state and local levels turn-out is even lower and can fall as low as 20 per cent. This seeming political apathy has long puzzled and disturbed American political scientists. Explanations usually fall into one of two categories – institutional and non-institutional. The institutional barriers to voting are, in fact, considerable, although claims that the formidable *number* of elections reduces turn-out are probably erroneous. After all, turn-out at presidential elections remains low in spite of their relative infrequency and the disproportionate amount of publicity and attention paid to them by political parties and the media. More significant are America's voter-registration laws. Under the laws of individual states, voters must themselves make the decision to register, and most states apply minimum residency requirements. Although for presidential elections this requirement has been reduced by Congress to only 30 days, the fact remains that in a mobile, open society many people fail to register or to register in time. Unlike most European countries, there is no automatic nationally organized compulsory registration system, and recent studies have shown that were such a system introduced, turn-out may increase by between 10 and 12 per cent. In 1993 Congress passed the so-called 'motor voter' law which encouraged states to allow people to register to vote whenever they applied to renew their driving licences. Although, by some estimates this increased the number of citizens registered to vote by 9 million by 1996, there is little evidence that these new registrees actually voted. Indeed, 1996 exit polls showed that the percentage of first-time voters (of all those voting) dropped from 11 per cent to 9 per cent.[3]

Non-voting may also be linked to the fact that the US has a first-past-the-post single-member-district electoral system rather than one based on proportional representation (PR). By closely relating votes cast to representation in assemblies, PR 'wastes' few votes. Under a single-member-district system, however, voters know that in many constituencies their vote will make no difference because of the large majority enjoyed by one party. Their incentive to vote is, therefore, reduced. In fact, if turn-out is measured in terms of the *number of people who are registered*, then the picture looks very different (table 7.3). Nonetheless, Americans remain concerned with their rate of voter

---

[3]   Quoted in *USA Today*, 8 November 1996, P. 3A.

participation. The data in table 7.3 are for presidential elections. Turn-out for House and Senate elections which are, after all, for national offices, are low by international standards. Moreover, an increasingly educated population should lead to an improvement in turn-out. However, 1992 excepted, the opposite has been the case. Very broadly, two schools of thought have attempted to explain this: the sociological and public choice. Public choice theorists argue that it is simply not rational to vote when the choice offered by parties is so limited. Certainly the relative absence of well-defined and deep-rooted social cleavages articulated by class-, ethnic- or regionally based parties reduces the direct and immediate interest the voter has in ensuring that 'his' or 'her' party is represented in government. American parties and candidates rarely promise social revolution; nor do they often promise to defend well-defined sectional, class, religious or ethnic interests. Moreover, recent research has shown that citizens often vote *retrospectively*; or they decide to vote for party A rather than party B by judging an incumbent's past performance – usually in terms of whether the party's period in office has increased the voter's real income. As

Table 7.3 Voting turn-out by voting-age population and registered voters, selected countries

	Vote as a percentage of voting-age population			*Vote as a percentage of registered voters*	
1	Italy	94.0	1	Belgium	94.6
2	Austria	89.3	2	Australia	94.5
3	Belgium	88.7	3	Austria	91.6
4	Sweden	86.8	4	Sweden	90.7
5	Portugal	85.9	5	Italy	90.4
6	Greece	84.9	6	Iceland	89.3
7	Netherlands	84.7	7	New Zealand	89.0
8	Australia	83.1	8	Luxembourg	88.9
9	Denmark	82.1	9	W. Germany	88.6
10	Norway	81.8	10	Netherlands	87.0
11	W. Germany	81.1	11	United States	86.8
12	New Zealand	78.5	12	France	85.9
13	France	78.0	13	Portugal	84.2
14	United kingdom	76.0	14	Denmark	83.2
15	Japan	74.4	15	Norway	82.0
16	Spain	73.0	16	Greece	78.6
17	Canada	67.4	17	Israel	78.5
18	Finland	63.0	18	United Kingdom	76.3
19	Ireland	62.3	19	Japan	74.5
20	United States	52.6	20	Canada	69.3
21	Switzerland	39.4	21	Spain	68.1
			22	Finland	64.3
			23	Ireland	62.2
			24	Switzerland	48.3

Source: Adapted from Nelson W. Polsby and Aaron Wildavksy, *Presidential Elections*, (New York, Free Press, 8th edition, 1991), tables 5.3 and 5.4. For qualifying notes, *see* original.

Morris Fiorina and others have shown, it is increasingly difficult to make this calculation when party programmes are so diffuse and when the appeal to voters is by individual *candidates* rather than by parties.[4] This more atomized, individualized politics may account for the decline of voting among all social groups since 1960. Interestingly, voter turn-out went up slightly in 1992 following a period when many voters' real incomes had declined. Many voters voted against President Bush on economic grounds and instead put their faith in Clinton (or Perot) as a vote for economic change. By way of contrast, turn-out declined in 1996 in the context of a relatively healthy economy. Although the very low turn-out of that year (48.8 per cent) could be interpreted as voter apathy or even alienation, it could also be that most voters were relatively happy with their economic lot and therefore saw little point in voting for change. Among those who did vote the appeal of the candidates rather than programmes and policies may have been paramount.

The sociological school argues, simply, that poorer, less well-educated citizens vote less than richer, better-educated citizens. The data certainly confirm this, with more than 50 per cent of manual workers apparently excluded from voting altogether.[5] Again this is a unique American phenomenon. In other democracies the (much smaller) number of non-voters is drawn from all social groups, with few citizens caught in a pattern of permanent non-voting. Non-voting among lower-status groups can also be linked to rational expectations. Their sense of political effectiveness tends to be lower because they are poorer and, as important, they find it difficult to identify with a party that fails to appeal to voters on class lines. Significantly, since 1968 the party which used to project such an appeal, the Democratic Party, moved further and further away from class-based politics and towards issue- and candidate-based politics.

Concern about non-voting in the United States is compounded by the fact that an increasingly educated and sophisticated population should have led to increased rather than decreased electoral participation. This phenomenon, above all, confirms the public choice theorists' claims that voters cannot easily make rational decisions when faced by inchoate parties and a politics based on individual office-holders unable to offer effective programmes of social and economic change.

---

[4]   Morris P. Fiorina, *Retrospective Voting in American National Elections*, (New Haven, Yale University Press, 1981).
[5]   For a full discussion, *see* Walter Dean Burnham, 'The turnout problem', in A. James Reichley (ed.), *Elections, American Style*, (Washington DC, Brookings, 1987), table A4.

'The American Voter' model and the New Deal coalition

During the 1950s and early 1960s a number of studies were published the findings of which established a 'model' of American voting behaviour. The unique contribution of this work was to explain the voting of individual citizens in terms of *psychological* orientations. By asking survey respondents how they felt about parties, candidates and issues and then relating these sentiments to actual political behaviour, it was possible to build up a cognitive picture of how individuals thought about politics. The results were surprising, to say the least. In a more recent study, Nie, Verba and Petrocik[6] summarized the findings thus:

> The American public had a remarkably unsophisticated view of political matters characterized by an inability to consider such matters in broad abstract terms . . . Citizens had inconsistent views when one looked across a range of issues . . . Most Americans had strong, long term commitments to one of the major political parties and this commitment served as a guide to their political behaviour . . . Citizens felt relatively satisfied with the political system and relatively efficacious.

Very few – a mere 2.5 per cent of the *American Voters'* sample – were categorized as ideologues, or people who thought about politics in abstract terms. Most evaluated candidates and parties in terms of the benefits they brought to social groups (42 per cent) or in terms of the 'nature of the times' (24 per cent). In other words, most voters had little sense of 'left' and 'right' or the role that parties and candidates might play in moving society in a particular direction. Instead, immediate or recent events or simple promises by politicians to lower taxation, say, or to increase social spending influenced voters. Reinforcement of this analysis was provided by studies showing that voters were often inconsistent in their views across issues. Some citizens favouring increased social spending also wanted a reduced role for government in society; anti-Communists were not always in favour of an increased role for the United States as international policeman. Most importantly of all, when attitudes on all issues were examined, it was not possible to find any pattern consistent with a coherently thought-out ideology, whether liberal, conservative, socialist or whatever.[7]

---

[6] Norman H. Nie, Sidney Verba and John R. Petrocik, *The Changing American Voter*, (Cambridge, Mass., Harvard University Press, enlarged edn, 1979), chapter 2. The main works summarized were: Angus Campbell et al., *The American Voter*, (New York, John Wiley, 1960); Gabriel Almond and Sidney Verba, *The Civic Culture*, (Princeton, New Jersey, Princeton University Press, 1963); Robert A. Dahl, *Who Governs?* (New Haven, Yale University Press, 1961); David E. Apter (ed.), *Ideology and Discontent*, (New York, Free Press, 1964).

[7] Philip Converse, 'The nature of belief systems in mass publics', in Apter, *Ideology and Discontent*, p. 543.

Table 7.4 Presidential election results, 1928–96

Year	Presidential candidates	Party	Electoral college vote	Popular vote	Percentage share	No. of states won[1]
1928	Herbert Hoover	Republican	444	21,392,190	58.2	42
	Alfred E. Smith	Democratic	87	15,016,443	40.8	6 (all Southern)
	Norman Thomas	Socialist	0	267,420	1.0	0
32	Franklin D. Roosevelt	Democratic	472	22,821,857	57.3	42
	Herbert Hoover	Republican	59	15,761,841	39.6	6 (all North Eastern)
	Norman Thomas	Socialist	0	884,781	2.2	0
36	Franklin D. Roosevelt	Democratic	523	27,751,597	60.7	46
	Alfred M. Landon	Republican	8	16,679,583	36.4	2 (Maine and Vermont)
	Norman Thomas	Socialist	0	187,720	0.5	0
40	Franklin D. Roosevelt	Democratic	449	27,244,160	54.7	38
	Wendell L. Wilkie	Republican	82	22,305,198	44.8	10
	Norman Thomas	Socialist	0	99,557	0.2	0
44	Franklin D. Roosevelt	Democratic	432	25,602,504	52.8	36
	Thomas E. Dewey	Republican	99	22,006,285	44.5	12
	Norman Thomas	Socialist	0	80,518	0.2	0
48	Harry S. Truman	Democratic	303	24,179,345	49.5	32
	Thomas E. Dewey	Republican	189	21,991,291	45.1	12
	J. Strom Thurmond	States' Rights Dem.	39	1,176,125	2.4	4 (all Southern)
	Henry A. Wallace	Progressive	0	1,157,326	2.4	0
	Norman Thomas	Socialist	0	139,572	0.2	0
52	Dwight D. Eisenhower	Republican	442	33,936,234	55.2	40
	Adlai E. Stevenson	Democratic	89	27,314,992	44.5	8 (all Southern)
56	Dwight D. Eisenhower	Republican	457	35,590,472	57.4	41
	Adlai E. Stevenson	Democratic	73	26,022,752	42.0	7 (all Southern)
60	John F. Kennedy	Democratic	303	34,226,731	49.9	23[2]
	Richard M. Nixon	Republican	219	34,108,157	49.6	26
64	Lyndon B. Johnson	Democratic	486	43,129,484	61.1	46
	Barry M. Goldwater	Republican	52	27,178,188	38.5	5 (Southern and Arizona)

Table 7.4 Continued

Year	Presidential candidates	Party	Electoral college vote	Popular vote	Percentage share	No. of states won[1]
68	Richard M. Nixon	Republican	301	31,785,480	43.3	32
	Hubert M. Humphrey	Democratic	191	31,275,166	42.7	14
	George C. Wallace	American Independent	46	9,906,473	13.5	5 (all Southern)
72	Richard M. Nixon	Republican	520	47,169,911	61.3	49
	George McGovern	Democratic	17	29,170,383	37.3	2 (DC and Massachusetts)
	John G. Schmitz	American	0	1,099,482	1.4	0
76	Jimmy Carter	Democratic	297	40,830,763	50.1	24
	Gerald R. Ford	Republican	240	39,147,973	48.0	27
	Eugene J. McCarthy	Independent	0	756,631	1.0	0
80	Ronald Reagan	Republican	489	42,951,145	51.0	46
	Jimmy Carter	Democratic	49	34,663,037	41.0	5
	John B. Anderson	Independent	0	5,551,551	7.0	0
84	Ronald Reagan	Republican	525	54,450,603	59.2	49
	Walter Mondale	Democratic	13	37,573,671	40.8	2 (DC and Minnesota)
88	George Bush	Republican	426	47,917,341	54.0	40
	Michael Dukakis	Democratic	112	41,013,030	46.0	11
92	Bill Clinton	Democratic	370	44,908,233	43.0	32
	George Bush	Republican	168	39,102,282	37.4	18
	Ross Perot	Independent	0	19,741,048	18.9	0
96*	Bill Clinton	Democratic	379	45,628,667	49.0	31
	Bob Dole	Republican	159	37,869,435	41.0	19
	Ross Perot	Independent	0	7,874,283	8.0	0

[1] From 1960 includes Alaska and Hawaii. From 1964 includes Washington DC.

[2] 15 electoral college votes were cast for segregational candidate Harry F. Byrd, including eight in Mississippi which he effectively 'won'.

* unofficial results reported in *The New York Times*, 7 November 1996, p. B5.

The image projected, therefore, is one of a rather ill-informed voter who thinks rather little about politics. In one important respect, however, American voters were found to be consistent – in their attachment to political parties, voters displayed enduring loyalties. Labelling this phenomenon *party identification*, voting analysts discovered that people acquired a positive or negative psychological attachment to a party early in childhood which remained with them throughout their lives.

In essence citizens were *socialized* by family and other social cues into thinking of themselves as Democrats or Republicans, a phenomenon which may account for the fact that 78 per cent of respondents to a 1958 survey had the same party identification as their parents.[8] Not all voters were found to be strong party identifiers. Some identified less clearly with a party, while others considered themselves either independent or independently supportive of one or other of the parties. (*See* fig. 6.2, p. 102.)

We will discuss this changing pattern of party identification later but, for now, note the consistency of Democratic support which constitutes a clear majority for most of the period. Because these figures are for voting in presidential elections, they raise an interesting question: how is it that the Republicans managed to win in 1952, 1956, 1968, 1972, 1980, 1984 and 1988 (table 7.4) given the in-built Democrat majority implied by the preponderance of Democratic identifiers?

In answering this question, political scientists at first stressed that party identification was very much a psychological orientation to politics. There may be elections when voters deviate from their normal identification because of the particular appeal of the candidate (as was the case in the 1950s with Dwight Eisenhower) or because of the importance of certain issues (for example, law and order in 1968). Obviously, however, the Democratic majority must come from somewhere; it cannot be purely psychological. The answer is that there have been certain periods in American history when rapid social and economic changes have forged new political coalitions. During these periods, orientations towards parties change as the parties themselves come to represent an emergent social group or region. By implication, during these years of turbulence, the voter is indeed guided by the issues and by objective economic and social circumstances. Political scientists have called such transitions periods of *realignment* when new electoral majorities are built. Between 1896 and 1928 the Republican Party reigned supreme. Urbanization, depression, the naturalization and integration of new immigrant groups and the emergence of

[8]   *The American Voter*, p. 147.

Plate 7.2 Bill Clinton faces a barrage of questions from New York media (about his avoidance of the draft) during the 1992 primaries.

an organized working class transformed party politics during the 1920s and early 1930s, however, and culminated in the resounding Democratic victory of 1932 (table 7.4). From the late 1920s, the Democrats became the party associated with the urban working class, trade unions and the underprivileged. The near invincibility of what was to be called the New Deal coalition was assured because of the support guaranteed by the traditionally Democratic South. By the mid-1930s the intellectual establishment and many members of an insecure middle class had joined the coalition, resulting in the *maintaining* elections of 1936, 1940, 1944 and 1948. Not until incumbent Democrats (most notably Harry Truman) began to support civil rights for Southern Blacks did the first cracks in the majority appear (in 1948).

The Republican victories of 1952 and 1956 were, according to the scholars, *deviating* elections. In other words, the Democrats remained the 'natural' majority party, but the specific circumstances of these elections allowed the Republicans to triumph. Eisenhower was an avuncular, charismatic war hero; in contrast, Adlai Stevenson, the Democratic candidate, projected an aloof, intellectual and narrowly Eastern establishment image. This personality contrast was, above all, responsible for the Republican victories. Significantly, these successes were only partly repeated at the Congressional level. Following Republican victories in 1946 and 1952, after 1954 Congress was firmly controlled by the Democrats.

The decline of partisanship and of the New Deal coalition

This neat and appealing theory of electoral behaviour seemed to be reinforced by the 1960 and 1964 presidential elections. Democratic victories returned, with the Republicans reverting to their normal status as the minority party. From about 1964 to the late 1970s, however, a number of developments appear which, in total, present a rather serious challenge to the accepted theory. In particular we note the following:

Partisanship declines

A popular interpretation of Richard Nixon's victory in 1968 was that it heralded a new Republican majority.[9] More citizens were suburban, middle class and conservative, so the Republicans should find themselves ascendant. Moreover, the South, so long solidly Democratic, could no longer tolerate the integrationist policies of Democratic presidents.

Superficially, the 1972 election seemed to reinforce these trends (table 7.4). Yet 1968 and 1972 were not classic *realigning elections* like 1932. The number of Republican Party identifiers, far from increasing, decreased slightly during these years (*see* fig. 6.2, p. 102) and the Democrats retained their dominance of Congress. Similarly, at the state level there was little evidence of an unstoppable Republican surge. Note, however, that Democratic Party identification also declined during the 1960s. This fact, together with the rise of Independent identifiers have led some commentators to speculate that what was occurring was party *dealignment*, or the slow demise of party identification as a key indicator of political preference.

By 1976, this process of dealignment seemed to have stabilized (fig. 6.2, p. 102), but at the same time neither party had recaptured the centre stage in the way in which the Republicans did after 1896 or the Democrats did after 1932.

Another indicator of declining partisanship is 'ticket splitting' or the tendency for voters to divide their loyalties between candidates of different parties. As can be seen from table 7.5, ticket splitting rose sharply from 1952 to 1980. By that year some 34 per cent of the voters split their tickets between presidential and house candidates. A

---

[9]   *See*, in particular, Kevin Phillips, *The Emerging Republican Majority*, (New York, Doubleday Anchor, 1970).

similar picture has emerged for state-wide offices (elections for senators, governors, state legislatures) in a number of states and regions.

Candidate and issue voting increases

A natural corollary to a decline in partisanship is that citizens (or at
least those of them who vote) are using some other criterion when
making a decision on who to vote for. Candidates and issues had
always played some part in the voting calculus, of course, but, from
the 1960s, they began to play a much more prominent role. It also
follows that, if people are voting for individual candidates or for particular issues, the electorate is much more sophisticated than implied
by the *American Voter* model. Indeed, in their 1976 work, *The Changing American Voter*, Nie, Verba and Petrocik discovered that, from
about 1964, voters showed a significantly increased consistency in
their views on domestic and foreign policy issues. Unlike the rather
unthinking citizen portrayed by *The American Voter*, the public
appeared more able to see the connections between issues, parties and
candidates and to view the world in terms of broad ideological
categories such as 'liberal' or 'conservative'. Certainly, presidential
elections took on a more ideological stance after 1964. The Gold-
water-Johnson contest of that year was clearly a conflict between conservative and liberal, as were the later contests between Humphrey,

Table 7.5 Key indicators of dealignment, 1952–88

	1952	1956	1960	1964	1968	1972	1976	1980	1984	1988
Percentage identifying with a party	75	73	75	77	70	64	63	64	64	63
Percentage splitting their ticket between president and House	12	16	14	15	26	30	25	34	25	25
Percentage splitting their ticket between Senate and House	9	10	9	18	22	23	23	31	20	27
Percentage neutral towards both parties	13	16	17	20	17	30	31	37	36	30
Percentage positive towards one party and negative towards the other	50	40	41	38	38	30	31	27	31	34

Source: SRC/CPS National Election Studies. Reproduced from Martin P. Wattenberg, *The Rise of Candidate Centred Politics*, (Cambridge Mass., Harvard University Press, 1991), table 2.2.

Nixon and Wallace and, more especially, between McGovern and Nixon. In 1976 there was a marked decline in ideological voting, almost certainly because the two candidates projected rather bland images and few issues clearly divided them. The year 1980 saw a return to a clear-cut choice, however, with the conservative Ronald Reagan facing an incumbent president, Jimmy Carter, identified – albeit reluctantly on his part – with the liberal cause. And 1984 also presented a clear-cut choice, with Ronald Reagan appealing directly to the right and Walter Mondale to liberals and the left. In 1988, however, the two candidates were much closer together on basic issues. So much so, in fact, that George Bush worked hard to label Dukakis a 'liberal' so as to secure the conservative vote. George Bush found his identification with conservative policies a *liability* in 1992, however, when the electorate called for new economic policies following a period of recession. Bob Dole tried to learn this lesson four years later in 1996 when he worked hard to capture the middle ground. Incumbent Bill Clinton also moved to the centre and, in the context of a healthy economy, this was sufficient for him to win re-election.

Declining partisanship and the rise of what has been called 'issue voting' raises a number of questions. One of the most important of these we addressed in the last chapter – the failure of the political parties to exploit the new interest in politics by providing coherent and ideologically consistent programmes to the electorate. Indeed, to a European observer, the combination of more ideological voters but declining parties and partisanship should be slightly baffling. Surely parties should be stronger in such a context? But as was pointed out in chapter 6, the complexity of the issues dominating the political agenda, together with recent changes in American society, have made it impossible for the parties to know what to say and to whom. Recall that to win, American political parties have to build broad coalitions of support. And research has shown that, although there has been a rise in ideological thinking among some of the electorate, it hardly dominates. The price of presenting to voters an unequivocally ideological programme was revealed in 1972, when George McGovern's evangelizing liberalism was rewarded by a landslide victory for his Republican opponent. So, rather than parties and issues coinciding and thus strengthening partisanship, the opposite has been happening. Issues and individual candidates have gained importance independently of parties and have often done so in a way that seriously damages a party's fortunes. Hence, in 1968 and 1972, Vietnam and the 'social issue' dominated – a combination of law and order, civil rights and civil liberties. Liberals within the Democratic Party found themselves seriously at odds with some of the traditional Democratic supporters on these questions. Southerners were conservative on civil rights, and a large number of blue-collar workers were consistently conservative on Vietnam and the social issue. This combination helps explain Richard Nixon's victories in 1968 and 1972. Nixon's success seemed to herald the beginning of the end for the New Deal coalition. At the level of presidential elections, the South was moving rapidly into the Republican camp, and the now dominant social issue divided, rather than unified, the Democrats.

Some have argued that Ronald Reagan's 1980 and 1984 victories were in a different category. He won, so the theory goes, because his economic policies coincided nicely with what the electorate wanted. Disillusioned with high levels of public spending and inflation, the public had acquired an *ideological* aversion to big government. Ronald Reagan's promise of a new prosperity based on free-market principles offered an irresistible alternative. Concomitant with the success of this issue appeal came a revival of the Republican Party and, because the party became identified with 'Reaganomics', some commentators claimed that a permanent realignment was under way.

Yet, as fig. 6.2 (p. 102) shows, the number of Republican identifiers did not increase markedly either in 1980 or in 1984. Moreover, the public's attitudes on economic issues are not as unambiguously ideological as the more optimistic of the Republican supporters claimed. Of course, everyone wants a healthy economy but, if the price of low inflation – the major objective of Reagan's programme – is high unemployment, then large sections of Republican support are likely to fall away. This is exactly what happened during the 1982 mid-term elections when Republican candidates associated with the administration's economic policies fared particularly badly. President Reagan's 1984 victory was no doubt attributable to a number of factors, including his personal popularity. But few commentators doubt that the rapid recovery of the economy in 1983 and 1984 was crucial. All this suggests that 1980 and 1984 were far from being realigning elections. Much the same could be said for the 1988 contest, when the Democrats made further inroads into the House and Senate while once again losing the presidency. In 1992, the Democratic victory was achieved in the context of what was widely perceived to be a damaging recession. The incumbent, George Bush, was accordingly punished by the voters. A revived economy and a move to the centre ground of American politics by Bill Clinton ensured his re-election in 1996.

Dealignment, Realignment and the Modern American Voter: Where Do We Go From Here?

Although the presidential election results of 1992 and 1996 suggest there is no realignment of the American voters towards the

Table 7.6 Party identification by election cycle, 1976–94, percentage

Party identification	1976–78	80–82	84–86	88–90	92–94	Change
Democratic	54	54	50	50	48	−6
Independent	14	12	12	11	11	−3
Republican	32	34	38	39	41	+9
Total	100	100	100	100	100	
(number of cases)	(4437)	(2960)	(4318)	(3934)	(4217)	

Note: Percentages based on average of presidential election year and following mid-term election year.
Source: American National Election Studies, Inter-University Consortium for Political Research, University of Michigan, various years.

Republican Party, some evidence of the beginnings of a realignment does exist. In particular, the Republican congressional victories in 1994 and 1996, together with major advances by the party at the state and local levels, led many commentators to believe that a 'real' realignment was under way.[10]

Such claims are boosted by the changing pattern of party identification since 1990. As can be seen from table 7.6, although by 1994 the Democrats remained the largest party in terms of identifiers, the Republicans were catching up fast. Note also the decline in the number of independents during the 1976 to 1994 period. Moreover, as can be seen from table 7.5, the indicators of dealignment peaked in 1980. Since then there seems to have been a small move back to 'old-style' party politics. In an important book published in 1992, a group of scholars based at the University of California, Berkeley and at Brigham Young University argue that the decline of party voting in the US has been greatly exaggerated.[11] Most people who may, in answer to survey questions, call themselves Independents, do in fact have some allegiance to one of the major parties. The number of *pure* Independents has changed little in the last 30 years (table 7.7).

While these data are interesting, we cannot dispute the rise of split-ticket voting or of the number of voters whose *strength* of commitment to one or other of the major parties has weakened over recent years. The parties continue to find it difficult to present coherent programmes to the electorate, and, as the Ross Perot phenomenon in

---

[10]   *See* Walter Dean Burnham, 'Realignment Lives: The 1994 Earthquake and its Implications,' in Colin Campbell and Bert A. Rockman, *The Clinton Presidency: First Appraisal*, (Chatham NJ, Chatham House, 1996).
[11]   Bruce E. Keith et al., *The Myth of the Independent Voter*, (Berkeley and Los Angeles, University of California Press, 1992).

Table 7.7 Composition of voters in presidential and House elections, 1956–90

	Presidential elections			House elections		
	Party-line voters[1]	Defectors[2]	Pure indeps	Party-line voters[1]	Defectors[2]	Pure indeps
1956	76	15	9	82	9	9
1958				84	11	5
1960	79	13	8	80	11	9
1962				83	11	6
1964	79	16	6	80	16	5
1966				76	17	7
1968	69	23	9	74	19	7
1970				76	16	9
1972	67	25	9	75	17	8
1974				74	18	8
1976	73	17	10	72	19	9
1978				67	23	10
1980	68	24	9	69	23	8
1982				76	17	6
1984	79	13	8	70	23	7
1986				72	22	6
1988	81	12	7	74	20	7
1990				75	20	5

Note: The entry in each cell is the proportion of all voters, except apoliticals, in the indicated election who voted for their own party's candidate, for another party's candidate, or were pure-independents.

[1] Strong, weak and independent partisans who voted for their party's candidate for president or for the House of Representatives.

[2] Strong, weak and independent partisans who voted for another party's candidate. All partisans who voted for George Wallace or John Anderson were defectors.

Source: Bruce E. Keith et al., *The Myth of the Independent Voter* (Berkeley and Los Angeles, University of California Press, 1992), table 10.1.

1992 demonstrated, disillusionment with parties or their candidates can persuade voters to defect to an Independent candidate. Perot's 19 per cent of the vote was the highest scored by a third-party candidate since Teddy Roosevelt's Progressive vote in 1912. This hardly looks like an indicator of party strength.

Political scientists and others have long expressed concern that these developments present a problem for democratic theory. It is at least feasible to expect parties presenting coherent programmes of change to be held accountable by the electorate. The voter can, after all, test the party's performance in government against electoral promises. Individual candidates, however, can hardly be expected to do this. If they are elected only on personality and appearance, then no programmatic element can exist. If candidates do take stands on issues, then at most levels of government, they cannot directly trans-late issue promises into policy changes. What difference can one member of Congress make to the rate of inflation, for example? Only presidents (and possibly governors) can be expected to deliver electoral promises, but most recent presidential candidates deliberately avoided taking clear issue stands because they knew that the electorate is divided on most issues in highly complex ways. In 1992 it looked, briefly, as though a return to 'old-style' politics was possible. George Bush lost because he was blamed for an economic recession and Bill Clinton promised bold new federal programmes to stimulate economic growth. In the event, however, these came to little and during his first term the president moved rapidly towards the centre ground of politics. By 1996 both candidates were vying for this centre ground and, on the most important issues of the day, including the deficit, law and order, welfare reform and foreign policy, there was little discernible difference between the two candidates.

Further trends in the American electorate

While the general problem applies, the electorate is not a broad undifferentiated mass; changes in voting alignments continue to occur, the most important of which are listed below.

1   A 'gender gap' has emerged among voters in presidential elections. In the last five elections more women voted Democratic than should have been expected from national trends. This applied with particular force in 1996 when women split their vote 54–37 per cent between Clinton and Dole, compared with a 44–44 per cent margin for men. This gender gap seems if anything to be growing. In 1992 only 46 per cent of women voted for Clinton compared with 41 per cent of men. Younger, educated and single women are especially prone to vote Democratic, reflecting, perhaps, an antipathy towards the tendency for Republican candidates to be conservative on a range of issues which resonate with women (abortion, child care, education, affirmative action). There is a number of other interesting aspects to this phenomenon. For one thing the personal behaviour of candidates seems to be less important then their stand on the issues. The scandals surrounding Bill Clinton, for example, some of which involved allegations about his sexual behaviour, seemed to do him little electoral harm among women. Another interesting dimension to the gender gap is the virtual disappearance of the foreign policy issue as a gender-related cue for voters. During the 1980s, one of the explanations of the gap was the distaste which many women had for the more aggressive and warlike stance of Republican candidates. Hence the contrast between Reagan and Carter or Bush and Michael Dukakis, the 1988 Democratic candidate. By 1996, however, 'strength abroad' as an electoral issue had all but disappeared from the campaign agenda, yet the gender gap actually increased. All this suggests that domestic rather than foreign policy issues are the driving force behind many women's preference for the Democrats.

2   Major changes in the regional pattern of voting have occurred since the 1960s. During the first half of this century the South was solidly Democratic, and, until the 1930s, New England was solidly Republican. Today the South

is markedly more Republican than Democratic, not just at the presidential level, but increasingly at the state and local levels as well. The region is far from being as solidly Republican as it used to be Democratic, however, even if it is conservative. In 1996 Bill Clinton, himself very much a Southerner, won five of the South and Border states to the seven secured by Bob Dole.

The West also tends to be Republican and conservative, although this applies only erratically in the Pacific states (Washington, Oregon and California) where the personality of particular candidates is often a better indicator of their success than their ideological position. Indeed, in 1996, Bill Clinton won all three states. What can be said is that the Mountain and Prairie states now look firmly committed to the Republican camp with victories for that party in the last five presidential elections, and an increasingly large congressional representation for the GOP.

Northern and Northern Eastern states are more Democratic and liberal – as should be expected from their industrial pasts. Bill Clinton managed a near sweep of these regions in 1992 and in 1996. We should be wary of assuming that the North and East can now be labelled Democratic. At the congressional, state and local levels the Republicans remain quite strong in many of the Northern states, and voter preference at the presidential level is as much to do with the attractiveness of individual candidates as it is to do with party label.

3   Finally, we should note the very high and consistent support for the Democrats among Black and some other minority voters. In 1984 a staggering 90 per cent of Blacks voted Democrat, 4 per cent up on 1980 and against the national trend. In 1996 83 per cent voted for Clinton and a mere 12 per cent for Dole. Two conclusions can be drawn from these figures. Either the vast majority of Blacks perceive themselves to be the direct beneficiaries of Democratic policies or they display a remarkable sense of group solidarity. On the former point, Democrats are more supportive of the civil rights and welfare policies from which many Blacks benefit. But by no means all Blacks are direct beneficiaries of these policies, and the high support for the Democrats implies that the party is always unambiguously in favour of welfare and civil rights, which is certainly not the case. Indeed, the Clinton administrations have proposed quite Draconian reforms to the welfare system involving reductions in welfare benefits for mothers with dependent children (*see* chapter 14). More feasibly, most Blacks feel a strong sense of racial solidarity and vote Democrat because they know that many of their number are more likely to benefit from Democratic policies than from Republican measures. No other social group of significant size shows such solidarity, which speaks volumes for the very special and troubled status of Blacks in American history and present-day society.

We can conclude then, that, most minority groups apart, the behaviour of the American electorate is now much more volatile and difficult to predict than during the 1950s and 1960s. Voters are also more sophisticated, better informed and make their electoral choices according to rational criteria – such as candidates' stands on issues. In the main, however, the political parties are less able to provide the voters with clear choices based on coherent programmes of social and economic change.

Non-electoral Political Participation

As implied earlier, elections must by their very nature represent limited means of control over those forming and implementing policy. A considerable degree of centralized political power is necessary even for a relatively low level of economic efficiency and social justice. With centralized power, individual citizens casting their votes in periodic elections can hope only to exercise an occasional veto influence over those at the apex of the constitutional system. This applies even in state and local elections where voters, although closer to the office-holders, are still several steps removed from day-to-day decision-making.

But elections are just one of a number of means whereby citizens can influence the decision-makers. As table 7.8 shows, participation extends to a number of other activities, particularly those associated with the local community. Historically, the local community was the primary focus of political life with both formal and informal access to local officials being the very essence of American democracy. In many respects this holds true today with some 34 per cent of a sample of citizens having worked on community problems and 24 per cent having contacted a local official on a particular issue (in 1987, table 7.8). For most Americans, then, non-electoral participation involves contact with local officials or community leaders over such questions as school management, zoning,[12] public works projects and law enforcement. This is a continuing, constantly changing interactive process. It is also perceived by all parties to be highly legitimate, and local policies *are* created, modified and vetoed through citizen involvement. Of course this process is not equivalent to direct or pure democracy. The earlier noted biases against participation by lower-income groups, women and ethnic minorities remain, and virtually no apparently local policy issue is entirely local today. Federal and state funding of local programmes ensures that local political activity is but one of a number of influences at work. Nonetheless, the importance of local community activity should not be underestimated especially in the light of the very high percentage of citizens (17 per cent in 1987) who have directly helped *form* a group or organization to solve a local community problem (table 7.8).

---

[12] Zoning is equivalent to local land-use planning powers in European countries and involves the division of land into different use-types: residential, industrial, commercial, recreational.

Table 7.8 Percentage engaging in fourteen acts of participations, 1967 and 1987

Specific activity	1967	1987	Absolute change	Relative change
Voting				
Regular voting in presidential elections	66	58	−8	−12
Always vote in local elections	47	35	−12	−26
Campaign				
Persuade others how to vote	28	32	+4	+14
Actively work for party or candidate	26	27	+1	+4
Attend political meeting or rally	19	19	0	0
Contribute money to party or candidate	13	23	+10	+77
Member of political club	8	4	−4	−50
Contact				
Contact local officials issue based	14	24	+10	+71
Contact state or national official: issue based	11	22	+11	+100
Contact local official: particularized	7	10	+3	+43
Contact state or national official: particularized	6	7	+1	+17
Community				
Work with others on local problem	30	34	+4	+13
Active membership in community problem-solving organization	31	34	+3	+10
Form group to help solve local problem	14	17	+3	+21

Source: Verba, Lehman Schlozman and Brady, *Voice and Equality*, table 3.6.

Table 7.8 provides further fascinating data on the *trends* in participation over a 20-year period. As noted earlier, voting rates have declined, but almost all other forms of participation have increased. Contacts with elected officials have seen particularly large increases, suggesting that many Americans become involved politically when they are concerned about particular *issues*. Indeed, the study from which these findings are drawn confirms that, while people may vote less than they used to, they are nonetheless often deeply involved in a range of political issues.[13] The same study shows the continuing strong relationship between income and education, on the one hand, and participation on the other. It should come as no surprise then that ethnic and racial minorities who tend to be poorer than whites participate much less in politics. (Table 7.9.) Note, however, that Latino Americans and, in particular, non-citizens have the lowest participation rates. This

[13] Sydney Verba, Kay Lehman Schlozman and Henry E. Brady, *Voice and Equality: Civic Voluntarism in American Politics*, (Cambridge, Mass., Harvard University Press, 1995).

Table 7.9 Political activities by race (per cent active)

Activity	Anglo-Whites	African-Americans	Latinos	Latino Citizens
Vote	73	65	41	52
Campaign work	8	12	7	8
Campaign contributions	25	22	11	12
Contact	37	24	14	17
Protest	5	9	4	4
Informal community activity	17	19	12	14
Board membership	4	2	4	5
Affiliated to a political organization	52	38	24	27

Source: Verba, Lehman Schlozman and Brady, *Voice and Equality*, table 7.9.

reflects the fact that many among these groups are recent arrivals and therefore have less involvement in community affairs.

In comparative context, American levels of non-electoral political participation are very high. As can be seen from fig. 7.1, while Americans may not be inclined to vote in elections, they are much more involved in community work and contact officials more frequently than the citizens of comparable countries.

There are two further varieties of political participation which table 7.8 either excludes or refers to only obliquely.

The first involves the activities of national interest groups. As chapter 12 will show, there is hardly an area of economic or social life that is not influenced by interest groups. How representative or democratic groups are is a point we will cover later but, as implied earlier, interest group membership and loyalties do cut across party allegiances, so their activities must be considered an additional part of the representative process.

Second, there are all those political actions usually viewed as external to the established channels of political access: demonstrations, marches, boycotts and, more rarely, acts of political violence and terror. Clearly the latter are evidence of the breakdown of democratic processes, and, at the national level, at least, have been remarkably rare in the USA. In recent history they have been confined largely to the actions of isolated individuals (assassinations, hijacks) or have been precipitated by a single, sometimes ephemeral issue (the Vietnam War, Black rights). At the local level the picture is somewhat different. Until the 1960s, political violence was a relatively common feature of some parts of Southern society, with the Black population being the victims of often systematic intimidation and random violence. Rarely, however, has local political violence been motivated by a desire for regime change. More often, the motivation has been the assertion of authority over a politically and socially subordinate

Figure 7.1 Comparative activity rates; five countries, by per cent

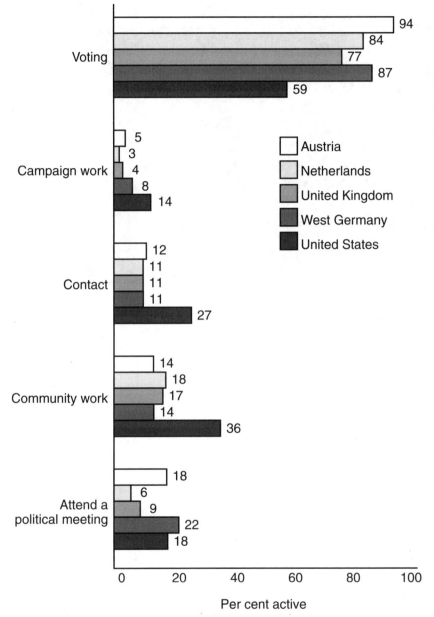

Source: Sydney Verba, Kay Lehman Schlozman and Henry E. Brady, *Voice and Equality* (Cambridge, MA, Harvard University Press, 1995), table 3.5.

minority group. Often, these illegal acts were implicitly endorsed by the legitimate authorities.

Partial exceptions to this generalization are the 'survivalist' and militia movements of the 1990s. Although for the most part these

Plate 7.3 Peace march, Washington D.C., 1967.

fiercely anti-government groups are non-violent, there have been some notable exceptions. The bombing of the federal building in Oklahoma City in 1995, which killed 168 people, is generally attributed to one of the more extreme of these groups. It is easy to exaggerate the size and importance of such organizations, however. They represent a tiny fraction of Americans and they lack ideological and organizational coherence.

More difficult to evaluate are acts of political protest – demonstrations, marches, boycotts, political strikes. These are very much a part of American life and, at certain times, have played a crucial role in politics. Starting in the 1940s and reaching a crescendo in the early 1960s, these were precisely the methods successfully employed by the civil rights movement – a fact which must help explain the greater proclivity for the African American community to partake in this type of political activity today (table 7.9).

Other than civil rights, however, it is difficult to find an issue where protest is successful and broadly accepted as legitimate, and even the civil rights movement helped inspire the urban riots of the 1960s which aroused bitter controversy and, eventually, a 'backlash' from many whites. This is not to deny that protest has been influential. In many instances – over unemployment in the 1930s and the Vietnam War in the 1960s – clearly it has. But it is almost impossible to *measure* its influence or, in some cases, to judge whether it actually helped or hindered the cause in question.

What we can conclude is that protest is very much a last resort. Only when the unambiguously legitimate means of access are either unavailable or exhausted do individuals and social groups take recourse to protest. In some cases, such as Southern Blacks in the 1950s and early 1960s, they had no choice because, within Southern states, normal channels of access were closed. But even in this example, the movement needed and received vital support from established political actors and institutions in the North. In other cases – protest over the Vietnam War, nuclear energy, the use of abortion, for example – some argue that direct political action was illegitimate because normal channels of access were available and the democratic process took its course. This last point demonstrates nicely the problems involved in discussing political participation. As emphasized, 'the democratic process', whether electoral or through interest-group activity, must always be an imperfect representative mechanism. Some individuals and social groups will win or lose more than others; some have disproportionately greater access and hence greater political power than others. What is perhaps remarkable about the American system is that, in spite of the obvious biases in the system in favour of certain interests and classes, there is a broad acceptance of basic constitutional arrangements. Protest and political violence are comparatively rare. Most Americans accept the legitimacy of the established channels of political access elections and the activities of interest groups.

Further Reading

The best analysis of political participation in the USA is Sidney Verba, Kay Lehman Schlozman and Henry E. Brady, *Voice and Equality: Civic Voluntarism in American Politics*, (Cambridge and London, Harvard University Press, 1995). For a discussion of changes in electoral behaviour, *see* Bruce Keith et al., *The Myth of the Independent Voter*, (Berkeley and Los Angeles, University of California Press, 1992); Martin P. Wattenberg, *The Rise of Candidate Centred Politics*, (Cambridge, Mass., Harvard University Press, 1991). The classic statement of the voter as rational actor is Morris P. Fiorina's *Retrospective Voting in American National Elections*, (New Haven, Yale University Press, 1981). Presidential elections are fully covered by Nelson Polsby and Aaron Wildavsky, *Presidential Elections*, (New York, Scribner's, 9th edition, 1996) and by Stephen J. Wayne, *The Road to the White House 1996: the Politics of Presidential Elections*, (New York, St Martin's Press, 1996).

8

US LEGISLATORS AND THEIR CONSTITUENTS

. . . Because [members of Congress] are vulnerable, they go to prodigious lengths to protect themselves. Like workers in nuclear power stations, they take the most extreme safety precautions. The fact that the precautions are almost entirely successful in both cases does not make them any the less essential. As David Mayhew remarks of the American Congress in a frequently quoted passage: 'If a group of planners sat down and tried to design a pair of national assemblies with the goal of serving members' electoral needs year in, year out, they would be hard pressed to improve on what exists.'

Anthony King, *Running Scared:*
Why American Politicians Campaign too Much and Govern too Little

The US Congress is usually – and accurately – referred to as the most powerful legislature in the world. While a common trend in other democratic countries has been the rise of powerful executives and the relative decline of assemblies and parliaments, the Congress has been remarkably successful in maintaining its independence from executive influence. This is not to deny that the powers and functions of Congress have changed over time. Clearly they have, and the particular way in which the institution operates today is very different even from 20 years ago. But, throughout its history, Congress has remained an essentially autonomous institution. Even during periods of executive ascendancy – most recently during the Johnson years – Congress never became the mere instrument of presidents.

The independence of Congress derives in part from its constitutionally defined powers and in part from the particular way in which the American party system has evolved. Constitutionally, Congress was given three main powers, all of which remain important today. First, all legislative power is vested in the House of Representatives and the Senate, and, within this broad function, Congress is given special powers to appropriate monies, to raise armies and regulate interstate commerce. Second, Congress has a constitutionally established right to declare wars and ratify treaties. Finally, the Senate is empowered to ratify treaties, approve appointments by the president to the judiciary and executive branch, and the House can impeach executive officers for wrong-doing. In addition, from very early in its history, Congress established the right to oversee and investigate the behaviour of the executive. In total, these powers are impressive, especially when it is remembered that originally Congress was expected to be the major initiator as well as approver of legislation. As with other legislatures around the world, Congress has partly (although by no means entirely) forfeited to the president the responsibility for initiating legislation. Unlike most other assemblies, however, Congress retains an independent power to approve legislation, appropriate monies and generally oversee the executive branch.

The simplest explanation of this autonomy is the distinctive constituency base which individual members of Congress enjoy. In contrast to parliamentary systems, the electoral fortunes of presidents and legislators are not directly linked. Presidents can, and often do, face a legislature dominated by a party other than their own. But this constitutional arrangement has been reinforced by the nature of the American party system. It is certainly possible to imagine a system characterized by bicameralism and the separation of powers where political party ties are strong and the electoral fortunes of legislators are interdependent with those of the executive. Only rarely has this been the case in the history of the United States. Much more common is a very loose party relationship between the president and members of Congress, with the legislators remaining essentially independent.

Representation and Congress

The sort of party government associated with parliamentary systems greatly restricts the representative function of individual legislators. In Britain, for example, the individual Member of Parliament is largely tied, through party discipline in the House of Commons, to the policies of either government or opposition. Crucially, his or her electoral survival depends on an official party endorsement.[1] So, while MPs may exercise some independent pressure on party leaders or

---

[1] Only very exceptionally do British MPs survive the removal of party endorsement; they may survive on personal appeal for one election, but rarely longer.

governments, it is limited. Clearly, this close organic link between executive and legislator limits the representative function of MPs. The electorate may benefit, at least in theory, from the coherent programmes and policies which party government produces, but the interests of individual constituencies do tend to become subordinated to national policy objectives. Curiously, British MPs are quick to insist that they come closest to what is called 'trustee' representatives, that is, they are elected by the people on trust to exercise their own judgement. They are not delegated to carry out a specific programme, to the letter, and without discretion. In reality they are closer to being party delegates than trustees. Members of Congress are patently not delegates, either in the sense of being slaves to a party programme or in the sense that they are mandated by their constituents to carry out specific policies. Indeed, the idea of a representative being a direct delegate of the people has relatively few applications in modern industrial societies. In small communities – and possibly in early New England town meetings – such a concept has meaning. But no member of Congress can accurately and continuously carry out the wishes of diverse and volatile electorates. Even if he or she knew what the electorate wanted, the individual member of Congress has but limited powers to influence what is a complex national policy process.

In truth, members are much closer to being trustees of their electorates. They are elected on the promise that they will exercise their judgement on behalf of their constituents' interests. And, in the opinion of the electorate, should they fail to defend and promote these interests, they are punished in subsequent elections. If members of Congress are not delegates, neither are they representative in the microcosmic sense. In fact, by this measure, they could hardly be less representative. An overwhelming majority of Senators and representatives are white, college educated, middle aged, middle class and male. In the 105th Congress (1997/8) only 49 women were elected out of the total 435 members of the House and only 9 Senators were women. Only one Afro-American Senator was elected and 37 members of the House (table 8.1). Lawyers and business people are greatly overrepresented among the members in both houses.[2]

To claim that members approximate most closely to a trustee form of representation is accurate, but tells us very little about the precise linkages between legislators, constituency and party, and how these have changed over time. Over the last 30 years, for example, it is

[2]   There are 435 members of the House of Representatives, 100 Senators, 3 delegates (District of Columbia, Guam, Virgin Islands) and a Resident Commissioner from Puerto Rico. The latter four cannot vote on the floor but can serve as committee members.

Table 8.1 Characteristics of the 104th and 105th Congress (1995/6 and 1997/8)

Incoming House compared with outgoing

	104th (outgoing)	105th (incoming)
Democrats	197	207
Republicans	235	227
Independents/vacant	3	1
Women	48	49
Men	385	385
Whites	375	375
Blacks	38	37
Hispanics[1]	17	18
Asian/Pacific Islander	3	3
College degree	92%	93%
Married	85%	84%
Have children	86%	86%
Years of House experience:		
Less than 2	21%	34%
2–6	31%	27%
7–12	17%	15%
13–20	21%	17%
More than 20	10%	7%
Leading religious preferences:		
Catholics	30%	30%
Baptists	13%	13%
Methodists	11%	11%
Presbyterians	10%	10%

Incoming Senate compared with outgoing

	104th (outgoing)	105th (incoming)
Democrats	47	45
Republicans	53	55
Women	8	9
Men	92	91
Whites	96	96
Blacks	1	1
Hispanics[1]	0	0
Asian/Pacific Islander	2	2
Native American	1	1
College degree	93%	94%
Married	90%	88%
Have children	94%	95%
Years of Senate experience:		
Up to 6	30%	43%
7–12	26%	25%
13–18	20%	12%
More than 18	24%	19%
Leading religious preferences:		
Catholics	21%	24%
Methodists	11%	13%
Episcopalians	14%	11%

[1] Hispanics can be of any race.

Source: USA Today, 8 November 1996, p. 6A.

commonly asserted that party has weakened its influence on members even further, with constituency pressures in the ascendant. The remainder of this chapter will be devoted to these questions and also to a preliminary discussion of the links between constituency influences on members of Congress and their work within the House and the Senate.

Congressional Elections

Representatives are elected every two years, Senators every six (with one-third elected every two years). This simple fact helps account for what are some starkly contrasting trends in the electoral dynamics of the two Houses, but there are also some common trends. Let us examine these first.

The spread of direct primaries

As with presidential elections, primaries are now the major means whereby members of Congress win their party's nomination for office. One major consequence of the demise of party conventions (the standard nineteenth-century form of nomination) has been to weaken the role of political parties in the nomination process. By being able to appeal directly to the electorate, the Senator or representative now owes much less allegiance to local and national party figures.

The rise and decline of Democrat dominance

Until 1994 it was widely believed that Democratic dominance of the House of Representatives was a near permanent feature of American politics. As can be seen from table 8.2, the Democrats managed to maintain a large majority in the House for many years. They were also strong in the Senate and controlled that House for all but six years in the 1961 to 1995 period. In the mid-term election of 1994, however, the Republicans swept the board winning back the House and the Senate. In the 1996 presidential election they kept control – although with a slightly reduced majority in the House.

This startling turnaround raises two important questions. Why did the Democrats manage to maintain their grip on Congress for so long – especially as the Republicans actually won most of the *presidential* elections during this period? Second, what accounts for the Republican victories in 1994 and 1996? As far as the first question is concerned, undoubtedly the Democrats benefited from being the majority party – more Americans identified with the Democrats than

Table 8.2 Composition of Congress, by political party, 1961–98

			House			Senate		
Year	Party and president	Congress	Majority party	Minority party	Other	Majority party	Minority party	Other
1961	D (Kennedy)	87th	D-263	R-174	–	D-65	R-35	–
1963	D (Kennedy)	88th	D-258	R-177	–	D-67	R-33	–
1965	D (Johnson)	89th	D-295	R-140	–	D-68	R-32	–
1967	D (Johnson)	90th	D-247	R-187	–	D-64	R-36	–
1969	R (Nixon)	91st	D-243	R-192	–	D-57	R-43	–
1971[1]	R (Nixon)	92nd	D-254	R-180	–	D-54	R-44	2
1973[1,2]	R (Nixon)	93rd	D-239	R-192	1	D-56	R-42	2
1975[3]	R (Ford)	94th	D-291	R-144	–	D-60	R-37	2
1977[4]	D (Carter)	95th	D-292	R-143	–	D-61	R-38	1
1979[4]	D (Carter)	96th	D-276	R-157	–	D-58	R-41	1
1981[4]	R (Reagan)	97th	D-243	R-192	–	R-53	D-46	1
1983	R (Reagan)	98th	D-269	R-165	–	R-54	D-46	–
1985	R (Reagan)	99th	D-252	R-182	–	R-53	D-47	–
1987	R (Reagan)	100th	D-258	R-177	–	D-55	R-45	–
1989[5]	R (Bush)	101st	D-259	R-174	–	D-55	R-45	–
1991[5]	R (Bush)	102nd	D-267	R-167	1	D-56	R-43	–
1993[5]	D (Clinton)	103rd	D-259	R-175	1	D-57	R-43	–
1995[5]	D (Clinton)	104th	R-235	D-197	1	R-53	D-47	
1997[5]	D (Clinton)	105th	R-227	D-207	1	R-55	D-45	

D = Democratic, R = Republican. Data for beginning of first session of each Congress.
Excludes vacancies at beginning of session.
– Represents zero.
[1] Senate had 1 Independent and 1 Conservative-Republican.
[2] House had 1 Independent-Democrat.
[3] Senate had 1 Independent, 1 Conservative-Republican, and 1 undecided (New Hampshire).
[4] Senate had 1 Independent.
[5] House had 1 Independent.
Source: US Congress, Joint Committee on Printing, *Congressional Directory* annual; beginning 1977, biennial.

with the Republicans. The Democrats also benefit from being the majority party in another sense. For, in single-member-district, first-past-the-post electoral systems, majority parties usually score more constituency victories than would be expected from their aggregate popular vote. Democrats also dominate state legislatures which are responsible for drawing up the boundaries of Congressional districts. Although the courts have been active on the question of malap-portionment (chapter 13, p. 278), a considerable amount of discretion remains – especially over the shape of constituencies rather than the balance of population between districts. As Gary Jacobson has pointed out, at least as far as the House is concerned, Democrats were actually better campaigners and politicians than their Republican counterparts. They were used to winning and to delivering the goods. As a result they continued to win.[3]

[3] *See* Gary C. Jacobson, *The Electoral Origins of Divided Government: Competition in US House Elections, 1946–1988*, (Boulder, Westview Press, 1990).

By the mid-1990s most of these advantages had been eroded. The number of people identifying with the Democrats declined and the number of Republican identifiers increased (fig. 6.2 p. 102). Their hold on the state legislatures also weakened. By 1997 the two parties controlled roughly the same number of state legislatures and the Republicans actually held a majority of the state governorships. As we established in the last chapter, these changes were greeted by many as evidence of a Republican realignment. What seems more likely is that a changing political agenda has resounded to the Republicans' advantage but not to the extent that they are in any sense the dominant or majority party. As far as congressional elections are concerned, the Republicans have benefited from public support for lower taxes, a balanced budget, an enhanced role for state governments, welfare reform and tougher law-and-order policies. But many issues on which the Democrats have the advantage – education, gender- and race-based questions, the environment, and protection of Medicare and Social Security – remain very important to the voters. In this sense we are likely to see much more competitive congressional elections in the future.

Regional change

While at the congressional level the Democrats continue to do better than would be expected from presidential election results, they have lost what was the solid support of the Southern states. As we noted in the last chapter, the electorate is now more volatile and most regions cannot be labelled as unequivocally Republican or Democratic. This said, the South is now effectively a Republican region as are the Mountain and Prairie states. The old industrial North East remains primarily Democratic while the Pacific and mid-western states are primarily Republican. Even these generalizations can be misleading. At any time a Democrat can win many Southern districts and a Republican many North Eastern districts. Much depends not only on the socio-economic and ethnic make up of the district in question, but also on the personal appeal and financial resources of the candidate running for office.

The importance of money

For both Senators and representatives, money has become a crucial resource in congressional elections. With voters acting in response to the appeal of individual candidates rather than to parties, incumbents and challengers must ensure that the voters know who they are and what their records are. This translates into buying television time for advertisements as well as spending money on mailings, meetings and other attention-seeking devices.

At one time, the personal efforts of candidates in raising money were less important than winning the party endorsement or the endorsement of the big corporations and labour unions. Large donations from such sources could help clinch the election of a particular candidate. With declining partisanship and the passage of the Federal Election Campaign Act (FECA) in 1974, however, candidates have been forced to rely more and more on their own capacity to raise funds or to persuade others to contribute to their campaigns. FECA was designed to reduce candidate dependence on money, but in fact the very opposite has happened. As can be seen from fig. 8.1 campaign spending has soared in recent years. Note also the rise in spending by House challengers particularly in 1994 when the Republican challengers did so well. What accounts for the ever-increasing importance of money? In part it is because the Supreme Court struck down a central provision in the Act which limited contributions by candidates, and in part because the law encouraged the growth of Political Action Committees (PACs). Although PACs are limited to giving $5000 per candidate per campaign they contributed 45 per cent of all campaign financing to Democrats in 1990. Individuals are limited to $1000 per candidate, but there are no limits on what candidates themselves can spend on their campaigns.

Fig. 8.1 shows only part of the picture because, under FECA, the rules for national party contributions on 'behalf of' candidates – that is, not going directly or exclusively to a particular candidate's campaign are much looser than for individual or PAC contributions. There are limits on this so-called co-ordinated spending but, by exploiting the law to the full, national party committees can contribute up to $73,620 to a House candidate and $1.73 million to a Senator from the most populous states. These loopholes can give to well-organized Republicans an enormous advantage. In 1994, for example, Representative Newt Gingrich mobilized the Republican national congressional committees to sponsor candidates supporting his *Contract With America* which itemized his programme of change for the United States.

Until quite recently it was common to contrast the advantages of incumbency in the House and the Senate. In 1980 of those seeking re-election to the House, a remarkably high and generally rising percentage were re-elected down to 1990 (90 per cent in that year).[4] The contrast with the Senate used to be considerable, where in 1980 only 53 per cent of those seeking re-election were successful. In the last

---

[4] Gary C. Jacobson, *The Politics of Congressional Elections*, (New York, Harper-Collins, 3rd ed. 1992).

Figure 8.1 House and Senate spending by incumbents and challengers, 1979–94

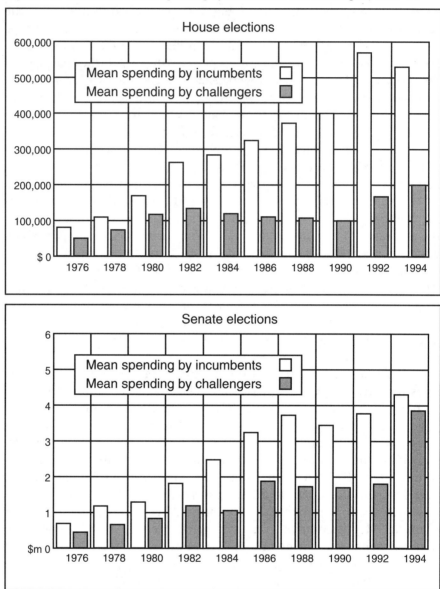

Source: Federal Election Commission, and reproduced in Michael Foley and John E. Owens, *Congress and Presidency: Institutional Politics in a Separated System*, (Manchester, Manchester University Press, 1996), figure 3.2.

several elections, however, the incumbency advantage has also been enjoyed by Senators – in 1990 97 per cent of those seeking re-election were successful.

In spite of this there is little doubt that congressional elections are becoming more competitive. For although incumbents usually win, they *believe* that, unless they raise a large amount of money, and organize and campaign well, they are in danger of losing. Indeed, as far as the House is concerned, incumbents virtually never cease to campaign. With elections every two years and the ever-present threat of an aggressive challenger, they cannot afford to let their guard slip. One consequence of this fraught environment is an increase in the number of vacant seats. Many representatives decide to quit after a few terms and to seek alternative careers. When this happens, the 'out' party is likely to build an impressive campaign organization in order to win the seat. As Burdett Loomis has noted:

> Only open seat candidates build organizations that resemble an incumbent's enterprise (with no accounting for congressional staff, district offices, communications capacities, and travel expenses). In the end, that is what much of the struggle for open seats is all about – to obtain the resources of incumbency for the future. One measure of the Republicans' 1994 success is that they won twenty one open seats previously held by House Democrats and six such seats in the Senate.[5]

Senators are, of course, more secure by virtue of their six-year term. Challengers will rarely manage to amass the money and staff to match incumbents (fig. 8.1) – although there are often celebrated exceptions to this rule. In 1996, for example, incumbent John Kerry of Massachusetts narrowly held off a challenge by Republican governor, William Weld. In the same election, conservative Republican incumbent Larry Pressler of South Dakota was defeated by Democrat Tim Johnson.

Given the personalized nature of Congressional electoral politics, how do members reconcile their commitment to campaigning and winning re-election, on the one hand, and their obligations to public policy-making on the other? To answer this question we have to look more carefully at the work of members and, in particular, at the sort of strategic choices they face, when seeking election or re-election.

Legislators as Rational Actors

Senators' and representatives' determined efforts to get elected or re-elected essentially involve an interaction between the candidate and the constituency. While not unimportant, party ties and contacts have long since ceased to dominate the nomination and campaign process. But this electoral interaction is not simply one of candidate projection and media promotion. Members are also required to tend to the

[5] Burdett A. Loomis, *The Contemporary Congress*, (New York, St Martin's Press, 1996), p. 108.

Table 8.3 Legislators' electoral vulnerability in nine countries

	Maximum legal life of largest house of national legislature (years)	Average actual life of largest house of national legislature 1960–94 (years)	Per cent of years 1960–94 taken up by legislatures the lives of which lasted three-and-a-half years or more[1]	Level of use of primaries for selection of party candidates for national office	Level of candidate centred,- as distinct from party-centred, voting among electorate[2]	Level of member-centred, as distinct from party-centred, voting in national legislature[3]	Level of individual candidate's reliance on own fund-raising efforts[4]
Australia	3	2.3	0.0	Non-existent	Low	Low	Low
Britain	5	3.3	94.3	Non-existent	Low	Low	Low
Canada	5	2.9	72.3	Non-existent	Low	Low	Low
France	5	3.5	76.7	Non-existent	Low	Low	Low
Germany	4	3.2	83.3	Non-existent	Low	Low	Low
Italy	5	3.2	85.6	Non-existent	Low	Medium	Low
Japan	4	2.8	31.4	Non-existent	Medium	Low	Medium
New Zealand	3	2.8	0.0	Non-existent	Low	Low	Low
United States	2	2.0	0.0	High	High	High	High

Source: Anthony King, *Running Scared* (New York Free Press, 1997), table 1.

needs and interests of their constituencies – a job that in the American context is complex and demanding. In no other comparable political system are legislators so electorally vulnerable as to have to devote themselves wholeheartedly to this task. As table 8.3 shows, in most other systems members of lower houses are relatively secure from immediate electoral pressures. They do not have to fight primary elections, they depend on party identities and financial support at the time of their election, voters tend to use national rather than local cues when voting, and the life of the typical parliamentary session is longer than in the USA.

Political scientists have attempted to characterize these efforts in terms of rational choice analysis. David Mayhew, for example, in his stimulating and influential book, *Congress: The Electoral Connection*,[6] argued that members of Congress are mainly motivated by one thing: re-election. Almost all their behaviour inside and outside Congress is shaped by this simple drive. A major a priori assumption here is that members can affect their re-election chances. While Mayhew accepts that there are limits to what a representative or Senator can do to please his or her constituents – no individual legislator can, after all, banish unemployment or solve the budget deficit problem – he does identify three broad strategies which can improve re-election chances. He or she can, first, advertise by spreading his or her name and reputation and generally creating a favourable image. Exposure on television and in the local press can be important, and, unlike the Washington/New York press, local newspapers are generally sympathetic to members of Congress.[7] Sometimes members go to unusual lengths in their efforts at self-promotion. Mayhew reports Charles Diggs Jr (Democrat, Michigan) as running a radio programme with himself as 'combination disc jockey-commentator and minister', and Daniel Flood (Democrat, Pennsylvania) apparently was 'famous for appearing unannounced and often uninvited at wedding anniversaries and other events'.[8]

It used to be the case that credit-claiming, or convincing constituents that the member has 'delivered the goods' was the key motivation of members. Indeed, 'pork barrel' politics is part of American folklore. Pork-barrel politics almost always involves particular rather than collective benefits to constituents. It would be very difficult for an individual member of Congress to claim credit for having reduced the rate of inflation, which everyone benefits from. Much more likely

[6]   New Haven, Yale University Press, 1974.
[7]   While there are no genuinely national newspapers in the USA, the *New York Times*, *The Wall Street Journal* and *Washington Post* act as forums for national debate.
[8]   Both quotes from David Mayhew, *The Electoral Connection*, p. 51.

is he or she to benefit from helping direct federal investment (for example, on a military installation or community development project) to his or her constituency. As we shall see later, the internal structure of power in Congress, not least the absence of strict party discipline, facilitates just such distributions.

Finally, members benefit from position-taking or being identified positively in the minds of constituents with a particular policy position. A predominantly Roman Catholic or fundamentalist Christian constituency would be gratified by public pronouncements or actual legislative action by their member against abortion. New York's large Jewish community would expect their Congress person to take a pro-Israeli stance, and so on. Most recently, legislators have formed caucuses to promote or defend a particular constituency interest. Typical examples are the House Automobile Task Force and the Steel Caucus, both of which have striven to counteract economic decline in these industries.

Senators and representatives have always tended their constituencies, but, in recent years, the pressures to do so have increased considerably. We have already noted the decline of political-party influence – one potentially major bulwark against an intimate constituency/legislator relationship. Less obvious is the impact of a number of political and technological changes on the information flow between the electorate and member. On the members' side, free mailing privileges, together with computerized mailing lists, enable legislators not only to send out a vast volume of letters (Senate offices, for example, send out about 1 million letters a month),[9] but also to target mail to particular groups of constituents. So, if a legislator wants to publicize his or her anti-abortion stand to all Roman Catholics and born-again Christians in the district he/she can do so. He/she can even hone down the target group to a particular neighbourhood or block. On the constituents' side, interest groups and political action committees increasingly 'rate' the legislative voting record of individual members. These group ratings enable groups and, via publicity back home, constituents, to identify their members as 'liberal', 'conservative', pro- or anti-environmental protection, labour, affirmative action or whatever.[10]

Predictably, Senators are less exposed to such highly focused pressures than are representatives, but Mayhew contends they are just as

[9]   *See* Michael J. Robinson, 'Three faces of Congressional media', in Thomas E. Mann and Norman J. Ornstein (eds), *The New Congress*, (Washington DC, American Enterprise Institute, 1981), pp. 55–96.
[10]   An excellent and comprehensive sample of ratings can be found in Michael Barone and Grant Ujifusa, *The Almanac of American Politics 1996*, (Washington DC, Barone and Co., 1997).

instrumental in their quest for re-election as House members. There is undoubtedly a great deal of validity to the rational-choice approach. Any observer of the Washington scene would have to concede that members are increasingly preoccupied with constituency matters. Richard Fenno, who spent several months with members of Congress as a participant observer, dubbed these activities 'home style'.[11] Fenno also noted another phenomenon, however, which does cast some doubt on the rational-choice thesis. The longer House members remained in Congress, the more concerned they became with Washington affairs and the less diligent they became in their pastoral constituency work. The implication here is that there are forces at work in the lives of members of Congress other than the simple drive to win re-election. It may be, of course, that these other forces complement, rather than compete with, constituency pressures. Most voters have very little knowledge of what representatives and Senators actually do in Washington. And given that the electorate is not so naive as to expect an individual member to transform society, a steady flow of positive messages linked to advertising, credit-claiming and position-taking may be enough to convince voters that 'their' representative or Senator is doing a good job.

Undoubtedly there is a number of activities important to the legislators which do not seriously conflict with constituency duties. On some issues – especially foreign-policy or technical financial questions – constituents do not have well-formed opinions. Yet, if members devote themselves to such issues, possibly they are at least indirectly neglecting their re-election chances by not putting their time to the most effective use. The rational-choice theorists' answer here is simple: members devote time to non-constituency questions because the internal dynamics of the House (or Senate) demand it. As separate and individual political actors they can achieve very little for the voters. So to ensure (say) the siting of a federal installation in their constituency, they are obliged to form coalitions with other members. Naturally, coalition-formation involves give and take. It is necessary for a legislator to spend time on apparently non-relevant legislative activity, to win support on those issues which are directly relevant. This is called log-rolling or the bargaining, vote-trading and exchange of favours which has long been a characteristic of Congress. It is principally in any one of the more than 100 work-groups (committees and subcommittees) in the Senate and 150 in the House which dominate day-to-day legislative business that what has come to be known in our political slang as 'log-rolling' takes place. We will return to log-rolling and the work of

[11]   Richard E. Fenno Jr, *Home Style: House Members in their Districts*, (Boston, Little, Brown, 1978).

Congressional committees later. For now it is important to stress that, though persuasive, the rational-choice view of the work of Congress has its limitations. It assumes that a legislator can know what the interests of his or her constituency are. Often this is difficult. Some districts are socially, ethnically and economically diverse. A Senator from Washington State may not need any prompting when voting on legislation affecting the aerospace industry – which dominates that state. But it is much more difficult for Senators from California, representing diverse and politically volatile populations, to respond in this way. Even the Senator from Washington State would today have to think twice about always serving the lumber industry given the size and the influence of the environmental lobby in that state. Moreover, as we will elaborate in the next chapter, it has become more and more difficult for members to deliver in terms of traditional pork-barrel politics. With almost all politicians agreed on the need for fiscal rectitude, the pork barrel has been reduced in size in recent years. Instead, members are more likely to play their part in providing programmes and policies that benefit most or all of their constituents – lower taxes, tougher policing, a return to family values and so on. In such a context members are better advised to indulge in general position-taking than claiming credit for *particular* constituency benefits.

More serious is the implication in the rational-choice approach that members of Congress are mere automatons responding to constituency demands. There is no place for ideology, party or individual preferences. Yet a wealth of empirical evidence exists to suggest that, at one point or another in a legislator's life, all of these can be – and usually are – important. As suggested, party influences are weak by European standards, but that does not mean they do not exist. Democrats have some policy positions and perspectives in common, as have Republicans. The next chapter will show, indeed, how party leadership within each House can be crucial in determining the outcome of legislation. Moreover, there is increased evidence of party solidarity – at least among Republicans in the House. In the 104th Congress, Speaker Newt Gingrich managed to persuade his Republican troops to vote the party line most of the time. We will return to this development in the next chapter. Similarly, appeals by a president to fellow party members in Congress can be effective. Lyndon Johnson used the Democratic majorities in the House and Senate to great effect when pushing through his Great Society social and civil rights programmes. More recently, Ronald Reagan appealed directly to party solidarity when endeavouring to persuade the Republican Senate to support his economic reforms in 1981–82. Assured of Republican minority support in the House, victory there was sealed by the additional support of conservative Democrats.

The existence of 'conservative' and 'liberal' groupings shows the importance of ideology. In itself this need not be significant – members may after all be simply mirroring their constituents' view – but constituencies are not always easily labelled conservative or liberal, and it is not uncommon for an established conservative or liberal member to represent a constituency which cannot accurately be described as either. Legislators are also influenced by other members and by their staff. In other words, in the context of a legislative process which is both fragmented and complex, they are exposed to a number of pressures and influences. Constituency demands may be on the ascendant but this does not mean that we should reduce the role of legislators to the vote-getting machines implied by some political scientists.

In sum, members are exposed to many influences. Given the importance of their constituents' preferences in deciding their electoral survival, it is unlikely that members will do anything directly to antagonize the voters. And, if particularly vulnerable or in a marginal seat, they may indeed devote all their energies to re-election. For some, and particularly members of the Senate, however, political life becomes much more complex, with constituency, party, committee, interest-group and ideological pressures competing for the members' favours.

The Work of Members of Congress

The changing pattern of influence on members has had important consequences on the internal structure of power in each House – and these changes will be analysed in the next chapter. A useful way to link discussion of the activities of members outside and inside the legislature is to examine the typical work-load of legislators and the support in staff, offices and other services provided for them.

Clearly representatives and Senators are not 'lobby fodder' as British MPs are often labelled. They have little choice but to take note of the needs and demands of their constituents and to act on them. Part of this function involves formulating and monitoring a mass of complex legislation. Given the sheer volume of legislation (some 10,000 bills are introduced every session, but only about 1000 become law), most members specialize in particular policy areas, often but not always related to their constituents' interests. Senator William Fulbright, for example, was for many years Chairman of the Senate Foreign Relations Committee. In this job he took a predominantly liberal stance, especially on the conduct of the Vietnam War – not a

Table 8.4 Senator Carl Levin's schedule, 24–29 May 1993

Monday 24 May	1.35 pm	Flight from Detroit to Washington
	3.00	Meeting with constituent and staff on labour legislation
	3.30	Meeting with staff on appointment of official to a Michigan state park
	4.00	Meeting with AFL-CIO and other senator on FDR Commission
	5.00	Reception with other senators sponsored by Senator Dodd
	5.00	Meeting with Clinton Administration nominee to Defense Department
	5.30	Meeting with Senate Armed Services Committee staff on foreign trip
Tuesday 25 May	8.15 am	Meeting with Senate Governmental Affairs Committee staff
	8.30	Meeting of Senators' Urban Issues Group
	9.30	Hearing of Nuclear Deterrence Subcommittee of Senate Armed Services Committee
	9.30	Nomination hearing of Senate Governmental Affairs Committee
	12.00	Photo session with Michigan school children on Senate steps
	12.15	Senator Dodd's Forum for Clinton ambassador Strobe Talbott
	12.30	Democratic Conference on campaign finance bill
	1.15 pm	Celebration for car manufacturers and unions with President Clinton
	2.30	Meeting with staff and lobbyist on health-care legislation
	2.30	Nomination hearings Senate Armed Services Committee
	4.00	Meeting with Michigan labour union members on health-care legislation
	4.45	Meeting with other senator on campaign finance legislation
	4.45	Record tape on NAFTA
	6.00	Buffet Dinner hosted by car manufacturers and unions
Wednesday 26 May	9.30 am	Hearing of Nuclear Deterrence Subcommittee of Senate Armed Services Committee
	12.00	Meeting with staff on gift legislation
	1.30 pm	Meeting with representative of National Cancer Society
	4.00	Meeting with staff and Michigan small-business people on NAFTA
	4.30	Meeting with Michigan electricity company on legislation
	5.00	Meeting with foreign government official on foreign trip
	5.30	Meeting with another senator on legislation
Thursday 27 May	8.35 am	Telephone call to Michigan TV station on auto industry celebration and NAFTA
	8.45	Meeting with Government Operations staff on Great Lakes

Table 8.4 Continued

	9.30	Telephone call to Treasury Under Secretary on legislation
	10.45	Meeting with Interior Secretary and congressman on legislation
	12.00	Photo session with Michigan school children on Senate steps
	12.30	Lunch with Democratic Policy Committee and Clinton administration officials
	2.30 pm	Meeting with executive from major company in Michigan
	2.30	Hearing of Defense Technology Subcommittee of Senate Armed Services Committee
	4.30	Meeting with Senator Riegle (MI) on federal appointments
	6.55	Television appearance
Friday 28 May	9.00 am	Meeting with law students in Court programme
	9.30	Meeting with staff on bonus legislation
	9.30	Briefing from CIA
	10.00	Meeting with Detroit city councilman
	11.00	Radio Phone Press Conference
	12.30 pm	Meeting with staff on National Security Council
	1.30	Record video tape on NAFTA
	2.00	Meeting of Friday Group
	4.25	Flight from Washington to Detroit

Source: Senator Levine's office. Reproduced in Foley and Owens, *Congress and Presidency*, table 3.7.

strategy which was linked in any obvious way to the interests of his rural and conservative constituency, Arkansas. Most of the crucial legislative work is conducted in the committees and subcommittees, yet, as table 8.4 shows, members spend rather little of their very heavy work-loads directly on committee work. The remainder is devoted to a number of tasks but in particular consulting with interest groups and aides on constituency-related matters. To assist the legislator perform all these functions, Congress has voted for itself a quite extraordinary number of services.

Office space, furnishings, stationery and postal allowances are generous. And all communication with constituents, primarily by mail, is free for Senators, and representatives are given generous mailing privileges. All of these benefits pale into insignificance compared with the provisions made for Congressional staff. In 1989, a staggering 23,400 people worked for Congress including, in the House, 7570 personal aides and, in the Senate, 3840. So each representative has approximately 17 people working for him or her, and each Senator enjoys the assistance of no fewer than 38 aides. Some of these positions are secretarial, but many are professionals including some (about two for each member in the House and five in the Senate) directly assigned

Figure 8.2 Growth in congressional staff, 1891–1991

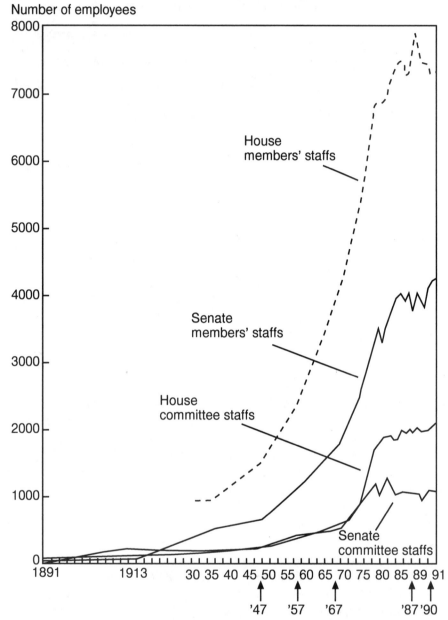

Number of employees

House
members' staffs

Senate
members' staffs

House
committee staffs

Senate
committee staffs

Source: Norman Ornstein, Thomas Mann and Michael Malbin (eds), *Vital Statistics on Congress, 1993–1994* (Washington, CQ Press, 1993).

the job of drafting and amending legislation.[12] In addition, 2000 staff work for House committees and over 1200 for Senate committees. Note how the growth in congressional staff has been exponential over the last 50 years (fig. 8.2).

There has also been a rapid increase in the number of subcommittees in recent years, reflecting an increase in the legislative work-load and the increasing independence of members of Congress; and staffs have risen correspondingly. As will be discussed in the next chapter, as the incoming Republican Speaker in 1994, Newt Gingrich pledged to reduce the number of subcommittees. Finally, members benefit from the work of a number of support agencies such as the Library of Congress (over 5400 staff) and the General Accounting Office (5300). Of course, these support agencies are rarely directly involved in legislation, but their presence does reinforce the claim that, probably uniquely among world assemblies,[13] Congress has acquired a formidable permanent bureaucracy.

So we can conclude that the typical member is a man or woman under pressure. But American national legislators are also uncommonly independent of party and executive, and to help them perform their legislative duties and retain this independence, they are uniquely privileged with staffing and other bureaucratic support. But the important questions remain. How does Congress influence the policy process? To what extent does it check executive power? Most important, is Congress truly the 'people's branch' in the sense that it expresses the democratic wishes of the population?

Further Reading

David Mayhew's *Congress: The Electoral Connection*, (New Haven, Yale University Press, 1974), remains the classic statement of the electoral connection. *Home Style*, (Boston, Little, Brown, 1978), by Richard E. Fenno Jr, is a book rich in anecdote on the same theme. Congressional elections are examined in Gary C. Jacobson, *The Politics of Congressional Elections*, (New York, Harper Collins, 3rd ed. 1992). Two textbook treatments of Congress are provided by Michael Foley and

---

[12] *See* Michael J. Malbin, 'Delegation, deliberation, and the new role of Congressional staff', in Thomas E. Mann and Norman J. Ornstein (eds), *The New Congress*, (Washington DC, American Enterprise Institute, 1981), pp. 134–77.

[13] Michael Malbin notes that the next most heavily staffed legislature is the Canadian Parliament, with a mere 3300 staff: Mann and Ornstein (eds), *The New Congress*, p. 135.

John E. Owens, *Congress and Presidency: Institutional Politics in a Separated System*, (Manchester, Manchester University Press, 1996) and Burdett A. Loomis, *The Contemporary Congress*, (New York, St Martins, 1996). An excellent comparative analysis of the electoral connection is Anthony King, *Running Scared: Why America's Politicians Campaign Too Much and Govern Too Little*, (New York, Free Press, 1997).

9

CONGRESS AS POLICY-MAKER

Let me say this about Congress . . . A Congress is not a President . . . A Congress should not be a President . . . A Congress should be nothing more, nothing less than what it is: a reflection of the will of our people and the problems that disturb them and the actions they want taken. The Congress ought to improve its ability to serve that function.

Senator Edmund S. Muskie quoted in John L. Steele (ed.), *The Role of Congress I: Study of the Legislative Branch*

It is impossible for either the internal or the foreign policy of great states to be strongly and consistently carried out on a collegial basis. Collegiality unavoidably obstructs the promptness of decision, the consistency of policy, the clear responsibility of the individual, and ruthlessness to outsiders in combination with the maintenance of discipline within the group.

Max Weber, *Theory of Social and Economic Organizations*

As was stressed in chapter 4, Congress was originally intended to be the key institution in the federal government. It was only through Congress that the people was given a direct control over policy. Members of the House of Representatives were directly elected, senators, president and vice-president were not. Moreover Congress was meant to formulate and pass laws – the president's main job being merely to implement them. Popular control of government was, of course, limited by the presidential veto and the territorial base of appointed senators. But it was the House of Representatives that controlled the purse strings and it was Congress as a whole that stood, as legislature, at the apex of the constitutional system.

The actual functioning of the institution never quite worked as intended. During the first 30 years of the nineteenth century, state legislatures voted to adopt what became effectively the direct election of the president, and, as the country grew and demands on government increased, president and executive took on the major responsibility for formulating legislation. This trend has occurred in almost every country and is an almost inescapable consequence of the vast information and work-force resources available to modern executive bureaucracies, but not to legislatures. Yet, unlike some national legislatures, Congress retains formidable power. It remains an indisputably important actor in the policy process. It is also an institution with powers and internal operations that are constantly changing. The main purpose of this chapter is to analyse the nature and significance of these changes so that an accurate understanding of the policy-making role of Congress in the 1990s can be achieved.

The Functions of Congress

As indicated in chapter 8, the first and most general function of Congress is one of representation. At its simplest, this means that members of Congress are held accountable for their actions through the electoral process. In complex societies the citizen/representative relationship must necessarily be limited, however, so, when we talk of the 'representative function of Congress', we are actually referring to a number of different functions, most of which are at least one removed from the direct influence of the voters. So the business of formulating and passing laws – the legislative function – involves constant interaction between members, and between members and staff, interest groups, executive officials, the courts and the media. Clearly the individual voter's influence in this process is limited although, as we have already established, the constant threat of electoral defeat does oblige US legislators to tend to the general pastoral needs of their constituencies. A second major function of legislatures, and especially the Congress, is to oversee the executive branch. Constitutionally and by convention, Congress has a number of established oversight powers. It controls finance, so appropriations bills originate in the House of Representatives and have to be approved by both Houses. As we will develop later, it is the president who initially produces the annual budget, so the appropriations process is an opportunity for Congress to approve, modify or criticize the executive's spending plans and also to monitor them during implementation. The Senate also approves presidential appointments and treaties, and both Houses have power to investigate inefficiency or wrong-doing in the executive branch. Finally, Congress has the power to veto all administrative reorganizations in the executive branch. Before we look at these functions in detail, it is necessary to outline the formal structure of power in the two Houses.

The Structure of Power in Congress

Two major focuses of power exist – committees and party leadership. Table 9.1 lists the standing committees of the Congress. Committees have always been central to the business of legislation in Congress and, if anything, their importance has increased over the years. As table 9.1 shows, the permanent committees are distinguished by function, and, as government has become more complex, so the number of committees and subcommittees has proliferated. Consolidation and reorganizations do occur – indeed the Republican 104th Congress, 1995/96 managed to reduce the number of subcommittees substantially (table 9.2). It remains the case, however, that the House and the Senate have large numbers of working groups – especially in comparison with other legislatures. Both internal and external pressures are at work to maintain this need. Internally, individual legislators build reputations by specializing in a particular subject. Often this specialization is linked to constituent needs. Moreover, Congress's own bureaucracy has to match developments in the executive branch, and, as departments and agencies have increased in number and function, so Congress has been obliged to respond. Often this is a two-way street. Members' career and constituency needs may benefit from executive fragmentation which legislation often encourages.

Note also the distinctions drawn in table 9.1 between policy committees which are primarily concerned with *general* policy and committees which are devoted mainly to servicing constituencies. In addition, the House has what might be called 'prestige' committees which are primarily concerned with money – an area where the House has special responsibilities – or with parliamentary procedure.

It is in the committees that the business of framing, amending and rejecting legislation occurs. Most committees *authorize* legislation while others provide funds to *finance* programmes. Hence, the Appropriations, House Ways and Means, Senate Finance and the Budget Committees are concerned with approving income (taxation) and expenditure bills. We will examine the budgetary process in more detail in chapter 15. By no means are all committees equal in power. The above-named finance committees are particularly prestigious and influential, especially so in the case of the House Appropriations Committee (which is the source of all appropriations bills), the House Ways and Means and Senate Finance Committees (which are responsible for tax bills) and the Budget Committees. Of the authorizing

Table 9.1 House and Senate committees types by preference motivations of new House members and senators

House	Senate
Prestige committees	**Policy committees**
Appropriations	Budget
Budget	Foreign Relations
Rules	Governmental Affairs
Ways and Means	Judiciary
	Labor and Human Resources
Policy committees	**Mixed policy/constituency committees**
Banking, Finance, and Urban Affairs (now Banking and Financial Services)	Armed Services
Education and Labor (now Economic and Education Opportunities)	Banking, Housing, and Urban Affairs
Energy and Commerce (now Commerce)	Finance
Foreign Affairs (now International Relations)	Small Business
Government Operations (now Government Reform and Oversight)	
Judiciary	
Constituency committees	**Constituency committees**
Agriculture	Agriculture, Nutrition and Forestry
Armed Services (now National Security)	Appropriations
Merchant Marine and Fisheries (now abolished)	Commerce, Science, and Transportation
Natural Resources (now Resources)	Energy and Natural Resources
Public Works and Transportation (now Transportation and Infrastructure)	Environment and Public Works
Science, Space, & Technology (now Science)	
Small Business	
Veterans' Affairs	
Unrequested committees	**Unrequested committees**
District of Columbia (now abolished)	Rules and Administration
House Administration (now House Oversight)	Veterans' Affairs
Post Office and Civil Service (now abolished)	
Standards of Official Conduct	

Source: Steven S. Smith and Christopher J. Deering, *Committees in Congress*, 2nd edn (Washington, DC: Congressional Quarterly Press, 1990), pp. 87 and 101. Reproduced in Michael Foley and John E. Owens, *Congress and Presidency: Institutional politics in a Separated System*, (Manchester, University of Manchester Press, 1996), table 4.10.

committees, the Senate Foreign Relations is of central importance in foreign policy, while the Agriculture, Banking and Judiciary Committees are prominent in both Houses. An equivalent hierarchy applies to most subcommittees with, for example, the House Appropriations Subcommittee on Defense being markedly more important than the Transportation and Infrastructure subcommittees. Because the House of Representatives is a larger and, by tradition, a more formal body than the Senate, complex rules have been formulated to govern day-by-day business. The Rules Committee is responsible for interpreting these regulations and in particular for helping to decide which bills, and in what form, come before the floor of the House. This power to withhold bills or to allow them to proceed only if certain amendments or provisions are omitted or included gives the Rules Committee considerable political clout. Indeed, during the late-nineteenth and early twentieth centuries, the Rules Committee was at the very centre of Congressional power. Today, although it continues to perform a gate-keeper function, it is less powerful, in part because the House is less formal than it was (of which more later) and in part because the Committee tends to be the voice of the majority party leadership rather than being an independent source of power in Congress.

Clearly, membership of committees is an important determinant of the status and influence of individual representatives and senators, and, accordingly, the processes whereby members are selected to sit on committees and eventually selected as chairpersons have long been the subject of debate and controversy. The most basic rule is that the party with a majority in the chamber automatically achieves a majority in the committees, with the minority party represented in rough proportion to its delegation in the chamber as a whole. Committee and subcommittee chairpersons are drawn exclusively from the majority party. In both House and Senate, members are allowed to sit on a maximum of two committees, although House members assigned to the important Rules, Ways and Means and Appropriations Committees are not normally permitted further assignments. In both Houses party committees selected by party caucuses (meetings of all party members in each House) choose the members of the standing committees. This process is predictably political, with seniority, experience, reputation and connections being the main determinants of assignments. Since the 1950s the Senate has ensured that all freshmen (new) senators are given at least one major committee assignment (the so-called 'Johnson Rule' introduced under the influence of the then senator majority leader, Lyndon Baines Johnson). By winning prestigious committee jobs, members can enhance their institutional reputations, gain access to legislative programmes of direct interest to their constituents, and, occasionally, attract national attention.[1]

During the first two years of the 1981–85 Reagan administration, for example, member of Congress James R. Jones (D. Oklahoma)

[1] *See* Richard Fenno Jr, *Congressmen in Committees*, (Boston, Little, Brown, 1973) for a vivid account of committee politics.

Table 9.2 Number of House and Senate subcommittees, selected Congresses, 1955–96

	84th (1955–56)	90th (1967–68)	94th (1975–76)	100th (1987–88)	104th (1995–96)
House subcommittees	99	154	172	160	77
Senate subcommittees	105	126	174	93	70

Source: Vital Statistics: 1993–1994, Congressional Quarterly's Players, Politics and Turf of the 104th Congress, special issue of *Congressional Quarterly,* 25 March 1995.

assumed a pivotal position as Chairperson of the House Budget Committee. Although he opposed many of the administration's economic policies, Jones was able to straddle party positions by proposing alternative, but by no means opposite, policies and by maintaining a friendly relationship with Pete Domenici, the Republican Chairperson of the Senate Budget Committee.

Within individual committees and subcommittees status is no less important, with the chairperson of each work-group at the very top of the pecking order. Both ranking within committees and the assertion of power by the chairpersons over committee members are largely determined by seniority. Until the early 1970s the seniority rule was condemned by liberals because of the enormous advantage it gave to the solidly Democratic – but conservative and often racist – one-party South. Indeed, the caricature image of elderly white-haired Southerners lording over all and sundry on Capitol Hill was not far from the truth, as such figures as Richard Russell of Armed Services, Russell Long of Finance and James Eastland of Judiciary in the Senate and Carl Vinson of Armed Services and Howard Smith of Rules in the House, testified.

Since the 1970s there have been two distinct waves of reform affecting committee power. Until the mid-1970s chairpersons were particularly powerful because of their control of the agenda. They could decide the order in which bills are discussed, the timing of committee meetings, the frequency of public hearings and the management of bills on the floor of the House. They used also to have a major say in the number and composition of subcommittees, together with the selection of subcommittee chairs. During the 1970s the Democrats instituted reforms that removed committee chairs from the very pinnacles of power. Their control of the work and membership of subcommittees was weakened. Moreover, seniority was removed as the only criterion for advancement within committees. In 1975 the House Democratic caucus, caught up in a general atmosphere of reform, removed three of the most powerful committee chairpersons at a stroke (Wight Patman of Texas, Banking and Currency; W. R. Poage of Texas, Agriculture; and F. Edward Hébert of

Louisiana, Administration). In fact, seniority remained central to any promotion within committees. From 1975 to 1994 chairpersons were obliged to treat subcommittee chairs (and committee members generally) more as equals than as feudal vassals. This was part of a general democratization and dispersal of power in the House and (to a lesser extent) the Senate which we will return to later.

The decentralization of power in the House (and to a lesser extent in the Senate) led many commentators to conclude that Congress was incapable of making quick decisions. Worse, decentralized committees were likely to pander to particular (or constituency), rather than general (or the public), interest. Republican presidents and congressional opposition spokespersons pointed to the fact that the Democrats' apparently permanent control of the House made it impossible to cut the budget deficit or to pass much-needed reforms in such areas as health care and the economy. Although these criticisms were almost certainly exaggerated (*see* pp. 180–3 below) they helped inspire a second major wave of reforms following the Republicans' capture of Congress in the 1994 mid-term elections. Newt Gingrich, the new Speaker, and Dick Armey, the new Majority Leader, were determined to push through the legislative programme outlined in their *Contract With America*. As a result, they persuaded the Republican Conference (the committee representing all the House Republicans) to push through a number of changes in committee operations (outlined on p. 184 below).

The major objective of these reforms was to strengthen party control over the committees. Judging by the success enjoyed by the Republicans in passing most of the *Contract With America* legislative programme (though most of it was eventually defeated in the Senate or by presidential veto), this objective seems to have been achieved.

In addition to the standing committees in each House, other workgroups exist, the most important of which are the Conference Committees. These are, simply, *ad hoc* bodies created to reconcile the differences that occur in the House and Senate versions of the same piece of legislation. Membership is drawn from those members in each House who have been most closely involved with the legislation – usually the relevant committee members – who then vote *en bloc* so as to represent the wishes of their chamber. A great deal of politicking goes on in conference, with bills often amended considerably and not always in line with the wishes of the House or Senate as a whole. Conference decisions can, however, be rejected by a subsequent vote on the floor of each chamber and sent back to the committee (see fig. 9.1 p. 174). In addition, *ad hoc* committees can be formed by the Speaker of the House to reconcile standing committees with overlapping jurisdictions, and select committees, appointed by presiding

Plate 9.1 Newt Gingrich, Speaker of the House of Representatives in his Capitol Hill office.

officers, can be created in either House to expedite a particular problem, often in association with a Congressional investigation. In recent years, for example, select committees on ageing and intelligence have been formed in both Houses. Such committees have to be renewed every two years and they cannot report legislation to the floor. In most cases select committees emerge as a forum for airing currently controversial issues.

The second focus of power in Congress is the party leadership. In the House the key figures are the Speaker and Minority Leader, and the key groups are the party caucuses, in particular the majority party caucus (presently the Republican Conference). The Speaker of the House used to have quite substantial formal powers. Until 1911, he was also Chair of the Rules Committee and he appointed committee chairpersons. This combination enabled Speakers to control the flow of legislation on to the floor. Concentration of such power in the personage of one particularly assertive Speaker, Joseph Cannon, led to a revolt in 1910–11 which resulted in the removal of the Speaker's control of the Rules Committee and of committee assignments. But the Speaker retains considerable authority. He or she continues to help control the flow of legislation, recognizes who is to speak on the floor, can create *ad hoc* committees, gives advice on assignments to conference and select committees, helps in assigning bills to committees and he/she votes in the event of a tie. While the Speaker has the greatest formal power of any individual in the House, his or her potential informal power is much greater. As leading parliamentarian and party leader he/she can become a crucial link between other centres of power – particularly committee chairpersons – as well as be the person most able to muster often disparate party forces behind a particular bill or the programme of a president. Whether these powers are utilized to the full depends on the personality, capabilities and political skills of the incumbent.

In recent years, for example, the office has come full circle as incumbents have changed. Between 1940 and 1960 the office was dominated by the forceful and highly political Sam Rayburn (with breaks in 1947–48 and 1953–54 when the Republicans had a majority in the House). Between 1961 and 1978 first John McCormack and then Carl Albert became Speakers, neither of whom had the skills or the charisma of Rayburn. Between 1978 and 1986 the highly partisan and politically astute Thomas (Tip) O'Neill partly returned the office of Speaker to its former glory. O'Neill's personality was ideally suited to the brokerage politics of the House, and he was aided by the 1975 reforms which gave to the Speaker the power to appoint Democratic members of the Rules Committee and to the Democratic Steering Committee, which assigns new committee members within the party. Given the Democratic dominance of the House, these amounted to considerable powers. On his resignation in 1986, O'Neill was replaced by Jim Wright of Texas, a long-time O'Neill supporter and, until 1986, Democratic House Majority Leader. In June 1989 Jim Wright was forced to resign after allegations of financial irregularities were brought against him by House Minority Whip, Newt Gingrich. Wright was replaced by Tom Foley who had a more accommodating style than the often confrontational Jim Wright. Following the 1994

mid-term Republican victory, Speaker Newt Gingrich took on a legislative leadership role unprecedented since the days of Joe Cannon. In
addition to the committee reforms (*see* above), Gingrich's formal
powers were enhanced. He was also widely perceived as partly responsible for the Republican victory so had built up considerable political
capital with House members. His dominance was to prove short lived,
however. In 1996 he was accused of a number of ethics charges and
was only narrowly re-elected Speaker in early 1997. It seems likely
that during the 105th Congress (1997–98) some power will return to
individual members and committee chairs at the expense of the party
leadership.

After the Speaker, the most important offices are the majority and
minority floor leaders, who are elected by the party caucuses and
whose main job is to monitor and organize party business on the floor
of the House. In fact, the Minority Leader is often a more crucial figure than the Majority Leader, largely because the Speaker is the effective majority spokesperson. Dick Gephart, the most recent Minority
Leader, saw his position and importance increase given Clinton's victory in 1996 and in the context of the difficulties encountered by
Speaker Gingrich in 1996 and 1997. Finally, both parties appoint
whips to help control floor business. These are in no way equivalent
to British parliamentary whips; they have no effective sanctions at
their disposal to oblige members to toe the party line (if there is one!).
Instead their job is to persuade, negotiate, bargain and cajole members into broad agreement on particular items of legislation.

The party caucus meets infrequently and then usually to agree on
procedure rather than to discuss substantive policy issues. As important today are the informal caucuses which have emerged over the last
20 years. These are usually organized around a particular interest
such as the Democratic Black and Hispanic caucuses, or around an
ideological orientation such as the Democratic Study Group representing liberal causes or the conservative Republican Study Group. In
the early 1990s the typical House member belonged to 16 caucuses
and the typical Senator to 14.

Leadership in the Senate roughly parallels that in the House, but
there are some important differences. Unlike the House, the presiding
officer, the vice-president of the United States, has few powers. Neither, indeed, has the President Pro-Tem who normally presides over
day-to-day business. Real power lies with the majority and minority
leaders, though even they can often do little to control the behaviour
of just 100 fiercely independent senators. Again, much depends on
the personalities of the incumbents. Some majority leaders, such as
Lyndon Johnson (1956–61), built reputations as power brokers, as
did a recent incumbent, Republican Howard Baker, whose manage-

ment of the Republicans' fragile majority in 1981–85 showed great political skill. Robert Dole of Kansas, who succeeded Baker in 1985, had to use all his political skill to hold together an even narrower Republican majority until the Democrats regained control of the Senate in 1986. In contrast to Johnson and Baker, some recent leaders, such as Mike Mansfield (1961–78) have been either unwilling or less able to assert authority over fellow party members. Following the Republican victory in 1994 Bob Dole became a highly effective Majority Leader. He eventually resigned to run for the presidency in 1996 and was replaced by Senator Trent Lott.

So far in our discussion we have concentrated on describing the formal powers of committees and party leaders. This tells us little about the dynamics of the policy-making process, however, and how the institution can be assessed in terms of its performance and effectiveness. To examine these questions, let us first look at the validity of the *criticisms* which have been directed at Congress over recent years, and then discuss the reform measures adopted in response to these criticisms.

Congress Under Fire

At least since World War II, Congress has been the subject of sometimes intense criticism. Very generally, we can divide these criticisms into broad categories – those which are historically specific and those which identify structural features of Congress that persist through time. Of course, the two sets of critiques are related, especially as the institution is constantly changing, but this simple distinction does facilitate a more subtle understanding of how the institution works.

1 Perhaps the most common and persistent criticism is that Congress is fragmented and unresponsive; that it is not a 'coherent' policy-making body but instead a forum for the defence and promotion of disparate, unrelated interests. That the policy-making process in Congress is fragmented cannot be disputed. Power is dispersed to committees and subcommittees, and the legislative process itself is cumbersome. When a bill is introduced, it faces a formidable number of potential veto points before it actually becomes law, and this is true even of those bills that are part of the president's programme, have substantial support in Congress and are recognized as important public questions. Fig. 9.1 shows the major obstacles that confront any bill when introduced into Congress. Committee action is the most difficult stumbling block, with only about 10 per cent of bills actually reported out. The presidential veto used to be a much rarer barrier but, since the advent of divided government, it is now exercised more frequently on important items of legislation (*see* chapter 10, p. 211). Even less common are successful attempts to

Figure 9.1 How a bill becomes law: the obstacle course for legislation in Congress

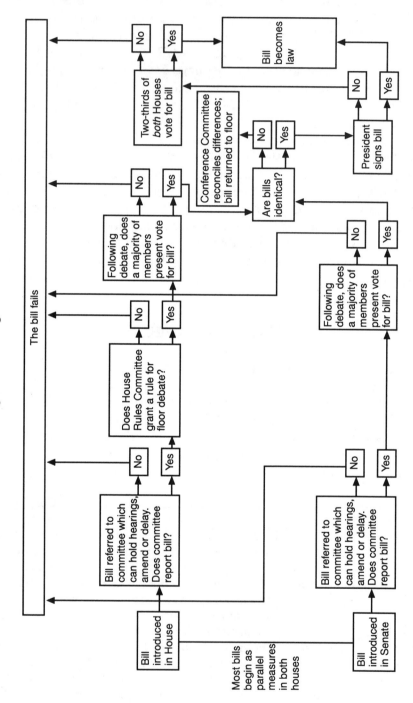

override a veto. The president can also exercise a *pocket veto* by failing to sign a bill passed within the last ten days of a legislative session.

Fig. 9.1 also omits reference to the Senate *filibuster* – a debating device which, although used infrequently, has ended the life of several controversial bills. Filibustering is the practice, allowed only by Senate rules, of speaking in unlimited debate and eventually forcing the opposition to back down. During the 1950s and 1960s many civil rights bills were killed by this method, with segregationist Southern senators speaking for many hours against the reform measures. A device, known as a *cloture* (or closure) rule, does exist for ending a filibuster; this can be invoked to end debate if three-fifths of the senators agree. Between 1917 (when the cloture rule was introduced) and 1990, 296 cloture votes were taken, of which 101 were successful. Since the 1970s, cloture has been voted much more frequently and is now successful in about 50 per cent of cases. During the 103rd Congress (1993–94), when the Republicans remained the minority party, they managed to produce an unprecedented 55 filibusters, many of which thwarted President Clinton's legislative measures.

In the House, the Rules Committee can constitute a further barrier to the passage of a law. Until 1975, Southerners dominated the Committee and frequently refused to grant rules to bills they disliked, irrespective of the support the measures may have won in the legislative committees. Again liberal, and especially civil-rights, legislation was the victim. In 1975, however, the Democratic caucus voted to give the Speaker the power to appoint Rules Committee members. As a result, although the Committee can still stop bills, it acts more in accordance with the general wishes of the House – and particularly with the relevant legislative committee – than before. Interestingly, debate on the floor used to be one of the least-significant aspects of the legislative process for, by the time a bill reached this stage, it was already roughly in its final form. Recent reforms, however, have increased floor activity with individual legislators now more able to attach riders and amendments to bills. Floor *votes* can also be crucial, of course.

Fig. 9.1 gives the slightly misleading impression that bills either proceed past a number of legislative hurdles or are simply killed off. The reality is that most bills are non-starters because they lack the support of key members – although some are initiated simply to attract public attention to an issue – and the remainder embark on a course which is beset with problems and pitfalls. But these do not always involve the possibility of a sudden death. As likely are the possibilities of amendment and delay. Delay can occur at almost any stage of the process, but it is in the committees that bills most often become buried, sometimes never to reappear. Given that Congress has a heavy work-load and is constantly under pressure, delaying a bill is often an expedient course to follow. For a bill's supporters, including presidents, this can be highly frustrating.

Few bills emerge from Congress in the precise form that they entered. They are amended – sometimes dramatically – from their original form, and this amendment process is the very essence of Congressional politics, for it is by changing the detailed provisions of bills that members can indulge in *log-rolling*, or the exchange of favours, which is so crucial to their electoral survival. So items are added to or deleted from bills in accordance with bargains struck between key legislators, usually within or between committees. Committee hearings, open to public scrutiny, also allow organized interests to air their views and generally to advertise particular points of view. And, of course, executive departments and agencies usually have crucial interests (with positions to defend or promote) in the detail of legislation. Finally, committees may compete one with the other for, as can be inferred from the list of committees in table 9.1, there is a number of areas where overlapping jurisdictions occur.

When all these influences are at work, as they are in major items of legislation, the potential for delay, obstruction and even confusion, can be appreciated. A classic example of what can happen to a vital piece of legislation is provided by President Clinton's health care reforms introduced in Congress in 1993. Given the enormous complexity of the bill – a fact that resulted from the need to consolidate a large number of existing federal health and welfare programmes – it was assigned to multiple committees. Two of these, the House Education and Labour and the Senate Labour and Human Resources, agreed on a reform package but only one that was too liberal for the Congress as a whole to accept. In addition, the key finance committee chairs found it difficult to win sufficient *committee* support for the reforms. As Burdett Loomis has noted, these failures tell us a great deal about congressional power given that the chairs of the committees involved included some truly formidable legislators – Representatives John Dingell (Energy and Commerce) and Dan Rostenkowski (Ways and Means) and Senator Daniel Patrick Moynihan (Finance). In the end Congress found it impossible to reconcile all the conflicting bureaucratic, health-care and insurance-company interests in a way that would produce a coherent legislative package. The bill died a year later during the 1994 mid-term election campaign.[2] There have, in fact, been remarkably few occasions when a major legislative package has not been delayed or obstructed by Congress. The early New Deal and Great Society (1965–66) periods are usually mentioned as the notable exceptions (*see* chapters 14 and 15). Some have argued that the first two years of the Reagan administration were also characterized by a responsive and responsible Congress, but the president by no means had it all his own way, and, by the end of 1982, Congress began to assert a more independent position, especially on economic policy. Similarly the much-publicized reform programme of the Republican 104th Congress came to little – mainly because President Clinton was able successfully to exercise the veto power.

Perhaps, indeed, Congress should assert its independence. How else, after all, could it be responsive to the demands of public opinion and voters? There are two answers to this question. The first, which is highly controversial, is the simple fact that, in a complex and pluralistic society beset with urgent domestic and international problems, democratically elected executives should not have to face open resistance from the legislative branch.

---

[2]   Burdett A. Loomis, *The Contemporary Congress*, (New York, St Martin's Press, 1996), chapter 10.

Executives in most Western states are relatively free from such pressures, and may be, as a result, more able to respond effectively to crisis. We will return to this contentious point in later chapters. The second response is more relevant to the argument in this section: fragmentation of power in Congress, multiple veto points and open access by myriad interests to centres of power render the institution *inefficient*. In other words, it cannot be responsive because its decision-making structure is clumsy, slow and confused. When it does appear to 'work', it is to resist change and pander to special, rather than collective or public, interests. Our brief survey of the legislative process suggests that there is considerable truth to this charge. Certainly more than one generation of House and Senate members have been aware of it, for they have repeatedly attempted to reform the institution. Before we examine these reforms, we should mention some of the other criticisms levelled at Congress.

2 *Congress has failed to perform the oversight function effectively.* In addition to passing legislation, Congress is charged with the job of overseeing the executive or holding the president, executive departments and agencies accountable for their actions. The appropriations process in part involves this job. In addition, Congress is responsible for monitoring executive appointments, holding formal investigations into the executive branch, and, as a last resort, it has the authority to impeach executive officers. The Constitution requires the Senate to approve presidential appointments, but it is not a power that the Senate has used in the strictly 'moral' sense, that is, rooting out inefficient, incompetent or corrupt appointees. As often, senators are concerned to ensure that incumbents in the more than 1500 major posts subject to Senate confirmation are men and women who are sympathetic to the legislators' political or constituency interests, or who are likely to defend an organized interest (such as labour or business) which senators are known to identify with. The appointment process is, in other words, not unlike the legislative process – it is highly politicized and subject to similar constituency interest group pressures.[3] Only rarely are appointees rejected or obliged to withdraw. In 1977, for example, only ten appointees were rejected or had to withdraw – the highest in the whole 1961–81 period – out of a total of 1529 nominations.[4] So Congress is accused of two failings in this area. First it favours many appointees, not because they are likely to serve the public interest, but because they will support particular or special constituency and group interests. And second that, independently of this problem, it has failed to root out some of the more obvious and colourful examples of incompetent presidential nominations. The Nixon administration was littered with such cases. But even the Carter presidency was able to produce its Bert Lance (the Budget Director who was eventually obliged to resign following exposure of illegal banking practices). More recently, the first Clinton administration has also had its share of dishonest or incompetent appointees with accusations

---

[3] For an excellent analysis of this subject, *see* G. Calvin Mackenzie, *The Politics of Presidential Appointments*, (New York, Free Press, 1981).
[4] Ibid., table 8.1, p. 177.

levelled at a number of cabinet secretaries, including Secretary of Housing and Urban Development Henry Cisneros and Commerce Secretary Ron Brown. While all this is true, Congress does now examine the records of the most senior nominees more carefully than in the past. This is particularly true of Supreme Court nominees who have the potential to shift the ideological complexion of the Court on a range of sensitive issues. Such perceptions certainly applied to Robert H. Bork, Reagan's 1987 nominee to the Court, who was opposed by the wide margin of 58 to 42 senators. Reagan's second nominee for the vacant position, Douglas H. Ginsberg, was obliged to withdraw following an admission that he had smoked marijuana while at law school. Eventually the president nominated a 'safe' candidate, Anthony Kennedy, who was quickly confirmed by the Senate. George Bush had fewer difficulties with his appointees, although his first choice as Defense Secretary, John Tower, was forced to withdraw following allegations that he was personally unsuitable for the job.

The investigative power of Congress consists of investigations by the standing committees, the work of special or select committees created for the specific purpose of enquiring into a particular problem, and the work of the General Accounting Office (GAO). GAO auditing of the executive spending is a continuous process, with the Office reporting its findings to Congress. Congress can also require the GAO to investigate a particular programme or agency at any time. Standing-committee investigations involve public hearings into alleged executive inefficiency or wrong-doing. One of the most famous was the Army-McCarthy hearings by the Senate Government Operations Permanent Investigations Subcommittee into communist influence in the Army, the CIA and Department of State. Subcommittee Chairman Joseph McCarthy became notorious as a red-baiter in this role, and his unfair and intimidating methods led eventually to his censure by the Senate in 1954.[5]

More typical are the several instances when Congress has created a select committee specifically to investigate a subject of public concern. In recent years, for example, the Senate Select Committee on Campaign Practices – known popularly as the (Sam) Ervin Committee after its Chairperson – won great public attention through its enquiries into the Watergate scandal. This in turn spawned further investigations into the security agencies (FBI, CIA, Defense Intelligence) the legality of whose activities had been questioned during the Watergate exposures. In 1987 the Reagan administration was also investigated by Congressional select committees set up in each House to investigate the origins and management of the Iran-Contra affair. In this case the House and the Senate decided to conduct joint hearings into the affair. This investigation led directly to a number of indictments and prosecutions, including the prosecution of former Defense Secretary, Caspar Weinberger. Weinberger, together with four other former officials, was pardoned by President Bush in late 1992. Most recently Congress has investigated President

---

[5] The institution of red-baiting, if not the actual practice, continued with the work of the House Unamerican Activities Committee (later the Internal Security Committee) until its abolition in 1975.

Clinton and first lady Hillary Clinton's involvement in the Whitewater property company which operated in Arkansas during Bill Clinton's tenure as Governor. Other notable Congressional investigations include enquiries into racketeering in trade unions, safety in atomic power stations, the conduct of the Vietnam War and standards in the pharmaceutical industry.

Note that it is not only government activities that come under Congressional scrutiny – although it is usually investigations into the executive branch which arouse the most feeling and controversy. The reason for this is simple: investigations (and oversight generally) raise awkward questions about where executive power begins and ends. With the rise of big government and the vast bureaucracy that accompanies it, Congress has found it increasingly difficult to perform the oversight function because it has limited access to exactly what goes on within the executive. Information is a valuable commodity and one jealously guarded by presidents and their bureaucrats. Even though Congress can subpoena witnesses and documents, presidents have repeatedly refused or been extremely reluctant to hand over information. In recent years they have claimed 'executive privilege' to certain information. Unfortunately, this concept has no clear constitutional status, so the legality of withholding information remains an open question. Since Watergate and Richard Nixon's unprecedented reluctance to furnish evidence to Congressional committees (he withheld information at least 19 times on matters unrelated to Watergate), presidents have been more pliant. But as the Iran-Contra affair confirmed, the executive continues to hold the trump card because the sheer volume and technical complexity of documentation often make it difficult for a hard-pressed committee even to know what to ask for.

Finally, Congress has the power to impeach executive officers. Impeachment is a formal accusation of wrong-doing which the House of Representatives carries out, while the Senate actually tries and convicts impeached officials. But on only 12 occasions has the House used this power, and on only four has the Senate convicted. One president, Andrew Johnson, was formally impeached although the Senate failed to convict, and of course the House Judiciary Committee voted articles of impeachment against Richard Nixon, who resigned before further action could be taken. Again, Congress has been accused of tardiness and indecision in this general area. The main criticism is that the impeachment process is so cumbersome and formalized that it is rarely used. Critics also point to the continuing evidence of executive wrong-doing which shows that impeachment is not an adequate deterrent. (Although the cumbersome impeachment process has also been praised for preventing hasty and partisan attacks on individual officials and politicians.)

In addition to these structural criticisms, Congress is at any one time criticized for its specific failure to deal with a contemporary crisis or problem. Or, observers infer that a structural feature of the institution is permanent when it is only temporary. So, in the ten years following World War II, it was common to accuse Congress of excessive partisanship. And, indeed, the red-baiting committees of the late 1940s and early 1950s did in part represent Republican attempts to indict the activities of past or present Democratic administrations. By the late 1950s and early 1960s the charge was somewhat different: Congress was dominated by conservative, segregationist Southerners. Following the reforms of the 1970s, the criticism has shifted once again. Now the accusation is that Congress is the creature of increasingly vocal and influential special- and public-interest lobbies – or simply that members serve their own, rather than the public, interest. Recent events seem to confirm this view in the minds of the American public. In 1989 five senators were found to have intervened in favour of Charles Keating of the Lincoln Savings and Loan Association. In 1991, the Senate Ethics Committee found evidence of wrong-doing by Senator Alan Cranston of California, and the other four were reprimanded. During the 103rd Congress (1991–93) 267 House members were found to have used an interest-free overdraft facility from a bank set up specifically for use by members of Congress. The public outcry at the extensive use of these 'rubber cheques' was considerable. Finally, in early 1997 Speaker Newt Gingrich was formally reprimanded and fined by the House for illegally using income from college courses he taught for partisan purposes. Although he was re-elected, this unprecedented action against a sitting Speaker weakened his position as House leader.

Reform and Change in Congress

The major criticisms of Congress prevalent in the late 1960s and early 1970s stressed two failings: legislative business was dominated by a few senior committee chairpersons; and, in its dealings with the executive, Congress was failing either to provide realistic policy-making alternatives or to check the burgeoning growth of executive power. Commentators had long noted that, if these problems were to be solved, political party organizations in the two Houses would have to take the lead. Indeed, if we think in terms of centralizing and decentralizing influences, party and party leadership are clearly centralizing forces, while the committee structure essentially disperses power. Party voting has not been strong in Congress since the 1890–1910 period, when over half the roll calls (votes on the floor) involved 90 per cent of one party voting differently from 90 per cent of the other.[6] As table 9.3 shows, even by the weakest measure of party unity – the

[6]   John F. Bibby, Thomas E. Mann and Norman J. Ornstein, *Vital Statistics on Congress 1991–92,* (Washington DC, American Enterprise Institute, 1992) p. 97.

Table 9.3 Votes in Congress showing party unity, 1954–94 (per cent of all votes)

How often a majority of Democrats voted against a majority of Republicans												
Year	*House*	*Senate*	*Year*	*House*	*Senate*	*Year*	*House*	*Senate*	*Year*	*House*	*Senate*
1954	38	47	1964	35	36	1974	29	44	1984	47	40
1955	41	30	1965	32	42	1975	48	48	1985	61	50
1956	44	53	1966	41	50	1976	36	37	1986	57	52
1957	59	36	1967	36	35	1977	42	42	1987	64	41
1958	40	44	1968	35	32	1978	33	45	1988	47	42
1959	55	48	1969	31	36	1979	47	47	1989	55	35
1960	53	37	1970	27	35	1980	38	46	1990	49	54
1961	50	62	1971	38	42	1981	37	48	1991	55	49
1962	46	41	1972	27	36	1982	36	43	1992	64	53
1963	49	47	1973	42	40	1983	56	44	1993	65	67
									1994	62	52

Source: Congressional Quarterly Weekley Report, 31 December, 1994, p. 3659.

percentage on which a majority of voting Democrats opposes a majority of voting Republicans – less than half of the roll-call votes in the period show any party cohesion; although a significant recovery of party solidarity is evident after 1983. And even on these occasions only between approximately 50 per cent and 70 per cent of members from the same party voted together. Note also that what little party unity there was declined markedly in the House from the mid-1960s to the mid-1970s when the Democratic Party, in particular, was riven with sectional and ideological conflict. But this simple index hardly gives an accurate picture of the frustration which most members increasingly felt at the way in which a few, often conservative, chairpersons dominated committee business and the legislative agenda. By the early 1970s this frustration had reached such a point that sweeping reforms were introduced, reaching a crescendo in 1975 following the election of the unusually liberal post-Watergate Congress in 1974. The major changes were:

1 In 1970 the House ended non-recorded teller voting and switched over to electronic voting on all roll calls. As a result the *number* of roll calls increased dramatically from 177 in 1969 to 541 in 1978.
2 In 1973 all bill drafting in committee was opened to public scrutiny, so exposing to organized interests and constituents the precise policy preference of members.
3 The Democratic caucus in the House voted in 1971 to permit ten or more members to demand a special vote on a disputed committee chairperson assignment. In 1975 all nominees for chairperson were subject to an automatic secret ballot by caucus members.
4 Also in 1975 the caucus voted to give the Speaker the power to appoint Rules Committee members, subject to caucus approval.
5 Since 1973 all Democratic House members have been guaranteed a major committee assignment and, since 1974, committee assignments

have passed from the Ways and Means Committee (traditionally dominated by Southerners) to the party's Steering and Policy Committee.

6 Subcommittees were greatly strengthened and increased in number by a
number of measures, beginning with the 1970 Legislature Reorganization
Act. In 1973 the subcommittees were provided with a 'Bill of Rights'
which gave to the full committee caucus the power to set subcommittee
jurisdictions and select chairpersons. Subsequently, subcommittees were
allocated extra staff.

7 Although the number of formal changes in the Senate has been fewer
than in the House, reforms have taken the same general direction and in
some cases have been quite radical. Committee meetings have been
opened up to the public, the Democratic caucus's power has been
strengthened in relation to the nomination of committee chairpersons,
and it is now much easier to end a filibuster than it was in the early
1970s. Also, the committee structure has been rationalized with the number of committees reduced and some overlapping jurisdictions eliminated.

All these reforms were designed to speed up the legislative process
and to weaken the entrenched power of committee chairpersons. By
so doing, members hoped to make Congress a more effective policy-
making body and therefore enhance its position in relation to the
executive. In fact, in the wake of the abuse of executive power
represented by the conduct of the Vietnam War and Watergate, Congress passed a number of laws specifically designed to curb such
excesses and to strengthen the legislative branch. The two most
important of these measures were the following:

The 1973 war powers act

Overriding a presidential veto, Congress acted in 1973 to limit the
president's ability to conduct war without the prior approval of Congress. Under this law the commitment of US armed forces could
occur only if Congress declared war or authorized the use of forces or
if the president acted in a national emergency. During emergency
actions, presidents were required to win Congressional support after
60 days, and a further 30 days could be granted. After the 90-day
period Congress could act to stop the use of troops in a law which is
not subject to a presidential veto.

The 1974 budget and impoundment control act

A perennial complaint of Congress-watchers in the post-war period
was the failure of the institution to match the executive's budget-
making capacity. Presidents presented annual budgets which had

effectively become national policy programmes. Congress, in contrast, seemed unable to see the budget as a coherent whole. Indeed, it dealt with finance in an incremental, piecemeal way, reflecting the fragmentation characteristic of bicameralism and the appropriations process. The 1974 Act attempted to compensate for these problems by creating budget committees in each House and a Congressional Budget Office to provide specialized technical information for both chambers and allow Congress to compete with the president as budget-maker.

We will expand on executive/Congressional relations in later chapters. But for now, what were the main effects of these reforms? Little was expected from them as they were being adopted; by the early 1990s, however, they had helped to contribute to what are now recognized as profound changes in the institution, as titles such *The New Congress*, *The Decline and Resurgence of Congress* and *Legislative Leviathan* suggest. The main changes can be summed up quite simply: power in Congress became even more dispersed than it was, but the institution was more professional, more concerned with the details of the legislative process and with oversight of the executive. Finally Congress was still essentially a conservative body – although not in the same ways as before.

The reform movement was fuelled by two main forces – the increasing electoral independence of individual members from party and regional ties which a more rapid turnover of members and other changes had produced, and the already noted disillusionment with the institution's ability to deal with executive power. Chapter 8 showed just how much constituency pressures have increased and how electoral success now depends less on traditional party organization and more on personal resources. In order to 'deliver the goods' to constituents, members needed two things: more control within Congress over legislation and more control over the executive policy-making process. While the reforms went a long way towards the achievement of both objectives, they also had the unintended effect of weakening party leadership in Congress. During the early 1990s Democratic congressional leaders were only too aware that their control over members was all too limited. The experience of the 103rd Congress (1993–94), when much of President Clinton's legislative programme died in a Democratic Congress, persuaded them of the need for further reform. Given the entrenched power of large numbers of Democratic congress-persons, however, this was not possible and reform had to wait until the arrival of a new cohort of Republican members in early 1995. As was mentioned earlier, the new Speaker, Newt Gingrich, was intent on reform which would strengthen party leadership. His own powers were enhanced and serious efforts were made to weaken committee power in relation to party influence. The main changes were:

a one-third reduction in staff;
the control of all staff by the chair;
a three-term limit for committee and subcommittee chairs;
a limit of five subcommittees on most committees, and an overall reduction from 118 in the 103rd Congress to 77 in the 104th;
abolition of the District of Columbia, Merchant Marine and Fisheries, and Post Office and Civil Service Committees;
limiting most members to serving on two committees and a total of four subcommittees;
requiring that all committee votes be published and no proxy voting be allowed;
requiring that almost all committee meetings be open and allowing coverage of television and radio, if requested;
speaker may no longer, with modest exceptions, refer bills to multiple committees simultaneously.[7]

Although in total these reforms constitute a shift away from committee power, the committees do remain the focal point of activity in Congress. Moreover, any weakness in the party leaders (such as occurred following Gingrich's formal reprimand in 1997) is likely to result in some return of authority to the committees. It should be mentioned that, although parallel moves have occurred in the Senate, reforms there have been much less radical. As has always been the case, power in the Senate tends to reside in the influence of individual Senators, rather than be determined by parliamentary rules and procedures.

Finally, how, given the claimed *decentralization* of power in Congress in recent years, can the increased degree of party unity since the early 1980s be explained? There are two possible answers here. First, the number of Southern Democrats has declined. These members were conservative and often voted with the Republicans rather than with their own party. Second, congressional politics has generally become more conflictual and ideological over the last 20 years. Often this means confronting the president in ways that were rare during the 1950s and 1960s. We will develop this point in the next chapter; a more abrasive executive/legislative environment has undoubtedly increased partisanship on all sides.

In one sense Congress is more efficient – for, although no more bills are passed, those that are tend to be more complex and comprehensive (fig. 9.2). In addition, committees do expedite bills more

---

[7]   Loomis, *The Contemporary Congress*, p. 81.

Figure **9.2** Public bills in the Congressional work-load, 80th–101st Congresses, 1947–90

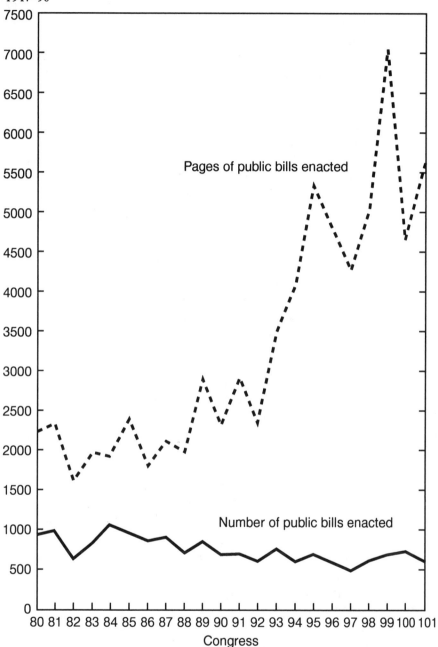

Source: Ornstein, Mann, Malbin, Schick and Bibby, *Vital Statistics on Congress*, 1991/92 edition, figure 6.3.

rapidly than before. But the process remains slow and cumbersome. In other words, Congress remains an institution where blockages, delays and vetoes can happen at several stages in the legislative process. As a result, it retains an inbuilt conservative bias – it is easier to prevent things happening than to pass bills. The increase in the number of 'omnibus' bills (fig. 9.2) represents an attempt to please as many members as possible. But each of these bills is passed only after an enormous amount of members' time and effort has been spent on them. In other words, coalition building – always a defining characteristic of Congress – has assumed an even greater importance during the 1980s and 1990s. Partly as a result of this institutional characteristic, though also because of the electoral changes outlined in chapter 8, a conservative coalition continues to exercise considerable influence. Until the early 1970s this consisted of Southern Democrats and Northern Republicans. During the 1980s it consisted of Southern Democrats and Republicans from every region. Since 1994 it has consisted of virtually all Republicans and a sizeable minority of Democrats.

Yet we should be wary of too harsh a critique of the way in which Congress operates. Congress today almost certainly reflects the moods and wishes of the nation more accurately than for many years. This is a direct result of a new, much more intimate Congressperson/constituency relationship and the easier access to legislators that organized interests now enjoy. Since the 1980s, public opinion has apparently moved to the right and Congress has accurately mirrored this trend. But, as we have already established, the American electorate is now highly volatile, and issues are much less susceptible to a simple identification on a left/right political continuum than they used to be. It may be that the Republican conservatism of the 104th and 105th Congresses will be short lived given the often rapid changes in the public mood.

We should also be cautious about assuming that, because Congress appears to pander to *particularistic* interests in American society (individual constituents and organized interests) rather than to the *public* interest, it is always incapable of effective collective action. On rare, but important, occasions it has shown unexpected resolve. In 1985 both Houses passed the Gramm, Rudman-Hollings Deficit Reduction Act which bound president and Congress to successive reductions in the budget deficit (although the Supreme Court struck down the compulsory provisions in the Act – for details *see* chapter 10, p. 204). A year later Congress passed the most sweeping overhaul of the American tax system in modern history. Moreover, against all expectations, the budget deficit *was* reduced in the early and mid-1990s.

Clearly the House and Senate can respond to outside pressures or to perceptions that the collective interest must take precedence over particular interests. Indeed, recent small signs of party revival (table 9.3) may help such reactions. Unfortunately, however, collective action of this sort is rare. In its everyday business, special and particular interest dominates, for the central dilemma for Congress in the late 1990s is, in fact, the same dilemma as of the 1950s and 1960s: building coalitions in a highly fragmented institution involves many trade-offs with costs in terms of time, coherence and efficiency mounting steadily as the legislative process lumbers on. And, although reforms have been initiated through party mechanisms, political-party influence on legislation remains relatively weak. Given the serious economic and international problems confronting the United States, the need for decisive and coherent policy-making is as great as ever. If Congress can contribute relatively little in this area, then this role must be played by that institution traditionally associated with national leadership – the presidency.

Further Reading

A good textbook treatment of Congress is Burdett A. Loomis, *The Contemporary Congress*, (New York, St Martin's, 1996). The reforms of the 1970s and 1980s are covered by James L. Sundquist, *The Decline and Resurgence of Congress*, (Washington DC, Brookings, 1981), and Roger H. Davidson (ed.), *The Post-Reform Congress*, (New York, St Martin's Press, 1992). The classic work on committees is by Richard Fenno Jr, *Congressmen in Committees*, (Boston, Little, Brown, 1973). An up-to-date and comprehensive account of the institution is provided by Michael Foley and John E. Owens, *Congress and the Presidency: Institutional Politics in a Separated System*, (Manchester, Manchester University Press, 1996). Facts and figures on the institution can be found in Congressional Quarterly's *Inside Congress*, (Washington DC, 6th edition, 1995) and also in Ornstein, Mann, Malbin, Schick and Bibby, *Vital Statistics on Congress*, (1995/96 edition).

10

PRESIDENTIAL POWER

The modern Presidency of the United States, as distinct from the traditional concepts of our highest office, is bound up with the survival not
only of freedom but of mankind . . . The President is the unifying force
in our lives . . . The President must possess a wide range of abilities: to
lead, to persuade, to inspire trust, to attract men of talent, to unite.
These abilities must reflect a wide range of characteristics: courage,
vision, integrity, intelligence, sense of responsibility, sense of history,
sense of humour, warmth, openness, personality, tenacity, energy,
determination, drive, perspicacity, idealism, thirst for information, penchant for fact, presence of conscience, comprehension of people and
enjoyment of life – plus all the other, nobler virtues ascribed to George
Washington under God.

Nelson A. Rockefeller, *Unity, Freedom and Peace*

The saddest life is that of a political aspirant under democracy. His failure is ignominious and his success is disgraced.

H. L. Mencken

These two quotations pinpoint the central dilemma of the modern
presidency: in the American political system the president is the only
national unifying force. He or she has, therefore, both great responsibilities and great power. But in recent years few incumbents have possessed the qualities necessary to carry out the job efficiently and
responsibly. Every president between the mid-1960s and 1992 was
associated to a greater or lesser extent with failure. Lyndon Johnson
was broken by the Vietnam War and Richard Nixon by Watergate.
Gerald Ford was little more than a caretaker president and Jimmy
Carter had been judged indecisive and politically inept. Ronald Reagan will probably not be deemed one of the great presidents given his

involvement in the Iran-Contra affair and the consequences of his economic policies (*see* chapter 14, pp. 320–1). George Bush lacked the charisma and authority associated with great presidents and, after one term, achieved the dubious distinction of being beaten by a larger margin than any incumbent president since Herbert Hoover in 1932. And while it is too early to pass judgement on Bill Clinton, his ambitious first-term legislative programme came to little and, at mid term, the Republicans captured both houses of Congress for the first time since 1952.

Curiously, this association of the office with mediocrity and the abuse of power is comparatively recent. Most texts on American government written during the 1950s and 1960s saw little wrong either with the nature of the office or with recent incumbents.[1] In retrospect the mid-century presidents – Franklin Roosevelt, Harry Truman, Dwight Eisenhower and John Kennedy – do seem impressive figures. So what has happened since? There are three possible answers to this question which will constitute the major part of discussion in this chapter. First, it could be argued that an accumulation of changes in American society and polity has made the job almost impossible to perform satisfactorily. Second, the process whereby presidents are recruited may have changed in ways that pre-select inappropriate – presidential candidates. Third, it could be simply that different – and inappropriate – personality types have occupied the office in recent years. Before we examine these claims in detail, it is necessary briefly to outline the formal and informal sources of presidential power and to trace the growth of the modern presidency.

Formal Sources of Power

To a European observer, one of the most remarkable features of the American political system is the concentration of governmental functions in one institution, the presidency. The Constitution is partly responsible for this, for it assigns to the presidency the roles of chief executive (Article 2, Section 1), commander-in-chief of the armed forces (Article 2, Section 2), chief diplomat (or the power to make treaties, Article 2, Section 2), chief recruiting officer to the executive and courts (Article 2, Section 2) and legislator [by making recommendations to Congress (Article 2, Section 3) and exercising the veto power under Article 1, Section 7]. As was emphasized in chapter 3, the framers did not expect the president also to become *chief* legislator

---

[1]   For a good review of this 'textbook' view of the presidency *see* Thomas E. Cronin, *The State of the Presidency*, (Boston, Little, Brown, 2nd edn, 1980), chapter 2.

but, over the last 100 years, he has assumed this crucial function. Finally, the president is head of state, so must carry out all those diplomatic and ceremonial duties normally performed by constitutional monarchs (in Britain, the Netherlands) or presidents (in Israel, India and Italy).

Given this panoply of powers it is not surprising that we automatically think of periods in American history in terms of incumbent presidents. The first years of the Republic are inseparable from the personality and influence of George Washington. Andrew Jackson's presidencies are closely associated with the democratization of American politics and the rise of a modern two-party system. Abraham Lincoln's personal conduct of the Civil War effectively shaped a whole era in American history, while Woodrow Wilson was the first president to elevate the United States on to the world diplomatic and military stage. Since the New Deal period – itself synonymous with the personage of Franklin D. Roosevelt – every president has made a lasting imprint on American and on world politics. Of course, presidents are constrained, sometimes seriously, by a number of domestic and international forces, but, within the United States, the chief executive is the natural and immediate focus of attention. As we saw in chapters 8 and 9, it would be difficult to consider Congress a natural leader or decision-maker. If anything the opposite is true. Federalism fragments political power and authority even further, leaving the presidency (and on rather rare occasions, the Supreme Court) as the sole unifying and centralizing influence in the system.

During the nineteenth and early twentieth centuries, it was the constitutionally assigned powers in military, foreign and diplomatic policy that tended to raise the visibility of the office. Indeed, through exercising these powers, some presidents greatly expanded and even exceeded the constitutional authority. In 1803 Thomas Jefferson authorized the purchase of the Louisiana Territories from France (*see* map 2.1, p. 9) without consulting Congress. Abraham Lincoln's conduct of the Civil War was almost authoritarian, involving as it did a blockade of the South, the suspension of habeas corpus, and unauthorized increases in the size of the army and navy. Much later Woodrow Wilson asked for, and was given, broad powers under the 1917 Lever Act to seize factories and mines and fix prices to help the war effort. But government, and especially the federal government, played a relatively minor part in economic and social life during this period. An assertive Congress could, and often did, dominate the political agenda. Without the vast bureaucratic and logistical resources of the modern executive, those presidents lacking political skills or unfortunate enough to preside over particularly difficult domestic events, such as the recriminations and confusion characteristic of the post-

Civil War period, were truly secondary political figures. From the New Deal period onward, no president has been able to take the back stage because the demands on the office have multiplied so dramatically.

Since World War II, commander-in-chief has meant control over several million men and women under arms and literally the power of life and death over humankind. As chief executives, modern presidents are responsible for numerous programmes and policies affecting every aspect of society. As chief legislator, the president takes to Congress a package of programmes, together with budget requests, which effectively mould the national political agenda. As we catalogued in chapter 5, the rise of federal grant programmes has meant that even local governments – those bodies so free from central control in the early Republic – now depend in part on the president's policies. Of course, the president is constrained when performing these functions and, of course, every industrial country has been required to centralize power in executives and greatly to expand the role of government. No Western country has acquired such formidable military and strategic power as has the USA, however, and in none has the role of state been transformed in quite the way as in America. The USA is, after all, the country where the state has traditionally been weak in relation to society; where the market was considered the most appropriate mechanism for distributing resources (chapter 3, pp. 37–9). Yet, by the 1990s, more than 30 per cent of national income was accounted for by government spending, and, in some areas of economic and social life, the federal government had become a major source of income and support for large numbers of individuals, subnational governments and corporations. It could be argued that American institutional arrangements, especially federalism and the separation of powers, are ill-suited to the sort of efficient and effective policy-making needed in a modern industrial society. If this is so, it increases the pressures on the executive even more for, to repeat the point, only the presidency has a truly national constituency and only the presidency is the natural co-ordinator and organizer of national policy.

Informal Powers

Given the president's position at the apex of the constitutional system, it is not surprising that the office has also attracted a number of informal powers or influences additional to those constitutionally assigned. These include his or her position as party leader, and as national and world leader. All three can provide presidents with valuable extra resources, but they can also burden the office with extra duties and responsibilities. Being party leader certainly sounds grandiose and impressive enough – and in the British system, for example, being prime minister and party leader is indeed a great political advantage. But, as we have seen, American political parties are fragmented and weak. Only very rarely in recent history have presidents been *guaranteed* party support in Congress, and lucky is the president who knows he or she can count on the support of governors, mayors and other party leaders in the federal system. This accepted, weak party ties are almost certainly better than none at all and presidents do use party connections to rally support (if not always successfully) during the nomination process and at mid-term elections. Party is also the vital cue available to presidents when they make appointments to the executive branch. Without the myriad party contacts at congressional, state and local events, it would be difficult to fill all the 50,000-plus jobs which are nominated annually. Presidents also use this process to pay off debts for electoral and other services rendered.

Americans expect something more than the efficient execution of policy from their presidents; they also expect them to embody the spirit of the nation or, in Clinton Rossiter's term, to be the 'voice of the people'.[2] It should not be forgotten that the United States has relatively few symbols of national unity, such as the monarchy in Britain or a long-established culture rooted in language and custom as in France. In some respects, the institution of the presidency helps fill this gap by providing Americans with a sense of national identity. When, at press conferences, an aide announces the entrance of 'The President of the United States', he is presenting a national symbol as well as chief executive, and the simple words of the announcement carry with them an almost religious respect that is notably missing when a British prime minister or German chancellor appears in public.

In recent years, the president's role as a national leader has been reinforced by America's emergence as a world power, a fact amply demonstrated by President Kennedy's famous speech at the time of the Cuban missile crisis:

> Let no one doubt that this is a difficult and dangerous mission on which we have set out. No one can foresee precisely what course it will take or what costs or casualties will be incurred. Many months of sacri-

[2] In the heady optimism of the late 1950s Clinton Rossiter's famous essay *The American Presidency*, (New York, Harcourt Brace Jovanovich, 1960), listed five informal powers, some of which now look unachievable, if still sought after: (1) voice of the party; (2) voice of the people; (3) protector of the peace; (4) manager of prosperity; (5) world leader (pp. 4–25).

Table 10.1 Awareness of political leaders on the part of adults and children, 1969–70

Office	Percentage correct by age		
	Adult	17	13
President (Nixon)	98	98	94
Vice-president (Agnew)	87	79	60
Secretary of State (Rogers)	16	9	2
Secretary of Defense (Laird)	25	16	6
Speaker of the House (McCormack)	32	25	2
Senate Majority Leader (Mansfield)	23	14	4
At least one senator from own state	57	44	16
Both senators from own state	31	18	6
Member of Congress from own district	39	35	11

Source: Fred Greenstein, 'What the president means to Americans', in James Barber (ed.), *Choosing the President*, (Englewood Cliffs, New Jersey, Prentice-Hall, 1974), p. 125.

fice and self-discipline lie ahead – months in which both our patience and our will will be tested, months in which threats and denunciations will keep us aware of our dangers. But the greatest danger of all would be to do nothing. The path we have chosen for the present is full of hazards, as all paths are; but it is the one most consistent with our character and courage as a nation and our commitments around the world. The cost of freedom is always high – but Americans have always paid it. And one path we shall never choose, and that is the path of surrender or submission.[3]

Such stirring rhetoric may seem inappropriate in the 1990s, but presidents continue to project themselves as the spirit of the nation, as an examination of George Bush's speeches on the Gulf War or Bill Clinton's on education or health care would show. In other words, presidents attempt to project themselves as defenders of the *public interest*. In contrast to the fragmentation and particularism of Congress and the federal system, the president alone claims to see policy in terms of what is in the interest of the whole country. In this sense, presidents attempt to elevate themselves above party, special interests and even ideology. Of course, they do not always succeed – indeed, few recent presidents have even come close to succeeding – but they are constantly striving for this very special status, and almost certainly the American public expect their presidents to play this part. Indeed, the public is dramatically more aware of the presidency (including the vice-president) than other public offices, and this consciousness is acquired early in life (table 10.1).

As world leaders, some recent presidents have had to attenuate their styles and rhetoric in line with the relative decline of American

---

[3] Quoted in Robert F. Kennedy, *Thirteen Days*, (Harmondsworth, Middlesex, Penguin, 1970), p. 37.

power. But they retain a special status in the international system. Certainly, what presidents say and do are significantly more important than the speeches and deeds of British and Japanese prime ministers, German chancellors and French presidents. This crucial international status adds yet another dimension to presidential power, and also to the pressures of the office.

The Presidency in Crisis

Presidential selection

Returning to our original questions, it seems reasonable to hypothesize that the crisis of the modern presidency is one of recruitment. It may be simply that the wrong people are being selected for the job. What is the nature of the presidential nomination process? And why is it now the subject of such criticism? We can divide presidential elections into four distinct phases: pre-primary, primary, convention and campaign.

Pre-primary It is often quipped that, no sooner is a president elected, than he has to start running for his second term. Although an exaggeration, this is not so far from the truth, for any candidate with even the slightest hope of winning nomination must plan his or her campaign several years ahead. In his build-up for the 1976 campaign, Jimmy Carter cultivated newspaper editors and political commentators more than a year before the convention. His strategy was simple: he had to raise his public visibility in order to neutralize the 'Jimmy who?' reaction whenever his name was uttered. Ronald Reagan announced himself more than two years before the 1980 election and, by late 1982, former vice-president Walter Mondale was already grooming himself for the 1984 contest. In 1985, vice-president Bush was beginning to build an organization ready for 1988, and Bill Clinton made no secret of his ambition to run for president many years before he formally announced his candidacy in October 1991. Merely announcing early guarantees nothing, of course. Much depends on the political resources, reputation, experience and skill of the candidate. The times are also important. Jimmy Carter's extraordinary journey from obscurity to president between 1972 and 1976 owed much to the prevailing disillusionment with 'Washington' and established party candidates. More typically, candidates must win the support of key political figures if they are to have any chance. In 1980 Ronald Reagan was endorsed by many of the leading Republicans and 'king-makers' of the political right; Gerald Ford notably lacked such support and was well advised to make an early retreat from the race.

Edward Kennedy, in contrast, had failed to win the unequivocal endorsement of the Democratic establishment but soldiered on nonetheless. In 1992 Bill Clinton did win support from established sections of the Democratic Party which almost certainly helped him to create the image of front runner early in the campaign. An incumbent president naturally enjoys a huge advantage in winning the party's nomination, and there is no instance in recent years of a president who wants to stand failing to secure nomination.

Curiously, few incumbent vice-presidents have been *elected* president in American history. George Bush was to prove an exception, in part because he won the support of many leading Republicans early in Reagan's second term. In 1992, however, he had to fight hard to win over the Republican right, and eventually only won their grudging support.

The primaries There was a time when a candidate with strong intra-party support could avoid the primary circuit. In 1968, for example, only 49 per cent of the votes cast by delegates at the Democratic convention were decided by primary election, the remainder was in the pocket of party caucuses. By 1976 this figure had risen to 75 per cent, thus making it absolutely essential for candidates to run in the primaries (*see* table 6.2, p. 104). So Hubert Humphrey's strategy of depending on his very considerable Democratic Party connections was successful in 1968, but suicidal just four years later when he entered the primaries late and was effectively beaten before the convention. Following reforms in the Democratic Party, the number of primaries was reduced in 1984 but increased again in the 1990s, so that today no candidate can afford to ignore them.

Today, there are 37 primaries in the Democratic Party and 41 in the Republican (figures are for the 1996 presidential election). While the primary season remains lengthy, running from February to June,[4] most of the important primaries, including those of California, New York and Texas, are now held in March. Unfortunately, the precise technicalities of primaries defy simple description because each state decides the timing, voter eligibility and general organization of its primary elections. The most important formal distinction is between *closed primaries*, operative in most states, which are open only to registered party members, and *open primaries* where voters can vote for either party, but not both, by asking for that party's ballot at the polling station. They do not, in other words, have to be registered as

[4] Puerto Rico is effectively first with its Republican primary scheduled in February, but it is not a meaningful guide to trends on the continental USA.

Democrats or Republicans to vote in that party's election. In those states without primaries for presidential nominations (all states have some form of primary for state-wide elections) party caucuses or meetings decide delegate selection. Over the last 20 years, primaries have become more important, not only because they have increased in number, but also because changes in party rules have had the effect of binding delegates more closely to candidates. Moreover, the partial switch back to caucuses in the Democratic Party in 1984 did not signal a return to 'old-style' party politics. For most of the new caucuses were very open and were as binding on delegates as primaries. So open were some of the caucuses – in many, almost anyone could participate – that some were replaced by primaries in the 1990s. There was a time when bargaining on the convention floor resulted in delegates switching their allegiances, so making the convention a key decision-maker in the nomination process. Today the primaries and caucuses proper play this role.

Because candidates *must* enter the primaries, they must have the political, financial and even physical resources to endure the long series of campaigns involved. They must also have the *time*, for staging a series of primary campaigns is effectively a full-time job. As will be developed later, this fact alone may pre-select certain sorts of candidates. Recent elections have also shown how important it is for candidates to make a good start. There is what might be called a 'media bandwagon effect', where a particular candidate is identified as a winner and this itself provides an essential impetus to his or her campaign. This may constitute a disadvantage for candidates with key support in those large industrial states where primaries come relatively late. Some commentators have even gone so far as to claim that Iowa (an early party caucus state) and New Hampshire (the first primary) hold the key to the fortunes of candidates – and these are hardly representative areas of the United States. Certainly, Jimmy Carter did well in early contests in 1976 and 1980, which helped him to head off opponents with support in larger states. And, in 1980, George Bush's late victories in such states as Michigan meant little when Ronald Reagan had already won most of the early primaries and therefore had accumulated a formidable number of delegate votes. Even if candidates do not win all the early primaries, they must at least enter and perform reasonably well. Such was the case with the successful nominees in 1988, George Bush and Michael Dukakis. In 1992, Bill Clinton bucked the trend of winning early primaries. He *lost* the New Hampshire primary to Paul Tsongas, the South Dakota primary to Bob Kerrey and the Colorado primary to Jerry Brown. Not until 10 March, with the 'Super Tuesday' series of Southern primaries, did he establish a lead.

The nominating conventions To foreigners, nothing better represents the sheer theatre of American politics than the nominating conventions. During the summer before the election, several thousand party delegates meet to choose their presidential and vice-presidential candidates in an apparently crazy few days of party festival. Although policy is discussed at conventions, they are more of a media event, where candidates and their supporters strive to achieve maximum public exposure. There was a time when the conventions actually chose candidates for the general election, with several ballots required before a majority (until 1936 two-thirds in the Democratic convention) of all the delegates could agree on a candidate. During this period, conventions were an accurate reflection of the vote trading and coalition formation typical of American politics generally. They were, in other words, highly political, involving deals, bargains and periodic deadlocks as party bosses switched their blocks of delegate votes or opted for a compromise candidate. In recent elections, however, the winning candidate is almost certainly identifiable before the convention begins as the primaries effectively decide the contest.

The spread of primaries was part of a general party reform movement prevalent in the late 1960s and 1970s. In the case of the Democrats, calls for reform were greatly aided by the events at the 1968 convention in Chicago when an old-style party organization nominated vice-president Hubert Humphrey, a candidate associated with organized labour and Lyndon Johnson's conduct of the Vietnam War. But this was the period when the social issue (the war, minority rights, the liberalization of society) was in the ascendant, and traditional Democratic Party organizations were notably unsympathetic to the new movement. Following violent scenes outside the convention hall when the young, radicals and other excluded groups demonstrated against the old-style machine politics, the party was plunged into a turmoil of recriminations.[5] The upshot was the appointment of a commission (the McGovern-Fraser Commission) to recommend changes in delegate selection. Since then the party has never been free of commissions, reforms and debate on how best to organize itself.

McGovern-Fraser resulted in two major changes. From 1972, representation at conventions from minorities and underrepresented groups – Blacks, women, youth – was greatly increased. Second, a system of proportional representation was recommended for primary elections. Previously, the person winning the primary took all the delegate votes ('winner take all'). McGovern-Fraser recommended

---

[5] For a graphic description of these harrowing events and the contrast with the Republican convention of that year, *see* Norman Mailer, *Miami and the Siege of Chicago*, (London, Weidenfeld and Nicolson, 1968).

that the delegates given to a candidate should be in proportion to his share of the vote. Between 1972 and 1984, the rules were modified further following the advice of more commissions, most notably the Hunt Commission which reported in 1982. From 1980 a minimum 20 per cent cut-off point was established in the primaries to discourage frivolous candidacies. (It has since been set at a minimum of 15 per cent). The original McGovern-Fraser idea of quotas for underrepresented groups has been replaced with affirmative-action requirements,[6] and, beginning in the early 1970s, the rules governing selection of delegates to party caucuses have been gradually modified to 'open up' meetings and committees to rank and file members.

Very generally, these reforms (which are paralleled in an attenuated form in the Republican Party) involved the struggle, which was discussed in chapter 6, between old-style party professionals and a new breed of party activists. As we established, the new party activists generally won out, yet it would be misleading to argue that somehow party influences are stronger as a consequence. In fact the opposite is true. Because delegates are now mainly chosen in primaries and are almost always tied to particular candidates, the voters, not party activists, decide the nomination. And given the rise of candidates' own vote-getting organizations, this effectively relegates political parties to a lesser position in the nominating process.

Not only has the drive for more democratic procedures in party nominations weakened the influence of party, it has also failed to correct the non-representativeness of convention delegates. In 1972, the delegates were certainly younger and more radical than in 1968, but in ideological and programmatic terms they were *not* typical of the average Democratic voter.[7] By 1980, Democratic delegates were markedly more female and Black than before, but they were also more middle class, had fewer links with industrial trade unions and traditional Democratic Party organizations, and stronger links with the growing public-sector unions. Aware of this, the Hunt Commission also recommended the creation of 'super-delegates' to the convention or regular party-elected or appointed officials.[8] It was assumed that state legislators, governors and members of Congress would be more

[6] In the American context affirmative action means a determination to increase the representation (in employment, access to housing and other services) of women and minorities. It can mean quotas, but as often is interpreted as taking positive action to help the underrepresented.

[7] *See* Jeane Kirkpatrick, *The New Presidential Elite*, (New York, Russell Sage, Twentieth Century Fund, 1976).

[8] One of the leading advocates of a return to party control was ex-Governor of North Carolina, Terry Sanford. *See* his *A Danger of Democracy: The Presidential Nominating Process*, (Boulder, Colorado, Westview, 1981).

Table 10.2 Representation of major elected officials at national conventions, 1968–92[1] (in percentages)

	1968	1972	1976	1980	1984	1988	1992
Democrats							
Governors	96	57	44	74	91	100	96[2]
US Senators	61	28	18	14	56	85	81[2]
US Representatives	32	12	14	14	62	87	88[2]
Republicans							
Governors	92	80	69	68	93	82	81
US Senators	58	50	59	63	56	62	42
US Representatives	31	19	36	40	53	55	30

[1] Figures represent the percentages of Democratic or Republican office-holders from each group who served as delegates.
[2] Unpledged delegates (i.e., 'super-delegates') only, not including those office-holders who went to the Democratic convention by other means.
Source: Figures provided by the Democratic and Republican National Committees, as reproduced in Stephen J. Wayne, *The Road to the White House 1996: The Politics of Presidential Elections*, (New York, St Martin's Press, 1996), table 4.6.

moderate in their views and would inject an element of peer-group review into the selection process. In 1984 and again in 1988 about one-seventh of all delegates to the convention were reserved for party and public officials and, as mentioned, caucuses replaced primaries in several states. Most observers agree that these changes did little to alter the fundamental nature of the nomination process. Although a 'traditional' candidate, Walter Mondale, was nominated, Gary Hart, a 'new-style' candidate, very nearly beat him. And the candidacy of civil-rights activist, Jesse Jackson, who did well in many primaries, showed how the system was basically unchanged since 1980. In 1988, neither of the two front runners was an old-style party candidate. Jesse Jackson's impressive showing in the primaries and caucuses came to nothing, not because Michael Dukakis had won the support of the party regulars (which he had), but because Dukakis won more primaries and caucuses than Jackson and therefore came to the convention with enough delegate votes to ensure victory.

By 1992 the number of 'super-delegates' was increased to nearly one-fifth of the total but, again, there is no evidence that their presence made any difference. For one thing, super-delegates are not necessarily more moderate than the typical Democratic voter.[9] For another, it is difficult to imagine how, in a media-infused process, they could make a difference. As Walter Dean Burnham has put it: 'They're little more than window dressing. There's not a lot of room

---

[9]   For a discussion *see* Nelson W. Polsby and Aaron Wildavsky, *Presidential Elections: Contemporary Strategies of American Electoral Politics*, (New York, Free Press, 8th edition, 1991), pp. 125–28.

for peer review in the television era . . . there's just no way super-delegates can exercise a credible veto'.[10] On the other hand, as table 10.2 shows, by the late 1980s almost all important party office-holders were at least attending the Democratic conventions even if their influence was not easy to measure.

The Hunt Commission also recommended that the primary season be shortened and that more primaries be held on the same days. In the event, the primary season was shortened slightly (state law, not party rules decide the timing of primaries, although the courts have given the parties the right to decide who is eligible to vote in primaries). Since 1988 most Southern states vote on the same day (the so-called Super Tuesday, 10 March in 1992). This last innovation did little to help Southerner Al Gore in 1988, but it gave Southerner Bill Clinton an essential boost in 1992. Finally, in 1996 California and a number of other states brought forward their primary dates from May and June to March. As a result, in future years it is highly likely that the winning candidate will be known by the end of March.

The campaign Before the campaign proper starts, nominated candidates have to choose their vice-presidential running mates. Until recently this decision was taken at the convention. Today, however, nominated candidates choose their running mates some weeks before the convention. Nominees use the opportunity to heal political wounds or to balance the ticket geographically or ideologically. In 1960 John Kennedy's choice of Lyndon Johnson helped to smooth relations between the two main contenders for the nomination; it also balanced the ticket between the urbane Catholic North Easterner and the more populist, Protestant Southerner. The choice is a crucial one for, although the office of vice-president is not itself very important, no fewer than five of the last ten vice-presidents eventually became presidents themselves (Harry Truman, Lyndon Johnson, Richard Nixon, Gerald Ford and George Bush), and Vice-president Al Gore remains the favourite for the Democratic nomination in the year 2000. Occasionally things go terribly wrong. George McGovern's initial choice of Thomas Eagleton in 1972 had to be changed with indecent haste once it was revealed that Eagleton had received psychiatric treatment. In 1980, Ronald Reagan's first preference, Gerald Ford, proved politically tactless when Ford, not unsurprisingly, laid down certain conditions for acceptance including a demand that the vice-president should be more an executive partner than subordinate. In 1984 Democratic vice-presidential candidate Geraldine Ferraro was constantly dogged by revelations of her husband's financial wrong-

---

[10] Quoted in *Congressional Quarterly*, 4 July 1992, p. 18 (supplement to vol. 50, No. 27).

doings. In 1988 George Bush's choice of Dan Quayle, the junior senator from Indiana, was greeted with surprise and incredulity among Republicans and Democrats alike. Quayle apparently did little to balance the ticket in geographical or ideological terms. In addition he proved an inept and inexperienced campaigner. After a few weeks, the Bush organization was obliged to shunt Quayle off into political sidings where any damage he might do would be kept to a minimum. In stark contrast, Bill Clinton chose Tennessee Senator Al Gore as his 1992 running mate. While Gore did not balance the ticket – he was close to being a political clone of Bill Clinton – he did add to Clinton's image of youth, moderation and vigour.

Both the pre-convention and post-convention campaigns are expensive. Advertising, and particularly television advertising, takes the lion's share. Indeed, spending on television has risen almost exponentially since the first major exposure of candidates during the 1960 campaign, when John Kennedy confronted Richard Nixon in live debates. What effect it has on the voters is, however, an open question. Some evidence exists to suggest that general television advertising has little effect; most voters apparently acquire positive or negative impressions towards candidates quite early on and then their perceptions are based on performance rather than image.[11] What advertising and the presidential debates almost certainly do, however, is *reinforce* public perceptions of candidates. In 1988, for example, the Bush campaign's efforts to label Dukakis as a liberal who was soft on law and order, almost certainly confirmed in the minds of many voters – Republican, Democratic and Independent – what they had suspected. Similarly, in 1996, Bill Clinton's constant reference to 'building a bridge to the 21st Century', contrasted with Bob Dole's references to the values of the past and helped reinforce his appeal as the candidate of youth and of the future. No candidate can afford to drop his or her guard, therefore; television is widely perceived as important even it its effects are difficult to measure.[12] In 1992 Ross Perot used television to quite remarkable effect. By July he was polling approval ratings as high as the party candidates. His subsequent withdrawal and re-entry reduced his support, but he still managed to win 19 per cent of the vote.

For most candidates, a high level of public exposure is maintained by constant travel, usually by air, but still a candidate may hire a train to re-enact the famous whistle-stop tours of an earlier era. Incumbent

[11]   Thomas E. Patterson and Robert D. McClure, *The Unseeing Eye: The Myth of Television Power in National Elections*, (New York, Putnam, 1976).
[12]   For an account of presidential communications, *see* Robert P. Hart, *The Sound of Leadership: Presidential Communication in the Modern Age*, (Chicago, University of Chicago Press, 1987).

presidents standing for re-election are usually less eager to engage in constant public image-building. They do, after all, enjoy the advantages of incumbency and can exploit their established positions as statesmen. In 1972, for example, Richard Nixon appeared in public infrequently and relied instead on the prestige of the presidential office when appealing to the voters.[13] Whatever the campaign strategy, all candidates continue during the last two or three months before the election to build political bridges, and to strengthen the coalition of support they must already have established to have won the nomination. To a European observer, the campaigns are remarkably free from reference to specific programmes and policies. Indeed, candidates score points against opponents or make reference to very broad issues and ideological labels. Michael Dukakis was condemned by George Bush as inexperienced and incapable of upholding American power and prestige abroad. Dukakis in turn criticized Bush for his insensitivity to the needs of ordinary citizens. Attacking opponents may not be the only focus. Reagan promised in 1980 to 'get America back to work'. Richard Nixon in 1968 pledged that he would pursue 'peace with honour' in Vietnam. In 1992, Bill Clinton repeatedly made references to the state of the economy and the need for change. George Bush steered away from the issues and emphasized the allegedly weak character of his opponent. In the context of a continuing economic recession this proved an ineffective strategy. In 1996 Clinton made few specific campaign pledges and instead relied on his record and on building bridges to the next century. Republican candidate Bob Dole's specific promise to reduce income tax by 15 per cent backfired on him. Few economists – or for that matter voters – believed that it was possible to achieve such a large reduction and balance the budget at the same time.

As we have already noted, the whole of the campaign, pre- and post-convention, has increasingly become an exercise dependent, not on traditional party organization, but on *personal* party organization and, in some cases, simply on personal followings. Again, this demonstrates the general trend towards essentially non-partisan elections, the implications of which we will discuss later.

Presidential selection: faults and foibles

Writing in 1981 and making direct comparisons with the selection process for British prime ministers, Anthony King listed eight appar-

[13]   And also, as we now know, on the illegal activities of CREEP (the Committee to Reelect the President).

ently serious flaws in the 1976 and 1980 presidential selection process. It is worth repeating these:

1   The two winners in the United States had entered politics in middle age, and neither had very much experience of government . . .
2   Neither winner in the United States had ever served in any capacity in the national government, whether in Washington or overseas. Moreover, at the time of their nomination, neither held any public office whatsoever . . .
3   The candidates in the United States were assessed and voted upon by party activists in some states but mainly by voters in primary elections. No special weight was attached to the views of those who had worked with the candidates or had had a chance to observe them at first hand . . .
4   The campaigns of would-be presidential nominees in the United States last for a very long time.
5   Campaigns for presidential nominations in the United States involve an enormous amount of wear and tear on the part of the candidates and their families . . .
6   The campaigns in the United States cost enormous sums of money, and the candidates and their staffs have to devote a great deal of time and effort to raising money.
7   The process of selecting presidential candidates in the United States is by no means an exclusively party process . . .
8   Electoral considerations may have loomed large in the minds of many of the party regulars who attended party caucuses in 1976 and 1980, but they probably figured scarcely at all in the minds of most voters in the primaries.[14]

Many of the charges have already been implied in earlier sections. In sum, they add up to a serious indictment of recent party reforms and also of those reforms in campaign finance which have almost certainly weakened candidates' ties with party organizations. Under the 1971 and 1974 Federal Election Campaign Acts, primary candidates receive matching federal funds up to a maximum of around $42.7 million (divided between both candidates in 1992) and an additional $11 million is available for each party for their party conventions (also in 1992). During the campaign proper a further subsidy is available provided candidates do not spend more than this from money raised from other sources. National and state local party committees can also spend a limited amount on the campaign. Crucially, candidates have to raise most of this money from large numbers of individual contributors. Voters can contribute no more than $1000 to candidates

---

[14]   Anthony King, 'How not to select Presidential candidates: a view from Europe', in Austin Ranney (ed.), *The American Elections of 1980*, (Washington DC, AEI, 1981), pp. 315–20.

per election (primary and general election) and only $250 of this qualifies for matching funds. Following a 1976 Supreme Court decision (*Buckley v. Valeo*) no limit exists on what candidates can themselves spend on their own campaigns. In 1992, Ross Perot spent *only* his own money. Although these reforms have reduced the dependence on a few large contributions they have also reduced candidate dependence on grass-root party activists and organizations. So, according to the critique, candidates are out of touch with the 'real' world of party organization and with day-to-day governmental activity.

Ronald Reagan and (in 1976) Jimmy Carter were 'unemployed' middle-aged (or even elderly) men with no experience of Washington and the wider international community. In 1988 Michael Dukakis was an incumbent governor, but again he lacked any Washington experience. They owed their success to undisputed political acumen devoted to winning their party's nomination. This involved mobilizing a personal party following and exploiting the uniquely open – even populist – nature of the 'new' American nomination process. As the critique bluntly asserts, such a system encourages the candidacy of a breed of politicians – the 'unemployed', wealthy, ambitious and instrumental – who are much less likely to make good presidents than those tested by peer-group pressures and the rigours of many years' experience in high office.

There is, without doubt, a great deal of truth to these charges. Certainly, few successful European leaders have assumed office with as little experience of the world of high politics as did Ronald Reagan or Jimmy Carter. But we should be wary of extrapolating from so small a sample; the same accusation would, after all, be difficult to level at the other three 'failures' among recent presidents – Lyndon Johnson, ex-Senate majority leader and vice-president; Richard Nixon, ex-member of Congress, senator and vice-president; and Gerald Ford, ex-House minority leader and established party man. In 1988 the American people elected a man of very broad experience, for George Bush had not only been vice-president for eight years, he had also been a member of Congress, chief of the CIA and the US ambassador to the United Nations. And while the relatively inexperienced small-state governor Bill Clinton won the Democratic nomination, in 1996, the Republican nomination went to the vastly experienced ex-Senate Majority Leader, Bob Dole.

Of course, at least four old-style party candidates (Hubert Humphrey, Gerald Ford, Walter Mondale and Bob Dole) did *lose* elections, which may vindicate the charges, but then so did George McGovern in 1972 (very much a non-party candidate) and Jimmy Carter in 1980 (an incumbent president with all the advantages that should bring). In 1992 an incumbent president was beaten by what at first sight looks like another 'outsider' candidate, the governor of Arkansas – a very small, poor Southern state. While in many respects Bill Clinton was an unusual outsider – he was well connected with the Democratic Party establishment, was widely travelled and had received an elite education at Yale and Oxford – he had all the attributes of the ideal late-twentieth-century candidate. His main advantage lay not in long-established party contacts and experience in government, but in the fact that he was a brilliant campaigner

We can, therefore, conclude that the American presidential selection process is far from ideal and has no doubt contributed to a succession of less-than-impressive presidents. But the very considerable problems associated with the office in recent years also have their origins in forces beyond the technicalities of the selection process, and it is to these we must now turn.

The presidency and structural changes in American society

As suggested, reforms in the selection process reflect deeper changes in the party system and in American society generally. It could well be argued that, almost irrespective of the quality of president, these and other developments have together made the job of chief executive much more difficult than ever before. We can identify three such developments, each of which has added to the burden of office.

The decline of party and the rise of issue politics In one sense, condemnation of recent presidential candidates because they have lacked close party ties and have failed to subject themselves to party peer-group review is unfair, for, if traditional party organizations have declined, candidates cannot be expected to have utilized this particular route to nomination. Once in the White House, however, the real problems of trying to govern in the absence of unifying party forces become painfully apparent. In chapter 6 we listed the functions of political parties, and among the most important were the provision of institutional cohesion and a means to staff the government. Jimmy Carter is usually quoted as the classic case of a president who failed on both counts, largely because he came to Washington with very limited executive experience (as Governor of Georgia) and with few connections in the traditional world of the Democratic Party (the unions, the big cities, elite universities, the North Eastern establishment). As a result, so the argument runs, his liaison with Congress was poor and his ability to fill key posts with the right men and women, wanting. Certainly, Carter had a rough time with Congress and was not personally inclined to create and nurture relationships with Congressional leaders. But he was not unique in experiencing difficulties with Congress. As we saw in chapter 9, *all* presidents have had such problems, including John Kennedy and even Franklin Roosevelt, both of whom had strong party contacts and support. In his first two years in office, Clinton enjoyed the advantage of a Democratic Congress and was undoubtedly more politically skilful than Jimmy Carter. Nonetheless, he achieved little in the way of enacting his legislative programme.

Worse still, the political vacuum left by the parties has in part been filled by 'issue politics', or the mobilization of political resources around particular issues and ideas. We will examine this phenomenon in more detail in chapter 12, but even the most casual observer of the American political scene will be aware of the rise of the minority caucuses, pro- and anti-abortion leagues, women's caucuses, the environmental lobby, the Christian coalition and so on. Each of these movements has its congressional supporters and advocates within administrations and state governments.

Issue politics has had a more subtle effect on the political agenda, however. For, when policy is defined in terms of discrete issues or one-dimensional ideologies (such as 'conservatism'), the effect is to fragment decision-making throughout the political system. Within the executive departments and agencies, each issue or position has its supporters, so compounding the already problematical business of getting bureaucrats to implement policy (of which much more later). In sum, in the absence of strong party linkages, presidents increasingly lack ideological and organizational 'connective tissue' when performing their duties – a fact that puts even more of a premium on the skills and political acumen of individual incumbents.

The nationalization of politics and society With improved communications and the spread of governments' responsibilities, the United States has become a much more centralized society over the last 30 to 40 years. Information is disseminated centrally by the three major television networks (NBC, CBS, ABC) and by the news services and syndicated columns of major newspapers and cable TV networks. Economically, society is more centralized and nationalized, with giant corporations providing the same goods and services uniformly throughout the country. It follows that the demands on governments have been centralized, with Washington increasingly the focus of political activity. Chapter 4's discussion of intergovernmental relations showed how state and local governments have become more interdependent with the federal government in recent years. And the same is true of unions, corporations, farmers and almost all those interests in society affected by federal government spending, regulation and arbitration. Naturally, the president is a major focus of all this attention, for he or she frames most major laws, draws up the budget and has the responsibility for implementing all laws. As chief executive, the president has to manage the vast bureaucracy responsible for these tasks, a bureaucracy that, in terms of powers and complexity, has grown considerably.

The changing nature of American economic and political power Although not always true, it does seem reasonable to suppose that governing is easier when a country's economy is growing in real terms and its status and power abroad are in the ascendant. Both applied in the case of the United States between 1942 and 1965. Between 1965 and the 1980s American international economic and military might experienced relative decline – although it is difficult to argue that this development has continued as a trend through the 1990s. Perhaps it is not entirely coincidental that the earlier period was associated with the era of 'successful' presidents, while the latter has witnessed the incumbency of executive 'failures'. While it would be foolhardy to accept this argument in full – was Harry Truman, after all, a 'success' and was Ronald Reagan a 'failure'? – there is no question that the management of the economy and the exercise of military and diplomatic power abroad are *more likely* to be difficult during periods of relative decline or when there is little consensus on management of the economy or on America's role abroad.

The Vietnam War was the first major demonstration of the limits to American military power and it effectively broke one president (Lyndon Johnson) and led another (Richard Nixon) to commit a series of illegal acts, including the secret bombing of Cambodia and the unauthorized surveillance of opponents of the war. More recently, Jimmy Carter's handling of the Iranian hostage situation dominated the final year of his presidency, and provided a poignant reminder of the limitations of American might. For recent presidents, ventures abroad have been problematical, for nothing increases presidential popularity more instantly than successful – or even unsuccessful but bold – military and diplomatic forays overseas. John Kennedy's popularity soared during the Cuban Missile Crisis, as did Jimmy Carter's following the signing of the Begin/Sadat/Carter Camp David accords in 1979, and Ronald Reagan's after the US invasion of Grenada and the bombing of Libya. In 1990/1991 George Bush's successful execution of the Gulf War led to approval ratings of over 80 per cent. When the USA is apparently 'humiliated' abroad as, eventually, with Vietnam, the hostage incident in Iran and perhaps over the clear limitations on America's global peace-keeping role, it puts pressure on presidents to do something about it. Whether the resulting actions are in the public interest or in the interests of world peace are, of course, another matter.

At home, managing the many distributional questions which are the very essence of the chief executive's job is obviously more difficult when the economy is stagnating or when, even if the economy is growing, the budget deficit is rising. In his book, the *Zero Sum Society*,[15] Lester Thurow identifies this as the key problem of modern society. In other words, when the national cake stays the same size or when federal spending is constant, distributional questions become a zero-sum game; when one person gains, another must lose because there is a strict limit to the total amount of resources available. So, if more women are employed, fewer men must be, or if South Carolina receives an increase in federal aid, other states must suffer a decrease. Of course, in reality, the number of decision points in the distributional system means that it is more complex than this. Even so, no single individual is more centrally placed to make these distributional decisions than is the president. He or she is responsible for producing an annual budget amounting to over $1400 billion, and for ensuring that this money is properly spent on literally thousands of programmes. Congress is, of course, also involved in this process and, when it comes to contested distributions, the courts become key actors. But neither Congress nor the courts are as politically visible as the president. Only the president is perceived as national leader and defender of the public welfare. Small wonder, then, that recent presidents have experienced such difficulties, both in domestic policy and with defence spending, which naturally affects the amount available for domestic programmes. Add to this zero-sum problem the increasingly strident demands of the single-issue lobbies, and the potential for conflict and failure can be appreciated. So no recent president has been able to balance the budget (in 1986 Ronald Reagan, a fiscal conservative, presided over a deficit of more than $180 billion), or has come anywhere near to satisfying the demands of social groups. Take Ronald Reagan's 1981 tax-cut measures. As passed by Congress, the cuts had a number of divisive consequences. They gave those earning between $15,000 and $20,000 a year (a majority of wage-earners) only $6 extra a week. But, for the rich the benefits were sizeable – $90 a week for those earning $100,000 a year, $257 a week for the super-rich in the $200,000-plus class. Organized labour was offended by this apparently unfair package, especially as it was accompanied by cuts in welfare and social security benefits. Together with tax cuts on corporate profits and increases in defence spending, this combination obliged Reagan to claw back some of the cuts with tax hikes during 1983. So the president's radical changes, which had been central to his 1980 electoral platform, ended up satisfying almost nobody.

[15]   Harmondsworth, Middlesex, Penguin, 1981.

Between 1983 and 1988 the quite dramatic recovery of the American economy certainly helped Ronald Reagan's popularity, but the basic distributional problem of how to cut expenditure and not offend almost anybody remained. This was amply demonstrated by the experience of the Bush administration. When the economy started to slow down in 1990, the budget deficit began to grow, reaching $300 billion by 1992. With the economy in recession, pressure to increase expenditures proved irresistible. At the same time, tax increases were politically as unpopular as ever. In the event George Bush did go along with a tax hike in 1991 which almost certainly contributed to his subsequent defeat in 1992.

During his first few years in office, Bill Clinton was fortunate to enjoy a growing economy which, combined with controls on federal spending, did result in a meaningful reduction in the federal deficit (*see* Chapter 15, table 15.2). After 1994, however, Republican control of Congress resulted in a serious deadlock over the Fiscal 1996 Budget and a temporary shutdown of some federal government activities. With the Republicans retaining control of Congress in 1996, further conflicts over the budget seem probable.

In effect, these changes in society and politics have made the country less easy to govern. Pressures on the central institutions are greater while the ability to respond effectively has been weakened. For the presidency, this unfortunate combination has been particularly serious and helps explain the waxing and waning of presidential power over the last 30 years. The era of the 'Imperial Presidency' coincided with the tail-end of American hegemony, and also, of course, with the incumbency of two especially imperious presidents. By the mid-1960s the office had grown enormously in power, and the pressures imposed by the Vietnam War and a declining economy tested the office to the full. The potential for the abuse of power was considerable. Unfortunately for the American people, Lyndon Johnson and, particularly, Richard Nixon fell to this temptation. The real importance of the Nixon period is not that the president, along with many of his aides and cabinet officers, broke the law, but that the chief executive wielded power in such a way that raised very serious questions on where, exactly, presidential power began and ended.

Richard Nixon impounded funds appropriated by Congress for programmes he disliked (impoundment is the setting-aside by the executive of funds appropriated by Congress). Towards the end of his presidency, he was exercising the veto power extensively and few of his vetoes were overridden by Congress. He invoked 'executive privilege' to justify the withholding of information from Congressional investigative committees, and he nominated a number of men to official posts who were unqualified or otherwise unsuitable. Even before

Plate 10.1 'Nixon Resigns': headline of the *Washington Post*, 1974.

Watergate, Congress began to fight back, notably by rejecting two of his more outrageous Supreme Court nominees (*see* chapter 13, p. 288). In 1972 the Congress attempted to control the president's discretion to make executive agreements – effectively treaties with foreign powers which could be concluded, sometimes in secret, without consulting the Senate. Under the Case Act, all such agreements have to be submitted to Congress. More far reaching was the 1973 War Powers Act passed by Congress over a presidential veto which put limits on the president's power to commit troops overseas (*see* chapter 9, p. 182). In 1973 Congress also insisted that the president's director and deputy directors of the vital office of Management and Budget be subject to Senate confirmation.[16]

Following Watergate, Congress asserted its power even more vigorously – in part because Watergate had precipitated a landslide victory for the Democrats in the 1974 mid-term elections. The Budget and Impoundment Control Act of 1974 obliges the president to report 'recission' to Congress when funds appropriated remain unspent. Congress then has to approve recission within 45 days. The same law created the Budget Committees in Congress to enable the legislature

[16]   The best history of the Nixon era is Jonathan Schell, *The Time of Illusion*, (New York, Vintage, 1975).

Table 10.3 Major bills vetoed, 1933–94

President	Total	Number involving appropriations	Number involving foreign and foreign economic policy	Major vetoes per year in office	Number overriden
Roosevelt	2	0	0	0.16	2
Truman	6	0	0	0.8	5
Eisenhower	2	2	0	0.25	1
Kennedy	0	0	0	0	0
Johnson	0	0	0	0	0
Nixon	13	10	1	2.4	4
Ford	11	10	1	4.4	7
Carter	5	2	2	1.3	1
Reagan	15	7	5	1.9	5
Bush	15	4	5	3.7	1
Clinton	0	0	0	0	0

Source: David McKay, 'Presidential strategy and the veto power: a reappraisal', *Political Science Quarterly*, 1989, table 5. Updated from *Congressional Quarterly*. For a definition of major bills and qualifying notes, *see* original.

to play a more constructive part in the budget process (*see* chapter 14 pp. 182–3).

As can be seen from table 10.3, Gerald Ford exercised the veto on major bills frequently and was overridden by Congress on no less than seven occasions. Note also the general tendency for the veto to be applied more frequently and in particular to appropriations and foreign policy bills which, in the past, almost never attracted the presidential veto. This reflects the much more difficult environment in which today's presidents have to work. Sometimes this means facing a Congress controlled by the opposition's party. Equally often it means that there are fundamentally irreconcilable interests represented by a fragmented Congress on the one hand and the president on the other. Although, during his first two years in Office, Bill Clinton did not use the veto power, he certainly did so thereafter and, by so doing, successfully thwarted the Republicans' attempt to pass their ambitious legislative programme in 1995 and 1996.

Finally, in 1976, Congress put considerable limits on the president's power to declare emergencies and assume special powers. Under the National Emergencies Act of 1976, Congress can terminate a declaration of emergency, and all declarations must be reported to Congress, together with legal justifications for them.

Following the adoption of all these measures and the incumbency of an unusually unassertive president, Jimmy Carter, presidency-watchers began to talk of the *decline* of presidential power and the resurgence of Congress. As we saw in chapters 8 and 9, there can be

no doubting that Congress has become more, rather than less, difficult for presidents to deal with. Presidents retain an enormous fund of
resources on which to draw, however. The next section concentrates
on those resources not covered in earlier sections and on the ways in
which successive presidents have adapted to the pressures and problems associated with the office.

Two main resources can be identified – the public and the presidential bureaucracy – to which a third, conceptually distinct resource,
personality, can be added.

Presidential Resources

The public

It may seem paradoxical in the light of the foregoing discussion to
view the public as a resource. Yet under many circumstances it can be
just that. As national leaders, presidents can make direct appeals to
the public through press conferences and special televised announce-
ments. In some instances, this amounts almost to a limited form of
direct democracy. In 1981 and 1982, for example, Ronald Reagan
made specific appeals to the public on television that they should
write to their members of Congress expressing support for the president's economic policies. Both the tax and spending cuts were passed
by narrow margins, and it seems reasonable to assume that Reagan's
pleadings had some effect – especially as many members cannot
afford to ignore a sudden influx of constituency mail. More recently,
Bill Clinton appealed to the public to oppose efforts by the Republican 104th Congress (1995–96) to cut Medicare and Social Security
benefits. His appeals were successful, not only in the sense that the
harshest cuts were unsuccessful, but also in that he could invoke this
experience as evidence of Republican hard heartedness in the 1996
presidential election.

Appeals to the public are not always successful, of course, as
Richard Nixon's sometimes painful public attempts to hide his guilt
over Watergate demonstrated. But earlier in his presidency, Nixon
had made highly effective use of this resource through his carefully
constructed public lectures on American disengagement from Vietnam.

Although still a potentially powerful weapon, the public-appeal
resource is beset with problems and pitfalls. As was established in
chapter 7, the American electorate is now highly volatile. Together
with a growing cynicism about public institutions, not least the presi-

dency,[17] this had made the president's public appeals more risky than they used to be. During Ronald Reagan's first two years, it seems reasonable to infer that the public was willing to provide support during what was effectively a 'honeymoon' period. Following the mid-term elections when the Democrats made deep inroads into the conservative coalition in the House, such support became more grudging, with the balance of public opinion shifting to the Congress rather than to the president. Although highly popular during the Gulf War when he made numerous public appeals, George Bush could do nothing to boost his popularity during the ensuing economic recession. This accepted, no other national institution – Congress, party, courts – can use the media quite like the president. He or she is, after all, just one person with a special national status. Given all the problems of governing in the 1990s, presidents will continue to make direct appeals to the public, for it is one of the few, if imperfect, means whereby the fragmenting influences in American politics can be overcome.[18]

Most commentators agree that the three most important indicators of presidential performance are the state of the economy, the extent of American involvement in foreign wars and the public's approval of the president. As can be seen from table 10.4, these three indicators can be closely associated – a weak economy and/or American soldiers dying abroad helped defeat the incumbent party in 1952, 1968, 1980 and 1992.

[17]   Both during and immediately after Watergate public rating of the office sank to a new low with, in 1974, only 13 per cent expressing 'a great deal of confidence in the executive branch'. Quoted in Louis W. Koenig. *The Chief Executive*, (New York, Harcourt Brace Jovanovich, 5th edn, 1986), p. 102. Since the mid-1970s public confidence in the office has increased a little, but ratings of individual presidents have generally been low. Comparing Reagan with his predecessors after 12 months in office, around 55 per cent of the public approved of the way he was handling his job as president, compared with 68 per cent for Eisenhower, 77 per cent for Kennedy, 69 per cent for Johnson and 61 per cent for Nixon. Both Ford (46 per cent) and Carter (52 per cent) fared badly by comparison (*Public Opinion*, vol. 4, No. 6, December January, 1982, pp. 30–1). Between 1982 and 1985 Reagan's popularity increased, only to decline following the revelations of the Iran-Contra affair in 1986 and 1987. By the end of his second term, however, Reagan had re-established his reputation with the public. President Bush started his term in office with higher ratings than most of his predecessors, his popularity then fell only to rise dramatically during the Gulf War. By the time of the election, however, and following an economic recession it dipped below 40 per cent. After just three months, Bill Clinton's ratings dipped to just 50 per cent – a historic low. Unlike most recent presidents, however, after an initial slide, his popularity increased during the second half of his first term, reaching over 60 per cent by the time of the election.
[18]   For a comprehensive account of how presidents use the public resource, see Sam Kernell, *Going Public*, Washington DC, Congressional Quarterly, 1986.

Table 10.4 Three indicators of presidential performance

Year	Real growth in GNP in the year before the election[1]	Number of deaths in a major war during the election year[2]	Approval rating in the summer before the election[3]
1952	2.30	4,437	30
1956	1.35	0	70
1960	2.22	0	59
1964	5.35	205	74
1968	4.34	16,588	39
1972	5.52	640	58
1976	4.03	0	45
1980	−1.94	0	33
1984	5.63	0	54
1988	3.84	0	51
1992	2.11	0	36
Range	7.57	16,588	44
Average	3.16	1,988	50

[1] Real growth in GNP was measured from the third quarter of the preceding year to the third quarter of the election year.
[2] Figures on war deaths are based on Combat Area Casualties file in the National Archives.
[3] Approval ratings were taken from Gallup Polls conducted during June and July of each election year. When more than one survey included the presidential approval question, the results were averaged.
Source: GNP data are taken from the US Department of Commerce, *National Income and Product Accounts* (multiple years), as reproduced in William G. Mayer, 'Changes in Elections and the Party System: 1992 in Historical Perspective', in Bryan D. Jones, *The New American Politics: Reflections on Political Change and the Clinton Administration*, (Boulder CO, Westview, 1995), table 2.6.

Bureaucracy

As the job of president has become more demanding, so incumbents have adapted their administrative resources accordingly. Every president has had a *cabinet* composed mainly of departmental heads at his disposal, but as we will see, the cabinet is but one of a number of administrative devices available, most of which have been introduced during this century to help presidents formulate and execute policy. In 1921 the Bureau of the Budget (now called the Office of Management and Budget) was established to help the president prepare the budget and co-ordinate spending policies. As can be seen from figure 10.1, since then other agencies have been created which collectively are known as the Executive Office of the President (EOP) (formally established by Congress in 1939). Quite distinct from the cabinet, the Executive Office consists of about 2000 individuals directly accountable to the president. This figure includes about 500 people who actually work in the White House as personal aides to the president – the White House Office in fig. 10.1. How presidents actually use the EOP, and in particular the White House staff, has aroused bitter controversy over the last 20 years. A major criticism, inspired mainly by Watergate, has concerned the extent to which the staff has grown in recent years and has increasingly insulated presidents from public opinion and political reality. A related theme centres on whether any personal bureaucracy can be an adequate administrative tool against the vast resources of executive departments and agencies and against a fragmented but powerful Congress.

There can be no disputing that some presidents have used their staffs unwisely. Richard Nixon, in particular, relied heavily on just a handful of personal aides, eschewing most cabinet officers, Congressional and party leaders. Three of his closest aides, John Ehrlichman, Bob Haldeman and Ron Zeigler, became so effective in acting as the president's mouthpieces that they earned the sobriquet 'The Berlin Wall'. And, in the Carter presidency, Stewart Eisenstadt, the domestic policy adviser, almost assumed the status of policy-initiator and spokesperson. During the second Reagan administration Donald Regan guarded his position as Chief of Staff jealously until he was forced to resign over the Iran-Contra Affair. George Bush's first Chief of Staff, John Sununu, was also widely regarded as imperious and insensitive. He, too, was forced to resign following allegations of misuse of government resources, including presidential jets. During this century, there have been at least three other instances of staffers assuming national prominence and even notoriety as 'the powers behind the throne'.[19] Critics have argued that the very considerable power of personal staffs is undemocratic – they are, after all, unelected and few are subject to Senate confirmation.

Personal staffs – and modern presidents all have domestic, economic and foreign policy advisers, a press secretary, legal counsel, and staff responsible for liaison work with Congress – often overlap with members of other agencies within the EOP. Hence presidents' national security advisers are also members of the National Security Council, a body consisting, among others, of the president, vice-president and Defense and State Secretaries set up by Congress in 1947 to help the formulation of foreign policy and aid crisis management. In some instances, the National Security Adviser becomes more important than the Secretary of State, as was clearly the case with Henry Kissinger before he effectively 'deposed' the incumbent, William Rogers, and assumed the office of Secretary of State himself during Nixon's second term. Similarly, the Director of the Office of Management and Budget can become a key figure, for the OMB is responsible for monitoring the spending of the various executive

---

[19]   Colonel House with Woodrow Wilson, Harry Hopkins with Franklin Roosevelt and Sherman Adams with Dwight Eisenhower.

Figure 10.1 The Executive Office of the President, 1994

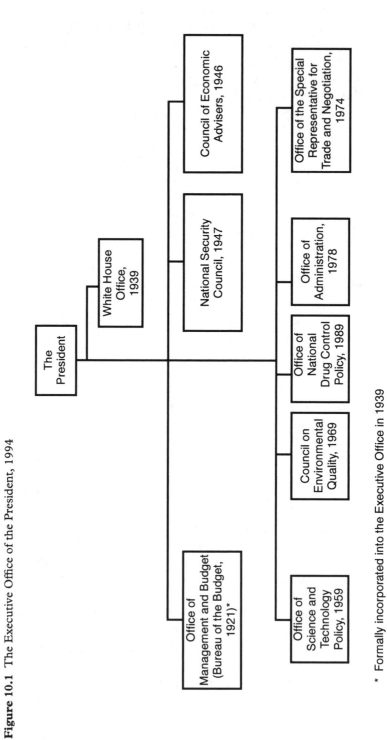

* Formally incorporated into the Executive Office in 1939

Source: Adapted from *US Government Manual 1994/95*, (Washington D.C., US Government Printing Office, 1994).

departments. In 1980 Ronald Reagan's choice of director, David Stockman, a bright young ex-member of Congress, was designed to ensure that the OMB Director would have direct responsibility for handling the budget and the cuts to be imposed on many of the departments and agencies.[20] In this sense, the OMB and its director resemble, although they are by no means identical to, the British Treasury and Chancellor of the Exchequer.

How presidents use the EOP and especially their personal staff varies greatly from administration to administration. Until Watergate it was common to contrast Franklin Roosevelt's style of creating an atmosphere of constructive competition, with aides deliberately positioned to provide contrasting information and advice, with Eisenhower's tendency to delegate responsibility and Kennedy's emphasis on intelligence and *esprit de corps*.[21]

Since Watergate, however, there is evidence that whatever management strategy is adopted by presidents, they will experience serious command problems. Certainly, presidents have felt obliged to innovate and reorganize the executive branch to improve management. Some presidents have adopted 'chiefs of staff' specifically to help management of the White House – although three recent incumbents in this position, Bob Haldeman of Watergate fame, Donald Regan in the Reagan White House and John Sununu in the Bush administration, have not been the best advertisements for the job. Ronald Reagan appointed Martin Anderson as chief of the Office of Policy Development, a new unit replacing the Domestic Policy Office and embracing some responsibility for economic affairs. Anderson had a special status within the White House, particularly in helping smooth relations between cabinet members. He left the White House after only a short period, however, and instead three of President Reagan's other staffers – Chief of Staff James Baker, President's Counsel Edwin Meese and Deputy Chief of Staff Michael Deever – acquired special status and became more centrally placed than other staffers or individual departmental secretaries. All three had left the White House by 1985, however, when ex-Treasury Secretary Donald Regan took over as Chief of Staff.

As mentioned earlier, Regan was obliged to resign in 1987 and was replaced by the more politically astute ex-Senate majority leader, Howard Baker. Indeed, Reagan's use of the EOP changed quite dramatically between his first and second terms. In his first term he relied

---

[20]   Significantly since 1973 the Director of OMB has been subject to Senate confirmation.
[21]   An excellent account of how different presidents have used their staff is John Hart, *The Presidential Branch*, (New Jersey, Chatham House, 2nd ed., 1995).

on at least three chief advisers and, in his second, just one (apart from his wife, who played an active role throughout). While praised for his management style in the first term, he was condemned for his failure to oversee the detail, and sometimes even the main thrust, of policy in the second. The Iran-Contra debacle resulted in part from this failing. Criticisms of George Bush's management style were of a different order. Although John Sununu was supposed to play the 'bad cop' to Bush's 'good cop', that is, to be the president's hit man, it soon became obvious that each was not fully aware of the policy position of the other. As a result, an impression of drift and indecision pervaded the Bush presidency. Sununu's replacement, Samuel Skinner, did little to help because he proved to be a grey, almost anonymous figure. Bill Clinton's experience with staffers was also fraught with difficulties. His first choice as Chief of Staff, Mac McClarty, proved ineffective and was replaced during the first term with the tougher and more political Budget Director, Leon Panetta. Neither McClarty nor Panetta took on a major executive or gatekeeping role, however. Clinton surrounded himself with numerous confidants, some of whom had little formal authority. Indeed, it could be argued that some of the most influential people in his first term were in this category. They included first lady, Hillary Clinton and staffers George Stephanopoulus and Dick Morris. Perhaps unsurprisingly, as the 1996 election drew closer, so Clinton relied more and more on the

Plate 10.2 Bill Clinton in the Oval Office at the White House.

advice of political consultant Dick Morris who urged him to move towards the centre ground of politics and thereby secure victory.

A more radical ploy has involved attempts to institutionalize the delegation of power through strengthening the cabinet. Although every president has had a cabinet, the Constitution unambiguously assigns executive power to the president, so whether the device is used or not is a matter of great discretion. Its membership consists of the heads of the executive departments plus individuals assigned by the president. Reinvigorating the cabinet is a natural option for presidents to choose, because a major part of executive leadership involves control and management of the vast federal bureaucracy. Much of the work of personal staff involves liaison with this bureaucracy, and the closer the communications and finer the line of command, the better. So presidents Nixon, Carter and Reagan pledged that they would strengthen their cabinets. Nixon patently failed to do this, but Carter did in fact use the cabinet quite frequently, as did Ronald Reagan. Indeed, during his first year in office President Reagan convened his cabinet no less than 37 times, a very high figure in historical perspective. It is doubtful that this smoothed relations between the White House and the executive departments. As we will see in chapter 11, a natural antipathy exists between the two, largely because departments and agencies have constituencies and interests of their own. Whatever the promises, presidents generally resort to using their own (usually reliable) staff rather than risk giving real power to departmental secretaries, and recent history is littered with examples of conflict between powerful staffers or EOP members and departmental heads. During his first term, Bill Clinton was no exception to this rule. As already indicated, he acquired an inner circle of advisers. Interestingly, this group contained cabinet secretaries, including Commerce Secretary Ron Brown and HUD Secretary Henry Cisneros. But they were involved as friends and confidants rather than as spokespersons for their departments.

Presidents' urges to reorganize extend to other areas and have included a major reorganization of the EOP by Jimmy Carter, who eliminated seven of the office's administrative units. And Jimmy Carter and Ronald Reagan promised to make greater use of their vice-presidents. Traditionally, the position has meant little in itself, or 'about as useful as a cow's fifth teat' as Harry Truman colourfully put it. Walter Mondale was, however, accorded a more central position in the Carter administration than many previous vice-presidents, and George Bush was given an unusual degree of public visibility. Similarly, Al Gore was accorded a special status in the Clinton White House. Gore not only assumed the mantle of heir apparent, he also became active in a number of policy initiatives.

All these efforts demonstrate the increasingly difficult political environment in which presidents have to work. As we have stressed time and again in earlier chapters, American politics has become increasingly fragmented in the post-war era. Together with the nationalization of political life, this has forced presidents to manage numerous centres of political power, each with its own policy network. As Hugh Heclo has emphasized, staff and other administrative assistance help, but cannot solve the central dilemma of the office:

> Whoever the President and whatever his style, the political and policy bureaucracies crowd in on him. They are there in his office to help, but their needs are not necessarily his needs. Delegation is unavoidable; yet no one aide or combination of aides has his responsibilities or takes his oath of office. However much the President trusts personal friends, political loyalties, or technocrats, he is the person that the average citizen and history will hold accountable.[22]

Personality

While no one could deny the importance of changes in the nomination process and the political environment as determinants of change in the nature of the presidency, some observers stress that the most crucial element in the office is the personality of the incumbent. With so much discretion attached to the job and such a premium on leadership skills – persuasion, manipulation, coercion, insight, charisma – personality is undoubtedly important. Indeed, even the most casual student of American politics has a cognitive picture of certain presidents – Truman as confrontational and combative, Eisenhower as kind and avuncular, Kennedy as inspirational, Reagan as reassuring, and above all, perhaps, Richard Nixon as devious and insecure. Borrowing heavily from psychology, one political scientist, James Barber, has attempted to formalize the 'Presidential character' by classifying presidents by personality type.[23] Barber's two dimensions are active-passive and positive-negative. Simplifying somewhat, the former describes how much *effort* presidents put into the job and the latter how much enjoyment or *satisfaction* they get from it. The resulting four categories are shown in table 10.5 along with the classification of a number of recent presidents. The key types are active/positives, representing individuals who receive enormous satisfaction from being

[22]   Hugh Heclo, 'The changing Presidential office', in Arnold J. Meltsner (ed.), *Politics and the Oval Office*, (San Francisco, Institute for Contemporary Studies, 1987), p. 177.
[23]   James David Barber, *The Presidential Character*, (Englewood Cliffs, New Jersey, Prentice-Hall, 4th edition, 1992).

active in the job, and active/negatives who put in intense effort but get little emotional reward for their pains. Beware, says Barber, of the active/negatives, who are likely to dig in when under pressure and display a sometimes paranoid inflexibility. Active/positives, in contrast, enjoy the cut and thrust of a highly demanding job and are likely to show that spirit of compromise and adaptability which is so essential to the politics of coalition formation. As with all simple psychological theories, Barber's typology is open to criticism.[24] *Events* often mould personality rather than the other way round. Who, after all, would have judged Lyndon Johnson 'inflexible' before he became so fatally obsessed with the war in Vietnam? And in many respects Richard Nixon, the epitome of the active/negative type according to Barber, was pragmatic and adaptable. Unlike Woodrow Wilson and Lyndon Johnson, Nixon had little moral commitment to causes or higher ideals. Moreover, to put Ronald Reagan in the same category as Warren Harding and William Taft seems misguided, for *every* modern president has to be 'active'. This may not mean working 18-hour days, but it must at least mean being *psychologically* active or aware of events and political priorities. While there is no doubt that George Bush was active, some doubt exists as to whether he drew great satisfaction from the job. Certainly, by the end of his term, he displayed an element of weariness and resignation that was not typical of an active/positive.

In sum, Barber's categories are not very useful guides to presidential *quality*. Highly successful and 'failed' presidents are put in the same category (Franklin Roosevelt and Jimmy Carter as

Table 10.5 Barber's classification of modern presidents

		Energy level in job	
		Active	Passive
Emotional attitude to satisfaction from the job	Positive	Franklin Roosevelt Harry Truman John Kennedy Gerald Ford Jimmy Carter George Bush Bill Clinton	William Taft Warren Harding Ronald Reagan
	Negative	Woodrow Wilson Herbert Hoover Lyndon Johnson Richard Nixon	Calvin Coolidge Dwight Eisenhower

Source: Adapted from various sources including James David Barber, *The Presidential Character.* Bill Clinton's classification is the author's.

[24] For a good critique, *see* Alexander L. George, 'Assessing Presidential character', in Aaron Wildavsky (ed.), *Perspectives on the Presidency*, (Boston, Little, Brown, 1975).

active/positives, Dwight Eisenhower and Calvin Coolidge as passive/negatives),[25] and the changes earlier analysed, especially those associated with presidential selection, appear to bear little or no relationship to Barber's idea of presidential quality.

What the typology does do is force us to think more carefully about the impact of personality on the office. There is no disputing that some men have been more suited to the job than others and that, irrespective of events, changes in the selection process and in American society, this simple fact continues to hold true. All the evidence suggests, for example, that Ronald Reagan enjoyed being president and had a talent for handling people around him which most other recent presidents have lacked. This does not mean to say that history will judge him a great president or even that his record in dealing with Congress and the public will be deemed successful. His casual style and willingness to delegate undoubtedly helped lead to the Iran-Contra affair in 1985 and 1986. But having a personality apparently suited to the job must at least help the incumbent come to terms with what possibly is the most demanding executive position in the modern world.

All the indications are that Bill Clinton, too, enjoys the business of being president. He is a naturally gregarious and extrovert personality who likes, and is liked by, most of the people who work with him. During his first term he may have become frustrated at the glacial progress of his legislative programme and his party's subsequent defeat at the mid-term congressional elections but, in response to these events, he did not become depressed and introspective. On the contrary, they inspired him to renewed enthusiasm during the last two years of his first term – an enthusiasm devoted not to legislation but to what Clinton does best – campaigning for re-election.

Assessing the Presidency: Presidential Power at Century's End

When, in 1960, Richard Neustadt described presidential power as the 'power to persuade', he accurately captured the need for presidents to be successful bargainers, negotiators and manipulators.[26] Coalition-building, in other words, is the very essential of the president's job, and incumbents must have the personal capacity not only to appreci-

---

[25] This pairing is particularly inappropriate given evidence claiming the high quality of Eisenhower's leadership. *See* Pred Greenstein, *The Hidden Hand Presidency: Eisenhower as Leader*, (New York, Basic Books, 1982).
[26] *Presidential Power*, (New York, John Wiley, 1960).

ate this fact (as Jimmy Carter constantly said he did) but also act accordingly (as Jimmy Carter repeatedly failed to do). Coalition-building skills are necessary at every level – within the White House, and in relations with executive departments, Congress, the media, interest groups and the public. Neustadt's famous essay was designed to show that formal command was not enough; that, indeed, it was sometimes quite was limited, unless supplemented by the more subtle political skills involved in the art of persuasion.[27] To reduce almost all of the president's job to bargaining skills is, of course, to oversimplify. Constitutionally, the chief executive has immense power of command – not least as commander in chief – which he can exercise without a finely honed aptitude for bargaining. The presidencies of Lyndon Johnson and Richard Nixon are proof enough of this. Yet both presidents are now considered less than successful, and, since the early 1970s, the number of power centres and policy networks in the American system has increased considerably. Moreover, changes in the selection process, while perhaps not pre-selecting certain personality types among candidates, have certainly affected the nature of their party and political contacts, and hence their access to major bargaining resources. Add to this the structural changes in society listed earlier and it is easy to appreciate why so many commentators complain of the office being 'overloaded'. While, in such a context, the premium of bargaining and leadership skills is greatly increased, there is also the danger that, under such enormous pressures, presidents will resort to confrontation or to clandestine and possibly illegal acts simply to get things done. Such was the case with the later years of the Nixon administration. As we saw, the veto power is now used more often than in the past, and presidents are also prone to go over the heads of congressional leaders with appeals direct to the American people. One thing is sure: no matter how difficult the job becomes or how recent presidents are judged by a fickle electorate, the position of president of the United States will continue to attract enormous attention both in the USA and abroad. For, to repeat the point yet again, alone in a highly fragmented political system, the presidency is the natural co-ordinating institution of national leadership. Given the inherent power of the federal government over the lives of many millions of Americans and non-Americans, this must ensure that the very special status of the presidency will continue.

---

[27] Neustadt showed how the commands of presidents on three occasions – Truman's sacking of General MacArthur, his decision to seize the steel mills in 1951 and Eisenhower's decision to send federal troops to Little Rock, Arkansas in 1954 – were as much a demonstration of failure rather than success, for they represented the failure of persuasion or the bargaining skills so crucial to the office, chapters 2 and 3.

Further Reading

A good account of presidential power is provided by Michael Foley and John E. Owens, *Congress and the Presidency: Institutional Politics in a Separated System*, (Manchester, Manchester University Press, 1996). The classic statement on the president's power to persuade is provided by Richard Neustadt, *Presidential Power, and the Modern Presidents. The Politics of Leadership from Roosevelt to Reagan*, (New York, Free Press, 1990). For accounts of the increasingly public nature of the office, *see* Sam Kernell, *Going Public*, (Washington DC, Congressional Quarterly, Second Edition, 1991) and Roderick P. Hart, *The Sound of Leadership*, (Chicago, University of Chicago Press, 1987). Presidential elections are covered in Nelson Polsby and Aaron Wildavsky, (*Presidential Elections*) 9th edition, (1995) and in Stephen J. Wayne, *The Road to the White House 1996: The Politics of Presidential Elections*, (New York, St Martin's Press, 1996). For an impressive historical sweep through the presidency, *see* Stephen Skowronek, *The Politics Presidents Make: Leadership from John Adams to George Bush*, (Cambridge, Mass., Harvard University Press, 1993). The most recent study of presidential bureaucracy is by John Hart, *The Presidential Branch*, (Chatham N.J., Chatham House, second edition, 1995). An interesting comparative perspective on the presidency is Richard Rose, *The Post Modern President: George Bush Meets the World*, (New Jersey, Chatham House, 1991).

11

THE FEDERAL BUREAUCRACY

The fully developed bureaucratic mechanism compares with other organizations exactly as does the machine with the non-mechanical modes of production. Precision, speed, unambiguity, knowledge of the files, continuity, discretion, unity, strict subordination, reduction of friction and of material and personal costs these are raised to the optimum point in the strictly bureaucratic administration.

Max Weber, *Essays in Sociology*

Our Government has no special power except that granted it by the people. It is time to check and reverse the growth of government which shows signs of having grown beyond the consent of the governed. It is my intention to curb the size and influence of the federal establishment . . .

Ronald Reagan

Our principles are clear. The government service is a noble calling and a public trust . . . There is nothing more fulfilling than to serve your country and fellow citizens and to do it well.

George Bush

Reinventing government requires ending overregulation and micromanagement. That implicitly demands that Congress give up its penchant for tinkering with bureaucracy and leave more of management to the managers.

Report of the National Performance Review [on Reinventing Government], 1993

Few areas of federal government activity come in for as much opprobrium as does the bureaucracy. As the Weber quote suggests, bureaucracies are supposed to work efficiently. Hierarchy, order,

Table 11.1 Public perception of efficiency of institutions, November 1981 (percentage)

Institution	Not efficient and well run	Efficient and well run	Don't know
Federal government	74	20	6
Local government	49	43	7
Large business corporations	33	56	10
Private voluntary organizations	23	60	17
Small business corporations	20	70	10

Source: Public Opinion, vol. 5, no. 1 (February/March 1982), p. 28. © American Enterprise Institute.

responsibility and professionalism are implied by the model of the 'rational' bureaucrat, yet, according to public folklore, typical federal administrators are the very opposite of this. They are overpaid, inefficient and wasteful. Worse, they are often the creatures of special interests, and occasionally they are simply corrupt. Surveys have shown, indeed, that the federal government is considered easily the most inefficient of all the major institutions in American society (table 11.1). While some of the more colourful charges levelled at the federal bureaucracy more closely resemble caricature than accurate portrait, the executive branch does seem unusually inefficient, fragmented and complex. So much so, indeed, that every president has pledged himself to simplify the executive branch and to root out wasteful and unnecessary programmes. Promises of this sort are popular with the electorate, and no doubt presidents genuinely believe that they can actually rationalize the bureaucracy. In spite of some changes, however, the complaints – and frustrated attempts at reform – continue. This issue raises a number of questions. Why is it that the executive branch attracts so much criticism? Is the criticism justified? To what extent *can* the federal bureaucracy be controlled and reformed? It may be that the structure and behaviour of the executive departments and agencies reflect other forces in American government which would have to be changed as a prelude to bureaucratic reform. Before we address these questions directly, it is necessary to provide some basic facts about the federal administration in the United States.

The Federal Bureaucracy: Organization and Function

The annual US *Government Manual* produces an organization chart of the government of the United States (fig. 11.1). While such charts can be misleading – they imply a hierarchical simplicity and equality

Figure 11.1 The government of the United States

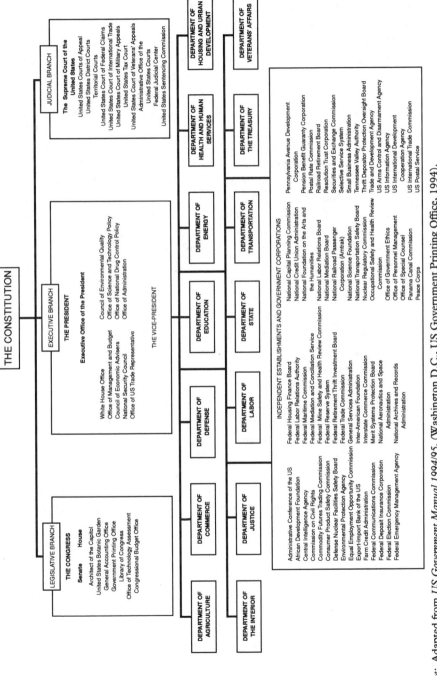

Source: Adapted from *US Government Manual 1994/95*, (Washington D.C., US Government Printing Office, 1994).

between units at the same level which is far from reality – they do reveal the bare bones of the system.

The most important distinctions are between the 14 executive departments, the independent establishments and the government corporations. Executive or cabinet departments are responsible for the major federal programmes, and their chiefs, the departmental secretaries, are directly answerable to the president. Given the growth in government over the last 60 years, cabinet departments have not proliferated as might have been expected. In 1997 only seven of the 14 departments were creations of the modern era and, of these, one (Defense) grew out of older departments. In fact, successive presidents have worked hard to reduce the number of departments or to rationalize existing ones. In 1949 the Departments of War, Army, Navy and Airforce were combined in one Department of Defense. In 1971 President Nixon proposed 'the most far-reaching reorganization of the executive branch that has ever been proposed by a President of the United States'[1] by amalgamating seven cabinet departments into four new ones. His plan was rejected by Congress, but Jimmy Carter and Ronald Reagan have continued the campaign to simplify the departments. Ronald Reagan went so far as to label the Departments of Education and Energy unnecessary, and, during 1982, bills were introduced into Congress proposing their abolition. Both were created by Jimmy Carter – the former because the existing Department of Health, Education and Welfare was so large and cumbersome, and the latter as a direct response to the nation's energy crisis. By 1988 they were still in existence, however, demonstrating Congress's resistance to major rationalizations. In the event, Reagan presided over an expansion of the cabinet departments with the creation of the Department of Veteran's Affairs in 1988.

Most presidents prefer a small, compact cabinet so as to facilitate smooth policy-making. Yet the number of departments for which they are responsible is but one of a number of management problems they have to face. Another involves the complexity characteristic of each department. This can be formidable, for, with the possible exception of the Department of State (responsible for the foreign service and foreign policy), each department is itself a collection of different agencies and services, each with its own interests and constituents. So the Department of Health and Human Services (HHS) was created in 1979 following an earlier incarnation as the Department of Health, Education and Welfare, which was itself a loose collection of disparate agencies. HHS's present organization is shown in fig. 11.2. Again the

---

[1] Quoted in Otis L. Graham, *Toward a Planned Society: From Roosevelt to Nixon*, (New York, Oxford University Press, 1976), p. 209.

Figure 11.2 Department of Health and Human Services

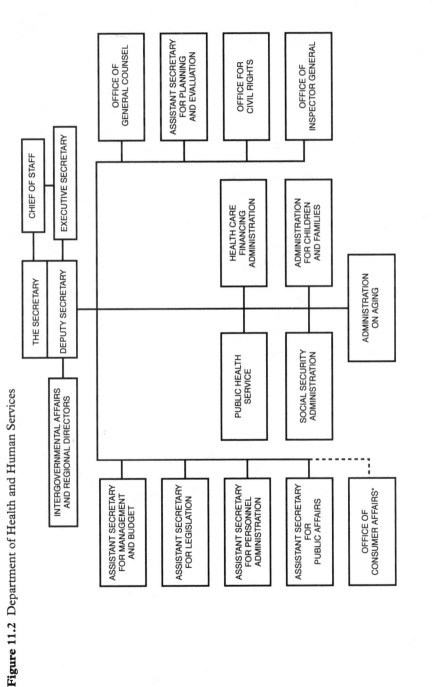

*Located administratively in HHS, but reports to the President.

Source: Adapted from *US Government Manual 1994/95* (Washington D.C., US Government Printing Office, 1994).

apparently simple hierarchical structure belies a reality of considerable complexity and competition – although the sheer number of different programmes does give some sense to the complexity of the department. In almost all cabinet departments there is a horizontal division of responsibilities and a vertical division organized geographically. Thus much of the day-to-day work of HHS is carried out at the regional and area levels. There are ten standard federal regions and, within these, a number of area offices, usually based on large cities. Fig. 11.2 also allows us to make some distinction between different sorts of bureaucrats. In the American system, a crucial distinction exists between the *competitive* service, which includes officials recruited by examination or on the basis of technical qualifications determined by the Office of Personnel Management, and the *excepted* service where appointment is decided, again mainly on merit directly by such agencies and departments as the FBI, Postal Service and the State Department. The excepted service includes the Senior Executive Service (SES) created by the 1978 Civil Service Act. SES appointees are the super-grade grade officials who can, in theory at least, be moved across agencies and given merit pay awards. The excepted service also includes *political* appointees who make up around 3 per cent of the total. In fig. 11.2 the secretary, undersecretary, the deputies and the top officials in each of the sub-units would be political appointees. Other very senior officials would be part of the SES, while the bulk of the remainder would be part of the competitive service. As will be developed later, the whole question of the role of political appointees has been highly controversial over the last 30 years.

The independent establishments and government corporations (fig. 11.1) include a vast number of agencies performing numerous functions. A very general distinction can be drawn between government corporations (broadly equivalent to nationalized industries in other countries) which include the US Postal Service and the Tennessee Valley Authority, and the regulatory agencies. But there are other institutions which fall into neither category, including the General Services Administration and Office of Personnel Management which deal, respectively, with the provision of buildings, equipment and other services for the whole executive branch, and the recruitment of staff to the cabinet departments. It is a little misleading to label all of these institutions 'independent' – the chief administrators (or in a few cases the boards of governors) are appointed by the president, subject to confirmation by the Senate. The president is also a key figure in helping decide the size of their budgets and in some cases he or she or the cabinet secretaries, take a very direct interest in their activities.

This is patently the case with the Central Intelligence Agency (CIA), and with the US Information Service which effectively functions as a propaganda service for the State Department.

The regulatory agencies are genuinely more independent, however, because most of them were originally set up by Congress to function as non-partisan organizations responsible for monitoring, controlling or regulating various aspects of economic and social life. Three waves of reform in American politics correspond to the three generations of regulatory agencies that exist. Between 1887 and 1915 a rising tide of reform sentiment led to the creation of agencies designed to tame the unacceptable economic and social activities of large corporations and natural monopolies, mainly the railroads. So, during this period, the Interstate Commerce Commission and Federal Trade Commission came into being. During the 1930s, most of the reforms were inspired by the Depression and its consequences. Hence, the Federal Deposit Insurance Corporation underwrites bank deposits to protect the public against bank failures, the Securities and Exchange Commission regulates the stock market, and the National Labour Relations Board helps regulate industrial relations. The final wave of reform, during the 1960s and 1970s, was inspired by, among other things, concern at environmental pollution (leading to the Environmental Protection Agency which is, incidentally, *not* an independent agency but a cabinet-level organization), civil rights (the Equal Employment Opportunity Commission), election malpractice (the Federal Election Commission) and consumer protection (the Consumer Protection Safety Commission). These agencies have sometimes been given formidable powers by Congress to exercise administrative, legislative and judicial powers over corporations, unions and the public at large. Until the 1960s, a common criticism was that they were anything but independent in the use of these powers. Instead the 'regulated controlled the regulators' or, to quote two celebrated cases, the Food and Drugs administration was in the hands of the drug companies and the Interstate Commerce Commission was deferential to the needs of the truckers and railroads.

Although sometimes exaggerated, there is little doubt that many of the regulatory commissions had established a *symbiotic* relationship with what had become their clients.[2] They needed each other, the clients for guidance on how best to operate in (or dominate) the market, and the regulators to ensure political independence and to justify their bureaucratic *raison d'être*. During the 1960s and 1970s, much greater public concern at the abuse of corporate power led to the

---

[2] *See* Murray Edelman, *The Symbolic Uses of Politics*, (Urbana, Illinois, University of Illinois Press, 1964) for a good analysis of this point.

Figure 11.3 Number of federal, state and local government employees, 1929–91

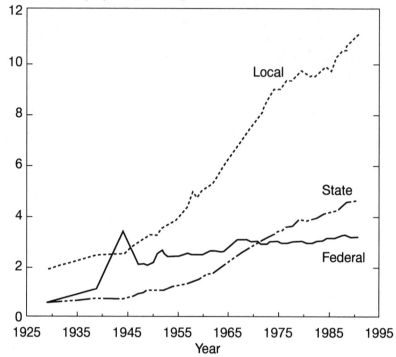

Source: Various, compiled by Harold W. Stanley and Richard G. Niemi, *Vital Statistics on American Politics*, (Washington D.C., CQ, 1994).

newer agencies (such as the Environmental Protection Agency) establishing a more *adversarial* relationship with the regulated.[3] This, together with limited reforms in the older agencies and a general increase in the amount of regulation in American life – especially of corporations – has led to a backlash by the corporate world and their political allies, the Republicans.

Contrary to popular belief, the burgeoning responsibilities of the federal government, together with greatly increased expenditure, have not been matched by dramatic increases in the *number* of federal employees responsible for implementing programmes and policies. As can be seen from fig. 11.3, the number of federal employees has remained roughly the same over the last 40 years, the big increases in total government employment being accounted for by state and local governments. Indeed, starting with the Carter administration and continuing under President Reagan, the absolute number of federal/civilian employees fell – although the decreases were modest

---

[3]   For a selection of case studies on regulation, *see* James Q. Wilson (ed.), *The Politics of Regulation*, (New York, Basic Books, 1980).

and were reversed during the later 1980s and 1990s. These reductions were part of the continuing campaign against big government, but the general failure of federal employment to rise in the post-war period takes more explaining. Part of the reason, at least until the early 1980s, was the rapid increase in the number and size of grant-in-aid programmes to state and local governments. As we saw in chapter 5, a fair percentage of the general increase in federal spending derives from this source. Devolved programmes increase employment at the lower, rather than federal, level. Second, increased expenditure does not necessarily require more federal employees – although it has almost certainly led to what is a considerable expansion of the number of professionals in federal employment. Professionals are the middle-grade employees, often scientists, or the highly trained personnel who have been increasingly recruited to help run more complex programmes, old and new. In fact (the Post Office excluded) the federal government employs relatively few less-qualified workers. State and local movements employ most of the lower grades (transport, hospital, municipal employees) and lower/middle grades (teachers, social workers, police and firefighters). A more professional civil service is harder to control because it can more easily fall back on technical and highly specialized information when challenged by the public, Congress or the president.

The Bureaucracy: How Uncontrollable?

Students of administrative behaviour are quick to identify certain characteristics of bureaucracy which are present whatever the political system involved or governmental function being performed. Some of these characteristics are labelled 'undesirable' – usually because they greatly reduce the accountability of bureaucrats to elected officials – and, as government becomes larger and more complex, so these undesirable features multiply. There is, of course, no reason to suppose that the United States is exempt from these trends. It is not, and that is problem enough. But critics go much further and argue that US government, and particularly the federal bureaucracy, has a number of additional, and uniquely American features that make the problem of accountability a particularly serious one. Unfortunately, unravelling cause and effect is difficult in this area, especially in a country where 'federal government' and 'bureaucracy' often hold negative connotations. With so many Americans deeply prejudiced against government, it is important to treat with caution some of the more colourful critiques levelled against bureaucracy, regulation, 'Washington' and the civil service.

The task of the remainder of this chapter is, therefore, to outline the major criticisms directed at the federal bureaucracy, to assess their validity and to record the ways in which presidents, Congress, the courts and the public have attempted to increase their control over administrators.

The Inherent Power of Bureaucracy

Simple theories of constitutional government and of administrative behaviour assign little or no independent power or discretion to administrators. Their job is to implement laws. The legislature passes the laws and the chief executive is responsible for managing and directing the administrators in the implementation process. According to classical theories of administration, bureaucrats can do this effectively if they operate in line with certain basic principles – hierarchical command, specialization and delegation of duties. The elected chief executives are at the apex of this system, they alone give commands; bureaucrats may advise them, but it is not their job actually to give orders. Reality is, of course, very far from this ideal type. In most systems, bureaucrats have two main powers, both of which can give them considerable control over the policy system.

Information

Bureaucrats function as administrative gatekeepers. When laws are being framed either by legislatures or executives, it is essential to find out what is achievable and what is not. A new law on lead levels in petrol (gasoline), for example, needs to be carefully informed about a host of technical questions, including the efficiency of internal combustion engines, pollution levels, the car industry's ability to compete internationally once their products are adapted, and so on. Politicians are obliged to heed the advice of their officials on such technicalities, and the officials themselves can, up to a point, select and organize information according to their own preferences and prejudices, or in favour of one interest rather than another. They may, for example, advise the politicians that certain options are simply not possible for technical reasons. Examples of administrative gatekeeping in highly technical areas may sound understandable, and possibly exceptional. But almost *all* law-making and implementation in modern industrial societies is technical and complex. From housing to transport to law enforcement to social security and defence, technical questions are paramount. No single president or cabinet secretary can possibly absorb all this information – even with the assistance of professional staffs. They have to rely on their bureaucrats.

Clientelism

Clientelism is the word used to describe the sort of symbiotic relationships between bureaucrats and their customers referred to earlier. Again, it is not unique to American politics; to a greater or lesser extent it occurs everywhere. It is also an entirely understandable phenomenon. Consider the case of defence agencies and defence contractors. In those Western countries with sizeable defence industries (Britain, Germany, France, the USA) intimate relations exist between contractors and officials in defence departments. Defence officials have, therefore, a continuing interest in particular corporations and defence systems – and also, perhaps, in ensuring that defence spending remains at certain levels. These interests may or may not be the same as those of the administrators' political masters. But there can be no doubting the independent political influence of officials in this context. Information is, again, the crucial resource, but it is not merely technical information; it is this plus all the advantages which daily personal contact and shared values give to the official and which are often denied to the politicians.

As government has increased in size and scope, so clientelism has spread. In modern societies all bureaucracies have their customers whose interests and needs must be tended to, whatever the government in power or the values and preferences of elected politicians.

The Bureaucratic Hydra: a Uniquely American Phenomenon?

Scholars of comparative government often refer to the extent to which different political systems are characterized by 'strong' or 'weak' states. Almost invariably, the United States is categorized as a weak state. In other words, rather than government being unified, resolute and separated from the rest of society, it is fragmented, indecisive and infused with social influence.[4] The aforementioned clientelism is a good indicator of the power and autonomy of the state. Although it exists everywhere, clientelism is likely to be more pervasive in weak state systems. In addition, weak states are likely to be characterized by competition between different parts of the administrative process. So sub-units – individual departments and agencies – display a marked degree of *autonomy* from the centre. They serve different interests,

---

[4] For a good comparative analysis *see* Peter J. Katzenstein (ed.), *Between Power and Plenty: the Foreign Economic Policies of Advanced International States*, (Madison, Wisconsin, University of Wisconsin Press, 1978).

and their officials do not all share the same values and policy objectives. We are not referring here to the absolute *size* of government. As noted, in terms of expenditure and function, American government is large by any standards. We are, rather, referring to the extent to which American government is fragmented and simply not amenable to central direction and control.

Much of recent criticism centres on this fact. Critics usually do not put the particular American situation in comparative context, but we have good reason to believe that the United States is different from many other countries; that certain institutional relationships make it especially difficult to exercise central control over public policy. Two basic critiques of American bureaucracy have been made in recent years – the 'iron triangle' and 'issue network' critiques.

Iron triangles

Starting with books written by Douglass Cater and Leiper Freeman in the mid-1960s came accusations that subgovernments working as iron triangles – Congressional subcommittee, administrative bureau and special interest – were the dominant actors in American politics.[5] The analysis was simple: Congressional subcommittees provide the money and monitor regulations, the bureau actually hands over the money or enforces the regulation, and the special interest is the beneficiary. All need one another and the system would break down without equal participation by all. Hence the 'iron triangle' metaphor. Empirical confirmation of subgovernments of this sort was readily at hand, especially in public works, defence, agriculture and water policy. Agriculture became a particularly appealing example with bureaux in the Department of Agriculture handing out subsidies to farmers who, in turn, had established intimate links with members of the several agricultural subcommittees. The triangle was 'iron' because it was impenetrable. The combined political clout of the leading subgovernment actors was formidable, with no individual president, public-interest lobby or Congressional leader able to break the pattern of distribution and public expenditure which the triangle had moulded. While the empirical validity of this case was convincing for certain sorts of public policy, it was clearly inappropriate in other areas. Appreciating this fact, Ripley and Franklin refined the thesis in an important book first published in 1976.[6] They pointed out that, in what they call redistrib-

---

[5]   Douglass Cater, *Power in Washington*, (New York, Vintage, 1964); J. Leiper Freeman, *The Political Process*, (New York, Random House, 1965).
[6]   Randall B. Ripley and Grace A. Franklin, *Congress, the Bureaucracy and Public Policy*, (Holmewood, Illinois, Dorsey Press, 1976, 5th edn, 1991).

utive domestic policy (where resources are taken from one group or class and given to another, as in social welfare programmes), presidents and top-level (politically appointed) officials, as well as Congress as a whole, play a more important part. And in some regulatory policies, bureaucracy and administration play a relatively small role. Other, more sophisticated refinements were added by the authors to the subgovernment theory, all of which demonstrated that the American administrative and political process is indeed unduly complex and often not amenable to simple, single-model characterizations.

Issue networks

A conceptually much simpler, yet almost certainly more accurate, picture of administrative politics in America has been drawn by Hugh Heclo.[7] Heclo argued that, as government programmes have grown in size and scope, so they have generated new lobbies, interests and, simply, a larger number of active participants in the policy process. Moreover, the networks of politicking and lobbying which develop as a consequence are constantly adapting and changing. So it is very difficult accurately to categorize where the policy system begins and ends:

> The notion of iron triangles and sub-governments presumes small circles of participants who have succeeded in becoming largely autonomous. Issue networks, on the other hand, comprise a large number of participants with quite variable degrees of mutual commitment or of dependence on others in their environment; in fact it is almost impossible to say where a network leaves off and its environment begins.[8]

As a result of this much more open and volatile system, no erstwhile secure subgovernment can afford to be complacent. The cosy relationships established between corporations and bureaucrats have been challenged by environmentalists, consumer-protection advocates and other public-interest lobbies (a point to be developed in the next chapter). The subgovernments continue to exist, of course, but they are increasingly buffeted by competing centres of power. Heclo does not view these developments as entirely negative – indeed, there may be greater scope for executive leadership when the system is more

[7] Hugh Heclo, *A Government of Strangers: Executive Politics in Washington*, (Washington DC, Brookings Institution, 1977); also his 'Issue networks and the executive establishment', in Anthony King (ed.), *The New American Political System*, (Washington DC, American Enterprise Institute, 1978).
[8] 'Issue networks', ibid., p. 102.

open. But he does view with alarm the increasing complexity of government and the fact that direct democratic accountability is difficult to achieve when the 'real' decisions are taken, not by president and members of Congress, but by numerous additional political actors including bureaucrats, lobbyists, the media and political consultants.

To the foreign observer, what is interesting about these critiques of bureaucratic power, is that they are comments, not only on administrators and administrative agencies, but also on the whole policy-making system. Many make the a priori assumption that more government is by definition a bad thing and that increasing public disenchantment with government derives from the constantly expanding volume of legislation and special regulations. Without commenting on the normative question of whether more government is good or bad, it is obviously the case that government, by whatever definition (number of policies, volume of regulations, amount of public expenditures) has increased in all modern industrial societies over the last 30 years. Though criticism of big government has occurred in other countries, however, it has been particularly vocal in the USA – a country where, as a percentage of GNP, government, though large, is hardly at the top of the international league table. No doubt this can partly be explained in ideological terms. As we noted in chapter 3, the USA has a long-established tradition of antagonism to government. But there are also important institutional differences between the USA and most other countries which may help us understand both academic and popular critiques of government in general and bureaucracy in particular.

Easily the most important is the independent role of Congress. Iron triangles and issue networks depend at least in part on an autonomous legislature and, within Congress, little legislatures (committees and subcommittees). Although this has long been appreciated – for example, in 1970 Harold Seidman noted that 'meaningful improvements in executive organization and in the management of the Federal system . . . will depend in the final analysis on reorganization of the congressional committee structure'[9] – it seems to have been partly forgotten amid all the talk of special-interest politics, political action committees and the generally more complex and confusing pattern of government typical of the 1980s and 1990s. Although it could be argued that autonomous legislative power increases accountability, it also greatly facilitates the sort of volatile issue-network politics where no single actor in the policy process can ever fully understand what is going on, let alone control events. Arguably, this is the very antithesis

---

[9]   Harold Seidman, *Politics, Position and Power: The Dynamics of Federal Organization*, (New York, Oxford University Press, 1st edn, 1970), p. 285.

of accountability. As we will discuss below, successive governments, including the Clinton administration, have recognized this problem but few have been able to do much about it.

A second unique feature of the American system is its openness. Access to Congress and members of Congress, as well as to officials at all levels, is remarkably easy compared with most other countries. Exploiting this fact, Washington has become a political consultants' and lobbyists' paradise. No interest, whether economic (corporations, unions), public interest (environment, consumer protection), or governmental (state and local governments), can afford to drop its guard by failing to make full use of the availability of policy-makers. Again, openness is at least partly a function of the proliferation of centres of autonomy or power. With subcommittees, bureaux, agencies and even individual officials competing with one another over particular areas of public policy, they are usually only too ready to make use of any resource that will enhance their autonomy further; in essence this means organized interests (together with their technical advisers, the lobbyists and consultants), and the media. A more open system received fresh impetus from the cathartic effects of the Watergate scandals. Freedom of information became a major public issue during the late 1960s and early 1970s, and the formal legal access of groups and individuals to government files and information was greatly strengthened as a result.[10] But these formal changes were almost certainly not as important in producing greater access as the changes in Congress, the party system and American society generally which earlier chapters have chronicled.

Reform Attempts

Perhaps the most common recent response to the problem of big government and bureaucratic power is simply to propose a reduction in the size and complexity of government. In his 1982 State of the Union Message, Ronald Reagan declared:

> Together, we have cut the growth of new federal regulations in half. In 1981, there were 23,000 fewer pages in the Federal Register, which lists new regulations, than there were in 1980 . . . Together, we have

[10] Under the 1966 and 1974 Freedom of Information Acts, Americans have the right to inspect all federal records. Certain information (for example, relating to criminal investigation, defence or inter-office memos) can be denied, but citizens can appeal against refusals in the courts. The substantive freedom of access in the USA is dramatically greater than in most comparable countries, and especially than in the United Kingdom.

created an effective federal strike force to combat waste and fraud in government. In just six months it has saved the taxpayers more than two billion dollars – and it's only getting started.[11]

As we noted earlier, the number of federal employees did decline during the late 1970s and early 1980s, since when the number has steadied and increased slightly. Does this mean that presidents are winning the battle against bureaucracy? Not necessarily. Federal employment may not have risen rapidly, but numbers are only loosely related to complexity and autonomy. Similarly, Ronald Reagan's reductions in *new* regulations did nothing to alter the fact of already established regulations, together with their policy networks. 'Waste and fraud' in the federal government undoubtedly exist, but this condemnation is more of a populist rallying cry than an attack on the central problems of complexity and autonomy. As we know, several presidents have attempted to reorganize the executive branch, the most dramatic proposal being Richard Nixon's 1971 plan to create four 'super departments' – Natural Resources, Human Resources, Community Development and Economic Affairs. Other, less-ambitious reorganizations have been attempted, some successfully, others not. Sometimes these involve the creation of new departments (HUD in 1965, Health, Education and Welfare (HEW) in 1953, the Department of Energy in 1977, the Department of Education in 1979, Veterans' Affairs in 1988). More common are *internal* reorganizations usually aimed at simplifying administration and reducing overlapping jurisdictions. Although well intentioned, reorganization is almost always a less than adequate reform measure. For one thing, Congress is reluctant to approve reorganizations that affect its own internal distribution of power, and accordingly has vetoed the more far-reaching reforms. Committees and, increasingly, subcommittees have vested interests in the continuing autonomy of departments, bureaux and agencies. Secondly, internal reorganization often involves 'shuffling the same old drones into new hives' as Robert Sherrill has put it, so no real change occurs.

In fact, Ronald Reagan eschewed the reorganization device, opting instead for more direct control of the executive branch. He did this in two ways: through control of agency and departmental rule-making and through the appointment power. In 1980 Congress passed the Paperwork Reduction Act, a law favoured by the Carter administration and designed to simplify federal regulations. The Act established an Office of Information and Regulatory Affairs (OIRA) within the Office of Management and Budget (OMB). Although not in itself

---

[11] *Address to Congress*, 26 January 1982, US Embassy Press Release, London, p. 3.

very significant, the Reagan administration used this new unit, in combination with two executive orders, to screen new agency regulations. In effect, this required the executive departments and agencies to submit any changes in policy to OMB. In turn OMB rejected any rules considered not in line with administration policy. Not surprisingly this particularly affected those agencies which, in the past, the administration had considered too progressive in such areas as environmental protection, affirmative action, occupational safety and health, welfare, education and social security. These centralized gatekeeping efforts provoked a storm of protest in Congress and almost certainly led to a loosening of regulations in a number of areas. As a number of commentators have noted, however, these changes did not amount to a fundamental shift in policy.[12]

The Reagan administration's use of the appointment power attracted a great deal of publicity because it represented a thoroughgoing attempt to politicize the executive branch. As well as placing Reagan supporters in the cabinet departments and regulatory agencies, the administration centralized the appointment, transfer and promotion of members of the Senior Executive Service. Utilizing the provisions of the 1978 Civil Service Act, the Office of Personnel Management, under direct instructions from Ed Meese in the White House, promoted, rewarded and transferred Reagan loyalists while punishing those considered liberal or disloyal. At the cabinet level, some of the Reagan appointees were so out of tune with their departments and with public opinion that they were forced to resign (Anne Gorsuch at EPA; James Watt at Interior). Lower down, the politicization strategy was also controversial and led to falling morale and frequent resignations among civil servants.[13]

Again, limits exist as to what can be achieved from such a strategy. If Congress establishes an Environmental Protection Agency, its job is to protect the environment. Officials recruited to the EPA will support this basic objective. Changing senior managers can undermine this policy but they cannot transform it. Congress, moreover, is ever vigilant and keen to exercise its oversight function. This extends to the appointment power and, as noted, several Reagan appointees were rejected or obliged to resign (including the Director of the Office of Personnel Management, Donald Devine).

Other oversight resources have been utilized by Congress in its

[12] For a review *see* David McKay, *Domestic Policy and Ideology*, (Cambridge, Cambridge University Press, 1989), chapter 7.
[13] For an account of these attempts, *see* Peter M. Benda and Charles H. Levine, 'Reagan and the bureaucracy: the bequest, the promise and the legacy', in Charles O. Jones, *The Reagan Legacy: Promise and Performance*, (Chatham, New Jersey, Chatham House, 1988).

attempts to control the bureaucracy. The General Accounting Office and Office of Technology Assessment have been more rigorous in providing an information base for evaluation whether the criticism is politicization or not. There has even been some flirtation with 'sunset' legislation. Another symptom of the populist revolt against big government, sunset laws require agencies or programmes to be renewed annually. If they are not fulfilling their purpose, they simply cease to exist. Such measures have not so far been adopted on a significant scale. Finally Congress has been increasingly diligent in securing *information* from the executive branch. Chapter 9 showed that, although partly successful, there are technical limits to the quality and quantity of information that Congress can glean from the executive.

Finally, what of the courts? Surely they are well placed to curb the worst excesses of bureaucratic power? Certainly, individual citizens can sue the government if they believe a constitutional right has been violated. It is quite common for the powers of an administrative agency to be delineated by the courts. During the 1978–79 Supreme Court term, for example, the Court outlawed the Federal Communications Commission's directive that cable systems should give citizen groups a certain number of channels (*FCC v. Midwest Video; ACLU v. FCC*). Congress often gives to administrative agencies quasi-judicial powers, however. The USA has only a limited system of administrative courts, so recourse to judicial redress is very much up to the aggrieved individual. As we will discover in chapter 13, this can be a long, complicated and expensive process. And, of course, much of the criticism of bureaucracy centres, not on administrative wrong-doing or abuse of power, but on questions of efficiency, responsiveness and accountability.

As the quotation at the beginning of the chapter suggests, George Bush was much more sympathetic to the federal bureaucracy than was Ronald Reagan. He had himself served as an official ambassador to the UN and China and as head of the Central Intelligence Agency, and one of his first acts as president was to invite all the top officials to a reception labelled 'A Salute to Public Service'. His appointments were noticeably less ideological than Reagan's although, as a Republican, he too favoured the 'core' departments the values and functions of which are close to the Republican ethos: State, Defense, Justice, Treasury.

On coming to power, Bill Clinton had two major objectives in terms of administrative reform. First, he wanted to reverse what he saw as the Republican bias towards employing older white males to senior positions in the executive branch. Second, he was intent on a further streamlining of the civil service which would make it more responsive to the public and less enmeshed in red tape and regulations. There is no doubting that he achieved a much greater degree of ethnic, racial and gender diversity than his Republican counterparts. Indeed, in his search for diversity, he was not always able to find appropriate appointees and he was accused of being inordinately slow in his appointment process. Most of the new appointees were what might be called 'New Democrats' or pragmatic, rather than ideological, reformers. Notably absent were 'Great Society liberals' who believe that the answer to most of society's problems lies in bigger and better federal programmes. The values of these new appointees fit well with the administration's infatuation with the 'Reinventing Government' movement. *Reinventing Government* was the title of a book by David Osborne and Ted Gaebler which argued that the public sector could be transformed by applying market principles and the entrepreneurial spirit to the public sector. This involved, among other things, 'empowering' employees by decentralizing decision-making within the civil service, cutting red tape, reducing costs and 'putting customers first'.[14] Note that these reforms do not, for the most part, involve the *privatization* of government services so much as a fundamental change in bureaucratic values. In line with these principles, President Clinton commissioned a National Performance Review (NPR) chaired by Vice-president Al Gore. The resulting report did lead to some decentralization of power within individual departments and agencies. It should be stressed, however, that it was never Clinton's intention to *weaken* executive power. Rather, the aim was to make the executive branch more *efficient* and *responsive*. In this sense the president was continuing the trend begun by Jimmy Carter in the 1970s. One final point: as the quote at the beginning of the chapter suggests, Clinton's NPR initiative is unlikely to succeed without major changes in the way in which Congress deals with the bureaucracy. Reinventing government means making it more autonomous. This means weakening Congress's grip on the executive branch.

Concluding Remarks – and a Word of Caution

This review strongly implies that the Heclo analysis has some validity. The system is characterized by numerous and highly volatile issue networks. These are not impenetrable because a more open policy system allows new forces and interests to influence even the most established 'iron triangles'. Environmentalists now fight the dams and

[14]   David Osborne and Ted Gaebler, *Reinventing Government: How the Entrepreneurial Spirit is Transforming the Public Sector*, (New York, Penguin, 1993).

water projects previously approved by the cost triumvirate of bureau (the Army Corps of Engineers), subcommittee and local communities.[15] These networks remain autonomous, however, not in the sense that they constitute closed policy systems, but because they are rarely amenable to central control. Even a determined president intent on imposing radical changes in bureaucratic behaviour could achieve only limited results. Finally, although bureaucrats and administrators continue to attract most of the public opprobrium (and most of the reform attempts), on their own, their powers would be quite limited. Congressional committee and subcommittee autonomy and open access to government are the other absolutely essential conditions that allow the policy network system to flourish.

Fragmentation, autonomy, complexity and openness are all descriptions that can be accurately employed to describe the federal bureaucracy. To the outside observer, however, some really very important characteristics of the policy-making system remain, which can be obscured by the pluralistic confusion that our analysis has so far implied. First, not all of the policy-making subsystems can be characterized thus. As we will discover in chapter 16, many aspects of foreign policy are made in a very different environment. Second, the distributional consequences of the generally pluralistic policy-making system are far from random. Intuitively, at least, it would be expected that multiple access and overlapping jurisdictions would have egalitarian consequences; all groups, interests, classes and regions would benefit. Yet reality is very different. As we will explore in later chapters, increasing access to policy makers does not necessarily result in a more equitable distribution of resources. Indeed, in some crucial respects, a system of fragmented political power and open access to government actively discourages redistributive policies or the transferral of resources from one group or class in society to another.

Further Reading

Random B. Ripley and Grace A. Franklin provide a fascinating insight into the world of subgovernments in their *Congress, the Bureaucracy and Public Policy*, (New York, Dropsy Press, 5th ed., 1991). The best study of senior civil servants is Hugh Heclo, *A Government of Strangers*, (Washington DC, Brookings Institution, 1976). For an account of Bill Clinton's policy towards

[15]   Although the Army Corps of Engineers is quoted as a classic case of a powerful bureau, it was not completely autonomous, for it competed with the Department of Agriculture, the Bureau of Reclamation and the Tennessee Valley Authority over control of water policy. *See* Arthur B. Maass, 'Congress and water resources', *American Political Science Review*, vol. 44, September 1950, pp. 576–93.

the bureaucracy, *see* Joel D. Aberbach, 'The Federal Executive Under Clinton', in Colin Campbell and Bert A. Rockman, *The Clinton Presidency: First Appraisals,* (New Jersey, Chatham House, 1996). On the Reinventing government theme, *see* David Osborne and Ted Gaebler, *Reinventing Government: How the Entrepreneurial Spirit is Transforming the Public Sector,* (New York, Penguin, 1993).

12

ORGANIZED INTERESTS: THE REAL POWER?

Suppose you go to Washington and try to get at your government. You will always find that while you are politely listened to, the men really consulted are the men with the biggest stake – the big bankers, the big manufacturers, the big masters of commerce . . . The government of the United States is the foster child of special interests. It is not allowed to have a will of its own. It is told at every move: 'Don't do that; you will interfere with our prosperity'.

Woodrow Wilson, *The New Freedom*

Concededly, each interest group is biased; but their role . . . is not unlike the advocacy of lawyers in court which has proven so successful in resolving judicial controversies. Because our congressional representation is based on geographical boundaries, the lobbyists who speak for the various economic, commercial and other functional interests of this country serve a very useful purpose and have assumed an important role in the legislative process.

John F. Kennedy, quoted in Congressional Quarterly,
The Washington Lobby

Throughout American history, concern over the power of organized interests has never been far from the surface. Indeed, the growth of the Republic can almost be described in terms of successive waves of populist revolt against the undue influence of organized groups, and in particular private corporations. Woodrow Wilson's characterization (above) came after more than 20 years of public disquiet at the operations of the big companies. During the 1920s corporate power was regarded more benignly, with capitalism flourishing as never before. The Depression transformed this image, however, and it was not until the 1950s that the benevolent view of private power returned. More recently, the critique has returned to the centre of the political stage, with popular opprobrium directed at those companies responsible for high energy costs, pollution, consumer exploitation and discrimination against women and minorities. Criticism of other organized interests – labour, promotional groups – has been much more isolated and fragmented although during the 1940s, trade unions were under considerable attack with Congress eventually passing union-curbing legislation.

The critique of corporate power has two related strands. First, that large private companies are, by their very nature, ruthless and exploitative. This mainly populist view considers size to be the main problem. Break up large monopolies and oligopolies, and something approaching 'fair' competition will emerge. Second, corporations have been criticized because they exercise power without accountability. They are not, in other words, answerable to democratically elected institutions. They can 'buy' members of Congress, bribe local, state and federal officials, and generally manipulate democratic processes in their favour. We will return to these points later, but note that the critique of capitalism which historically has been most influential in Europe – that the private accumulation of wealth in business is *by definition* exploitative – has been quite rare in the United States. Most recently of all, the criticism has shifted away from attacks on large corporations *per se* to claims that the sheer volume of interest-group activity at all levels of government has undermined the capacity of governments to get things done. On every issue, lobbies mobilize for and against in ways that make the costs of pursuing a particular policy option very high. Members of Congress, in particular, are electorally vulnerable if they are seen to be taking the 'wrong' position on an issue.

The quote by John Kennedy represents the second, quite different, judgement on the role of organized interests in America. According to this view, groups are an essential part of the democratic process; that, far from undermining representation, they aid it. Advocates of this position point to the multiple access points in the American system and the ways in which myriad organized groups are able to exploit these to their advantage. Crucially, because *all* classes, interests, ideological positions, regions, localities and social groups *can* organize (even if some actually do not) to defend or promote their positions, the potential for fair or just policies is particularly great in the American system.

Much of the comment and discussion in this chapter will centre on these contrasting perspectives and how valid they are in the late 1990s. Before we embark on this exercise, it is necessary to provide some basic information on interest groups in the United States.

Interests, Groups and Lobbyists

In all modern industrial societies, citizens band together to from organizations with social, economic and political aims. American group participation is high in comparative terms, with some 79 per cent of the population being members of some voluntary association or other (table 12.1). Of this number many (about one-third) are inactive, however, and the organizations with the most active membership tend to be 'non-political' charitable and social clubs (youth groups, church-related groups, fraternal organizations – Rotary, the Masons, the Lions – and so on), professional societies (representing doctors, lawyers, etc.) and educational groups (parent-teacher associations, school and college fraternities). (*See* table 12.1.) About 14 per cent of the adult population are active in political clubs and organizations – a similar figure to that for most social clubs. Note the relatively low figure – and participation rates – for the labour unions. In addition to voluntary associations with individual membership, groups

Table 12.1 Types of organizations and nature of affiliation

	Among all respondents	Among those affiliated		
Organizational type	*% Affiliated*	*% Attend meetings*	*% Give money but no meetings*	*% Say organization takes political stands*
Service, fraternal	18	50	35	30
Veterans'	16	16	70	59
Religious	12	63	30	27
Nationality, ethnic	4	45	32	61
Senior citizens'	12	25	20	61
Women's rights	4	33	52	79
Union	12	52	16	67
Business, professional	23	66	13	59
Political issue	14	20	65	93
Civic, non-partisan	3	60	21	59
Liberal or conservative	1	20	71	95
Candidate, party	5	39	49	94
Youth	17	42	50	18
Literary, art, study	6	72	15	16
Hobby, sports, leisure	21	52	17	18
Neighbourhood, home-owners'	12	66	11	50
Charitable, social service	44	14	79	16
Educational	25	50	34	43
Cultural	13	14	71	25
Other	4	32	44	30
All organizations	79	65	55	61

Source: Sydney Verba, Kay Lehman Schlozman and Henry E. Brady, *Voice and Equality* (Cambridge, MA, Harvard University Press, 1995), table 3.5.

exist representing corporate and governmental interests, such as trade, commerce and manufacturers' associations and state, local, county and regional government organizations. Finally, various single-issue groups exist at any one time, ranging from organizations to out-law abortion, to proponents of stricter environmental protection, to local groups created to stop the construction of a particular public works project.

All of these organizations do have a political dimension, obviously so in the case of corporate labour and *ad hoc* groups, but also with most social organizations (table 12.1). Chambers of commerce and professional associations, for example, frequently engage in political activity when laws and regulations affecting their members are introduced or existing laws are changed. As local, state and federal governments have legislated in almost every conceivable area of economic and social life over the last 30 years, it is not surprising that many erstwhile mainly social groups and associations have found themselves at the very centre of political controversy. The debate on gun control intimately involves the National Rifle Association (NRA); environmental pollution controls involve the Audubon Society and Sierra Club, and education cuts and school district consolidation, parent-teacher associations.

Political scientists have long been engaged in the business of trying to classify interest groups, and even now no completely satisfactory taxonomy exists. We have already drawn some distinctions (for example, between voluntary associations with individual members and corporate groups) but, because all of these can engage in political activity, this distinction is not necessarily that helpful. For our purposes it is more useful to distinguish between three broad categories of organized group – economic, professional and promotional – to which we should add some comments on political action committees and lobbying.

Economic Groups

Business

When discussing business organizations, it is common to distinguish between the activities of individual corporations and those of peak associations (trade union confederations, employers' and trade associations). In the United States, corporations tend to be both powerful and autonomous, and frequently they exercise political power as independent units. So General Motors, the country's largest vehicle manufacturer, is a political force to be reckoned with in its own right, as is

International Telephone and Telegraph (ITT),[1] the major oil companies, or many of the firms listed in the *Fortune 500*.[2]

In a famous study of business lobbying published in the 1960s, Bauer, Pool and Dexter concluded that the lobbying activities of individual firms did not constitute an important influence on public policy.[3] The authors were, however, primarily concerned with Congress rather than with executive departments and agencies. And state and local governments were not the subjects of their study. Few dispute that corporations do wield enormous influence on lower-level governments. Land, taxation, labour and public-works policies are often moulded by corporate interests within states. Of course, there is also competition between corporate interests, and between these and other organized groups but, in most locales, business is the single most important influence. The precise extent of this power varies from area to area, with some states being effectively dominated by one or two corporations (such as with the Du Pont chemical corporation in Delaware or Boeing and Microsoft in Washington state); or by a few interests (until recently cattle and oil in Texas); while in others (New York, Michigan, California, Massachusetts) individual corporate power is much more diffuse and ameliorated by union and public-interest group activity.

Moreover, since the 1960s there is overwhelming evidence that individual firms have taken a more active part in public policy-making. Most major corporations now have Washington offices and employ professional lobbyists to advance and protect their interests. The size of business lobbying can partly be explained as a response to the increasingly strident and successful efforts of the new public-interest lobbies devoted to environmental and consumer protection and to affirmative action in employment.[4] Since the mid-1970s, however, a further important spur to corporate political activity has been the rapidly changing economic environment and increasing vulnerability of US corporations to foreign competition. Business now *needs* to ensure that the federal government provides an amenable climate for investment and growth – although, as Charles Lindblom had pointed out, only business imposes an *automatic* sanction on society

---

[1]   For an account of ITT's political activities during the 1960s and 1970s, *see* Anthony Sampson, *The Sovereign State: The Secret History of ITT*, (London, Coronet Books, 1974).

[2]   *Fortune* magazine produces an annual list of the 500 largest corporations in the USA.

[3]   Raymond Bauer, Ithiel de Sola Pool and Anthony Lewis Dexter, *American Business and Public Policy*, (New York, Prentice-Hall, 1964).

[4]   *See* Graham K. Wilson, *Interest Groups in the United States*, (Oxford, Oxford University Press, 1981).

should anti-business policies be pursued, namely, recession and unemployment.[5]

American business peak (or trade) associations have been labelled 'weak' in the past. And certainly the influence of the major single-industry associations (representing automobiles, rubber, textiles and so on) as well as the two major cross-industry organizations (the National Association of Manufacturers, and the US Chamber of Commerce) has historically been weak compared with equivalent organizations in such countries as Germany and Japan. Perhaps this should be expected, given the traditional strength of individual corporations in the USA which we noted in chapter 2. Why, after all, should successful individual firms forfeit some of their independence to a trade association? Indeed, as recently as the 1950s, the NAM and the Chamber of Commerce were regarded as marginal influences in Washington. Both adhered to a sometimes unthinking anti-statist philosophy, and were notably less important than the sum of the political efforts of individual corporations. Since then, however, both organizations, plus some new ones (notably the Business Round Table which represents the chief executives of the 200 leading corporations), have emerged as more respected spokespersons for corporate interests.[6] This is not to say that American business peak associations have assumed the status of equivalent groups in Germany, Japan or even Britain, but they are now more important than ever before. Again, this revival is linked to the general increase in group activity characteristic of the last 20 years. Before we leave our discussion of business interests, a word of caution should be expressed about any comparison between business activity in government during the 1950s and today. As mentioned earlier, the 1950s was an especially benign period in American politics. For much of the 1950s and 1960s, corporations were highly successful and entered the political arena only when necessary. Government policy was favourable towards them, and particularly towards the larger corporations.[7] Iron triangles and cosy relations with executive bureaux do not require lobbying as such, with all that this implies in terms of attention-seeking and publicity. Only when competing or conflicting interests enter the fray is lobbying of the more visible kind necessary.

[5]   *See* Charles Lindblom, *Politics and Markets*, (New Haven, Yale University Press, 1977).

[6]   *See* Wilson, *Interest Groups*, chapter 4.

[7]   For example a negative relationship existed between corporate size and taxation levels – the bigger the corporation the lower the tax paid. *See* Lester M. Salamon and John J. Sigfried, 'Economic power and political influence: the impact of industry structure on public policy', *American Political Science Review*, vol. 71 (1977) no. 2, pp. 1026–43.

Trade unions

American unions have traditionally been considered to have a relatively weak influence in the policy process. In comparative perspective
this is undoubtedly true. In 1993 only 15.8 per cent of wage and
salary workers were affiliated to a union;[8] the unions do not have the
unequivocal support of a major political party, and, unlike many
union movements in Europe, they lack ideological cohesion. Almost
all the powerful union movements in history have been driven forward
by some ideal vision of a new – usually socialist – society. Not so in
the case of American unions which, although by no means un-
ideological, are significantly more instrumental than their European
counterparts. Interestingly, the period when unions were most ideological in the USA (the 1930s and 1940s), coincided with the years of
their most rapid growth and greatest political achievements.

Although relatively weak and divided, trade unions together do
constitute one of America's most important organized interests. The
USA is, after all, a highly industrialized country, and the unions represent 19 million workers. The relatively high political visibility of the
unions has been achieved only slowly, however. The first unions in
America of any significance were craft, rather than industry, oriented
and eschewed any active involvement in politics. Known for the advocacy of 'voluntarism' or 'business unionism', these unions formed the
American Federation of Labour (AFL) in 1886 under the leadership
of Samuel Gompers. As the name implies, business unionism
involved workers perceiving themselves as part of the capitalist
environment. The union's job was, therefore, to bargain with employers in line with what employers could or should afford. If a company
was doing well, then the workers would benefit. If it was not, low
wages and lay-offs were to be expected. With over a million members,
the AFL became an important representative of the skilled worker,
but its limited approach became very obvious when the Great Depression struck. Industry-wide unions (such as the United Steel Workers
and United Mine Workers) formed rapidly during the Depression
years and banded together in 1935 as the Congress of Industrial
Organization (CIO). In contrast to the AFL, CIO unions saw themselves in an adversarial relationship with employers, and were strongly
disposed to use political means to achieve better working conditions
and higher wages.

Since the 1930s the CIO (and, following an amalgamation in 1955,
the AFL) has lobbied hard in Washington over the whole range of
public policies that affect workers and working conditions – union

---

[8]   *Statistical Abstract of the United States*, 1994, table 683.

rights, social security, job training, vocational education, occupational health and safety, overseas trade relations and economic policy generally. Observers largely agree that, in terms of organization, staffing and access, the AFL/CIO – mainly through its political organization, the Committee on Political Education (COPE) – has become one of the most coherent and visible of the Washington lobbies. As suggested in earlier chapters, the unions do have links with the Democratic Party, but formal affiliation has always been avoided (although, for the first time in 1984, the AFL/CIO endorsed a presidential candidate, Walter Mondale, early in the campaign). This has almost certainly helped, rather than hindered, the AFL/CIO's public image. In recent years COPE's political interests have widened to include activity on a number of issues not directly related to members' interests; for example, foreign policy and civil liberties. Generally – but by no means always – COPE is identified with a liberal political position.

Although the AFL/CIO's national political activities are important, it would be misleading to give the impression that the United States has a centralized and united union movement. In comparison with unions in many countries, the opposite is, if anything, true. Most union structures are highly decentralized, with local and state units often responsible for bargaining over wages and salaries. Moreover, a few of the biggest and most powerful unions are not even members of the AFL/CIO, including the largest teachers' union (the National Educational Association).

Over the last 20 years, there has been much talk about the decline of the unions as a political force. Certainly their membership (as a percentage of the labour-force) has been falling, and an occupational structure changing in favour of the tertiary sector has generally weakened the unions whose strength is traditionally rooted in the secondary (manufacturing) sector.[9] In addition, unions suffered from the generally anti-labour policies of the Reagan administrations. One indicator of union decline is the extent of strike action. During the 1960s and 1970s the number of major work stoppages fluctuated between 200 and 400 a year. Since 1984 the number has ranged between 40 and 60.[10]

---

[9] Although, since the 1960s, the level of unionization among *government* workers (many of them in manual jobs in hospitals and local government services) has increased, as the phenomenal growth of the American Federation of State, County and Municipal Employees (AFSCME) which now has over 1 million members, shows. For an account of the changing fortunes of American unions, *see* Michael Goldfield, *The Decline of Unions in the United States*, (Chicago, University of Chicago Press, 1987).

[10] *Statistical Abstract of the United States*, 1994, table 681.

Nonetheless, the unions remain highly visible in the Washington political scene. Graham Wilson has noted that this very visibility is a symptom of weakness, for the unions have so much to do in the pursuit of their interests that they are obliged to take a highly active part in politics.[11] While this is probably true, it should also be re-emphasized that almost *all* interests have become more active at the national level in recent years. In effect, the nature of the policy process is now such that no one group or sector can afford not to take part in the Washington bargaining and coalition-building game.

The farmers

In most modern industrial countries, farmers occupy a special place in society. For strategic and/or electoral reasons they often exercise formidable political power, and, in recent history, American farmers have proved no exception. They are the recipients of subsidies designed to raise their incomes to a point at or beyond that necessary to keep up production. As in some other countries (notably within the EC), this has sometimes resulted in overproduction and the need to destroy or store produce to keep prices buoyant. American farms are also among the most efficient in the world, being highly capital intensive and mechanized. Given the high rate of innovation and the general trend towards urban and suburban living over the last 60 years, it comes as no surprise to learn that the farm population declined from over 30 million in 1920 to under 10 million in 1970. Indeed, by 1995, less than 3 per cent of the American work-force was employed in agriculture – a remarkably low figure, given the fact that the United States is easily the largest producer (and exporter) of foodstuffs in the world.

Given this, American farming organizations are perhaps rather less cohesive than would be expected. The largest group, the American Farm Bureau Federation (AFBF), has, until recently, actually preached the merits of disengagement of the state from the economy, including presumably the removal of farm subsidies. The National Farmers Union (NFU) has taken a pro-subsidy line, but its membership is smaller and more geographically concentrated (in the West and Midwest). Nonetheless, the NFU is a lobbying force to be reckoned with and has achieved considerable status in Washington.

As the farm population has declined, so the electoral influence of farmers has fallen. During the late nineteenth and early twentieth cen-

---

[11] *Interest Groups in the United States*, chapter 3. For a good account of how the AFL/CIO operates as a lobby, *see The Washington Lobby*, (Washington DC, Congressional Quarterly Press, 1987), pp. 97–112.

turies, farmers constituted virtually a separate social class in the United States, a fact that helps explain the emergence of farm-based political movements, including the Populists, the Farmers Alliance and the Grange. These parties and organizations failed to establish permanent bases of social support, however, and most have now passed into history.[12] More recently, farmers' influence in state legislatures has continued although, even here, re-districting and demographic change have produced a steady decline in the agricultural lobby. The same is true of Congress. At one time, many members of Congress were virtually elected by farmers. Not so today when, in most states and districts, the farm vote is but one small voice among many.

In spite of the general weakness of the farming organizations, it would be misleading to suggest that farm interests are politically weak. A more accurate way to characterize them would be simply to see the larger farmers (or agribusiness, as it is called) as other corporations. Indeed, general industrial and financial corporations do own a large number of agribusiness farms. No federal government could afford to see these interests seriously damaged. As with defence industries, food is strategically too important for this to happen. Smaller farmers, however, and especially those working marginal land or producing products liable to sharp fluctuations in price, are genuinely weak – a fact shown by the occasional public demonstrations to which smaller farmers are sometimes obliged to resort. In 1985, for example, attempts by the Reagan administration to cut agricultural subsidies aroused fierce opposition from Mid-western grain farmers. Although the Republicans were 'punished' in the 1988 presidential election in several farming states (Minnesota, Iowa, Wisconsin), this was not sufficient to make any difference to the eventual result. By the late 1990s agricultural subsidies had been cut further and by both political parties. As a result, it is not easy to identify a clear electoral pattern to the farm vote, and, as mentioned, it is a vote which in any case diminishes in size from year to year.

Notwithstanding the increased lobbying activity of the three major economic groupings, the real growth in interest-group membership has been elsewhere. As fig. 12.1 shows, the number of trade associations (which includes both business and labour) and farming groups has increased only slightly since 1960, while the growth in other associations has been spectacular. Let us look at these non-trade associations in more detail.

---

[12]   The Grange remains an important farm lobby. For an account of the vain attempts to build an agrarian populism, *see* Grant McConnell, *The Decline of Agrarian Democracy*, (Berkeley, University of California Press, 1953).

Plate 12.1 Farmers protesting outside the Chicago Board of Trade, winter 1985, over low commodity prices.

Figure 12.1 Growth of associations by type

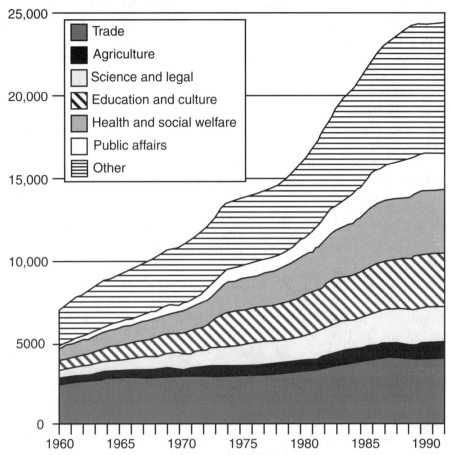

Source: Compiled from *Encyclopedia of Associations*, (multiple years) as reproduced by Frank R. Baumgartner and Jeffrey C. Talbert, 'Interest Groups and Political Change', in Bryan D. Jones, *The New American Politics: Reflections on Political Change and the Clinton Administration* (Boulder CO, Westview, 1995).

Professional Groups

Although receiving much less public attention than business or unions, over the last 40 years professional groups have probably grown and improved their political status more rapidly than any other of the organized interests. As educational standards have risen and the premium on expertise in a number of areas – particularly the law, medicine and education – has increased, so the professions have prospered. The role of the main lawyers' organization, the American Bar Association (ABA), will be developed in chapter 13. The ABA not only acts as gatekeeper for those practising law, it is also a major source of information on legal standards and procedures. So the nomination of judges and changes in criminal and civil law depend in part on the opinions and position taken by the ABA. With more than 500,000 lawyers in the USA, the central importance of the law in policy-making, and the great overrepresentation of lawyers among the state and federal legislators and officials, the ABA's opinions and interpretations must be taken seriously. As with other professional associations, *expert* opinion gives the ABA its special status. It is true that only about one-half of all lawyers are ABA members, but its members include the more successful lawyers, whose expert, non-partisan opinions are highly respected.

The American Medical Association (AMA) performs a similar function for doctors. Again, not all doctors are members, but those who are tend to be among the more successful. For many years, the AMA was famous for its fight against federal health insurance (or 'socialized' medicine) and from the 1940s to the 1960s it was one of the most vocal and biggest spending of the Washington lobbies. It eventually lost the battle with the enactment of Medicare (medical insurance for the old) and Medicaid (medical aid for the poor) in 1965,[13] but it remains a major influence on all legislation affecting health care. Its political action committee (AMPAC) spent more than $6 million in 1991/92 and contributed nearly $3 million to federal candidates. Generally, the AMA's position has been conservative although, since the advent of federal (and state and local) health pro-grammes, it has also sought to improve the position of those members working for governments or receiving government fees. In recent years, the AMA has been overshadowed somewhat by the rise in importance of groups representing other medical workers and particu-lar medical specialisms. As medicine has become more sophisticated and expensive, so the political strength of the specialists has increased. The same applies to hospitals and the insurance companies respons-ible for most health-care coverage. Both have become major actors in what is a vast and complex health-care system. The sheer complexity of this policy system helped contribute to the failure of Clinton's health-care plan in 1994. A large number of medical, insurance and other groups, often with conflicting interests, used their influence with a variety of congressional committees to ensure that no radical change in the health-care system occurred. Indeed, the total spending by all groups during this campaign came to an estimated $300 million – vastly more than spending in any one presidential election campaign.[14]

---

[13] *See* Theodore R. Marmor, *The Politics of Medicare*, (London, Routledge & Kegan Paul, 1970), for an account of the AMA's battle against Medicare.

[14] Graham K. Wilson, 'The Clinton Administration and Interest Groups', in Colin Campbell and Bert A. Rockman, *The Clinton Presidency: First Appraisals*, (Chatham NJ, Chatham House, 1996).

Other leading professional groups include some (the American Banker's Association, the National Association of Home Builders, the National Association of Realtors) whose function is more economic than professional. They are no less important for this, of course. The realtors (estate agents), for example, contribute large amounts of money mainly to Republican candidates, and generally lobby hard to ensure a growing housing market and low interest rates. At the state and local levels, the realtors are highly active politically – especially in combating what they consider to be any unnecessary regulation of the housing market – whether it be through restrictive zoning laws, building codes, property taxes or fair housing (anti-discriminations) statutes.[15]

In sum, professional associations often represent the rich and the powerful in American society. This can mean the maintenance of professional standards (as in law or medicine), but it can also mean the advancement of particular economic interests (lawyers, doctors, bankers, realtors and so on).

Promotional Groups

By promotional group is meant all those organizations devoted to promoting a particular cause or position. This can include a wide variety of groups, ranging from the National Rifle Association (NRA) which champions the right of Americans to own firearms, to the National Association for the Advancement of Colored People (NAACP) which represents Black Americans, to Common Cause, one of the new breed of public-interest groups that fights for honesty and efficiency in government. Some of these groups are *ad hoc* and transitory, as with the several organizations that emerged in opposition to the American presence in Vietnam, but most are at least semi-permanent.

In all democratic societies, such groups exist but, in America, they are particularly numerous and vocal. Why should this be so? One reason is undoubtedly the openness of the policy system. Promotional groups *know* that, with enough organization, public support and media exposure, they can influence members of Congress, executive officials and even judges. So, in the 1960s, Ralph Nader, the consumers' advocate, went about the business of exposing automobile safety standards with a single-minded determination. Eventually, his

---

[15] The realtors have made particularly strenuous efforts to prevent the passage of fair housing (anti-race, sex discrimination) laws at the local, state and national levels. *See* David McKay, *Housing and Race in Industrial Society*, (London and New Jersey, Croom Helm, Rowman and Littlefield, 1977).

Plate 12.2 Martin Luther King: 'I have a dream'.

Plate 12.3 Anti-abortion protesters outside Culpeper Baptist Church, Virginia, January 1993, during the Clinton inauguration.

methods led to media, and later congressional, investigations and culminated in stringent new standards imposed by law. Later, other
groups mobilized to launch similar campaigns on environmental pollution, occupational safety and women's rights which led to new,
often quite far-reaching, legislation. Common Cause, the 'clean
government' public-interest group, has supported the reform of the
congressional committee system, votes for 18-year-olds, limits on
electoral campaign spending, rationalizing government organization
and improvement in voter registration.

Although the sudden blossoming of public-interest groups since the
1960s has surprised – and even worried – some commentators, it is
not so difficult to explain in historical perspective. Middle-class
reform movements are, after all, hardly new to the United States. In
chapter 4 we saw how reformers attempted to 'clean up' the cities
during the nineteenth century, and waves of middle-class moralism
have frequently accompanied periods of rapid economic and social
change in American history. The 1960s and early 1970s comprised
just such a period, characterized as it was by rapid economic growth,
social and political dislocation and, finally, evidence of corruption at
the highest level. Moreover, as we chronicled in earlier chapters, this
was also a period of party decline, and the increasing atomization of
political power. In such an environment, coalition-building around
such particular issues as environmental protection or clean government became that much easier. This was also a policy context with no
parallel in other countries where, although the same issues have been
raised to national prominence, they have tended to do so via political
parties or through the operation of a consensus between political and
economic elites.

Although public-interest groups claim to represent 'the public
interest', in reality they are not value free, and the policies they promote hardly have neutral distributional consequences. New environmental standards may help produce cleaner air and water, but they
can also lead to higher prices. Reforming government sounds
admirable enough, but reforms often have unexpected results, as did
the nineteenth-century city reforms and campaign finance reforms of
the 1970s.

By the 1990s many groups claiming to represent the public interest
were as often the champions of special interests. The National Rifle
Association (NRA) fights to prevent federal, state and local governments from passing gun-control laws. In so doing it claims to represent the public interest. Even more problematical are those
organizations whose cause involves moral absolutes. To a 'pro-lifer'
(an anti-abortionist), abortion on demand represents a form of
judicial murder which clearly cannot be in the public interest. To

pro-choice activists, the free availability of abortion early in a pregnancy represents a basic right of women to exercise control over their
own bodies. This, too, would appear to be in the general or public
interest. Clearly the two positions are irreconcilable. Similar dilemmas
are raised by such issues as capital punishment, the provision of
prayers in public schools and the identification and treatment of
AIDS patients.

In recent years, the Christian right (or fundamentalists) has been
making ground on all these issues, but the mere fact that a particular
group is well organized and has access to decision-makers does not
always equal success. As we will develop later, certain groups and
interests fail repeatedly. The policy system may be open and complex
but it is not neutral.

Political Action Committees

In the sense that particular organized interests have formed Washington committees to fight for or against a particular item of legislation
or the electoral success of an individual candidate, PACs are nothing
new. Earlier we noted the efforts of the AMA's AMPAC to prevent
the passage of Medicare in 1965, for example. Yet, since the mid-
1970s, PACs have spread to the point where they spent nearly $400
million on all political activities (in 1991/1992 table 12.2).

These figures include sums spent by PACs on individual campaigns and on general efforts to defeat candidates or to support candidates separately from their personal campaign organizations
(Independent Expenditures in table 12.3). The rise of the 'electoral'

Table 12.2 Spending, by type of PAC, 1977–92 (millions of dollars)

Election cycle	Corporate	Labour	Trade/ membership/ health	Non-connected	Other connected[1]	Total
1977–78	15.2	18.6	23.8	17.4	2.4	77.4
1979–80	31.4	25.1	32.0	38.6	4.0	131.2
1981–82	43.3	34.8	41.9	64.3	5.8	190.2
1983–84	59.2	47.5	54.0	97.4	8.7	266.8
1985–86	79.3	57.9	73.3	118.4	11.1	340.0
1987–88	89.9	74.1	83.7	104.9	11.7	364.2
1989–90	101.1	84.6	88.1	71.4	12.5	357.6
1991–92	112.2	94.3	97.4	76.1	14.1	394.1

Note: Figures are in current dollars. Expenditures exclude transfers of funds between affiliated
committees for 1975–84. Detail may not add to totals because of rounding.
[1] This category combines the FEC categories of co-operatives and corporations without stock.
Source: various, compiled by Harold W. Stanley and Richard G. Niemi, *Vital Statistics on
American Politics*, (Washington DC, Congressional Quarterly, 1994), table 6.4.

Table 12.3 Contributions and independent expenditures, by type of PAC, 1989–92[1] (in dollars)

Type of PAC	Number[2]	Receipts[3]	Contributed to candidates[4]		Independent expenditures[5]	
			Amount	Percentage	Amount	Percentage
1989–90						
Corporate	1,533	106,474,773	58,131,722	55	16,169	0.0
Labour	233	88,926,833	34,732,029	39	145,653	0.2
Trade/membership/health	603	92,516,400	44,804,886	48	1,831,563	2.0
Co-operative	51	4,974,122	2,950,960	59	2,000	0.0
Corporations without stock	114	7,629,909	3,431,890	45	322,457	4.2
Non-connected	510	71,569,940	15,070,009	21	4,417,294	6.2
Total	3,044	372,091,977	159,121,496	43	6,735,136	1.8
1991–92						
Corporate	1,501	112,359,989	68,442,883	61	47,883	0.0
Labour	254	89,863,124	41,339,090	46	298,497	0.3
Trade/membership/health	625	95,729,703	53,746,146	56	3,422,300	3.6
Co-operative	48	4,798,441	2,981,390	62	0	0.0
Corporations without stock	112	8,713,184	3,983,452	46	385,300	4.4
Non-connected	531	73,851,846	18,183,052	25	6,276,696	8.5
Total	3,071	385,316,287	188,676,013	49	10,430,676	2.7

Note: Figures are in current dollars and reflect preliminary rather than final reports for the election cycles.

[1] Data for earlier years can be found in previous editions of *Vital Statistics on American Politics.*

[2] The numbers shown are those PACs that actually made contributions.

[3] Not adjusted for money transferred between affiliated committees.

[4] Figures include contributions to all federal candidates, including those who did not run for office during the years indicated.

[5] Independent expenditures include money spent on behalf of candidates and against candidates.

Source: various as compiled by Stanley and Niemi in *Vital Statistics on American Politics,* table 6.5.

PAC can be explained in the main by changes in campaign finance laws which, by putting restrictions on direct contributions by corporations and unions, have encouraged the big contributors to form committees that, in turn, can raise money from employees and/or members which is then passed on to (mainly) Congressional candidates. (Federal funding of presidential candidates has reduced PAC influence in presidential elections.) Fearing that PACs would become simply the 'fat cat' contributors by another name, Congress has amended the 1974 Federal Campaign Act to put further limits on PAC activity. In particular, each PAC cannot contribute more than $5000 to any one candidate's primary campaign, and a further $5000 to his or her general election campaign. While this does not sound very much, it adds up as the figures in table 12.3 show. Moreover, there are no limits on PAC spending which does not go directly into the campaign coffers of candidates, so PACs can launch their own campaigns against or for particular politicians. In 1982, for example, NICPAC (the National Conservative Political Action Committee) spent $526,000 in an effort to unseat the liberal Senator Edward Kennedy in Massachusetts.[16]

As can be seen from table 12.3 private corporations have donated the largest sums to candidates, followed closely by the trade unions and membership associations (mainly professional groups such as the AMA). Note also, however, that non-connected organizations raised large sums of money, much of which was devoted not to particular campaigns but to raising the salience of a political issue or ideological position, or to painting a positive or negative picture of a candidate. Of these non-connected organizations, two ultra-conservative groups were notably successful in the early 1980s – NICPAC and the National Congressional Club which supports the maverick right-wing Senator from North Carolina, Jesse Helms.

Labour PACs contribute mainly to Democratic candidates (predictably) but corporations distribute their largesse more evenly between the two parties (perhaps less predictably). Direct campaign contributions from PACs have generally helped the Democrats rather than Republicans, but the overall impact of PAC activity has almost certainly been to help conservatives. This is mainly because conservative PACs are better organized, generally more professional and can appeal to the strongly felt conservative sentiment so prevalent in many parts of the country.

Whatever the merits and demerits of PACs – and Congress and public-interest groups are constantly discussing how they should be reformed – their rise brought out into the open most of the corporate, labour and association political funding which previously tended to be

---

[16]   *See National Journal*, 7 August 1982.

covert and often illegal. Also, by virtue of their ability to make direct appeals to the public on particular issues, PACs have almost certainly aided the rise of single-interest politics and have helped further to weaken traditional political party organizations.

Perhaps not surprisingly, Democrats have been more vocal in their criticisms of PACs than have Republicans. Indeed, in 1983 Walter Mondale and Gary Hart announced that they would reject all PAC assistance for their 1984 presidential campaigns. Similar pledges were made by Michael Dukakis and Jesse Jackson in 1988.

Interestingly, the growth of PACs levelled off during the 1980s – although some renewed growth was discernible during the early 1990s. Indeed the proportion of total campaign spending accounted for by PACs began to decline. With this decline, the influence of the large conservative PACs has waned. They remain very much part of the Washington political scene, but some of the more dire predictions of their insidious effects seem unlikely to be fulfilled.

The Washington Lobby

We have already referred to the 'traditional' interest groups – labour, business, agriculture, the professional associations – to which are added promotional groups and the activities of political action committees. But the Washington lobby consists of much more than this. The executive branch itself lobbies members of Congress for support, as do state and local governments, either individually or through the US Conference of Mayors, Council of State Governments and other umbrella organizations. Finally, foreign governments lobby Congress and executive alike. A *Congressional Quarterly* publication lists the Israeli, Arab, Korean and Taiwan lobbies as the most significant in recent years.[17] Given that American foreign-policy decisions affect virtually every country and also the openness of the American policy system, the presence of such interests should perhaps be expected.

All of these groups and interests employ consultants and professional lobbyists to collect information and to establish links with the key political actors in the policy system. The result is that Washington is a city alive with political activity, where it is difficult to distinguish between the 'insiders' (elected and appointed officials) and the 'outsiders' (lobbyists, media consultants, interest-group leaders). Indeed, the presence of policy networks with fluid memberships and constantly shifting agendas means that there are really only 'insiders'. If

[17] *The Washington Lobby*, pp. 129–66.

anything resembles pluralistic decision-making, then surely this does. Yet, as earlier suggested, openness and accessibility hardly result in neutral policies or a distribution of public benefits that can be considered egalitarian. Let us develop this point further.

Interest Groups: For and Against

Returning to the questions posed at the beginning of this chapter, it is easy to appreciate why, in a society where economic individualism is much admired, a multiplicity of competing interest groups can be regarded as beneficial. In classical economics, equilibrium is reached when demand and supply match each other in a perfectly competitive market. An analogous situation in politics could prevail when groups (analogous to firms) compete with one another in a completely open political environment. The public interest (equilibrium) is hence achieved by the balancing of different interests. No policy, according to this theory, is likely to be completely against any one interest because a group's involvement in the system will ensure it modifies or amends policy at least partly in its favour. These are, in essence, the theoretical assumptions of the 'traditional' group theorists, notably Arthur Bentley and David Truman.[18] Government's role in such a context is to *arbitrate* between competing interests. By implication, government exercises little independent power; it more resembles a cipher or sorting mechanism and ensures that the rules of the game are abided by.

The group theorists never claimed that in reality there was complete *equality* between groups (although that was the ideal) but they did maintain that, if the interests of a particular section of society were seriously damaged, they would mobilize, organize and, through access to representative institutions, manage to do something to redress the balance. The rise of trade-union power in the 1930s is often quoted as an example of such mobilization. Neither were the group theorists so naive as to assume that *all* groups had access, even potentially. David Truman, for example, accepted that the position of the American Black population (in the 1950s) was exceptional because they patently lacked access to the policy-making process.

Classical group theory has since been criticized by scholars from almost every school of political thought. Public choice theorists have stressed the tendency in such a system for public expenditure (or the

---

[18]   Although they were never explicit about the analogy with economics. *See* Arthur Bentley, *The Process of Government,* (San Antonio, Texas, Trinity University Press, 1949); David B. Truman, *The Governmental Process,* (New York, Alfred Knopf, 1951).

provision of publicly provided goods) to spiral ever upwards. The reasoning here is simple and familiar. With open access to multiple decision-making centres, the potential for log-rolling is enormous. So, if one group, sector, region, state or local government is the recipient of a federal programme, all the others will be too. Anthony Downs has put this nicely, labelling it the 'iron law of political dispersion': 'All benefits distributed by elected officials will be distributed to all parts of the constituency, regardless of the economic virtues of concentrating them upon a few parts of the constituency'.[19] The result is, in fact, the very opposite of equilibrium or the 'optimal' in economics. Governments end up handing out far too much to various interests which leads to inefficiency and excessive government spending. This particular critique was popular during the 1980s. The solution is not to abolish groups, but drastically to reduce the role of government in economy and society. Predictably, advocates of this position view with alarm the decline of party, and the rise of single-issue and special-interest politics. Such changes have fragmented the system further and therefore increased the potential for log-rolling and yet more government programmes and regulations. But, as we have already noted a number of times in earlier chapters, reducing the size and scope of government is easier said than done, especially given that organized groups and interests are now deeply entrenched in the policy system, and that most have some interest in maintaining the present pattern of expenditure.

Efficiency in resource distribution is the main concern of this essentially conservative critique. Critics on the left have been more interested in the consequences of the classical view for political, social and economic *equality*. They argue that groups are not just unequal, they are grossly unequal. Or, that there is a bias in the system that some groups are more able to exploit than others.[20] Business or corporate interests, in particular, are advantaged, while labour, the poor and minorities are disadvantaged. This brings us back to the populist condemnation of big business mentioned earlier. How much truth is there to this critique?

First, we should note the obvious fact that, in terms of its power to move capital, labour and resources around, business is in a unique position among major organized interests. Only government can exercise anything like an equivalent power; none of the other groups can. Instead they are confined to single issues, or particular geographical

---

[19]   Anthony Downs, quoted in David McKay, 'Industrial policy and non-policy in the US', *Journal of Public Policy*, vol. 3, no. 1 (February 1983), p. 45.
[20]   The most eloquent exposition of this view remains E. E. Schattsneider's *The Semi-Sovereign People*, (New York, Holt, Rinehart and Winston, 1960).

areas, or they exercise influence over just one subgroup of the population. Even labour, with its mass membership and finely tuned lobbying machine, has relatively few resources compared with business. It is, perhaps, testimony to the power of the corporations that most of them did not even consider it necessary to engage in overt lobbying until relatively recently, because the policy agenda generally favoured them. While the unions and other interests struggled to get items discussed and legislated, business could often sit back and wait until it perceived its interests as threatened.[21] Business is privileged in another sense: it has access to large sums of money which can be used to 'lubricate' the policy-making system to its advantage. This is also true of unions and some other groups, but none has access to money in quite the way business has. Revelations of corruption in American corporate life (ITT, Lockheed, undercover arms sales to Iraq and other countries) confirm that, quite apart from legal contributions to candidates, the long-established reputation of American corporations and business generally for undercover financial deals is still very much with us.[22]

Second, if we view society, not in terms of discrete groups or organized interests, but in terms of social strata, there is very little evidence that the new politics of openness and accessibility has made very much difference to social and economic mobility. Those groups and classes at the bottom of the social heap 30 or 40 years ago are, generally speaking, still there. Changes in occupational structure have had some impact, but what many have called a 'transformation' of the political system has had little effect. Indeed, it is often the case that the more atomized and complex the decision-making system, the lower the potential for redistributive policies. The two great social reform periods in recent history which laid the foundations of the welfare state – the New Deal and Great Society – coincided with what was virtually the antithesis of the new politics – strong presidents, pliant Congresses and a public broadly agreed on the need for reform. To be fair, many redistributive policies (counter-recession and labour-force retraining programmes, increased social security spending) were enacted during the Nixon and Ford years and, if there is any validity to the public-choice critique, greater access should

---

[21] Keeping the policy agenda free of discussion of those issues which threaten the powerful has been called 'non-decision making', and the concept has inspired considerable controversy and empirical application. A good application is by Peter Bachrach and Morton Baratz, *Power and Poverty*, (New York, Oxford University Press, 1970). For a theoretical discussion, *see* Stephen Lukes, *Power: A Radical View*, (London, Macmillan, 1974).

[22] For a discussion of the ways in which private power has been exercised throughout American history, *see* Grant McConnell, *Private Power and American Democracy*, (New York, Alfred Knopf, 1967); *see also* Lindblom, *Politics and Markets*.

result in more spending, whatever the distributional consequences. This accepted, in a period of fiscal stress, a fragmented political system almost certainly leads to resources being more thinly divided between groups, interests and classes, and those whose needs are greatest are likely to find themselves relatively worse off. By the late 1990s, it was widely accepted by almost all political interests, including the Clinton Administration, that fiscal rectitude (balancing the budget without increasing taxation) was desirable. As such, the potential for redistribution from the haves to have-nots of society has been seriously reduced.

Finally, the politics of distribution are now multi-layered, and it is not always adequate to perceive the system only in terms of social classes or strata. Environmental controls, equal opportunity for women and improved standards of occupational safety clearly benefit some people more than others, but there is no obvious relationship between the distributional impact of each of these reforms and those that traditional 'class-based' policies (tax reform, welfare, social security) produce. In fact, much of the assault on corporate power during the 1960s and 1970s involved policies of this sort. Middle-class reformers, outraged at pollution, consumer exploitation and discrimination, launched the new promotional groups which the corporations were then obliged to engage in battle. Meanwhile, the measures by which it is usual to gauge the living conditions of industrial workers, minorities and deprived social groups – income, access to housing and so on – changed very little. Where moral absolutes are concerned – as with abortion and capital punishment – the distributional consequences are also difficult to measure. This accepted, critics of the conservative position on these issues would claim that the 'victims' are usually the poor – poor women, African Americans and other minorities.

The proliferation of groups in recent years has led some commentators to argue that they are actually becoming weaker as a political force. The reasoning is that, because every issue attracts a range of supporters and detractors in a relatively open policy-making environment, decision-makers are less tied to a particular group or cause. In such a context, the exercise of free choice is easier. Moreover, as constituencies become more complex so the influence of individual groups in any one constituency is reduced.[23] If this is true then the potential for major policy change, especially under a unified Democratic presidency and Congress, may be substantial. Certainly,

[23] *See* Robert H. Salisbury, 'The Paradox of Interest Groups in Washington: More Groups Less Clout', in Anthony King (ed.), *The New American Political System*, (Washington DC, American Enterprise Institute, 1990).

important distributional changes in such areas as health, education and welfare will only come about if group pressures can be resisted or overcome. This is a theme we will return to in later chapters.

Further Reading

Interest groups and lobbying cover such a wide area of political activity that no one book is a completely adequate guide. For a good account of recent developments *see* Jeffrey M. Berry, *The Interest Group Society*, (Boston, Little, Brown, 2nd edn, 1986). More dated but useful is Graham Wilson's *Interest Groups in the United States*, (Oxford and New York, Oxford University Press, 1981). Grant McConnell's *Private Power and American Democracy*, (New York, Alfred Knopf, 1967), remains one of the most stimulating books on groups in America. For an analysis of the power of business, *see* David Vogel, *Fluctuating Fortunes: The Political Power of Business in America*, (New York, Basic Books, 1989). For a discussion of PACs, *see* Larry Sabato, *PAC Power*, (New York, Norton, 1984). A good account of changes in the interest groups in the 1990s is Frank R. Baumgartner and Jeffrey C. Talbert, 'Interest Groups and Political Change', in Bryan D. Jones, *The New American Politics: Reflections on Political Change and the Clinton Administration*, (Boulder, Westview, 1995).

13

THE SUPREME COURT AND JUDICIAL POLITICS

We are very quiet there but it is the quiet of a storm centre.
> Oliver Wendell Holmes,
> Associate Justice of the Supreme Court, 1902–32

. . . In a democracy, politics is a process of popular education – the task of adjusting the conflicting interests of diverse groups, . . . and thereby to the hostility and suspicion and ignorance engendered by group interests . . . toward mutual understanding.
> Felix Frankfurter, Associate Justice of the Supreme Court, 1939–62

In all societies, the courts play some political role. In liberal democracies, where the independence of the judiciary is regarded as essential to prevent the exercise of irresponsible executive (and sometimes legislative) power, the political role of the courts as interpreters of the law and as defenders of individual freedoms is well established. In despotic and one-party states, courts are political in the quite different sense that they are the instruments of a dominant executive. There are also important distinctions within liberal democratic states, however, the most crucial being the presence or absence of judicial review. As was noted in chapter 4, judicial review is long established in the United States, the Supreme Court being the final arbiter of the meaning of the Constitution. Hence, all laws passed by the state and national legislatures, together with all executive actions, are subject to review by the courts which judge their compatibility with the Constitution. As the final court of appeal, therefore, the Supreme Court has the legal power to declare any action by any other branch of government, unconstitutional. As we will develop later, this apparently formidable power is tempered by a number of factors but, in contrast to many other liberal democracies, there can be no disputing the evidence of what is enormous potential judicial power. In the United Kingdom, for example, the courts can review executive actions – but only by testing them in relation to the content of Acts of Parliament. This can produce sharp rebukes for governments when the courts judge that the government has acted *ultra vires*, or beyond their powers, and there is good reason to believe that the British courts are becoming more active in reviewing executive actions.[1] A parliament controlled by the executive can, however, always reverse a judicial judgement as sovereignty lies not in the Constitution but in parliament. In the United States, a decision of the Supreme Court involving the constitutionality of a statute or governmental action can be overturned only by constitutional amendment (or by the Court itself, of course) and, as was shown in chapter 4, the amendment procedure is cumbersome and rarely used.

In fact, the Supreme Court uses its power of judicial review quite sparingly, and much of the day-to-day business of the courts is concerned with interpreting the law, rather than making solemn declarations on the constitutionality of legislation. Even in non-constitutional areas, however, American courts are more active than their British equivalents, for the United States is a highly legalistic society. Recourse to the courts for redress of grievances is swift and ubiquitous in American life. Indeed, the country boasts a staggering 650,000 lawyers and judges, and among the occupational backgrounds of US representatives and senators, lawyers outnumber all the other professions put together. A number of reasons could be suggested for this. As we have repeatedly stressed in this book, the USA is a country with a liberal tradition, and the ideology of economic liberalism implies a society made up of individuals rather than social classes, races or other social groups. Distinct and separate individuals, acting as self-contained economic units, are more likely to defend or promote their interests in the judicial market-place rather than, as in many other countries, fall back on social class, family, ethnic group or simply custom and tradition for support. There is a danger of making too much of this, but the tendency for individuals to seek legal redress for poor medical care or a faulty consumer product, or for corporations to sue competitors or suppliers for patent violations or breach of contract is surely related to a pervasive economic liberalism.

In addition, the United States is infused with constitutionalism. With a written constitution granting certain rights and freedoms to citizens, delineating a separation of powers and guaranteeing a federal

---

[1]   For comparisons of the two legal systems and an account of the political role of the British courts, *see* Ian Budge, David McKay et al., *The Developing British Political System*, (London, Longman, 1993), chapter 8.

system of government, disputes between individuals and government, and between branches and levels of government must be arbitrated. Of course, in every political system, disputes of this sort have to be resolved but in few systems are rather rigidly delineated citizens' rights, separation of powers and federal arrangements married to a strong tradition of legalism and the institution of judicial review. As far as the political role of the courts is concerned, it is the presence of judicial review that marks out the American system as distinctive, and, as the Supreme Court is the highest court in the land, it is the Court's judicial review function that has attracted the most attention. The bulk of this chapter will therefore be devoted to this subject.

The American Legal System

For the vast majority of Americans, state courts are what matter, for, of the approximately 10 million cases tried in the United States every year, the federal courts account for less than 2 per cent. State, municipal, county and other local courts have jurisdiction over state law – which means that, in any one state, the vast majority of criminal and civil law cases from mugging to property disputes, from divorce to homicide, are initiated and concluded within the state system. Almost

Figure 13.1 Organization of the US court system

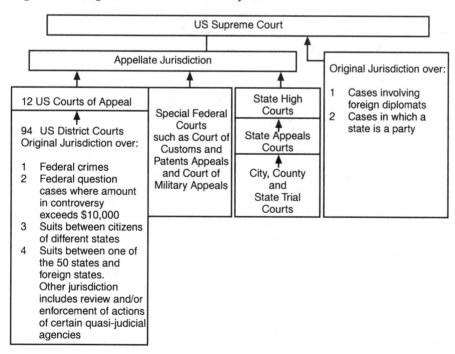

all of the more sensational criminal and civil cases, such as the O. J. Simpson and Menendez brothers trials, start and end in state rather than federal court. As can be seen from fig. 13.1, however, federal courts can play a crucial part in state law because, if a decision by the highest state courts of appeal is controversial and if the case involves a federal question, then it can be appealed to the US Supreme Court. Effectively, this gives the Supreme Court the power to interpret and judge state law, for 'a federal question' can mean almost anything that is contentious or controversial. In law it means any state court decision which is potentially incompatible with federal law or with the US Constitution. If, for example, a state high court hands down a decision extending the power of state police to search a suspect's house for evidence, this would have to be compatible with the 4th Amendment of the Constitution which prohibits unwarranted search and seizure. Only the US Supreme Court can judge whether the state law is unconstitutional or not.

In one sense, the Supreme Court's power of judicial review over state law is its most important function. Without it, the country would cease to be a united nation state. Instead, a loose confederacy would prevail with each state going its own way in economic and social affairs.

The power to review state high court decisions is part of the *appellate* jurisdiction of the Court. In addition, the Court hears cases on appeal from within the federal court system. As shown in fig. 13.1, most federal cases originate in the federal district courts (94 in number), the decisions of which can be appealed to one of the 12 crucial Courts of Appeal, and thence to the Supreme Court. The Court[2] also has original jurisdiction on a number of minor areas such as cases involving ambassadors.

Most citizens involved in federal litigation, therefore, have contact with the District Courts which are responsible for cases involving federal criminal and civil law. Compared with state law, federal criminal law is limited to a relatively few areas, the most notable being bank robbery, kidnapping, currency forgery, drug trafficking and assassination. Most of the work of the District Courts is in the area of civil law, with taxation, regulation and civil rights and liberty cases dominating. Few of these cases are appealed, and those that are are usually settled in the Appeal Courts which, on a day-to-day basis, are the most important judicial policy-makers in the country. They are not, however, the key judicial policy-makers because their decisions can always be overruled by the Supreme Court.

---

[2]   For the remainder of the chapter Supreme Court and the Court will be used interchangeably.

Table 13.1 Cases filed, US District, Appeals and Supreme Courts, 1970–93

	1970	1975	1980	1985	1989	1993
District Courts	87,300	117,300	168,800	273,700	233,500	228,600
Appeal Courts	11,662	16,658	23,200	33,360	39,734	49,770
Supreme Court	4,212	4,761	5,144	5,158	5,746	7,245*

Source: Statistical Abstract of the United States, 1994, tables 328–31.
* 1992

As can be seen from table 13.1 the District Courts' case-load showed an inexorable rise between 1970 and 1985. A greatly expanded federal role in part accounts for this, and, although the precise relationship between spreading federal legislation and litigation is hard to establish, there is no doubt that a more active federal government has greatly increased the case-load of the District Courts and of the Appeal Courts. By 1978 the overload of the courts had reached crisis proportions, and Congress increased the number of district judges from 281 to 398 and appeal judges from 62 to 97. By 1991, there were almost 600 district judges and more than 150 appeal judges. Since the mid-1980s the number of cases filed has decreased and levelled off at around 230,000 although an increasing number of these cases is now successfully appealed to the Courts of Appeal (table 13.1).

As table 13.1 shows, the Court also experienced a sharp rise in its case-load until the mid-1980s followed by a levelling off and a renewed increase during the 1990s. Increases in the number and use of law clerks (each justice has up to four clerks assigned to him or her), and improved administration of the Court by the last chief justice, Warren Burger, probably account for the institution's ability to manage. Even so, demands for the creation of a National Court of Appeals to screen cases coming before the Court, remain.

As with lower courts, new legislation in civil rights and liberties, and in the general area of federal regulation, largely accounts for the new demands on the Court.[3] So, as with the Congress and presidency, an ever-expanding federal role has produced new pressures on the Supreme Court which have made its operations more complex and difficult and, crucially, more politically visible.

The Supreme Court: Decision-making

Each year about 150 cases are actually decided by the Supreme Court, and, while most of these will be of relatively minor political or

---

[3] For a discussion of this point *see* Richard Hodder-Williams, *The Politics of the US Supreme Court*, (London, Allen & Unwin, 1980), chapter 3.

constitutional import, some will have profound consequences for the American polity and society. Since 1950, for example, the Court has decided that racially separate educational and other facilities are inherently unequal; that almost exact mathematical equality should be applied to the size of state legislative and congressional districts; that indigent arrested persons should be provided with the services of a lawyer at the government's expense; that tapes of presidential conversations were not so private as to be protected by executive privilege and therefore could be used in court against presidential staff accused of dishonesty; and that the bussing of school children to achieve racial integration is constitutionally required to overcome a historical pattern of legally imposed educational segregation. The very fact that all of these decisions have aroused intense controversy demonstrates their political significance, and the questions of how far and in what ways the Court can hand down decisions that are at odds with public opinion or with the other branches of government are topics we will return to later. Clearly, *how* the Court makes decisions is important. How does it decide which cases to hear? What criteria does it employ when deciding a case?

It is misleading to talk of *the* Supreme Court. Rather than being a unified organic body, the Court consists of nine individuals, each with his or her (in 1981 Sandra Day O'Connor was the first woman to be appointed to the Court) quite distinctive view of law, politics and society. Justices are appointed by the president with the advice and

Plate 13.1 The United States Supreme Court.

University of Winchester
Tel: 01962 827306
E-Mail: libenquiries@winchester.ac.uk

Borrowed Items 23/03/2018 14:37
XXXX403X

Item Title	Due Date
American politics : research and readings	14/05/2018
Developments in American politics 6	14/05/2018
American politics and society	14/05/2018

Indicates items borrowed today

Thankyou for using this unit

www.bibliotheca.com

consent of the Senate. Unlike other executive appointments, they are appointed for life. Once on the Court, then, they are free from the political, financial and other pressures which insecurity of tenure inflicts on most political actors. Of course, only a small percentage of cases coming before the Court are actually heard; most are denied review or, in the language of the Court are denied *certiorari*. *Certiorari* is, simply, that act whereby the losing party in the lower court appeals the record of the case to the Supreme Court so that details of the case can be made 'more certain'.[4] More than 90 per cent of cases are appealed in this way; in most of the remainder, the court is required to hear cases by a statutory appeals process.[5] The granting or denial of *certiorari* is clearly an important decision, and the court is legally beholden to no one to justify which cases are heard and which are not. From a strictly legal perspective, the criteria for granting *certiorari* are relatively easy to identify. Loren Beth lists seven:

1   How fundamental is the constitutional (or other) issue presented by the case?
2   How many similar cases have been or are being litigated?
3   Is there a conflict of opinion in the lower courts on this particular issue?
4   Does a lower court decision seem to conflict with an earlier Supreme Court decision?
5   Is there a significant individual right involved?
6   Has the lower court departed significantly from the accepted and usual course of judicial proceedings?
7   Does the case involve the interpretation of a statute never before construed?[6]

At least four of the nine justices have to agree to grant *certiorari* – a fact that strongly implies that the decision is not so clear-cut as the list suggests. Indeed, not one of points 1 to 7 is completely unambiguous or not open to serious disagreement or argument. How many cases in the civil rights and liberties areas – a good proportion of the total – do *not* involve a significant individual right? Almost certainly none. Similarly, many cases claim to involve a 'fundamental constitutional issue', yet few of these are granted *certiorari*. The fact is that while points 1 to 7 may be a legally correct list of criteria, they tell us very little of the political context in which decisions are taken. Why did it take until the 1940s and 1950s before the Court started regularly to hear civil

---

[4]   For a good discussion of this point, *see* Loren P. Beth, *Politics, the Constitution and the Supreme Court*, (New York, Harper and Row, 1962), chapter 3.
[5]   The most important class of cases here are those where *state* high-court decisions declare a federal law unconstitutional, or where the constitutionality of state law is in doubt.
[6]   Beth, *Politics*, pp. 31–2.

rights cases? Why did it take to the 1960s for criminal defendants' rights cases to come to the fore, and until 1973 for the Court to deliberate on the constitutional status of bans on abortion?

There are two possible answers here. First, that the philosophy and outlook of the justices change over time, either as a result of turnover or because individual justices change their minds; and second, that the political and social context in which the Court operates has changed over time, thus forcing certain issues, which were previously excluded, on to the judicial policy agenda. Taking the second point first, it is certain that the Court is influenced by the broader society. In the civil rights area, World War II 'nationalized' a number of social issues and brought into sharp focus, both for whites and Blacks, the injustices of segregation in the American South. Publicity on conditions in the South was advanced by a number of interest groups, in particular the National Association for the Advancement of Colored People (NAACP) which also acted as a judicial interest group by providing financial and legal support for litigants involved in civil rights cases.[7]

Although it is impossible to measure the influence on the Court of the 'social and political environment' or of the work of interest groups intent on promoting a particular cause or defending a special interest, the justices are undoubtedly swayed by such factors, at least in terms of letting them influence the policy agenda, or what sorts of cases are actually heard.

But it would be misleading to leave the impression of a Court granting *certiorari* only to classes of cases currently subject to public attention. Many cases are heard when the public pressure is minimal or absent. Reapportionment, for example, was not a matter of intense public debate when the Court implied in the famous 1962 case, *Baker v. Carr*, that the Tennessee State Legislature was constitutionally bound to organize its legislative districts according to the principle of mathematical equality. Later, in *Reynolds v. Sims* (1964), the Court made re-districting mandatory at the state and congressional levels. Also, the business of getting a case before the Supreme Court is long and hard. It may be years from the time a case is first filed in the District Court before it eventually reaches the Supreme Court. Such a process does not always lend itself to instant decision-making in response to public or interest-group pressure.

The judicial agenda is also influenced by the philosophies and attitudes of the justices themselves. Generally speaking, a decision not to

[7] For a good account of the early lobbying efforts of the NAACP *see* Clement E. Vose, *Caucasians Only*, (Berkeley and Los Angeles, University of California Press, 1967).

hear a case which in some way does meet one or more of the criteria 1 to 7 and which is currently controversial, is a conservative decision. It can reflect a justice's desire to keep the Court out of the 'political thicket' by leaving a lower court's decision or judicial precedent to settle the matter. The fact that the Court did not hear many civil rights cases in the 1920s and 1930s might be explained in this way, as might the reluctance of the Court to get involved in economic policy during the 1940s and 1950s. We should be wary here, however, for, so far, discussion has been confined to the influences shaping the Court's policy agenda, that is, which cases are heard and which are not. Naturally, the crucial question is, how does the Court decide those cases granted *certiorari?* Even the most conservative justice would have to recommend the issue of a writ of *certiorari* when a Circuit Court of Appeals had decided a case that fundamentally contradicted judicial precedent as represented by an earlier Supreme Court decision. More interesting are those instances when the Court decides to uphold such a radical departure from precedent, or decides that a particular act of Congress or executive action is unconstitutional.

One basic fact must be appreciated when discussing the Court as a political actor: it uses its power sparingly. It exercises *judicial self-restraint* (although, as we shall see, some Courts have been more restrained than others). It follows the doctrine of 'assumption of constitutionality'. In other words, it will use its power of judicial review very selectively, arguing a case on procedural grounds when it can, rather than declaring a law unconstitutional. As can be seen from table 13.2 the Court has, in fact, used its power of judicial review over federal law sparingly – especially down to 1920. Since then it has been more prone to strike down federal law, and this tendency has

Table 13.2 Number of federal statutes held unconstitutional by the Supreme Court, 1790–1993

Period	Number	Period	Number
1790–99	0	1900–09	9
1800–09	1	1910–19	6
1810–19	0	1920–29	15
1820–29	0	1930–39	13
1830–39	0	1940–49	2
1840–49	0	1950–59	5
1850–59	1	1960–69	16
1860–69	4	1970–79	20
1870–79	7	1980–89	16
1880–89	4	1990–93	3
1890–99	5	Total	127

Source: various, as compiled by Lawrence Baum, *The Supreme Court*, (Washington DC, Congressional Quarterly Press, 1995), table 5.3.

Table 13.3 Number of state laws and local ordinances held unconstitutional by the Supreme Court, 1790–1993

Period	Number	Period	Number
1790–99	0	1900–09	40
1800–09	1	1910–19	118
1810–19	7	1920–29	139
1820–29	8	1930–39	93
1830–39	3	1940–49	57
1840–49	9	1950–59	61
1850–59	7	1960–69	149
1860–69	23	1970–79	193
1870–79	36	1980–89	162
1880–89	46	1990–93	24
1890–99	36	Total	1,212

Source: various, as compiled by Baum, *The Supreme Court*, table 5.4.

increased since 1960. As far as state laws are concerned, the Court has been more active (table 13.3). Note that here, too, the rate has increased in very recent years.

As noted earlier, the Supreme Court consists of nine individual justices, and the final decision of the Court reflects the interaction of the opinions of these nine people. The formal decision-making process goes like this. Once *certiorari* is granted, the justices first receive written and then hear oral argument from the lawyers on both sides of the case. Later a case conference is convened at which the justices, sitting in private, make a preliminary decision. Five of the justices must agree to constitute a decision, and one of these will be assigned to write the majority opinion. If the chief justice is part of the majority he or she or another majority member assigned by him/her will write the opinion. If the chief justice is part of the minority, the most senior member of the majority will make the assignment. Once the assignments have been made, the opinion of the Court is written. This can take many weeks to complete and, once published, the names of other members of the majority may be added to it. Some members, however, while they may agree with the author of the opinion of the Court, may do so for *different* reasons, in which case they will write *concurring* opinions. Finally, those in the minority may choose to write a dissenting opinion, or even a number of dissenting opinions. Usually members will join just the majority or dissenting opinion, but it is quite possible for the Court to publish up to nine separate opinions: an opinion of the Court, four concurring opinions which may support the Court opinion on four different grounds, and four dissenting opinions which dissent on four different grounds. In the celebrated 1978 *Bakke* decision, which limited the use of racial quotas to discriminate positively in favour of minorities when admitting them to university courses, the

Court published no less than six separate opinions.[8] In this case – and this often applies when the justices are split – the variety of concurring opinions made it difficult to infer the exact meaning of the Court's decision; an outcome possibly preferred by the Court in this politically sensitive and technically complex area.

To the more casual observer of the judicial process, how a justice decides in a particular case may seem obvious. Precedent, and a careful interpretation of congressional statutes would be the immediate answer. Naturally, the justices do refer to precedent and they do spend much of their time interpreting legislation. In this respect their behaviour is little different from that of the British House of Lords (the highest court of appeal in Britain). But even reference to precedent can be problematical. What historical precedents are there for cases involving electronic bugging? Or genetic engineering? Or racial quotas, for that matter? Very few that could be considered even vaguely relevant. And interpreting statute law when it involves overruling executive actions can be politically sensitive, to say the least. In both instances the courts have very considerable discretion, not only to follow precedent, but to create it; not only to interpret statutes, but to direct the executive branch to change policy. When the formidable power of judicial review is added, the discretion available to the Court widens dramatically. Again, the reflex response to the question 'What guides the Court when it uses judicial review?' is: the Constitution. But, as was stressed in chapter 4, there is very little in the Constitution that is unambiguous, and the Supreme Court has reversed itself on a number of occasions when interpreting constitutional provisions.

If the justices cannot rely on precedent or the literal meaning of statutes or constitutional provisions, what does guide their judicial opinions? This is a complex and difficult question. We have already mentioned the political and social environment and there can be no disputing that the Court has been influenced by pressures from public opinion, presidents and interest groups. Instances of such pressures will be recorded later. Partly independently of such forces, however, different Courts and justices have acquired reputations for being 'conservative' or 'liberal', 'active' or 'passive'. These labels often refer to the jurisprudence or legal philosophy adhered to by different justices. Certainly, no self-respecting Supreme Court justice would rationalize his or her decision in terms of 'political pressures' or 'political expedience' – even if these were truly the main influences. Instead, justices would indeed refer to the Constitution and the ways in which the

[8] For a good account of this and associated cases *see* Alan P. Sindler, *Bakke, Defunis and Minority Admissions: The Quest for Equal Opportunity*, (New York, Longman, 1978).

wording of the Constitution should be interpreted. By so doing they are obliged to look, not only at the actual wording of the document, but also to the meanings and motives behind the words. If, along with such a 'positivist' approach, the justice also believes that the Court has an unbending duty always to 'discover' the Constitution's true meaning, then an activist Court is implied. For relating the events in a particular case to the true meaning of the Constitution and then testing whether (say) a law on censorship is reconcilable with the Constitution, invites the Court to declare on the constitutionality of that law. Such was the approach of the two outstanding jurists of the early part of this century, Oliver Wendell Holmes and Louis Brandeis. In a number of celebrated cases[9] both argued that some federal and state laws on internal subversion were incompatible with the 1st Amendment's general prohibition of laws abridging freedom of speech – although they accepted that absolute freedom of speech was clearly not intended by the framers of the Constitution. In Justice Holmes's famous example, 'the most stringent protection of free speech would not protect a man in falsely shouting fire in a theater and causing a panic', they argued that if the 1st Amendment was to mean anything, some principle inherent in the provision must be detected and invoked. By this reasoning, Holmes elaborated the 'clear and present danger test', or 'the question in every case is whether the words used in such circumstances are of such a nature as to create a clear and present danger that they will bring about the substantive evils that Congress has a right to prevent'. Of course, problems remain here – discovering exactly when the danger is clear and present must in part be a subjective exercise, perhaps especially so when Congress (or a state legislature) has passed a law attempting to prevent subversion in time of war. Indeed, Holmes and Brandeis sometimes believed there was a clear and present danger, as they did in the *Schenck* case[10] from which the above quotation is taken. But the very fact of attempting to find some principle inherent in the Constitution implies a legal philosophy that is largely independent of the vagaries of social and political pressures prevailing at any one time.

In marked contrast, one of the most prominent jurists of the 1940s and 1950s, Felix Frankfurter, believed that the representatives of the American people – Congress and president – should be left to interpret the Constitution, the Court's involvement being confined to mediating disputes between the branches or between federal and state governments. Even then, Frankfurter argued, the Court should

---

[9]   *See* Henry J. Abraham and Barbara A. Perry, *Freedom and the Courts*, (New York, Oxford University Press, 6th edn, 1994).
[10]   *Schenck v. United States (1919)*.

attempt to *balance* the various competing interests in society rather than search for some 'inherent principle' or 'higher meaning' behind the wording of the document. Clearly, a passive Court is implied by this approach, or one that steers clear of politics, letting representative institutions sort out conflict in society. The activism of Holmes and Brandeis and the passivity of Frankfurter represent two of the more coherent of a number of philosophical positions taken by the Court, and the labels 'active' and 'passive', 'liberal' and 'conservative' usually correspond to the perceived philosophy of the Court at a particular time. We should not, however, be deceived into thinking of different Supreme Courts as representing distinct and coherent philosophies. To repeat, nine individuals make the decisions and each may vary quite dramatically in outlook.

Some Courts, then, have lacked an identifiable philosophy. More important, it is impossible to separate the decisions of the justices from the political and social environment in which they operate. The 'positivism' of Holmes and Brandeis, with its search for a consistency and justice inherent in the Constitution, irrespective of political and social pressures, failed to dominate even the Court on which they sat, let alone be the main approach of subsequent Courts. Like any other political institution, the Court has to interact with society and polity. It is subject to a number of pressures and constraints. What makes the institution so interesting, however, is the mix of judicial philosophy and external constraint that has produced an ever-changing political role for the Court in American history. The remainder of this chapter will be devoted to studying this role, by analysing the constraints on the Court's power and, in particular, by asking whether the institution can be the equal of the other branches of government.

The Court and Political Power

There can be no doubting that Supreme Court decisions have political impact. From the momentous *Marbury v. Madison* decision in 1803 when, by declaring Section 13 of the 1789 Judiciary Act unconstitutional, Chief Justice John Marshall effectively established judicial review, through to the landmark civil rights cases of the last 40 years, the attention of public and polity alike has been riveted by the political implications of the Court's decisions. But, as suggested earlier, this does not mean that these solemn judicial deliberations take place in isolation from society. On the contrary, many have argued that the Court rarely deviates from the prevailing weight of political or public opinion; that, in fact, its main function has been to legitimize dominant political influences, and, when it has gone against these, it has soon found itself in trouble. In one rather obvious sense, this is always true, for courts depend on their authority rather than on naked power. They have no police force or army – or even bureaucrats – to enforce their decisions. For this they have to depend on the other branches of government. Perhaps the most dramatic example of the dangers inherent in fundamentally disagreeing with the other branches of government was the 1857 *Dred Scott* case. In this, the Court effectively declared unworkable the 1820 Missouri compromise which gave Blacks free status in the territories. If Blacks were to revert to slave status in these Northern and Western territories, a forced extension of the culture and values of the South was implied, a change completely unacceptable to Lincoln and the dominant Republican Party. The decision was never enforced because the Civil War soon followed, as did the 13th and 14th Amendments that specifically granted equal legal status to all citizens. For the other branches of government simply to ignore the Court is the most serious challenge to its power, for, once ignored, its authority and legitimacy are undermined. Without these it loses all influence. After the Civil War the Court did, in fact, soon reassert its authority, and it has never been seriously undermined since. But there have been ebbs and flows of judicial power, crises of confidence and periods of intense controversy. A useful way to study these is to document the constraints or limitations on the Court's power, or to record those instances when the scope and substance of judicial decisions have, in one way or another, been circumscribed.

Constitutional amendment

Amending the Constitution to overturn the Court is the ultimate legal weapon available to the other branches and to the states. As we know, however, amendments have been few and far between, and just four have been employed to overrule the court. In one of these – the 26th Amendment ratified in 1971 to extend the vote to 18-year-olds – the Court's *Oregon v. Mitchell* (1970) decision was overturned. Another (the 11th Amendment which prohibited a citizen of one state to sue the government of another state) has passed into historical obscurity.[11] Only two amendments stand out as changes crucial to preserve the integrity of the union and the smooth running of government – the 14th Amendment which overturned *Dred Scott*, and the 16th Amendment sanctioning a graduated federal income tax. Ratified in 1913 when the need for increased defence spending was widely per-

---

[11]   Although the Supreme Court decision which sanctioned such cases, *Chisolm v. Georgia* (1793), aroused great controversy at the time.

ceived as necessary, the 16th Amendment overturned the 1895 *Pollock v. Farmers' Loan and Trust* decision which had declared a graduated or progressive federal income tax unconstitutional. In more recent years, calls for constitutional amendments to overturn Supreme Court decisions have been equally rare, although a movement exists to amend the Constitution to overturn the 1973 *Roe v. Wade* decision sanctioning abortion. More recently, in a 1989 decision (*Texas v. Johnson*), the Court struck down a state law banning the burning of the American flag and a year later struck down a federal law on the same issue (*United States v Eichman*). In response, a movement for a constitutional amendment making it a crime to burn the flag gathered pace. In the end, however, Congress proved reluctant to overturn the Court on what was an issue of entirely emotional and symbolic importance.

Congressional control

The Constitution grants remarkably wide discretion to Congress over the composition and organization of the federal judiciary. Article 3 states, quite simply: 'The judicial power of the United States shall be vested in one Supreme Court, and in such inferior Courts as the Congress may from time to time ordain and establish'. So Congress has the power to determine the size and administration of the federal machinery of justice. Additionally, the Constitution specifically gives to Congress discretion over the Court's appellate jurisdiction and implicitly, at least, over the number of justices and when the Court should actually sit. Only rarely, however, has the Congress exercised these very substantial discretionary powers. Easily the most important item of legislation in these areas is the 1789 Judiciary Act which established the Court's power to review state court decisions denying federal rights to citizens. Apart from this, Congress has regularly increased the number of federal judges and courts in line with population and case-load increases, and the number of Supreme Court justices fluctuated between six and ten until 1870, since when it has remained at nine. During the 1930s, President Roosevelt attempted to increase the size of the Court to overcome opposition to his New Deal legislation, but Congress was disinclined to tinker with the Court in this way (*see* p. 287 below). By the 1930s the figure of nine justices was regarded as almost a part of the Constitution.

If Congress has been reluctant to alter the Court's composition and jurisdiction, it has shown little hesitation in reversing Court decisions via statutory reversals, or legislating to invalidate a particular judicial interpretation of federal law. Between 1946 and 1968, for example, some 111 roll-call votes in Congress reversed Court statutory interpretations. Few of these were of great import, however, and, of course, Congress cannot touch those decisions which are based on *constitutional* interpretation.

Perhaps Congress's most important function in relation to the Supreme Court is as a forum for public opinion. Senators and representatives quite often openly attack the Court or even introduce bills designed to curb its power. During the 1950s and 1960s, for example, Southerners incensed at the Court's desegregation decisions, and conservatives at its civil liberties and reappointment decisions, regularly did both. More recently, the 'pro-life' lobby in Congress has attempted to change the law on abortion, following the Court's liberal *Roe v. Wade* decision in 1973. Indeed, moral outrage at Court decisions on abortion, obscenity and school prayers inspired no less than 30 bills designed to curb the Court's jurisdiction during 1980 and 1981. While these attempts may fail, we cannot claim that constant attacks in the national legislature have no effect on the justices. In some contexts they may well influence the Court, especially if the justices are effectively isolated in their policy position, as was the case in 1937 when few sources of power or influence in American society sided with the Court. Finally, the Senate has to confirm all nominations made to the judicial branch by presidents. As will be discussed below, this is a power the Senate has used with increased vigour in recent years.

Presidential control

Presidents have two main means whereby they can influence the Court. First and most important, via the appointment power; and second, by appealing to public or Congressional opinion to reinforce their opposition to, or support for, a particular position. All federal judges are political appointees, and the vast majority nominated by a president share his political party label if not his total political and social philosophy. In the case of District and, to a lesser extent, Appeals Court nominations, presidents used to be guided by the advice and influence of the Senate (via the confirmation power) but also by state and local party leaders and dignitaries. Today, however, lower court and Supreme Court nominations are very much a matter of presidential preference. Broadly speaking, presidents have appointed justices whose political views are similar to their own. This does not mean to say that presidents deliberately manipulate an appointment in order to change the complexion of the courts – although often they do – nor does it mean that they are always successful in their attempts to change the courts' outlooks and philosophies. As far as the Supreme Court is concerned, they are circumscribed by chance for, although a vacancy on the Court has on average come up about every two years, some presidents have been denied the privilege of receiving their 'quotas' of two nominations. In his four years as president, poor Jimmy Carter made no appointments, while, in his first three years in office, Richard Nixon made four and, in his first two years, Bill Clinton made two. Interestingly, it was President Carter who explicitly stated an intention to remove political considerations from the appointment of all federal judges although, as far as the Supreme Court was concerned, his pledge went untested.

On three occasions in recent history, presidents have been given and taken the opportunity to try to change the political complexion of the Court. Roosevelt did so after 1937, Nixon after 1969 and Reagan after 1981. In Roosevelt's case, the Court had repeatedly struck down New Deal legislation on the grounds that it was an unconstitutional exercise of the Interstate Commerce Clause and violated 'substantive' due process under the 14th Amendment. In the face of the possible collapse of his economic recovery programme, Roosevelt attempted to 'pack' the Court by asking Congress to increase the number of justices by one for every existing justice over 70 years old, up to a maximum of 15. His strategy was clear – to tip the ideological balance of the Court away from the so-called 'Four Horsemen of Conservatism' (Justices Butler, McReynolds, Sutherland and Van Devanter) towards a more liberal stance. He failed in the Court-packing plan largely because, by the time it reached the critical stage in a not-too-enthusiastic Congress, one of the conservatives, Van Devanter, had retired. Roosevelt then proceeded to fill this and other vacancies, which came thick and fast during the next few years, with 'New Dealers' or justices sympathetic to an enhanced federal role in economy and society. He was remarkably successful. Almost all of his nine appointees toed the New Deal line, and the Court kept well out of economic affairs during the 1937–53 period.[12]

The second quite dramatic instance of political use of the appointment power occurred during the first two years of the Nixon Administration. One of Richard Nixon's 1968 campaign pledges had been to replace the liberals of the Warren Court with 'strict constructionists' or conservatives less prone to the advancement of civil rights and liberties characteristic of the Warren era. He was given a golden opportunity to do just this, for four vacancies occurred during the 1969–71 period. One of these was for chief justice, and the president lost no time in nominating Warren Burger, Chief Judge of the District of

[12] And in many respects the Court still keeps out of major economic controversies, especially those relating to federalism (*see* chapter 5).

Columbia Court of Appeals to the position. Burger, a conservative Republican from Minnesota, remained chief justice until 1986.[13] Nixon's next two nominees ran into serious trouble in the Senate. Only rarely in the twentieth century have Supreme Court nominations been rejected, and it is a remarkable testimony to Nixon's political insensitivity that his second and third nominations, Clement Haynsworth and Harrold Carswell, were voted down in the upper chamber. Both were undistinguished as jurists, and Carswell, in particular, had acquired a dubious record on civil rights in the Southern courts from which he hailed. Their rejection illustrates well the simple fact that presidential discretion over appointments is limited. A president may nominate a conservative or a liberal, but not an incompetent or a bigot. A Senate judiciary committee well versed by the American Bar Association, leading jurists and interested groups will see to that. Richard Nixon did, however, succeed with his next three appointments, Harry Blackmun, Lewis Powell and William Rehnquist. Rehnquist was a solid conservative (but a respected jurist) while the others were known at least as moderately conservative.

The Reagan experience was different again. Sandra Day O'Connor, nominated in 1981, was a respected judge who was chosen largely because she was a woman. A conservative, but no ideologue, O'Connor replaced the moderate Potter Stewart, an Eisenhower appointee. In 1986, when Chief Justice Burger retired, Reagan elevated William Rehnquist to the chief justiceship and nominated Judge Antonio Scalia to fill the vacancy. Both moves were highly strategic. Rehnquist was known as a conservative on all major questions. His nomination inspired considerable opposition in the Senate but he was eventually confirmed. Scalia was also known to favour the Reagan agenda, but his nomination met with little resistance.

These controversies pale into insignificance compared with the nomination of Robert Bork following the resignation of Justice Lewis Powell in June 1987. Powell had long held the pivotal vote against the New Right agenda favoured by the administration involving such issues as affirmative action and abortion. Robert Bork's tenure on the Court of Appeals was marked by a 'strict constructionism' or a consistently conservative interpretation of the Constitution. During the lengthy nomination proceedings, Bork worked hard to convince the Senate Judiciary Committee that he was, in fact, a centrist rather than

---

[13] The chief justice position became vacant quite fortuitously for Nixon. President Johnson had nominated Abe Fortas as Warren's successor but, during the Senate hearings into Fortas's suitability, it was revealed that, among other things, in 1966 he had received a $20,000 fee from a millionaire who at the time was being investigated (and later was convicted) for fraud. *See* Bob Woodward and Scott Armstrong, *The Brethren: Inside the Supreme Court*, (New York, Simon and Schuster, 1979), Prologue.

an ideologue of the right. It was this inconsistency that helped produce his eventual defeat by the widest margin ever (58 to 42). Reagan's next nominee Douglas Ginsburg was also a conservative but was obliged to withdraw following revelations that he had once smoked marijuana while in law school. Eventually, the Senate confirmed the nomination of Anthony Kennedy, a moderate and pragmatic conservative from California.

At the Appeal and District Court level, Ronald Reagan pursued a more overtly political strategy than any previous president. As one commentator put it: 'The striking feature about Reagan's lower-court judges is that they are predominantly young white upper-class males, with prior judicial or prosecuting experience and reputations for legal conservatism established on the bench in law schools, or in politics'.[14] By appointing large numbers of conservatives to the lower courts, President Reagan almost certainly changed the nature of lower-court decisions, and therefore the sorts of cases that are appealed to the Supreme Court. During his presidency, George Bush was able to make two appointments. In 1990 he nominated David H. Souter to replace William Brennan, almost the last of the Court's liberals and first appointed in 1956. Souter was quickly confirmed by the Senate. In 1991 Bush nominated Clarence Thomas to replace Lyndon Johnson nominee Thurgood Marshall. Thomas was also confirmed in spite of allegations that he had sexually harassed a former employee, Anita Hill. Marshall was the first Black member of the Court and Thomas the second. Both Souter and Thomas became identified with the dominant conservative representation on the Court.

On coming to office, Bill Clinton was determined to make his administrative and judicial appointees 'look like America'. As far as gender and ethnicity are concerned, the President was true to his word. Relatively few of his judicial appointments, however, have been so liberal as to transform the judiciary from the conservative stance acquired during the Reagan and Bush years. Indeed, his first two appointments to the Court, Stephen Breyer and Ruth Bader Ginsburg, were widely regarded as moderates. Both nominations were easily confirmed by the Senate. In fact, the justices they replaced (Byron White and Harry Blackmun) were, on the face of it, more liberal than the new appointees.

There can be no doubt that the Burger Court was very different from the openly liberal Warren Court and that the Rehnquist Court has in turn proved more conservative than the Burger Court.

---

[14]   David M. O'Brien, 'The Reagan judges: his most enduring legacy?' in Charles O. Jones (ed.), *The Reagan Legacy: Promise and Performance*, (Chatham, New Jersey, Chatham House, 1988), p. 75.

Personnel changes partly account for these shifts, but presidents can never be sure that, once appointed, a justice will fulfil expectations. Appointed for life to the most respected forum in the land, many justices change their political philosophies once on the Court. Such was the case with Earl Warren, one-time conservative Republican governor of California, expected by his patron President Eisenhower to continue the self-restraint of the Stone and Vinson Courts. In civil rights and liberties and reapportionment he did just the opposite. And, although the Nixon appointees generally moved the Court to the right, they did not do so in a coherent and consistent manner. Liberal civil rights and liberties decisions did not suddenly cease in 1971, even if they have become infrequent and interspersed with more conservative judgements.[15]

Public and political opinion

Appointment power must by definition be limited because, even when presidents have made appointments, they have no direct control over the justices once they are on the Court. They can, of course, appeal to Congress (as with the Court-packing plan) or to public opinion but, once this happens, the independent influence of the president is lost. As we noted in earlier chapters, public opinion is hard to define and almost impossible to measure. Scratch beneath the surface and what most commentators mean by public opinion is a particular configuration of political power, expressed either through representative institutions or through the media or organized groups. If we accept this approach, we can state confidently that only very rarely in American history has the Court challenged a dominant climate of opinion. Between the Civil War and 1937, for example, the Court acquired the reputation for defending the burgeoning capitalist interests of the period by striking down state and federal legislation designed to regulate industry or to protect workers from exploitation. The regulation of interstate commerce did not, the Court argued, extend to such things as federal laws regulating child labour. Or, more importantly, entitlement of 'due process of law' under the 14th Amendment did not extend to *state* attempts to regulate industrial and commercial life. It applied directly only to federal-citizen relationships. As a result, between 1900 and 1937, some 184 decisions invalidated state regulatory provisions.[16] To be fair, some state laws were also upheld during

---

[15]   *See* Woodward and Armstrong, *The Brethren*; also Herman Schwartz (ed.), *The Burger Years: Rights and Wrongs in the Supreme Court, 1969–1986*, (Harmondsworth, Middlesex, Penguin, 1988).
[16]   Quoted in Hodder-Williams, *The Politics of the US Supreme Court*, p. 138.

Figure 13.2 Number of economic and civil liberties laws (federal, state and local) overturned by the Supreme Court by decade, 1900s–1980s

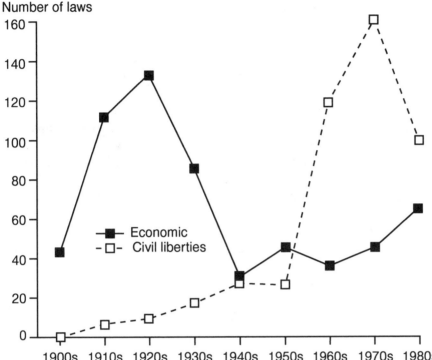

Source: Various as compiled by Lawrence Baum, *The Supreme Court*, figure 5.2.

these years, but the general stance of the Court was anti-regulation or anti-government 'interference' in economic affairs. Crucially, however, so generally was public opinion, at least until 1929. Most presidents, Congress and many state legislatures accepted the Supreme Court's judgements with relative equanimity. It was not until the coming of the Great Depression in the early 1930s that the climate of opinion changed dramatically. And, when the Court began regularly to strike down federal New Deal legislation, it became politically isolated. Within two years, and following intense pressure from unions, Congress and president,[17] the Court had made its 'switch in time that saved nine' and thereafter followed, rather than led, the other branches in the general area of economic policy. Fig. 13.2 shows this transition well. From the early 1940s the Court overturned few laws in the economic policy area although it has become more active in this area in very recent years.

[17]   See Beth, *Politics*, chapter 6.

During the 1940s and up to about 1957, the Court was deferential to Congress and to president on questions of 'subversion' and national security. In case after case, the Court accepted the restrictions placed on citizens by the 1940 Smith Act, the 1950 McCarren Act and, in the case of the Japanese Americans, by executive fiat.[18] Not until the late 1950s, when public fears about communist subversion began to subside, did the Court begin to relax the restrictions on communists and others perceived to be subversive.

Even in civil rights it would be difficult to argue that the Court was acting in isolation from broader political and public opinion. *Brown v. Board of Education*, the landmark 1954 decision, which argued that racially separate facilities in education and other facilities were inherently unequal, may have been highly unpopular in the South, but it was welcomed in the North by many members of Congress, and was not unpopular with the president. What can be claimed for *Brown*, is that it helped push opinion towards the desegregation of the South although, enforcement problems apart (of which more later), it was not until 1964 that Congress, goaded on by a determined and proselytizing president, passed the first major federal civil rights act.

The apportionment decisions of the early 1960s, extending the principle of representation according to mathematical equality, first to state legislatures and then to Congressional districts, were probably more widely unpopular with politicians than the civil rights decisions. But they were not unpopular with the public, most of whom stood to gain from a removal of the bias in representation towards rural areas. And how could state and national politicians justify the gross inequities that had accumulated over time? This is not to deny that the Court was a genuine innovator in this area,[19] however, as it was in the realm of criminal defendants' rights. Starting with *Mapp v. Ohio* in 1961 and continuing through to Earl Warren's resignation in 1969, the Court handed down a remarkable succession of decisions granting defendants the right to state-provided counsel, access to police files, extending the freedom from unlawful search and seizure, and gener-

---

[18]   The Smith Act made it unlawful to advocate the overthrow of the US Government, and the McCarren Act required 'subversive organizations' to register with the Subversive Activities Control Board. In 1942 West Coast Americans of Japanese origin (many of them citizens) were arbitrarily interned in concentration camps by the Governor of California (ironically Earl Warren, later the champion of individual freedom on the Court) as a threat to internal security. The Court failed to hear the cases arising from this until 1944 and then argued them on procedural rather than constitutional grounds.

[19]   It is interesting to note that the Burger Court modified the original apportionment decisions to allow community of interest as well as population to determine the size of districts.

ally providing much greater protection to arrested persons. Coming as they did during the disruptions of the 1960s, these changes were welcomed only by what eventually was a diminishing band of liberals. The dramatically increased activism of the Court in the civil rights and liberties area is shown by the number of acts declared unconstitutional from the late 1950s onwards (fig. 13.2).

Undoubtedly, the Warren Court moved well ahead of public opinion in this area. Perhaps predictably, the Burger Court did not continue the crusading spirit of the Warren era. In civil rights and liberties it was careful to qualify some of the more dramatic decisions of the 1960s. In one sense, the Burger Court was placed in a much more difficult position than the Warren Court was, for it had to clarify what were highly complex and difficult questions raised, but not settled, by Warren. Hence, in school desegregation, the thorny problem of distinguishing between *de jure*, or legally sanctioned, and *de facto*, or naturally evolving, segregation emerged as the main civil rights issue. Generally, the Court argued that a past pattern of *de jure* segregation should be reversed via bussing, but not (as generally prevails in the North) if the segregation is *de facto* in nature. Similarly, on the use of other affirmative action measures, such as quotas, the Court had to grapple with the problem of choosing between *individual* rights under the 14th Amendment and the *collective* rights of Blacks and other minorities who have sought redress for a pattern of past discrimination. Individual rights generally prevailed. In criminal procedural rights, the Court limited the application of the 'exclusionary rule' or the admissibility of evidence culled during unlawful searches and seizures. And, in a number of other areas, the protection afforded arrested persons was reduced.

Often the Court cannot predict what the impact of its decisions on public opinion will be. The Burger Court, for example, handed down a decision on abortion in 1973 (*Roe v. Wade*) which looked clear enough. The Court effectively outlawed all state laws that prohibited abortion during the first three months of pregnancy, liberalized them during the next three months and banned abortions during the last ten weeks. This compromise has, however, been seized by the pro-life anti-abortion interest groups and branded as a further example of the federal courts undermining public morals and the sanctity of family life. Little doubt exists that the decision precipitated debate and political controversy on an issue the salience of which increased enormously during the 1970s and 1980s. The Court's decisions on capital punishment which, though laying down quite strict guidelines, have effectively left to the states the final decision on when (and how) a person should be executed, have also aroused great controversy. In both instances, debate on the issues has been passed on to the broader political stage. But they hardly left the judicial policy agenda. Controversy on where individual rights begin and end must by necessity concern the courts, and, given governments' intimate involvement in granting and in denying rights to citizens (indeed, in exercising a power over life and death in the two examples cited above), the court's involvement must also continue.

With the appointment of Souter and Thomas, the Rehnquist Court moved clearly to the right. Indeed, the two most liberal members of the Court in 1993 were Nixon appointees, Harry Blackmun and John Paul Stevens. As earlier noted, the Clinton appointees, Stephen Breyer and Ruth Bader Ginsburg, did not shift the Court leftwards in ideological terms because they replaced liberals rather than conservatives. Predictably, therefore, the Rehnquist Court has advanced the conservative agenda especially on moral and social issues and in the general area of federalism. It has been very reluctant, however, to strike down any of the landmark liberal decisions of the Warren and early Burger Courts such as *Roe v. Wade* or *Miranda v. Arizona* (on the rights of accused persons) as unconstitutional. Instead, it has argued cases on narrower grounds, often leaving to state and local officials the final decision on how the law should be interpreted. By avoiding constitutional precedents, the Court has left open to Congress the opportunity to pass laws reversing its own decisions. Just this has happened. In the 1991 Civil Rights Act, Congress overturned the 1989 *Patterson v. McLean Credit Union* decision which limited an employee's ability to sue for damages if subject to racial harassment at work. The Court has also been reversed by statutory interpretation over laws involving abortion and affirmative action. The reduced judicial activism of the Court in the civil rights and liberties areas is demonstrated by the data in fig. 13.2. Note also the Court's increasing role in economic policy – a fact that reflects the increasingly complex and controversial nature of policy-making in this area. It should be pointed out that, on many of the social issues, the 'moderate conservatism' of the Rehnquist Court has not been particularly out of tune with public opinion, partly, it is true, because of its reluctance to set headline-grabbing constitutional precedents.

We can conclude that only rarely has the Court consciously moved against prevailing public and political opinion, and, when it has done so, it has not been for long. Two important qualifications have to be applied to this generalization. First, the Court has been reluctant to challenge, or has never for long challenged, a programme or policy supported by the other branches, and which is perceived to be crucial to the integrity of the union (the status of slavery in the North), national security in wartime or 'emergency' conditions ('subversion' in the two world wars and afterwards) or to the running of the economy (the New Deal legislation). When, however, there is no consensus on a policy – especially when Congress and president are in serious disagreement – then the Court plays a central role in arbitrating the conflict. We have two dramatic examples of the Court playing just such a role in recent history. In 1952 President Truman seized the nation's steel mills on the grounds that industrial disputes were undermining production and the Korean War effort. The Court quickly condemned the seizure as an unconstitutional infringement on the legislative powers of Congress. In 1974, the Court declared that executive privilege did not protect President Nixon's taped conversations which could be used in the courts and Congress to investigate the Watergate wrong-doings. On both occasions, Congress was unsympathetic to the president's position and, significantly, so was broader public opinion.

More recently, the Burger Court showed little reluctance to make deliberations affecting the separation of powers. In *Buckley v. Valeo* (1976) some key features of the 1974 Campaign Finance Act were struck down (*see* chapter 10, p. 204). Later, in *Immigration and Naturalization Service v. Chadha* (1983), the legislative veto was declared unconstitutional. Following this decision, the capacity of Congress to control the discretionary powers given to executive agencies was greatly curtailed. In 1985, the Court effectively established that Congress and the president, rather than the Court and the Constitution, should be the final arbiter of the economic relationship between the federal government and the States (*Garcia v. San Antonio Metropolitan Transit Authority*). Finally, in 1986, the Court declared the mandatory spending cuts required by the Gramm-Rudman-Hollings Deficit Reduction Act an unconstitutional violation of the separation of powers.

The second qualification to the Court's deference to prevailing public and political opinion is that, when it does challenge them in areas involving the behaviour of myriad individuals rather than a few institutions or political leaders, it tends to experience serious problems in enforcing its decisions or in predicting their precise impact on public opinion.

Lack of enforcement powers

As noted earlier, without their own police force, army or bureaucracy, the courts cannot enforce their decisions unless their authority is accepted by those who do exercise coercive powers. Moreover, the Supreme Court depends on lower courts (federal and state) to implement its decisions, and these may not always interpret or accept the Court's judgements in an unambiguous fashion. The most celebrated examples of judicial recalcitrance and obstruction involved the enforcement of civil rights in the South. Following *Brown v. Board's* 1954 directive that Southern schools should desegregate 'with all deliberate speed', Southern District Courts were assigned the job of enforcing the order. Appointed by presidents on the advice of local politicians and party faithfuls, district judges reflect local conditions, interests – and prejudices. Very few of the Southern district judges of the 1950s and 1960s were integrationists, and most resisted – mainly through delays – the order to desegregate. In fact, not until 1969 in the *Alexander v. Holmes County Board of Education* decision – some 15 years after *Brown* – did the Supreme Court finally make it mandatory to desegregate immediately, and by then, of course, the Court was supported by the not inconsiderable weight of the 1964 Civil Rights Act with its array of compliance and enforcement procedures. The figures on racial segregation demonstrate this point well. In 1963, nine years after *Brown*, only 45 per cent of Black students in Southern schools went to schools where any whites were present. By 1971 this figure had increased to 85.6 per cent.[20]

More rarely, a state or local political actor may openly defy a Court order, as happened in Little Rock, Arkansas, in 1957 when Governor Faubus used the local militia forcibly to prevent Black children from entering a high school. Only the eventual use of federal troops on the instruction of President Eisenhower enabled the Black children to enter the school. Much more common is evasion of the directives of the Supreme Court, not only by other courts or by outright defiance, but through ignorance, deception or the simple fact that complete enforcement is technically impossible to achieve. Such has been the case with criminal law decisions such as *Miranda* and *Gideon* which laid down strict procedures for the interrogation of suspects. As research has shown, arrested persons often do not know their rights, police officers are frequently ignorant of the correct procedures and, even when informed, can compromise them. Similarly, the decisions of the early 1960s outlawing special prayers and bible reading in public schools (*Engel v. Vitale, Abington School District v. Schempp*) as infringements of the 1st Amendment's freedom of religion clause, have proved very difficult to enforce. Indeed, though neither the Burger nor the Rehnquist Courts had (by 1997) seriously compromised the principles laid down in *Engel* and *Schempp*, both were under considerable pressure to do so.

---

[20]   Quoted in Baum, *The Supreme Court*, p. 223.

Conclusion

It is often argued that the greatest limitation on the political power of the Court is 'judicial self-restraint' or a conscious decision by the justices to avoid the political thicket by deferring to the other branches (or to public opinion) rather than causing great controversy by departing from the dominant opinion. Our earlier discussions suggest strongly that this is true, although self-restraint is more a matter of political common sense than, as some jurists have argued, something that can be justified solely on philosophical grounds. Judges may search for a 'higher principle' inherent in the Constitution, or they may be convinced that government 'interference' in the economy is always a bad thing. Sooner or later, however, they have to take cognizance of the political and social environment in which decisions are made. As we noted, the Supreme Court is seriously constrained by this environment; it is not an institution apart from politics, but one which is an organic part of the polity and society.

If the Court rarely challenges the dominant political forces in society, what use then is the institution of judicial review? From our discussion we can identify three crucial functions:

1　The Court arbitrates between federal and state law. In terms of the stability and integrity of the union this is undoubtedly its most important function.
2　Judicial review provides the Court with an apparently neutral point of reference (the Constitution) for arbitrating between the different branches of government – although historically this has tended to work only when one branch (the executive) is relatively isolated from Congressional and public opinion.
3　Judicial review can help defend individual freedoms under the Bill of Rights and 14th Amendment. Of course, there have been numerous occasions when the Court has clearly failed to defend such freedoms, as with the internment of the Japanese Americans in 1942. But – and this is the strongest argument in favour of judicial review under bills of rights – the legislative and executive branches would have denied these freedoms even in the absence of judicial review. Its presence is usually beneficial, therefore, in the sense that, when it deviates from the other branches, it does so by favouring the individual. As the civil rights, and especially civil liberties, cases of the 1950s and 1960s demonstrate, this can involve quite radical, if sometimes temporary, departures from prevailing political and public opinion.

Finally, how has the Court responded to the much more fragmented polity and society characteristic of the 1980s and 1990s? In a word, uncertainly. As suggested, the Burger and Rehnquist Courts had to confront questions involving moral absolutes where *any* compromise would have been unacceptable to some. Issue politics, combined with the increasingly technical nature of cases, can produce a situation where the Court hands down decisions that are highly contentious. Issue politics produces odd, unpredictable political coalitions where it is almost impossible to please everybody. The Court's decisions on abortion and capital punishment, for example, involved issues where the subsequent lines of opposition and support were complex and unpredictable. In some other areas – campaign finance for instance – the technicalities of the question are so formidable that the Court has produced decisions where the consequences have been unexpected, and perhaps undesirable. In fact, as mentioned, the Burger Court proved to be quite active on political questions generally, including such issues as federalism and the proper constitutional limits to legislative power. The Rehnquist Court, the conservatism of which was little changed by the Clinton nominations, faces the same dilemmas, and has, as noted, been reluctant to make precedent-setting constitutional decisions on such questions as affirmative action, the treatment of illegal immigrants and abortion in the face of a public opinion that is deeply divided. The Court will, however, be forced into taking decisions in these and other areas, given that during the mid-1990s, state legislatures and state initiatives passed highly controversial, and possibly constitutionally unsound, measures on such questions as the medical use of marijuana, the legal rights of homosexuals, the provision of state benefits for illegal immigrants and the status of affirmation programmes.

Throughout all these changes the Supreme Court and the whole judiciary strive to perform what is perhaps their most vital function – the legitimization of the system in the eyes of the citizenry. In the words of Felix Frankfurter:

> A gentle and generous philosopher noted the other day a growing 'intuition' on the part of the masses that all judges, in lively controversies, are 'more or less prejudiced.' But between the 'more or less' lies the whole kingdom of the mind, the differences between the 'more or less' are the triumphs of disinterestedness, they are the aspirations we call justice . . . The basic consideration in the vitality of any system of law is confidence in this proximate purity of its process. Corruption from venality is hardly more damaging than a widespread belief of corrosion through partisanship. Our judicial system is absolutely dependent upon a popular belief that it is as untainted in its workings as the finite limitations of disciplined human minds and feelings make possible.[21]

---

[21]   Quoted in David F. Forte, *The Supreme Court in American, Politics,* (Lexington, Mass., D. C. Heath, 1972), pp. 93–4.

To perform this function adequately the Court cannot deviate too much from the mainstream of political opinion, a fact that has not been lost on many recent justices, including most on the present Court.

Further Reading

The best single introduction is Lawrence Baum, *The Supreme Court*, (Washington DC, Congressional Quarterly Press, 5th edn, 1995). *See also* Henry J. Abraham, *The Judicial Process*, (New York, Oxford University Press, 6th edn, 1993). A good, although somewhat dated non-American interpretation of the Supreme Court is Richard Hodder-Williams, *The Politics of the US Supreme Court*, (London, Allen & Unwin, 1980). For a vivid journalists' account of how the Court operates, *see* Bob Woodward and Scott Armstrong, *The Brethren: Inside the Supreme Court*, (New York, Simon and Schuster, 1979). An analysis of the Burger Court is Herman Schwartz (ed.), *The Burger Years. Rights and Wrongs in the Supreme Court, 1969–1986*, (Harmondsworth, Middlesex, and New York, Penguin, 1988). On the Rehnquist Court, *see* David G. Savage, *Turning Right: The Making of the Rehnquist Supreme Court*, (New York, Wiley, 1992). For a compendium of Supreme Court information *see* Kermit L. Hall, *The Oxford Companion to the Supreme Court*, (New York, Oxford University Press, 1992). The classic work on the Court and civil rights and liberties, is Henry J. Abraham and Barbara A. Perry, *Freedom and the Court*, (Oxford and New York, OUP, 6th edn, 1994).

14

SOCIAL POLICY IN AMERICA: SELF-RELIANCE AND STATE DEPENDENCE

Sooner or later cuts in Social Security and Medicare which provide benefits for older Americans are unavoidable, because the alternatives – huge tax increases or peacetime budget deficits – are worse and probably politically unacceptable,

Robert J. Samuelson

Don't be bold; crawl before you walk . . . And give up the idea of dramatic reform.

Clinton task-force member commenting on the feasibility of welfare reform

Introduction

It would be easy to infer from earlier chapters that decision-making in the American political system is so fragmented and dispersed that the resulting policies are simply not amenable to simple characterization; that the open and pluralistic nature of the system produces a politics of confusion and unpredictability. While there is no doubt a great deal of truth to this, it would be wrong to leave the analysis without enquiring further into the nature and consequences of policy-making in the United States. The purpose of the next three chapters is, therefore, to add perspective and balance to earlier conclusions by examining how policy-making has developed in three important areas – social, economic and foreign policy. Discussion will focus particularly on the following three questions:

1 To what extent do policy systems differ in style and substance one from another?

2 How does policy develop over time? How do changes in administration and the domestic and international environment change the ways in which policy is formulated and implemented?

3 Related is the crucial question of the role that political institutions and processes play in the policy system. To what extent do institutional relationships mould public policies as opposed to broader structural forces in economy and society? This question is important because if institutions' independent roles are limited, then so is the potential for institutional reform. In other words, it may be that, whatever the institutional context, governing a large complex industrial society, such as the United States, would be a difficult business.

Obviously we cannot provide definitive answers to these questions, and obviously our discussion of each of the policy areas must, of necessity, be brief. Because we can only touch on the main issues involved, references to more detailed analyses will be provided when appropriate.

Social Policy

Governments have always been more reluctant to intervene in the general area of social policy in the US than they have in Western Europe. Indeed, it was not until the 1930s that the federal government laid down a framework of law providing for welfare and social security benefits for the poor and the old. Even then, the extent and level of welfare coverage were limited. Contributory earnings-related pensions applied only to certain kinds of workers. Welfare was restricted to families with dependent children (effectively mothers and children) and was distributed through the states on a matching federal-state basis. As a result, great disparities in the provision of welfare from state to state developed – disparities which remain to this day. Housing and health, moreover, were not considered legitimate parts of federal social policy until the 1960s, and, since then, housing subsidies have been subject to periodic cuts to the point where, during the Reagan years, they all but disappeared – if only temporarily. Only education has been universally accepted as a legitimate part of the social-policy agenda. But, until very recently, it was always local and state governments rather than the federal government, that provided for elementary, secondary and higher education.

The roots of the American antipathy to anything but limited and selective social benefits are not difficult to identify. They lie in the strongly held notions of self-reliance which have been discussed a number of times in earlier chapters. By the 1970s, however, some areas of social policy had become established as proper and legitimate roles for the federal government. Almost all of these involved earnings-related social security benefits for widows, widowers, the disabled, the blind and, above all, the old. Most Americans now consider these benefits as rights, not hand-outs by the government. There is, in fact, a sizeable 'hand-out' element in the social security programme, as benefits often bear little resemblance to what has been paid in. In addition, Medicare, the programme providing medical aid for the old, is also now considered a right, even though the redistributive element in the programme is very considerable. Finally, many Americans, even those on the right, look more benignly on the welfare programme for the old (Supplementary Security Income) than they do on other welfare programmes. Clearly the elderly are given a special status as a group who cannot be expected to help themselves.

The same sympathy is not, paradoxically, extended to children in poor families who, though provided with a range of welfare benefits, do not fare as well as do the old. One reason for this is the problem of ensuring that benefits received by parents do actually reach needy children. Because of this and the belief among many politicians that many of those on welfare can and should be capable of supporting a family through work, the two main welfare programmes, Food Stamps and Aid for Families with Dependent Children, have always been politically vulnerable. Similarly, medical care for the poor (Medicaid) is less well protected than Medicare.

As can be seen from table 14.1, most of the major social-policy bills were enacted during the New Deal and the Great Society period of the 1960s. Since then, there have been numerous amendments to the original legislation but, until 1996, no wholesale reform. In fact, reform attempts have come from left and right, with the most recent assault on the system from the right being led by the Republican 104th Congress. In 1996 Congress did pass a welfare-reform bill which President Clinton eventually signed. The bill imposed new restrictions on welfare benefits, and in some respects made the administration of welfare more, rather than less, complex. Few question that what is essentially an *ad hoc*, inefficient and inadequate range of benefits is in need of further reform. What then accounts for the repeated failure to rationalize the system? Both institutional and ideological explanation can be used to answer this question. Let us look at each of these in turn.

Federalism As far as the welfare programmes are concerned, any reform would have to rationalize the greatly varying benefit levels presently applicable in the 50 states. Such an exercise would prove expensive unless benefit levels in the richer states were to drop to pay for higher benefits in the poorer states. Such a strategy would be politically unacceptable. Reforming the 'welfare mess', therefore, would

Table 14.1 Major federal social policy legislation, 1935–95

1935	Social Security Act – established the basic old age, survivors and disabled insurance programme, as well as unemployment insurance and the main welfare programme, Aid for Families with Dependent Children (AFDC)
1937	Public Housing Act – provided limited grants for the construction of municipal housing.
1964	Food stamps – the provision of stamps which the poor can exchange for food
1965	Creation of Medicare (medical care for the old) and Medicaid (medical care for the poor)
1965	Elementary and Secondary Education Act – federal aid for local school authorities in disadvantaged areas
1968	Housing Act – the provision of housing subsidies for the owners and renters of low- and modrate-income housing
1971	Supplementary Security Income (SSI) – the provision of welfare benefits for older citizens
1988	Family Support Act – requires states to provide work or training programmes for welfare recipients
1996	Welfare reform limits recipients to five years' benefits (with some exceptions). Consolidates federal programmes as block grants for the states. Limits welfare benefits for young mothers

cost a lot of money. Co-ordinating benefits across programmes would also prove very difficult. AFDC, Food Stamps and Medicaid, as well as myriad educational, social service and housing benefits, would require rationalization. Given the expense involved in the most 'rational' reforms, the Congress and the Clinton Administration have opted for cuts in programmes and limitations on eligibility. Indeed, the most recent legislation is 'work' rather than 'welfare' driven, the assumption being that most people presently on welfare are capable of supporting themselves through employment.

Social security, Medicare and the electoral connection As suggested earlier, social security has a special status as a protected set of measures in the United States. In 1982 President Reagan attempted to cut benefits but was unable to do so because of fierce opposition from Congress and public opinion generally. More recently, Newt Gingrich and the Republican 104th Congress made a serious attempt to cut back on the *increase* projected in the cost of Medicare over the next several years. This threat provoked a storm of anger from older Americans and their organizations. Most Americans, regardless of their economic position, expect to receive Medicare benefits at some time during their lives. By attacking the burgeoning cost of the programme (see fig. 14.1) Gingrich was taking a considerable political risk. And even though he was not planning to cut social security, there was a wide-spread impression that this would be next on the list. Meanwhile President Clinton could project himself as the guardian of these pro-grammes and accuse Gingrich and the Republicans of being mean

Figure 14.1 Composition of Federal Spending. Relative to GDP, discretionary spending has fallen during the past two decades, while entitlement spending and interest on the debt have grown

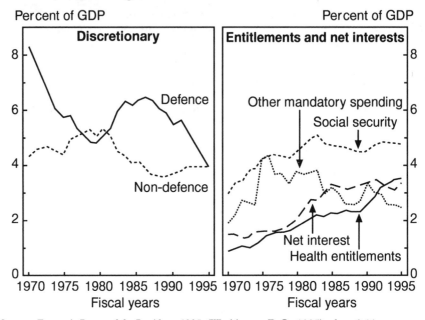

Source: Economic Report of the President, 1995, (Washington D.C., 1995), chart 2.11.

spirited and insensitive to the needs of the old. It seems likely that these events helped Clinton to victory in the 1996 presidential elections.

Social insurance (mainly old age pensions) is easily the largest item in the non-defence federal budget (fig. 14.1), and, as entitlement programmes, it is effectively uncontrollable. Increasingly, however, benefits for the old, which have little or no contributory element (SSI, Medicare and Supplementary Medicare), are also electorally protected. As fig. 14.1 shows, health benefits are also increasing very rapidly in cost, and it was this very rapid growth that inspired Gingrich to propose what were in effect modest cuts. While the Republicans may have been politically foolish to propose such measures, there is no doubt that, in the longer run, they are needed. The fundamental problem with Social Security and with Medicare is that the numbers of *contributors* to the programmes through payroll taxes will gradually decrease sometime early next century while the number of *beneficiaries* increases. To put it another way, when the 'baby-boom' generation (those born between about 1945 and 1965) retires there will be fewer workers in the labour-force to replace them.

This is an actuarial problem facing all welfare states at century's end, and in fact it is not as serious in the USA as in some countries,

Figure 14.2 Social security receipts, spending and reserve estimates, 1992–2035

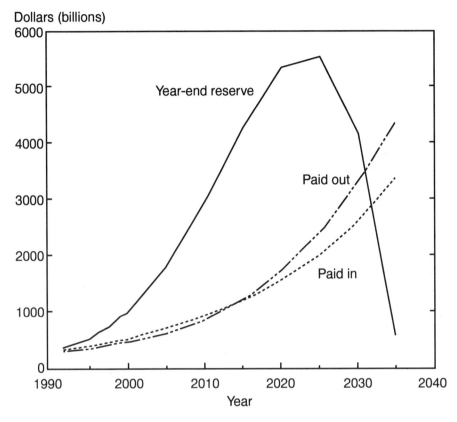

Source: Harold W. Stanley and Richard G. Niemi, *Vital Statistics on American Politics*, (Washington D.C., Congressional Quarterly, 1994), figure 12.2.

given that the American birth rate is one of the highest among richer countries. Nonetheless *something* will have to be done about the problem over the next decade. This is amply demonstrated by fig. 14.2 which shows what will happen to the Social Security Trust Fund by 2040 if no reforms are instituted. Congress originally created a trust fund to ensure that the programme was self-financing and immune to 'raids' by the federal government. A large surplus will build up as the baby-boom generation pays in more and more as their incomes increase. build up as the baby-boom generation pays in more and more as their incomes increase. After about 2025, however, the programme slides inexorably towards insolvency. Aware of this, President Clinton has made the reform of Medicare and of the social security system a priority for his second term. As a 'lame-duck' president he will personally incur no political costs in attempting such reforms. Whether Congress will go along with what will have to be sizeable cuts and/or tax increases is another matter, however. One thing is certain: the spiralling cost of these entitlement programmes will remain firmly at the centre of the political agenda for some years to come.

The continuing importance of self-reliance While the old and disabled are protected, younger, able-bodied citizens are under increasing pressure to take jobs and support themselves. The 1988 Family Support Act requires the states to provide work or training programmes for all welfare recipients, and the 1996 Welfare Act introduced further measures designed to encourage welfare recipients to work. Indeed, Democrats and Republicans are now committed to some version of what is called 'workfare', or the linking of benefits to training and jobs. The 1996 act went so far as to abolish AFDC benefits and instead devolved responsibility for the provision of welfare to the states. It remains to be seen how this will work out in practice, but for families, workfare is not a realistic option unless accompanied by comprehensive child care. And, while the 1996 Act did include some provision for child-care spending, this was widely perceived to be inadequate.

One of the most interesting aspects of the widespread public concern at the alleged growth in welfare expenditure and the related belief that most welfare recipients are scroungers rather than the deserving poor is that, in relation to the size of other federal programmes, public-assistance spending is quite low. As can be seen

Figure 14.3 Federal outlays by function, fiscal 1995. Social security, defence, medicare and net interest on the debt comprise 65 per cent of federal spending, dwarfing outlays on international affairs and social insurance programmes

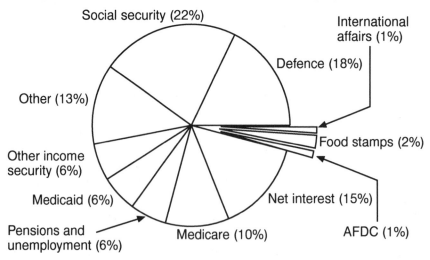

Note: AFDC is aid to families with dependent children.
Source: Economic Report of the President, 1995, chart 2.12.

from fig. 14.3 the major welfare programmes (food stamps and AFDC) account for just 3 per cent of federal spending. The category 'other income security' also contains a number of programmes for the poor, but the major item here is Supplementary Security Income (SSI) which provides welfare for older Americans. This programme has not been the main butt of public objections. Whatever the objective situation, Democrats and Republicans have shown a determination to cut the welfare rolls. Whether the 1996 Act, and other measures that may be introduced in Clinton's second term, have this effect, remains to be seen.

Health-care Reforms

When he came into office, Bill Clinton was determined to reform America's health-care system. His motives were twofold. First, as a reforming Democrat, he wanted to extend medical coverage to the 15 per cent of Americans who were totally without medical insurance. Second, he wanted to stem the spiralling cost of medical care. He delegated the job of producing a health-care plan to his wife Hillary and to Ira Magaziner an old confidant and author of books on industrial policy in the US. It took them 15 months to produce an outline Health Care Security Act which, among other things, required employers to provide health-care coverage, extended coverage to the whole population, created an internal market device called alliances to purchase coverage and services, and placed price controls on insurance policies.

The plan was submitted to Congress in October 1993. Twelve months later it was still in Congress never to emerge as legislation. What went wrong? Most commentators agree that some of the blame must be attributed to the plan itself. It did propose the creation of a new bureaucracy; it was unpopular with business and especially with smaller companies; and it was not at all obvious that it would cut costs. As a result, it was heavily criticized in Congress where it was referred to a number of committees, each with *different* priorities. Alternative plans were eventually drawn up by congressional Democrats and Republicans but these proved unacceptable to the White House. Indeed, the President and his team proved less than apt at guiding the legislation through Congress – although, to be fair, *any* major reform of the health-care system, however well steered through Congress, would have encountered difficulties.[1] The major problem

---

[1] *See* Bryan D. Jones and Billy Hall, 'Issue Expansion in the Early Clinton Administration: Health Care and Deficit Reduction', in Bryan D. Jones, *The New American Politics: Reflections on Political Change and the Clinton Administration*, (Boulder CO, Westview, 1995).

with the policy area is that most Americans receive very good health care, and the sizeable minority who do not can only improve their coverage at the expense of the majority. Such a situation is not amenable to easy solutions – and especially not when the major priority of government is to reduce the budget deficit without increasing taxation. It now seems, indeed, that a major overhaul of health-delivery systems is unlikely to occur for some years.

Conclusions

Perhaps the most remarkable development in American social policy over the last twenty years is the virtual abandonment by Democratic leaders of the sort of redistributive measures associated with the New Deal and the Great Society. For, while social security and Medicare remain politically sacrosanct, welfare and a number of other income support programmes are now viewed with hostility. For Republicans and those on the right, it was always thus. Today, they have been joined by many Democrats including a Democratic president.

In this sense, the status of a major aspect of American social policy has returned to its pre-New Deal position. Income support should be provided for the 'truly needy' who are unable to work. Any adult who is able to work must do so, or forfeit the support of the state. Notions of self-reliance remain very powerful in the United States.

15

MANAGING ECONOMIC CHANGE

Sometimes magic works, sometimes it doesn't. For a generation after World War II, America had (as Tom Wolfe put it) a 'magic economy.' . . . In less than thirty years everything doubled. That is the real earnings of the typical worker, the real income of the typical family, consumption per capita. 'In 1973 the magic went away.'

Paul Krugman, in *Peddling Prosperity*

As recently as 35 years ago, a section on economic policy in a textbook on American politics would not have been considered necessary. Today it is essential. Not since the 1930s have economic issues dominated the policy agenda as they do now. Abroad, America's standing has changed in a new and often hostile international economic order. At home, the budget and foreign trade deficits have become perennial problems. It hardly needs stressing that the state of the economy is vitally important, not only for the economic role of governments in society and the ways in which they tax citizens and allocate expenditure, but also for the health of the polity. Small wonder, then, that economic policy has come to dominate the agenda of the 1980s and 1990s. Governments, moreover, are now irrevocably involved in economic affairs. Some 35 per cent of gross domestic product is accounted for by government expenditure; federal regulation of industrial and commercial affairs, from environmental protection to antimonopoly law, is widespread; and, by manipulating aggregate levels of expenditure and taxation and altering the supply of money in the economy, all federal governments now accept the need to 'manage' the economy. Regulation has been discussed elsewhere (chapter 11), and this section's aim is to study economic management policies and in particular to identify those forces that shape the economic policy-making agenda.

State and Economy in the United States

As chapter 2 emphasized, the traditional view of the United States is of a country where the state plays a relatively minor role. In contrast to the burgeoning welfare states and mixed economies of Europe, convention has it that Americans prefer market to public mechanisms to distribute goods and services in society. By most simple quantitative measures this view has some validity. The United States is low on scales measuring the percentage of GNP accounted for by public expenditure and of taxation's share of GNP.

Note also, however, that America is closer to such countries as Australia and Spain than it is to Japan, so we might be better advised to label Japan rather than the United States as the 'exception' (table 15.1). And although the trend in expenditures has been upwards, there has been no dramatic change since the late 1950s, the increase being from about 27 to 35 per cent of GNP. Of course, if a longer time-span is taken, then the growth of public expenditure has been dramatic. In 1930 the percentage of GNP accounted for by public expenditure was less than 10 per cent. Much of the increase since

Table 15.1 Public expenditure as percentage of GDP and in per capita $ (late 1980s)

			Per capita expenditure	
	% GDP	*% OECD mean*	*PPP $*	*% OECD Mean*
USA	35.3	81	6,473	121
Canada	42.8	99	7,368	138
Norway	48.1	111	7,410	139
Switzerland	30.1	69	4,767	89
Sweden	60.0	138	8,262	155
Denmark	55.7	128	7,375	138
Germany	43.2	99	5,755	108
Japan	27.2	63	3,585	66
France	48.4	112	6,197	116
Finland	38.2	88	4,904	92
Australia	35.0	81	4,414	83
United Kingdom	42.9	99	5,293	99
Netherlands	54.0	124	6,616	124
Italy	45.2	104	5,538	104
Belgium	50.6	117	5,972	112
Austria	47.3	109	5,517	104
New Zealand	41.9	97	4,475	84
Spain	36.1	83	3,134	59
Ireland	50.4	116	3,801	71
Greece	43.0	99	2,736	51
Portugal	37.6	87	2,368	44
Average	43.4		5,331	

Source: OECD, reproduced in Richard Rose, 'Is American Public Policy Exceptional?' in Byron Shafer (ed.), *Is America Different?* (Oxford University Press, 1991), table 7.2.

Figure 15.1 Federal outlays as a percentage of GNP/GDP, 1869–1998

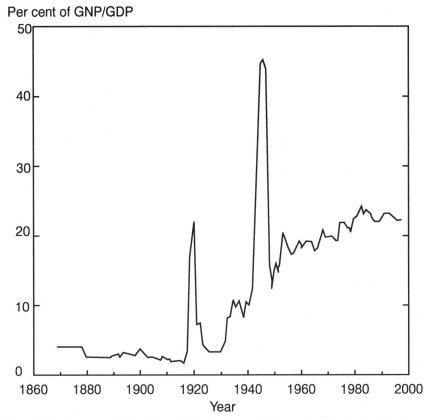

Source: Various, as compiled by Harold W. Stanley and Richard G. Niemi, *Vital Statistics on American Politics*, (Washington D.C., Congressional Quarterly, 1994), figure 13.1.

then is a result of massively enhanced defence spending and, since the early 1960s, of the partial replacement of defence expenditure with spending on a range of domestic programmes. If we examine federal government expenditures alone, what stands out is the rapid growth in spending precipitated by the two world wars and by the New Deal. Until the early 1930s, less than 5 per cent of GNP was accounted for by federal spending. Since 1945 it has been rising slowly and erratically, and today it is around 22 per cent of GNP (fig. 15.1).

Whatever the relative position of the USA, the sheer size of the government budgets should not be underestimated. In 1997 the federal government alone will spend over $1700 billion, and total expenditures of all governments will come to over $2400 billion. As table 15.2 shows, the gap between this expenditure and income – the federal debt – increased rapidly until 1992 so that, by the mid-1980s, the size of the deficit had become the number-one economic issue. As in every other developed economy, American governments – and

Table 15.2 Federal receipts, outlays and deficits 1979–96 (billions of dollars)

	Receipts	Outlays	Deficit	Deficit as a % of GDP
1979	463	503	−40	1.6
1980	517	591	−74	2.7
1985	734	946	−212	5.3
1989	990	1,144	−154	2.9
1990	1,031	1,251	−220	4.0
1991	1,054	1,323	−269	4.7
1992	1,090	1,380	−290	4.9
1993	1,153	1,408	−255	4.1
1994	1,257	1,461	−203	3.1
1995[1]	1,364	1,539	−192	2.7
1996[1]	1,415	1,612	−197	2.6

[1] = estimated
Source: Economic Report of the President, 1995, Washington DC.

particularly the federal government – have enormous potential power over economic activity. By increasing spending and lowering taxation the economy can be stimulated. Conversely, lower spending and higher taxes can lower the level of economic activity. Used in this way, fiscal policy is a major tool of macro-economic policy. Other tools include control over credit and money supply, both of which are currently in fashion as means of fighting inflation.

American government affects the economy in a number of other ways, most of which can be contained under the general description of micro-economic policy. Micro-economic policy is concerned not with pulling fiscal and monetary levers to affect the general direction in which the economy moves, but rather with a range of policy instruments that affect the specific behaviour of individuals, firms, sectors and regions. Hence, industrial policy, labour relations, education, training, and regional and urban policy are typical micro-economic tools.

Regulatory policy can also be a micro-economic device, although, as we saw in chapter 11, it is often motivated by non-economic considerations such as the promotion of equality or the protection of the environment. It hardly needs mentioning that this range of macro- and micro-policies is not perceived by policy-makers as a coherent set of interrelated instruments. Neither do the policies always complement one another according to some coherent economic rationale. If anything, the very opposite applies. Politicians and bureaucrats are not in agreement as to which policy should be applied at any particular time; and the policies themselves often compete with, rather than complement, one another; or as the economists would put it, *trade-offs* exist between (say) education and training policy and taxation, or between inflation and unemployment.

When attempting to identify the scope and limitations of economic policy in any society, institutional and ideological factors are important. How do these constrain economic policy-making in the United States?

Ideology and Economic Policy

As our discussion in earlier chapters showed, ideology plays an important part in shaping the policy agenda or in influencing which issues or alternative policies are available for debate and discussion at any one time. In most Western countries economic policy has been influenced by three distinct philosophies, each of which has its defenders among economists as well as its political champions. On the right, economic liberals look to the market for salvation. In the centre, Keynesians believe that, when the market fails to provide full employment and steady growth, governments should step in and, via increased spending and borrowing, stimulate demand. On the left, socialists place the market in a subordinate position in relation to a public sector that would plan the allocation of resources in society. Socialist solutions are effectively excluded from the policy agenda in the United States and now almost everywhere else. They carry connotations of collectivism unacceptable in a society so infused with economic individualism. Until the 1980s, most debate involved clashes between liberals and Keynesians. Much of the politics of economic policy, then, centred on levels of taxation and spending, and on the extent to which credit and the money supply should be controlled. Prior to 1933, liberal economics dominated; it was not until the New Deal and World War II that federal governments began to 'borrow and spend their way out of trouble', either to stimulate a depressed economy or to produce war *matériel* on a massive scale. To the economic liberal, high levels of government expenditures are bad enough, even if they are covered by taxation. But deficit spending and loose money-supply policies are even worse, for these lead directly to inflation and, so the argument runs, eventually to disaster. Economic liberals' antipathy even to government expenditure adequately financed by taxation derives from their conviction that the market is the only efficient and acceptable allocator of resources. When governments allocate they do so wastefully and inefficiently. Of course, the free marketeers accept that governments have to play some role, especially in defence. But the essence of their philosophy is to reduce what has become a very intrusive role in society and always to ensure that what expenditure remains is recovered by taxation.

During the late 1930s and 1940s Keynesian thinking dominated, and successive federal governments ran up large deficits, the peak being reached in the admittedly unusual conditions of wartime in 1943 when, in one year, a $54.8 billion deficit amounted to some 35 per cent of GNP. Interestingly, though most of the post-war period is usually labelled 'Keynesian', total federal debt as a percentage of GNP declined steadily until 1970, although it rose sharply thereafter until levelling off in the early 1990s. If debt has been increasing, spending has been rising sharply. Moreover, there has been a tendency towards increased domestic, rather than defence, spending. To the economic liberal the latter may be justifiable, the former rarely is. The liberal position was given further stimulus by the events of the early and mid-1970s. During the 1971–73 period, loose money-supply policies were accompanied by steep rises in commodity prices, culminating in the 1973–74 fourfold increase in oil prices. These fuelled inflation and wrought serious damage on the supply side of the economy. Producers, in other words, found their costs increasing rapidly. Their incentive to produce and invest was greatly undermined, resulting in a drop in output and rising unemployment. The ensuing recession convinced many in the Ford and Carter administrations that the way back to economic health lay in recreating the right production and investment environment – low taxes, inflation and interest rates. This, they argued, could be achieved only if governments avoided overstimulating demand through expenditure and borrowing. But neither president was very successful in keeping government spending down, and, when elected in 1980, President Reagan made a much stronger pledge to cut expenditure, borrowing and taxes, and therefore provide an amenable investment environment. We will examine how Ronald Reagan's new economic programme fared later.

Although, by the late 1990s, we can conclude that a near consensus on the need for liberal economics existed, conflicts over the consequences of liberal policies remain. Many in the Democratic Party and in the labour unions continued to advocate Keynesian solutions, and most commentators remained wary of the *political* feasibility of exclusively free-market solutions, whatever their economic merits. In addition, many political leaders are concerned about the social consequences of expenditure cuts. As established in earlier chapters, federal, state and local governments are now irrevocably involved in the business of providing a wide range of economic and social services whether they like it or not. The tension between this plain fact and the prevailing liberal economic philosophy is considerable and unlikely to disappear in the immediate future.

The liberal-Keynesian conflict in economic policy is essentially about macro-economic management. What then of the relationship between ideology and micro-economic policy? In some respects, adopting interventionist micro-strategies to solve economic problems is more of a challenge to liberal ideology than is Keynesian demand management. For, industrial or regional policy assumes that governments can and should interfere with individual economic actors or sectors by providing incentives, subsidies, loans or guidance. Perhaps for this reason, the United States has less consciously planned and developed industrial, regional and labour-market policies than any comparable country. Indeed there *is* no federal industrial or regional strategy worth the name, and training and labour-force policies are more ameliorative *ad hoc* measures than true labour-market strategies. Japan and France, by way of contrast, have had highly developed industrial policies involving centrally co-ordinated resource and investment planning. In Japan's case, industrial planning by sector involved close linkages between government, corporations and unions. Such corporatist arrangements were, until recently, quite alien to the American way of doing things.

Nonetheless, during the 1970s, a number of commentators, noting the relatively poor economic performance of the United States, called for a federal industrial policy. These calls went unheeded and all but faded away amidst the free-wheeling economic boom of the middle and later Reagan years. By the early 1990s, however, industrial policy had returned to the centre of the economic stage. Slow or even negative economic growth continued for several years, and increasingly invidious comparisons were made between the performance of American as opposed to Japanese and German industry. By 1993 the incoming Clinton administration was committed to an economic strategy that could be interpreted as industrial policy, including an economic-stimulus package: infrastructure investment, a federal training programme and special help to facilitate innovation in high-growth industries such as microchips and genetics. Very early in the first Clinton term, however, the advocates of industrial policy, and especially Labor Secretary Robert Reich, were eclipsed by economic and political events. The economy recovered rapidly from 1993, thus partly removing the need for an economic-stimulus package. This recovery was, moreover, steady and non-inflationary. Further government expenditure may have resulted in 'overheating' and renewed inflation. As important for the fate of the package were dissenting voices from within the administration. Deputy Director of the Office of Management and Budget, Alice Rivlin, had written a book, *Reviving the American Dream*, which argued that what the economy needed was less, not more, federal government expenditure and regulation. Although her perspective was at first unpopular, by the middle of 1993 it was her views, rather than those of Robert Reich, which were on the ascendant within the White House.[1] Finally, there was deep disquiet among Republicans in Congress that the stimulus package represented a giant pork-barrel give-away. This combination of factors killed the stimulus package in Congress. Indeed, by the end of 1993, the whole industrial-policy question had slipped from the policy agenda.

Of course, the US has had a range of industrial policies for many years, from loans provided by the Small Business Administration to aid for urban transport schemes, to employment-creation programmes for poor cities and rural areas to investment incentives for commercial and industrial development. At the state and local levels, similar programmes and schemes exist. Crucially, however, these have in the main been *ad hoc* and unco-ordinated, and have emerged as a result of the lobbying and bargaining processes outlined in earlier chapters. They cannot, therefore, be considered as part of an economic or industrial *strategy*.

Institutions and Economic Policy

The relationship between ideology and political and social institutions has inspired debate within social science for many years. In American politics, for example, whether federalism is a cause of a limited federal-planning and co-ordinating role in society or whether it has been maintained as a result of the power of liberal ideology, has never been resolved. Whatever the causal directions, there can be no doubting that institutional arrangements continue to have a profound effect on economic policy-making. Indeed, some would argue that the institutional constraints are such that no administration can effectively manage the American economy. What are the constraints?

Federalism and localism Chapter 5 referred to competitive interdependence in US intergovernmental relations and showed how the federal government is now locked in a symbiotic relationship with lower-level governments. So, although federal governments continue to hand out large sums of money to states and localities, it is no easy thing to withdraw this largesse in line with economic imperatives. State and local governments have multiple channels of access to officials in Washington and, notwithstanding recent cutbacks in federal aid, formidable political resources can be harnessed to defend federally funded programmes. Of course, to a greater or lesser extent, this goes on every-

---

[1] For a discussion of these events, *see* Paul E. Peterson, *The Price of Federalism*, (Washington DC, Brookings, 1995), Chapter 8.

Plate 15.1 Panic on Wall Street. Frenzied traders on the floor of the New York Stock Exchange, September 1986.

where but the institution of federalism gives to individual states added legal weight in their efforts to maintain federal funding. Federalism also encourages 'highest common denominator' options when funds are being allocated. In other words, federal governments find it very difficult to discriminate between states according to some rational economic principle. When providing regional economic or research and development aid, for example, who gets what depends more on lobbying, criteria of equity or mere chance than on the needs of economy. The failure to develop a coherent micro-economic strategy must in part be related to this phenomenon.

State and local governments also have independent revenue sources, which can weaken the scope and substance of federal fiscal policy. Federal revenues account for only about 60 per cent of all government income in the USA, the remainder deriving from state and local sales, property and income taxes. Constitutionally, and in marked contrast to the situation in a country like Britain, the federal government cannot *directly* affect these revenues. It is easy to make too much of this point, however. Runaway spending by subnational governments is uncommon. Many state constitutions prohibit deficit spending, and the bulk of government debt in the USA is incurred at the federal level. But, in a rather indirect sense, the fiscal goings-on of state and local governments do affect federal budgets, for their fiscal problems, together with opposition by publics to increased state and

local taxes, can lead to calls for federal revenues to fill the gaps left by
tax-limitation measures. Some commentators have, indeed, pointed
to the paradoxical possibility that antipathy towards impersonal
government and high taxes will lead to greater centralization at the
state and at federal levels.

Separation of powers When studying economic policy-making in the
USA, foreign observers usually look first to the budgetary process and
in particular to the conflicts between Congress and president that the
spending power produces. Given the American concern with macro-
policy and with controlling spending, this is perhaps not surprising.
Indeed, as chapters 8–11 showed, battles over spending are the very
essence of presidential and of congressional politics. Much of the conflict derives from a simple constitutional fact: Congress, and in particular the House of Representatives, was given the power to raise taxes
and appropriate monies for the executive branch to spend. As the role
of the government has expanded, so the need for institutional mechanisms to co-ordinate and control spending has also increased. So
president and Congress have improved and streamlined their budgetary bureaucracies, each intent to provide the other branch with a
coherent spending and taxing policy.

On the executive side, the first important item of legislation was the
1921 Budget and Accounting Act which created the Bureau of the
Budget, a bureaucracy designed to provide improved budget advice
and review for the president. At first, the Bureau of the Budget was
intended to help control spending – an objective in line with the prevailing *laissez-faire* or liberal philosophy that spending was essentially
a bad thing. All changed with the coming of the New Deal, when,
under the leadership of Franklin Roosevelt, the Bureau became a partisan for increased spending in opposition to a sometimes hostile Congress. The Bureau was also formally incorporated into the Executive
Office of the President during this period, and its staff increased from
40 to over 600. The next significant law was the 1946 Full Employment Act, a piece of legislation that effectively endorsed Keynesian
demand management by pledging the federal government to full-
employment policies. Among other measures, the Act created the
Council of Economic Advisers, a further White House innovation but
this time designed to encourage presidents to pursue 'rational economic policies to foster and promote free competition, to avoid economic fluctuations or to diminish the effects thereof, and to maintain
employment, production, and purchasing power'. The 1946 Act also
mandated the president to produce an annual Economic Report to
document economic performance over the past year and to provide
Congress with a programme for the coming year.

Since 1946, successive presidents have experimented further with the budget machinery, usually to inject rationality into burgeoning federal budgets. Lyndon Johnson ordered the adoption of planning programming-budgeting systems, effectively a technique to link spending with preconceived planning priorities. Jimmy Carter, in turn, adopted zero-base budgeting, or budget plans organized from the bottom up according to spending limits rather than according to specific programme objectives. The latter adapts spending to (say) the construction of so many miles of interstate highway or to a particular objective in the space programme and thus tends towards expenditure rising incrementally. The point about these and other innovations is that they reflect presidents' growing concern with the sheer size of the budget and the need to present Congress with a coherent spending plan.

Congress has responded with its own innovations. The 1946 Act, for example, created a Joint Economic Committee consisting of seven senators and seven members of Congress to provide Congress with a total view of the economy and aid the legislature's response to presidential initiatives. More recently, the 1974 Budget Reform Act created a Congressional Budget Office, together with Budget Committees, to provide each House with a coherent view of budget-making and instil a sense of spending priority, rather than proceed as had been the case in the past on an incremental basis. Judging by the first few years of the new budget process, congressional control has improved but the fundamental problems of budget-making remain. These are simply that Congress's role is negative rather than positive. Or, as we discovered in chapter 10, 'the president proposes and Congress disposes'. Economic management is first and foremost an executive responsibility. Until the reforms, the role of congress was confined to trimming, tinkering or otherwise modifying the president's budget on an *ad hoc* basis. After the reforms, the congressional budget committees played a more prominent role which almost certainly made the budget process more cumbersome. The budget timetable remained effectively the same. In the spring of Year One the departments and agencies submit their expenditure estimates to OMB. OMB then spends several months reviewing – and often cutting – these estimates until the president formally submits the budget to Congress in late January of Year Two. During the ensuing nine months, the budget committees work with the legislative and appropriations committees to reconcile competing interests and objectives until a final budget resolution or reconciliation is passed in September before the beginning of the financial year on 1 October. During the first years of the Carter presidency, the system seemed to work moderately well, but then the economy was growing rapidly and deficits actually ended up quite close to the president's projections. Since 1980, the situation has been transformed, first by deepening recession, and later by deficits far exceeding expectations (table 15.2). This period has also seen the most radical and frenzied activity in the politics and procedures of Congressional budget-making ever experienced.

This started in the first few weeks of the Reagan administration, when the president submitted major changes for spending in 1982, 1983 and 1984. Large increases in defence spending and cuts in domestic programmes were proposed. Parallel, quite radical cuts in taxation were also introduced into Congress. On the budget side, a new resolution, known as Gramm-Latta I (after Delbert L. Latta, the ranking Republican on the House Budget Committee, and Phil Gramm, a leading Democratic conservative on the committee), actually instructed 15 House committees and 14 Senate committees on how their budgets would be slashed over the next three years. The amounts involved – 36, 47 and 56 billion dollars in each of these years – were huge. Finally, the resolution was framed in such a way that any subsequent supplementary appropriations would be very difficult to achieve.[2] In reaction to these Draconian measures, congressional committees submitted a mass of new legislation designed to reassert traditional congressional power. The administration, fearing a sudden increase in spending, accepted a modified resolution (Gramm-Latta II) which was finally passed, very speedily, in August.

Although the final bill imposed less extensive cuts than those originally planned, this particular budget experience was almost the antithesis of the slow, incremental, deliberative process for which Congress is famous. In retrospect, we can conclude that president Reagan was fortunate to have the support of three key groups in Congress – the conservative Republicans, conservative Southern Democrats (the 'Boll Weevils') and, crucially, moderate Republicans (the 'Gypsy Moths'). It was this coalition that also helped the administration achieve quite startling tax cuts in the same session. Always a fragile arrangement, signs of collapse were evident even by late 1981, and after 1982 the administration was much less successful in handling Congress.

Within Congress, the 'traditional' centres of budgetary power, the appropriations committees and subcommittees, reasserted their influence. During his last few years in office, Reagan found it easier to deal directly with these committees rather than work through the budget committees which were prone endlessly to tinker with the details of the budget. The events of 1981 were, in other words, exceptional.

---

[2] For a full discussion, *see* Robert W. Hartman, 'Congress and budget making', *Political Science Quarterly*, vol. 97, Fall 1982.

Underneath all the dramatic events of those first few months of the new administration, the policy networks, clientelism, and fragmented and autonomous centres of power, which earlier chapters have described, did not somehow miraculously disappear. What the 1981 experience does show is that Congress was at least capable of rapid response to presidential economic initiative. It also demonstrated the growing influence of the Office of Management and Budget which, under the leadership of David Stockman, assumed a very central position as designer and as manager of government-spending priorities.[3]

The problem of dealing with the deficit was sufficiently serious to inspire Congress, under pressure from the administration, to pass the Gramm-Rudman-Hollings Deficit Reduction Act in 1985. By imposing on Congress a timetable for mandatory spending cuts, the law would indeed have solved the budget deficit, with major cuts falling on defence and the discretionary programmes. In 1986, however, the Supreme Court declared the mandatory provisions of the law unconstitutional violations of the separation of powers. As a result, that which is now an advisory law has produced much smaller cuts than originally anticipated.

George Bush faced a Democratic Congress intent on defending a range of entitlement and other domestic programmes. In each of Bush's four years in office, Congress and president were at loggerheads on the budget which, together with a weakening economy, resulted in the ballooning of the deficit during 1989–92 (table 15.2).

Budget drama continued with the first Clinton Administration. During his first two years in office, things went relatively smoothly. Congress was still in the hands of the Democrats, the economy was growing steadily and, during 1993, the President's budget included expenditure cuts that helped reduce the budget deficit (table 15.2). All changed with the election of a Republican Congress in 1994, however. Under the leadership of House Speaker Newt Gingrich, the Republicans were intent on extensive cuts in federal social spending for fiscal year 1996. President and Congress failed to agree on a budget by the October 1995 deadline, and this resulted in a much-publicized partial close-down of the federal government. 'Non-essential' workers were laid off, national parks closed, and the crisis was not resolved until early 1996. These events were not repeated in 1996 – mainly because of the political costs to all parties of being seen as unco-operative during an election year – but the potential for conflict remains. This is especially true in an era of divided government.

[3] Although even Stockman's glittering reputation was tarnished somewhat following the publication of a magazine article which revealed his misgivings about the rationality of the policy process. *See* William Greider, 'The education of David Stockman', *Atlantic Monthly*, December 1981. Stockman was eventually to resign in 1985.

The economic problems of the 1980s and 1990s highlighted another important institutional relationship which is peculiarly American: the unique political position of the American central bank, the Federal Reserve System. Created in 1913, the Federal Reserve is a 'decentralized' central bank consisting of 12 Federal Reserve Districts governed by a board in Washington. Congress deliberately gave the board some autonomy from the president and, in recent years, the chairmen of the board have asserted their independence to some effect. This is important because the Federal Reserve has special responsibility for implementing monetary policy, and in particular for setting interest-rate levels. With budget deficits increasing, one recent chairman, Paul Volcker, insisted on controlling the money supply through a policy of high interest rates. Although at first the Reagan administration accepted the Federal Reserve's policy in this area, by late 1982, serious disagreement had emerged between Volcker and Donald Regan, the Treasury Secretary. Volcker continued to insist on a tight money policy, while some members of the administration wanted some relaxation to help lift the economy out of recession. Later, Volcker became a vocal critic of the rapidly appreciating dollar, while the administration generally viewed this as a problem for other countries. In these countries, central banks, if not the creatures of executives, are often significantly less autonomous than the Federal Reserve System.

George Bush had an easier time with a Federal Reserve under the chairmanship of Alan Greenspan – although the president did call for a more rapid reduction in interest rates during the recession of 1991/92 than the Federal Reserve eventually sanctioned. Greenspan continued as chairman during the Clinton Administrations. Bill Clinton was fortunate, however, that during the whole of his first term, the economy grew steadily without threatening inflation. As a result, interest rates were kept relatively low, and the Federal Reserve's fine tuning of the economy remained essentially non-controversial.

Conclusion

In many respects, the economic policy-making system resembles the social policy system. In both, the chief executive has the major responsibility for policy formulation and implementation, and in both he or she faces competition from other centres of power – notably Congress, executive departments and agencies, state and local governments, and organized interests. There are, however, some important qualitative differences between the two policy areas. Economic policy is obviously more important in the sense that most other domestic and foreign policies depend on it. All parties and politicians have interests in economic performance and all believe that the federal government has to play a key role in economic management. They may disagree – sometimes radically – on what that role should be but no one disputes the need for economic policy. Social policy, in contrast, is considered by many on the right not to be a legitimate concern of the federal government. The great paradox of social policy is the incontrovertible fact that dozens of federal programmes exist in the absence of central co-ordination and control. Control problems apply to economic policy, too, of course, but not in quite the same way. Measures of performance – inflation, growth, interest-rate levels, the deficit, unemployment – exist to provide a focus of activity for policy-makers, as does the budgetary process itself. Nonetheless, macro-economic management is shared between at least three major institutions – presidency, Congress and Federal Reserve – which is highly unusual in comparative context. And micro-economic policy-making is as confused and incoherent as social policy. What the two policy systems do share in common is that both are attempting to solve apparently intractable problems. Most other countries are experiencing similar difficulties of economic and social management, but in few are institutional arrangements organized in such an apparently inconvenient manner.

Before ending our discussion of economic policy, some reference to the growing consensus on economic management during the late 1990s should be mentioned. Much of this consensus revolves around two themes. First, the almost universal perception that the budget deficit must be brought down to zero without increasing taxation. Holding this consensus together may prove relatively easy while the economy is growing. Should it falter, however (as it always has in the past), then the institutional conflicts inherent in the American system will receive fresh impetus. The second and related dimension to the consensus is the wide acceptance that free markets at home and abroad are the only mechanisms that can produce lasting prosperity. This means less government interference at home and the achievement of open markets in international trade. While every recent administration has been committed to both, the costs of such policies can be high. Less government is not always compatible with other values such as clean air, an educated work-force, affirmative action and consumer protection. Free trade can lead to the demise of local industries and the 'export' of American jobs to lower-cost countries such as Mexico. The apparent economic consensus of the late 1990s does not somehow magically remove these conflicts. Indeed, as with the deficit, should the economy falter badly, they will return to the top of the political agenda.

16

THE AMERICAN WORLD ROLE

Oliver Cromwell once said that a man-of-war is the best ambassador. That's not really quite true. As the negotiations with North Korea proved, the best approach is a good ambassador backed up by a man-of-war.

Defense Secretary William Perry, 1994

Today, as an old order passes, the new world is more free but less stable. Communism's collapse has called forth old animosities and new dangers. Clearly America must continue to lead the world we did so much to make.

President Clinton, Inaugural Address, 1992

Over the last 60 years the United States has been transformed from one of six or seven world powers with a standing army of under 200,000 and few foreign alliances or military bases, into a country with a military machine of almost three million men and women under arms (over a million of whom are stationed overseas), alliances with nearly 50 countries and unrivalled military and diplomatic status and capacity. From being isolationist and contemptuous of the 'corruption' and imperialism of the old European powers, the United States is itself, in spite of recent reverses, now in a position to exploit and dominate other countries and, unlike the pre-war powers, literally to determine the fate of all humankind.

The country's political processes and institutions have not always handled these new responsibilities well. Indeed, one school of thought argues that a country infused with a past characterized by a combination of isolationism and idealism is ill suited to playing the role of world police officer. Certainly, there have been many foreign and military policy mistakes in the post-war era, including the Vietnam War, which caused serious domestic conflict and terrible suffering and instability throughout Indo-China. This section will not, however, concentrate on normative questions of fortune and folly in American foreign policy. Instead, our discussion will focus on the policy-making process and on the constraints imposed on foreign policy by institutional arrangements and public opinion.

The Institutional Context

As with social and economic affairs, it is somewhat misleading to refer to an American foreign *policy*, for there are at least three distinct types of foreign and defence policies. There is, first, strategic foreign policy, or the general stance of the United States in relation to other countries over time. Scholars have been quick to identify two competing themes in the post-war period – realist and idealist. Realism[1] is, simply, the pursuit of 'national self-interest' and is associated with international power politics and the implementation of policies that have clear military, diplomatic or economic benefits. Idealism, in contrast, injects a moral or normative element into policy, as such presidential rhetoric as 'making the world safe for democracy' or achieving 'peace with honour' in Vietnam implies. We will return to these two characterizations of strategic policy later. Although strategic policy is influenced by the broader society and polity, its main institutional context comprises the presidency, National Security Council and State Department.

Second, crisis management is a crucial part of foreign policy. Since World War II, the Berlin airlift, Suez, the Cuban missile crisis, the Gulf of Tonkin incident, a number of subsequent military actions in Indo-China, American reactions to military activity in the Middle East including the Gulf War and the Iranian hostage crisis, have all involved the United States in quick crisis-management decisions.[2] Generally, the presidency and National Security Council are the institutional foci of these decisions although, the longer the crisis drags on, the more likely are Congress and the public to become involved. Just this happened with the year-long Iranian hostage crisis in 1979–80.

Third, logistical or structural defence policy involves the deployment of billions of dollars-worth of material and over one million

[1]   The classic account of the realist position is by Hans J. Morgenthau, *In Defense of the National Interest*, (New York, Alfred Knopf, 1951).
[2]   For a good account of post-war foreign policy, *see* James A. Nathan and James K. Oliver, *Foreign Policy Making and the American Political System*, (Boston, Little, Brown, 1983).

Plate 16.1 The United States' armada en route for the Gulf. An F.A. 18 jet is catapulted from a US Navy carrier, 1990.

personnel around the globe. As we established in earlier chapters, this process entails voters, organized interests (defence contractors), state and local governments and congressional committees, as well as the more obvious institutions of Department of Defense and presidency. While this policy system is much more open and accessible than strategic and crisis-management policy, it is almost certainly less fragmented and pluralistic than the processes associated with social or economic policy. Oligopolistic defence industries are protected by government contracts,[3] and the defence budget has a powerful base of support in Congress.

These three contrasting institutional settings for foreign and defence policy do impinge on one another. Logistics and weapons systems can influence strategic thinking (the Cruise missile) and crisis management (the Iranian hostage crisis, the bombing of Libya, the Gulf War), while strategic considerations are obviously important determinants of logistical policy. Similarly, crisis management is profoundly affected by the strategic context. During the Cuban missile

[3] The big eight arms contractors, Boeing, General Dynamics, Grumman, Lockheed, McDonnel Douglas, Northrop, Rockwell International and United Technologies, receive almost one-third of defence contracts, and most depend on government contracts for their survival.

crisis, for example, President Kennedy referred constantly to the infringement of an American sphere of influence (the Western hemisphere) which was a long-established part of American foreign policy.

How has decision-making in each of these policy areas changed over time? Perhaps obviously, crisis management has always primarily been the prerogative of the president and his closest aides in the National Security Council. Quick response requires tightly knit decision-making structures, and, as commander-in-chief, the president has the constitutional, as well as political, position to assume the leadership of such structures. Not that this means that the president and the aides are completely insulated from the outside world during a crisis and make their choices according to strictly rational criteria. As Graham Allison has shown in his brilliant study of the Cuban missile crisis, at least three competing models of decision-making can be used to explain the events of the crisis, two of which put great premium on outside information and political and bureaucratic procedures and pressures.[4] But crisis management is, compared with other policy-making processes in American government, remarkably free from political and societal pressures.

The main development in strategic foreign policy-making has been the gradual centralization of power in president and National Security Council, at the cost of State Department influence. This has shown itself most graphically in the eclipse of some recent secretaries of state in the shadow of national-security advisers – most notably Henry Kissinger and Zbigniew Brzezinski. As research has shown, presidents have increasingly eschewed state departments and their secretaries, because they can represent independent sources of authority and control over particular issues and areas. Certain countries or policy options are championed within the department, and it is simply not convenient for presidents to have to join battle with the professional bureaucrats when foreign policy is formulated.[5] White House/departmental antagonism occurs in other areas, of course, but, within foreign policy, presidents do at least have the option of, if not ignoring the State Department, at least of bypassing it. For the State Department effectively has no domestic constituency, and its officials are unusually neutral and apolitical, versed as they are in the arts of diplomacy and moderation. So while presidents may find it almost impossible to disregard the Departments of Defense, Agriculture or

---

[4] Graham T. Allison, *Essence of Decision: Explaining the Cuban Missile Crisis*, (Boston, Little, Brown, 1971).
[5] *See* Bert A. Rockman, 'America's Department of State: irregular and regular syndromes of policy making', *American Political Science Review*, vol. 75, no. 4, December 1981.

Commerce, they can almost do this in the case of State. Foreign policy is also more insulated from the other 'traditional' centres of power in American government. House and, particularly, Senate Foreign Relations Committees are important forums for discussion and criticism, but their function is qualitatively different from (say) those of the Armed Services and Agriculture Committees with their entrenched relationships with big spending bureaux and powerful corporate clients.

In other words, foreign-policy decision-making is different. Within the White House the NSC is uniquely important and, in theory at least, consistency and coherence are almost certainly more achievable in foreign affairs than in many domestic areas. It may be, of course, that clarity and coherence can lead to greater errors of judgement and strategy, and that more pluralistic arrangements would lead to greater moderation. Perhaps. But it should be noted that in *cross-national context*, American presidents are *not* particularly free from institutional and political constraints in foreign policy-making. Public and Congressional opinion has been exerted on presidents with increasing intensity since the events of Vietnam and Watergate. Earlier chapters have catalogued some of these constraints, including the 1973 War Powers Act. President Reagan's 1983 remark, when he heard of British Prime Minister Thatcher's carefully disguised visit to the Falklands, that he 'couldn't even go to church in secret' reveals a great deal. Presidents and their policy-makers are constantly exposed to public scrutiny; they may be able to secrete themselves away in the NSC and plan general strategy. They may also be relatively free from direct and immediate congressional or bureaucratic pressure. But they still have to operate in the context of the American political system, with all that this implies in terms of openness and accessibility. So individual ethnic groups, such as Americans of Cuban or Jewish origin, constantly monitor the administration policy towards Cuba or Israel. Right-wing caucuses, such as Jesse Helms's National Congressional Club, campaign strongly in favour of a hard line towards Cuba. Since the Vietnam War, the involvement of American troops in counter-insurgency wars abroad has become especially difficult because of the ever-present potential for serious domestic political opposition.

The openness of the official system has led to the evolution of an 'unofficial' foreign-policy system on at least two occasions. Such was the case during 1969–73 when illegal acts were committed in southeast Asia. More dramatic were the events of the Iran-Contra affair which involved the creation of an alternative foreign-policy machinery in the White House under the guidance of NSC Adviser John Poindexter, CIA Chief William Casey and Colonel Oliver North. By agreeing to secure the release of American hostages in the Lebanon by selling arms to the Iranians, the proceeds from which would go to help the Contras fighting for the overthrow of the Sandinista regime in Nicaragua, these officials were acting contrary to the spirit and to the letter of the law. President Reagan and Secretary of State George Schultz either did not know of these events or were only vaguely aware of them, thus demonstrating the extent to which the president had lost control of this particular policy system during his second term.

But the culprits in the Iran-Contra affair were discovered, thus perhaps demonstrating how much more public and press opinion can do to expose the errors of foreign policy compared with the situation in Britain and France.

American Foreign Policy in the Post-Cold War World

Until recently, the most striking feature of American foreign policy was the overwhelming influence of the realist, as opposed to idealist, school. In the context of the Cold War, American policy was couched in terms of self-interest, indeed in terms of national survival. The ideological struggle between East and West centred on territory (in Europe and in the Third World) and on economic interest (was capitalism or communism to be the model for world development?). During the early and mid-1980s, the Reagan administrations elevated this competitive struggle to the top of the policy agenda. Increased defence spending and military action in the Middle East, Grenada, Libya and Central America were all justified in terms of the national interest. By the late 1980s, signs that this particular perspective on international relations was becoming obsolete were clearly evident, and by 1992, conditions had changed to the point where presidents were making reference to what was called 'the new world order'.

The crucial change was, of course, the demise of the Soviet Union and more generally of communism as a viable alternative to capitalism. Even in China, the last major redoubt of political communism, a rejection of the centralized resource-allocation of economic communism had occurred. Communism's collapse did not transform the realist focus of American foreign policy. The Gulf War, for example, was fought at least in part to protect the West's oil supplies. But it did greatly complicate the business of identifying where, exactly, America's national interest lay.

When there was an identifiable enemy whose economic and political system was so obviously alien to the American, justifying high defence spending and the deployment of US troops abroad was

Figure 16.1 Perceptions of the Soviet Union and too-little-defence-spending attitudes

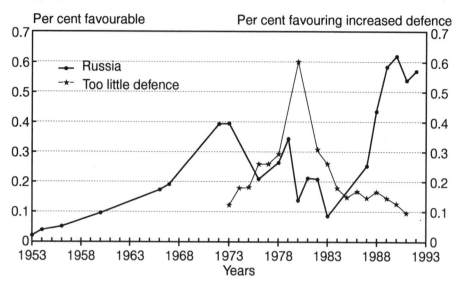

Source: William R. Thompson, 'Foreign Policy, the End of the Cold War and the 1992 Election', in Bryan C. Jones, *The New American Politics: Reflections on Political Change and the Clinton Administration*, (Boulder CO, Westview, 1995), figure 11.4

relatively easy. Today, such justification is harder. Instead of appealing to self-interest, the new world order appeals to humanitarian motives. In Somalia and Bosnia no American interests were directly threatened, yet American troops, aircraft and ships were deployed under the auspices of a UN-sponsored humanitarian mission. It remains to be seen whether the US can continue to play this role – especially in terms of winning the support of the American people.

The change in public attitudes towards defence spending and how these relate to the Cold War is amply demonstrated by fig. 16.1. Note the dramatic change in attitudes towards the Soviet Union in the late 1970s and the early 1980s, and the associated rise in the need for increased defence expenditure. When, in the late 1980s and the early 1990s, communism collapsed in Eastern Europe, a steep rise in public regard for the Soviet Union (or Russia) and a sharp decline in the perceived need for defence spending occurred. Defence spending did indeed decrease following these events. Expressed as a percentage of GDP, defence spending fell from well over 6 per cent in the mid-1980s to just over 4 per cent in 1994 (table 16.1). Defence spending is now no longer the largest item on the federal budget. As recently as 1960, it accounted for more than 50 per cent of *all* federal spending. By 1994 it had shrunk to 18.9 per cent (table 16.1).

Even so, the United States remains easily the world's most powerful military force. In terms of rapid deployment, the US has no peer.

Table 16.1 Defence outlays as a percentage of federal outlays and GDP, 1960–94

Year	Defence outlays (percentage of)	
	Federal outlays	*Gross domestic product*
1960	52.2	9.5
1965	42.8	7.5
1966	43.2	7.9
1967	45.4	9.0
1968	46.0	9.7
1969	44.9	8.9
1970	41.8	8.3
1971	37.5	7.5
1972	34.3	6.9
1973	31.2	6.0
1974	29.5	5.7
1975	26.0	5.7
1976	24.1	5.3
1976	23.2	5.0
1977	23.8	5.1
1978	22.8	4.8
1979	23.1	4.8
1980	22.7	5.1
1981	23.2	5.3
1982	24.9	5.9
1983	26.0	6.3
1984	26.7	6.2
1985	26.7	6.4
1986	27.6	6.5
1987	28.1	6.3
1988	27.3	6.0
1989	26.6	5.9
1990	23.9	5.5
1991	20.6	4.8
1992	21.6	5.0
1993	20.7	4.6
1994, est.	18.9	4.2

Source: Statistical Abstract of the United States, 1994 (Washington DC, 1994), table 537.

Only the American forces can be moved rapidly around the world to meet a crisis or emergency. No other country has this capacity. This fact alone puts pressure on American politicians to play the role of global policing and to take on a humanitarian, rather than realist, role. Post-Gulf War American involvements in Somalia, Bosnia and Haiti are best understood in these terms. In addition, the American role in brokering peace, whether it be in Israel or Bosnia, is facilitated by a background of US military and economic power. Such missions will no doubt continue. The danger comes when the costs of intervention, whether measured in terms of expenditure or in terms of American lives, become too great for public opinion to tolerate. Should this happen, there is always the possibility that America will revert to an isolationist stance.

Conclusions

It is important to stress that realist thinking has not been *replaced* with idealist values. It is more that both are now important in explaining the motives behind American actions abroad. As emphasized earlier, militarily, the US is now more privileged than ever before. Ten years ago who would have remotely guessed that the United States would, by 1997, be negotiating with Russia over the eastward expansion of NATO? Where the US is more circumscribed is in terms of defining its new mission and in building domestic support for an active role abroad. This applies to 'traditional' foreign policy and to foreign *economic* policy. As indicated earlier, the US now lives in a much more interdependent world. It is in relations with the EC, negotiations over GATT and the North American Free Trade Area (NAFTA), that some of the more important foreign-policy questions are raised. Clearly these have a much greater input from domestic politics than do most 'traditional' foreign-policy areas.

This interdependence often makes it difficult to distinguish clearly between different policy systems, and there is no doubt that it makes the business of government more burdensome. Given the external constraints imposed by interdependence and the internal pressures resulting from a fragmented and open political system, it is not surprising that presidents have sought to centralize decision-making in the White House. Unfortunately, we cannot easily pass judgement on this development (which, in any case, represents only a relative and partial change towards centralization). For, in a world fraught with tensions and dangers, the costs of policy errors and misjudgements can be startlingly high, and the relationship between 'rational' policy-making and institutional arrangements is obscure. As Bert Rockman has put it:

> The problem of reconciling 'the persistent dilemmas of unity and diversity' remains to be solved as much in the foreign policy sphere as in the domestic one, especially as the distinction between these areas erodes. In unity lies strategic direction and clarity, but also the dangers of monocled vision. In diversity lies sensitivity to implementation and to nuance, but also the dangers of producing least common denominators.[6]

---

[6] 'America's Department of State', p. 925.

17

CODA: THE FUTURE OF THE AMERICAN POLITICAL ECONOMY

Since the mid-1970s increasing numbers of commentators have expressed serious doubts about the capacity of the American political system to deal with a world characterized by economic instability, a sometimes ruthlessly competitive international trading environment and an increasingly destabilized Eastern Europe, Middle East and Asia. Most of the misgivings have centred on the particular institutional arrangements of American governments or on broader questions of ideology. In this and in earlier chapters we have made reference to these critiques which, very generally, can be divided into three related themes.

1   Politics in the United States is too pluralistic. Open access to multiple centres of power ensures that public goods are distributed inefficiently. Institutionally, this means that the separation of powers, federalism and a weak party system prevent central direction and control. As a result, the sort of tough decisions needed to cope with economic dislocation and world instability cannot easily be made in the American context. Another way of putting this, perhaps, is to argue that the US system is simply too democratic. All social groups, jurisdictions and corporations have *some* influence on policy and need to be 'bought off', before anything actually gets done. This leads to inefficient and often excessive public expenditure.[1] In other countries, strong central executives, unitary government and cohesive political parties are better able to direct economy and society decisively and

---

[1]   Many books and articles have been written on this theme. *See*, for example, Jonathan Rauch, *Demisclerosis; The Silent Killer of American Government*, (New York, Times Books, 1994); Kevin P. Phillips, *Arrogant Capital: Washington, Wall Street and the Frustration of American Politics*, (Boston, Little, Brown, 1994).

efficiently.[2] Related are claims that the United States has a 'weak state' system, or that government policy is a result of myriad societal influences, rather than being imposed on society by a strong government or by a state which has nurtured a corporatist consensus with leading economic actors within society.[3] This pluralistic indecision and confusion may not be damaging when there is little need for state action. But, so the argument runs, in an interdependent world where governments in all of the competing economies play crucial roles, the United States is at a serious disadvantage, for *strategic* thought and action are all but impossible in a pluralist context.

2   A slightly different critique dwells on the gap between promise and performance characteristic of the American system. In other words, the dominant beliefs and values in the United States – liberty, equality, participation – lead to expectations that cannot be met by the institutional framework of politics.[4] The political system is not particularly efficient at translating into actual policies and programmes the demands that these values encourage. Again, the USA is different from many other countries in this respect. In few countries are egalitarianism and opportunity so deeply embedded in the national culture, and in few do these values persist even when the economy is changing rapidly, and when the ability of the system to meet public demands is so apparently inadequate. Proponents of this view point to the declining parties, failed presidents, capricious Congress and, above all, voter apathy and declining trust in government as evidence of the malaise.

3   Critics on the left are more concerned with the consequences of a volatile capitalism and fragmented political system for social and political equality. With even greater pressures for cuts in expenditure and a political system that puts great premium on distributing largesse according to political access and lobby power, rather than according to criteria of social justice or need, the position of those already disadvantaged will surely deteriorate, and the prospects for racial minorities look especially bleak.[5] In partial

---

[2]   This is one of the assumptions of the critics of divided government, *see* James L. Sundquist, *Constitutional Reform and Effective Government*, (Washington DC, Brookings Institution, 1986). *See also* Gary W. Cox and Samuel Kernell (eds), *The Politics of Divided Government*, (Boulder, Colorado, 1991).

[3]   *See* Peter J. Katzenstein (ed.), *Between Power and Plenty*, chapters by Katzenstein and Krasner. *See also* Lester Thurow, *Head to Head: The Coming Economic Battle Among Japan, Europe and America*, (New York, Morrow, 1992).

[4]   The most virulent statements of this view are presented in Nathan Glazer and Irving Kristol (eds), *The New American Commonwealth*, 1976, 10th Anniversary Issue of *The Public Interest*, New York, Basic Books, 1976. For a more recent analysis, see Samuel P. Huntington, *American Politics: The Promise of Disharmony*, (Cambridge, Mass., Harvard University Press, 1981).

[5]   *See* Andrew Hacker, *Two Nations: Black and White, Separate, Hostile and Unequal*, (New York, Charles Scribner's Sons, 1992); also Kenneth M. Dolbeare, *Democracy at Risk: The Politics of Economic Renewal*, (Chatham, New Jersey, Chatham House, revised edition, 1986). Interestingly, the American left is primarily concerned with questions of equality and justice, rather than with more theoretical or abstract issues, thus reflecting the influence of peculiarly American ideas on radical thinking.

contradiction of the promise/performance critique, advocates of this position see little prospect for improvement because of the pervasive strength of the dominant ideology which diverts the deprived masses from collective action by immersing them in a culture of shallow consumerism and misguided self-reliance.[6]

Although the normative base of each of these three critiques is quite distinctive – the first dwells on questions of economic efficiency, the second on problems of legitimacy and political control, and the third on equality and justice – all are pessimistic about the capacity of American government to adapt to a new domestic and international environment by providing its citizens with an acceptable degree of economic security and social justice. How much credence can be attached to these critiques?

We must, first, acknowledge that the American political system has experienced particularly serious problems in recent years. Earlier chapters catalogued the difficulties that each of the main political institutions has confronted, and our discussion of social, economic and foreign policy confirmed that, in a fragmented and open political system, 'efficient' and 'just' policy-making is remarkably difficult to achieve. While acknowledging this, we should be wary of too unqualified an acceptance of these three interpretations. They are, first of all, not always mutually compatible. The radical critique assumes a passivity on the part of the masses which is directly disputed by those who see increasingly strident public demands as the source of social disharmony. In comparative perspective, the latter view seems slightly misplaced. By most measures (regime and governmental stability, politically motivated violence, the strength of radical political parties) the USA is remarkably stable, and the populace has accepted with equanimity economic change and the relative decline of American economic power. Second, problems of economic dislocation and governmental overload are hardly unique to the USA. Indeed, one country, the UK which, with unitary, party government, patently lacks some of the institutional disadvantages of America, has experienced a similar crisis. Admittedly, like America, Britain has a liberal tradition which militates against a dominant state, but the relationship between the strength of the state and an 'effective' political and economic system is uncertain. Indeed, at century's end there is a growing body of opinion claiming that the two are negatively related: the weaker the central government the more efficient the economy. Critics point to

---

[6] For a summary of this perspective, *see* Ira Katznelson and Mark Kesselman, *The Politics of Power: A Critical Introduction to American Government*, (New York, Harcourt Brace Jovanovich, 3rd edn, 1987).

the problems currently being encountered by many European countries with large state sectors that are now considered an impediment to economic growth.

Discussion of governmental 'effectiveness' involves competing values. A truly successful economy, able to adjust to technological change and a highly competitive international trading environment, may be hard to reconcile with a democracy built on equality of opportunity and pluralism. Democracy, participation and accountability are desirable objectives in themselves and, to many, some sacrifice in political or economic efficiency is justified to achieve them.

Unfortunately, however, the trade-offs between accountability and effectiveness and between equality and efficiency are complex and difficult. Until recently it was common to argue that, in the context of global economic interdependence and rapid technological change, the fragmented and pluralistic political system which characterizes the United States works against efficiency *and* responsiveness and equality. If this is so, radical reform of the American system is urgently needed. More recently, however, audits of American political and economic performance have come to different conclusions. Pointing to the difficulties experienced by most of the other leading industrial states, including France, Germany and Japan, many have concluded that, for all its imperfections, the American political system has been performing moderately well. The budget deficit has almost been brought under control; economic growth has been impressive; the US has one of the lowest unemployment rates of all the OECD countries. At the same time, the US continues to absorb large numbers of immigrants every year. The great paradox at century's end is that, in spite of these achievements, many Americans remain disillusioned with the working of their system of government and many are angry that the numerous and complex distributional questions that pervade American political life have not been resolved.[7] The latest panacea for the country's ills are lower taxes and less government – solutions that even a Democratic president has all but embraced. The problem is, of course, that government continues to perform a wide range of functions in the USA as it does in other states. The crucial question for the next century is how to reconcile this enhanced state role with increasingly strident calls for a return to the era of minimum government.

---

[7]   *See* Susan J. Tolchin, *The Angry American: How Voter Rage is Changing the Nation*, (Boulder, CO, Westview, 1996).

APPENDIX

THE CONSTITUTION OF THE UNITED STATES

[PREAMBLE]

We the people of the United States, in order to form a more perfect union, establish justice, insure domestic tranquility, provide for the common defense, promote the general welfare, and secure the blessings of liberty to ourselves and our posterity, do ordain and establish this Constitution for the United States of America.

ARTICLE 1 [THE LEGISLATURE]

Section 1

All legislative powers herein granted shall be vested in a Congress of the United States, which shall consist of a Senate and House of Representatives.

Section 2

1. The House of Representatives shall be composed of members chosen every second year by the people of the several States, and the electors in each State shall have the qualifications requisite for elections of the most numerous branch of the State legislature.
2. No person shall be a representative who shall not have attained to the age of twenty-five years, and been seven years a citizen of the United States, and who shall not, when elected, be an inhabitant of that State in which he shall be chosen.
3. Representatives and direct taxes[1] shall be apportioned among the several States which may be included within this Union, according to their respective members, which shall be determined by adding to the whole number of

[1] See the Sixteenth Amendment.

free persons, including those bound to service for a term of years, and excluding Indians not taxed, three-fifths of all other persons.[2] The actual enumeration shall be made within three years after the first meeting of the Congress of the United States, and within every subsequent term of ten years, in such manner as they shall by law direct. The number of representatives shall not exceed one for every thirty thousand, but each State shall have at least one representative; and until such enumeration shall be made, the State of New Hampshire shall be entitled to choose three, Massachusetts eight, Rhode Island and Providence Plantations one, Connecticut five, New York six, New Jersey four, Pennsylvania eight, Delaware one, Maryland six, Virginia ten, North Carolina five, South Carolina five, and Georgia three.

4.   When vacancies happen in the representation from any State, the executive authority thereof shall issue writs of election to fill such vacancies.

5.   The House of Representatives shall choose their speaker and other officers; and shall have the sole power of impeachment.

Section 3

1.   The Senate of the United States shall be composed of two senators from each state, chosen by the legislature thereof,[3] for six years; and each senator shall have one vote.

2.   Immediately after they shall be assembled in consequence of the first election, they shall be divided as equally as may be into three classes. The seats of the senators of the first class shall be vacated at the expiration of the second year, of the second class at the expiration of the fourth year, and of the third class at the expiration of the sixth year, so that one-third may be chosen every second year; and if vacancies happen by resignation, or otherwise, during the recess of the legislature of any State, the executive thereof may make temporary appointments until the next meeting of the legislature, which shall then fill such vacancies.[4]

3.   No person shall be a senator who shall not have attained to the age of thirty years, and been nine years a citizen of the United States, and who shall not when elected, be an inhabitant of that State for which he shall be chosen.

4.   The Vice-President of the United States shall be President of the Senate, but shall have no vote, unless they be equally divided.

5.   The Senate shall choose their other officers, and also a President *pro tempore*, in the absence of the Vice-President, or when he shall exercise the office of President of the United States.

6.   The Senate shall have the sole power to try all impeachments. When sitting for that purpose, they shall be on oath or affirmation. When the President of the United States is tried, the chief justice shall preside: and no person shall be convicted without the concurrence of two-thirds of the members present.

7.   Judgement in cases of impeachment shall not extend further than to

[2] Partly superseded by the Fourteenth Amendment.
[3] See the Seventeenth Amendment.
[4] See the Seventeenth Amendment.

removal from office, and disqualifications to hold and enjoy any office of honor, trust or profit under the United States: but the party convicted shall nevertheless be liable and subject to indictment, trial, judgement and punishment, according to law.

Section 4

1. The times, places, and manner of holding elections for senators and representatives, shall be prescribed in each State by the legislature thereof; but the Congress may at any time by law make or alter such regulations, except as to the places of choosing senators.
2. The Congress shall assemble at least once in every year, and such meeting shall be on the first Monday in December, unless they shall by law appoint a different day.

Section 5

1. Each House shall be the judge of the elections, returns and qualifications of its own members and majority of each shall constitute a quorum to do business; but a smaller number may adjourn from day to day, and may be authorized to compel the attendance of absent members, in such manner and under such penalties as each House may provide.
2. Each House may determine the rules of its proceedings, punish its members for disorderly behavior, and, with the concurrence of two-thirds, expel a member.
3. Each House shall keep a journal of its proceedings, and from time to time publish the same, excepting such parts as may in their judgment require secrecy; and the yeas and nays of the members of either House on any question shall, at the desire of one-fifth of those present, be entered on the journal.
4. Neither House, during the session of Congress, shall, without the consent of the other, adjourn for more than three days, nor to any other place than that in which the two Houses shall be sitting.

Section 6

1. The senators and representatives shall receive a compensation for their services, to be ascertained by law and paid out of the Treasury of the United States. They shall in all cases, except treason, felony and breach of the peace, be privileged from arrest during their attendance at the session of their respective Houses, and in going to and returning from the same; and for any speech or debate in either House, they shall not be questioned in any other place.
2. No senator or representative shall, during the time for which he was elected, be appointed to any civil office under the authority of the United States, which shall have been created, or the emoluments whereof shall have been increased during such time, and no person holding any office under the United States shall be a member of either House during his continuance in office.

Section 7

1. All bills for raising revenue shall originate in the House of Representatives; but the Senate may propose or concur with amendments as on other bills.

2. Every bill which shall have passed the House of Representatives and the Senate, shall, before it become a law, be presented to the President of the United States; if he approve he shall sign it, but if not he shall return it, with his objections to that House in which it shall have originated, who shall enter the objections at large on their journal, and proceed to reconsider it. If after such reconsideration two-thirds of that House shall agree to pass the bill, it shall be sent, together with the objections, to the other House, by which it shall likewise be reconsidered, and if approved by two thirds of that House, it shall become a law. But in all such cases the votes of both Houses shall be determined by yeas and nays, and the names of the persons voting for and against the bill shall be entered on the journal of each House respectively. If any bill shall not be returned by the President within ten days (Sundays excepted) after it shall have been presented to him, the same shall be a law, in like manner as if he had signed it, unless the Congress by their adjournment prevent its return, in which case it shall not be a law.

3. Every order, resolution, or vote to which the concurrence of the Senate and House of Representatives may be necessary (except on a question of ajournment) shall be presented to the President of the United States; and before the same shall take effect, shall be approved by him, or being disapproved by him, shall be repassed by two thirds of the Senate and House of Representatives, according to the rules and limitations prescribed in the case of a bill.

Section 8

1. The Congress shall have the power to lay and collect taxes, duties, imposts, and excises, to pay the debts and provide for the common defense and general welfare of the United States; but all duties, imposts, and excises shall be uniform throughout the United States;

2. To borrow money on the credit of the United States;

3. To regulate commerce with foreign nations, and among the several States, and with the Indian tribes;

4. To establish an uniform rule of naturalization, and uniform laws on the subject of bankruptcies throughout the United States;

5. To coin money, regulate the value thereof, and of foreign coin, and fix the standard of weights and measures;

6. To provide for the punishment of counterfeiting the securities and current coin of the United States;

7. To establish post offices and post roads;

8. To promote the progress of science and useful arts, by securing for limited times to authors and inventors the exclusive right to their respective writings and discoveries;

9. To constitute tribunals inferior to the Supreme Court;

10. To define and punish piracies and felonies committed on the high seas, and offenses against the laws of nations;

11. To declare war, grant letters of marque and reprisal, and make rules concerning captures on land and water;

12. To raise and support armies, but no appropriation of money to that use shall be for a longer term than two years;

13. To provide and maintain a navy;

14. To make rules for the government and regulation of the land and naval forces.

15. To provide for calling forth the militia to execute the laws of the Union, suppress insurrections and repel invasions;

16. To provide for organizing, arming, and disciplining the militia, and for governing such part of them as may be employed in the service of the United States, reserving to the States respectively the appointment of the officers, and the authority of training the militia according to the discipline prescribed by Congress;

17. To exercise exclusive legislation in all cases whatsoever, over such district (not exceeding ten miles square) as may, by cession of particular States, and the acceptance of Congress, become the seat of the government of the United States, and to exercise like authority over all places purchased by the consent of the legislature of the State in which the same shall be, for the erection of forts, magazines, dockyards, and other needful buildings; and

18. To make all laws which shall be necessary and proper for carrying into execution the foregoing powers, and all other powers vested by this Constitution in the government of the United States, or in any department or officer thereof.

Section 9

1. The migration or importation of such persons as any of the States now existing shall think proper to admit, shall not be prohibited by the Congress prior to the year one thousand eight hundred and eight, but a tax or duty may be imposed on such importation, not exceeding ten dollars for each person.

2. The privilege of the writ of *habeas corpus* shall not be suspended, unless when in cases of rebellion or invasion the public safety may require it.

3. No bill of attainder or *ex post facto* law shall be passed.

4. No capitation, or other direct, tax shall be laid, unless in proportion to the census or enumeration hereinbefore directed to be taken.[5]

5. No tax or duty shall be laid on articles exported from any State.

6. No preference shall be given by any regulation of commerce or revenue to the ports of one State over those of another: nor shall vessels bound to, or from, one State be obliged to enter, clear, or pay duties in another.

7. No money shall be drawn from the treasury, but in consequence of appropriations, made by law; and a regular statement and account of the receipts and expenditures of all public money shall be published from time to time.

[5] See the Sixteenth Amendment.

8.   No title of nobility shall be granted by the United States: and no person holding any office or profit or trust under them, shall, without the consent of the Congress, accept of any present, emolument, office, or title, of any kind whatever, from any king, prince, or foreign State.

Section 10

1.   No State shall enter into any treaty, alliance, or confederation; grant letters of marque and reprisal; coin money, emit bills of credit; make anything but gold and silver coin a tender in payment of debts; pass any bill of attainder, *ex post facto* law, or law impairing the obligation of contracts, or grant any title of nobility.
2.   No State shall, without the consent of the Congress, lay any imposts, or duties on imports or exports, except what may be absolutely necessary for executing its inspection laws: and the net produce of all duties and imposts laid by any State on imports or exports, shall be of the use of the treasury of the United States; and all such laws shall be subject to the revision and control of the Congress.
3.   No State shall, without the consent of Congress, lay any duty of tonnage, keep troops, or ships of war in time of peace, enter into any agreement or compact with another State, or with a foreign power, or engage in war, unless actually invaded, or in such imminent danger as will not admit of delay.

ARTICLE 2 [THE EXECUTIVE]

Section 1

1.   The executive power shall be vested in a President of the United States of America. He shall hold his office during the term of four years, and, together with the Vice-President, chosen for the same term, be elected, as follows.[6]
2.   Each State shall appoint, in such manner as the legislature thereof may direct, a number of electors, equal to the whole number of senators and representatives to which the State may be entitled in the Congress: but no senator or representative, or person holding an office of trust or profit under the United States, shall be appointed an elector.
   The electors shall meet in their respective States, and vote by ballot for two persons, of whom one at least shall not be an inhabitant of the same State with themselves. And they shall make a list of all the persons voted for, and of the number of votes for each; which list they shall sign and certify, and transmit sealed to the seat of the government of the United States, directed to the president of the Senate. The president of the Senate shall, in the presence of the Senate and House of Representatives, open all certificates, and the votes shall then be counted. The person having the greatest number of votes shall be the President, if such number be a majority of the

---

[6] See the Twenty-second Amendment.

whole number of electors appointed; and if there be more than one who have such majority, and have an equal number of votes, then the House of Representatives shall immediately choose by ballot one of them for President; and if no person have a majority, then from the five highest on the list the said House shall in like manner choose the President. But in choosing the President, the votes shall be taken by States, the representation from each State having one vote; a quorum for this purpose shall consist of a member or members from two-thirds of the States, and a majority of all the States shall be necessary to a choice. In every case, after the choice of the President, the person having the greatest number of votes of the electors shall be the Vice-President. But if there should remain two or more who have equal votes, the Senate shall choose from them by ballot the Vice-President.[7]

3.   The Congress may determine the time of choosing the electors, and the day on which they shall give their votes; which day shall be the same throughout the United States.

4.   No person except a natural born citizen, or a citizen of the United States, at the time of the adoption of this Constitution, shall be eligible to the office of President; neither shall any person be eligible to that office who shall not have attained to the age of thirty-five years, and been fourteen years a resident within the United States.

5.   In case of the removal of the President from office, or of his death, resignation, or inability to discharge the powers and duties of the said office, the same shall devolve on the Vice-President, and the Congress may by law provide for the case of removal, death, resignation, or inability, both of the President and Vice-President, declaring what officer shall then act as President, and such officer shall act accordingly, until the disability be removed, or a President shall be elected.[8]

6.   The President shall, at stated times, receive for his services a compensation, which shall neither be increased nor diminished during the period for which he shall have been elected, and he shall not receive within that period any other emolument from the United States, or any of them.

7.   Before he enter on the execution of his office, he shall take the following oath or affirmation: 'I do solemnly swear (or affirm) that I will faithfully execute the office of President of the United States, and will to the best of my ability, preserve, protect and defend the Constitution of the United States.'

Section 2

1.   The President shall be commander in chief of the army and navy of the United States, and of the militia of the several States, when called into the actual service of the United States; he may require the opinion, in writing, of the principal officer in each of the executive departments, upon any subject relating to the duties of their respective offices, and he shall have power to grant reprieves and pardons for offences against the United States, except in cases of impeachment.

---

[7]   Superseded by the Twelfth Amendment.
[8]   See the Twentieth Amendment and the Twenty-fifth Amendment.

2. He shall have power, by and with the advice and consent of the Senate, to make treaties, provided two-thirds of the senators present concur; and he shall nominate, and by and with the advice and consent of the Senate, shall appoint ambassadors, other public ministers and consuls, judges of the Supreme Court, and all other officers of the United States, whose appointments are not herein otherwise provided for, and which shall be established by law; but the Congress may by law vest the appointment of such inferior officers, as they think proper, in the President alone, in the courts of law, or in the heads of departments.

3. The President shall have power to fill up all vacancies that may happen during the recess of the Senate, by granting commissions which shall expire at the end of their next session.

Section 3

1. He shall from time to time give to the Congress information of the state of the Union, and recommend to their consideration such measures as he shall judge necessary and expedient; he may, on extraordinary occasions, convene both Houses, or either of them, and in case of disagreement between them with respect to the time of adjournment, he may adjourn them to such time as he shall think proper; he shall receive ambassadors and other public ministers; he shall take care that the laws be faithfully executed, and shall commission all the officers of the United States.

Section 4

The President, Vice-President, and all civil officers of the United States, shall be removed from office on impeachment for, and conviction of, treason, bribery, or other high crimes and misdemeanors.

ARTICLE 3 [THE JUDICIARY]

Section 1

1. The Judicial power of the United States shall be vested in one Supreme Court, and in such inferior courts as the Congress may from time to time ordain and establish. The judges, both of the Supreme and inferior courts, shall hold their offices during good behavior, and shall, at stated times, receive for their services, a compensation, which shall not be diminished during their continuance in office.

Section 2

1. The Judicial power shall extend to all cases, in law and equity, arising under this Constitution, the laws of the United States, and treaties made, or which shall be made, under their authority; to all cases affecting ambassadors, other public ministers and consuls; to all cases of admiralty and maritime jurisdiction; to controversies to which the United States shall be a party;

to controversies between two or more States; between a state and citizens of another State,[9] between citizens of different States, between citizens of the same State claiming lands under grants of different States, and between a State, or the citizens thereof, and foreign States, citizens or subjects.

2.   In all cases affecting ambassadors, other public ministers and consuls, and those in which a State shall be party, the Supreme Court shall have original jurisdiction. In all the other cases before mentioned, the Supreme Court shall have appellate jurisdiction, both as to law and to fact, with such exceptions, and under such regulations as the Congress shall make.

3.   The trial of all crimes, except in cases of impeachment, shall be by jury; and such trial shall be held in the State where the said crimes shall have been committed; but when not committed within any State, the trial shall be held at such place or places as the Congress may by law have directed.

Section 3

1.   Treason against the United States shall consist only in levying war against them, or in adhering to their enemies, giving them aid and comfort. No person shall be convicted of treason unless on the testimony of two witnesses to the same overt act, or on confession in open court.

2.   The Congress shall have power to declare the punishment of treason, but no attainder of treason shall work corruption of blood, or forfeiture except during the life of the person attained.

ARTICLE 4 [INTERSTATE RELATIONS]

Section 1

Full faith and credit shall be given in each State to the public acts, records, and judicial proceedings of every other State. And the Congress may be general laws prescribe the manner in which acts, records and proceedings shall be proved, and the effect thereof.

Section 2

1.   The citizens of each State shall be entitled to all privileges and immunities of citizens in the several States.

2.   A person charged in any State with treason, felony, or other crime, who shall flee from justice, and be found in another State, shall on demand of the executive authority of the State from which he fled, be delivered up, to be removed to the State having jurisdiction of the crime.

3.   No person held to service or labor in one State under the laws thereof, escaping into another, shall, in consequence of any law or regulation therein, be discharged from such service or labor, but shall be delivered up on claim of the party to whom such service or labor may be due.

---

[9] See the Eleventh Amendment.

Section 3

1. New States may be admitted by the Congress into this Union; but no new State shall be formed or erected within the jurisdiction of any other State; nor any State be formed by the junction of two or more States, or parts of States, without the consent of the legislatures of the States concerned as well as of the Congress.
2. The Congress shall have power to dispose of and make all needful rules and regulations respecting the territory or other property belonging to the United States; and nothing in this Constitution shall be so construed as to prejudice any claims of the United States, or of any particular State.

Section 4

The United States shall guarantee to every State in this Union a republican form of government, and shall protect each of them against invasion; and on application of the legislature, or of the executive (when the legislature cannot be convened) against domestic violence.

ARTICLE 5 [AMENDMENT PROCESS]

The Congress, whenever two-thirds of both Houses shall deem it necessary, shall propose amendments to this Constitution, or, on the application of the legislature of two-thirds of the several States, shall call a convention for proposing amendments, which, in either case, shall be valid to all intents and purposes, as part of this Constitution when ratified by the legislatures of three-fourths of the several States, or by conventions in three-fourths thereof, as the one or the other mode of ratification may be proposed by the Congress; Provided that no amendment which may be made prior to the year one thousand eight hundred and eight shall in any manner affect the first and fourth clauses in the ninth section of the first article; and that no State, without its consent, shall be deprived of its equal suffrage in the Senate.

ARTICLE 6 [DEBTS, SUPREMACY]

1. All debts contracted, and engagements entered into, before the adoption of this Constitution, shall be as valid against the United States under this Constitution, as under the Confederation.
2. This Constitution, and the laws of the United States which shall be made in pursuance thereof; and all treaties made, or which shall be made, under the authority of the United States, shall be the supreme law of the land; and the Judges in every State shall be bound thereby, anything in the Constitution or laws of any State to the contrary notwithstanding.
3. The senators and representatives before mentioned, and the members of the several State legislatures, and all executive and judicial officers, both of the United States and of the several States, shall be bound by oath or affirmation to support this Constitution; but no religious test shall ever be required as a qualification to any office or public trust under the United States.

ARTICLE 7 [RATIFICATION]

The ratification of the conventions of nine States shall be sufficient for the establishment of this Constitution between the States so ratifying the same.

Done in Convention by the unanimous consent of the States present the seventeenth day of September in the year of our Lord one thousand seven hundred and eighty-seven, and of the independence of the United States of America the twelfth. In witness whereof we have hereunto subscribed our names.

[Names omitted]

ARTICLES IN ADDITION TO, AND AMENDMENT OF, THE CONSTITUTION OF THE UNITED STATES OF AMERICA, PROPOSED BY CONGRESS, AND RATIFIED BY THE LEGISLATURES OF THE SEVERAL STATES, PURSUANT TO THE FIFTH ARTICLE OF THE ORIGINAL CONSTITUTION.*

[The first 10 Amendments were ratified 15 December 1791, and form what is known as the 'Bill of Rights']

AMENDMENT 1 [FREEDOM OF RELIGION, SPEECH, ASSEMBLY, PETITION]

Congress shall make no law respecting an establishment of religion, or prohibiting the free exercise thereof; or abridging the freedom of speech, or of the press; or the right of the people peaceably to assemble, and to petition the Government for a redress of grievances.

AMENDMENT 2 [RIGHT TO BEAR ARMS]

A well regulated Militia, being necessary to the security of a free State, the right of the people to keep and bear Arms, shall not be infringed.

AMENDMENT 3 [QUARTERING OF SOLDIERS]

No Soldier shall, in time of peace be quartered in any house, without the consent of the Owner, nor in time of war, but in a manner to be prescribed by law.

AMENDMENT 4 [SEARCH AND SEIZURE]

The right of the people to be secure in their persons, houses, papers, and effects, against unreasonable searches and seizures, shall not be violated, and

*Amendment 21 was not ratified by state legislatures, but by state conventions summoned by Congress.

no warrants shall issue, but upon probable cause, supported by Oath or affirmation, and particularly describing the place to be searched, and the persons or things to be seized.

AMENDMENT 5 [CRIMINAL PROCEDURAL RIGHTS]

No person shall be held to answer for a capital, or otherwise infamous crime, unless on a presentment or indictment of a Grand Jury, except in cases arising in the land or naval forces, or in the Militia, when in actual service in time of War or public danger; nor shall any person be subject for the same offence to be twice put in jeopardy of life or limb; nor shall be compelled in any criminal case to be a witness against himself, nor be deprived of life, liberty, or property, without due process of law, nor shall private property be taken for public use, without just compensation.

AMENDMENT 6 [CRIMINAL COURT PROCEDURES]

In all criminal prosecutions, the accused shall enjoy the right to a speedy and public trial, by an impartial jury of the State and district wherein the crime shall have been committed, which district shall have been previously ascertained by law, and to be informed of the nature and cause of the accusation; to be confronted with the witness against him; to have compulsory process for obtaining witnesses in his favor, and to have the Assistance of Counsel for his defence.

AMENDMENT 7 [TRIAL BY JURY IN COMMON LAW CASES]

In suits at common law, where the value in controversy shall exceed twenty dollars, the right of trial by jury shall be preserved, and no fact tried by a jury, shall be otherwise re-examined in any Court of the United States, than according to the rules of the common law.

AMENDMENT 8 [BAILS, FINES AND PUNISHMENT]

Excessive bail shall not be required, nor excessive fines imposed, nor cruel and unusual punishments inflicted.

AMENDMENT 9 [RIGHTS RETAINED BY THE PEOPLE]

The enumeration in the Constitution of certain rights, shall not be construed to deny or disparage others retained by the people.

AMENDMENT 10 [RIGHTS RESERVED TO THE STATES]

The powers not delegated to the United States by the Constitution, nor prohibited by it to the States, are reserved to the States respectively, or to the people.

AMENDMENT 11 [SUITS AGAINST THE STATES]

[Ratified 7 February 1795]

The judicial power of the United States shall not be construed to extend to any suit in law or equity, commenced or prosecuted against one of the United States by Citizens of another State, or by Citizens or Subjects of any Foreign State.

AMENDMENT 12 [ELECTION OF PRESIDENT AND VICE-PRESIDENT]

[Ratified 27 July 1804]

The Electors shall meet in their respective states and vote by ballot for President and Vice-President, one of whom at least, shall not be an inhabitant of the same state with themselves; they shall name in their ballots the person voted for as President, and in distinct ballots the person voted for as Vice-President, and they shall make distinct lists of all persons voted for as President, and of all persons voted for as Vice-President, and of the number of votes for each, which lists they shall sign and certify, and transmit sealed to the seat of the government of the United States, directed to the President of the Senate; The President of the Senate shall, in presence of the Senate and House of Representatives, open all the certificates and the votes shall then be counted; The person having the greatest number of votes for President, shall be the President if such number be a majority of the whole number of Electors, appointed; and if no person have such majority, then from the persons having the highest numbers not exceeding three on the list of those voted for as President, the House of Representatives shall choose immediately, by ballot, the President. But in choosing the President, the votes shall be taken by States, the representation from each state having one vote; a quorum for this purpose shall consist of a member or members from two-thirds of the States, and a majority of all the States shall be necessary to a choice. (And if the House of Representatives shall not choose a President whenever the right of choice shall devolve upon them, before the fourth day of March next following, then the Vice-President shall act as President, as in the case of the death or other constitutional disability of the President.)* The person having the greatest number of votes as Vice-President, shall be the Vice-President, if such number be a majority of the whole number of Electors appointed, and if no person have a majority, then from the two highest numbers on the list, the

*Superseded by Section 3 of the Twentieth Amendment.

Senate shall choose the Vice-President; a quorum for the purpose shall consist of two-thirds of the whole number of Senators, and a majority of the whole number shall be necessary to a choice. But no person constitutionally ineligible to the office of President shall be eligible to that of Vice-President of the United States.

AMENDMENT 13 [ABOLITION OF SLAVERY]

[Ratified 6 December 1865]

Section 1

Neither slavery nor involuntary servitude, except as a punishment for crime whereof the party shall have been duly convicted, shall exist within the United States, or any place subject to their jurisdiction.

Section 2

Congress shall have power to enforce this article by appropriate legislation.

AMENDMENT 14 [CITIZENSHIP, DUE PROCESS, EQUAL PROTECTION]

[Ratified 9 July 1868]

Section 1

All persons born or naturalized in the United States, and subject to the jurisdiction thereof, are citizens of the United States and of the State wherein they reside. No State shall make or enforce any law which shall abridge the privileges or immunities of citizens of the United States; nor shall any State deprive any person of life, liberty, or property, without due process of law; nor deny to any person within its jurisdiction the equal protection of the laws.

Section 2

Representatives shall be apportioned among the several States according to their respective numbers, counting the whole number of persons in each State, excluding Indians not taxed. But when the right to vote at any election for the choice of electors for President and Vice-President of the United States, Representatives in Congress, the Executive and Judicial officers of a State, or the members of the Legislature thereof, is denied to any of the male inhabitants of such State, being twenty-one years of age,* and citizens of the United States, or in any way abridged, except for participation in rebellion, or other crime, the basis of representation therein shall be reduced in the proportion which the number of such male citizens shall bear to the whole number of male citizens twenty-one years of age in such State.

*Changed by Section 1 of the Twenty-sixth Amendment.

Section 3

No person shall be a Senator or Representative in Congress, or elector of President and Vice-President, or hold any office, civil or military, under the United States, or under any State, who, having previously taken an oath, as a member of Congress, or as an officer of the United States, or as a member of any State legislature, or as an executive or judicial officer of any State, to support the Constitution of the United States shall have engaged in insurrection or rebellion against the same, or given aid or comfort to the enemies thereof. But Congress may by a vote of two-thirds of each House, remove such disability.

Section 4

The validity of the public debt of the United States, authorized by law, including debts incurred for payment of pensions and bounties for services in suppressing insurrection or rebellion, shall not be questioned. But neither the United States nor any State shall assume or pay any debt or obligation incurred in aid of insurrection or rebellion against the United States, or any claim for the loss or emancipation of any slave; but all such debts, obligations and claims shall be held illegal and void.

Section 5

The Congress shall have power to enforce, by appropriate legislation, the provisions of this article.

AMENDMENT 15 [THE RIGHT TO VOTE]

[Ratified 3 February 1870]

Section 1

The right of citizens of the United States to vote shall not be denied or abridged by the United States or by any State on account of race, color, or previous condition of servitude.

Section 2

The Congress shall have power to enforce this article by appropriate legislation.

AMENDMENT 16 [INCOME TAX]

[Ratified 3 February 1913]

The Congress shall have power to lay and collect taxes on incomes, from whatever source derived, without apportionment among the several States, and without regard to any census or enumeration.

AMENDMENT 17 [DIRECT ELECTION OF SENATORS]

[Ratified 8 April 1913]

The Senate of the United States shall be composed of two Senators from each State, elected by the people thereof, for six years; and each Senator shall have one vote. The electors in each State shall have the qualifications requisite for electors of the most numerous branch of the State legislatures.

When vacancies happen in the representation of any State in the Senate, the executive authority of such State shall issue writs of election to fill such vacancies: *Provided,* That the legislature of any State may empower the executive thereof to make temporary appointments until the people fill the vacancies by election as the legislature may direct.

This amendment shall not be so construed as to affect the election or term of any Senator chosen before it becomes valid as part of the Constitution.

AMENDMENT 18 [INTRODUCTION OF PROHIBITION]

[Ratified 16 January 1919]

Section 1

After one year from the ratification of this article the manufacture, sale, or transportation of intoxicating liquors within, the importation thereof into, or the exportation thereof from the United States and all territory subject to the jurisdiction thereof for beverage purposes is hereby prohibited.

Section 2

The Congress and the several States shall have concurrent power to enforce this article by appropriate legislation.

Section 3

This article shall be inoperative unless it shall have been ratified as an amendment to the Constitution by the legislatures of the several States as provided in the Constitution, within seven years from the date of the submission hereof to the States by the Congress.*

AMENDMENT 19 [WOMEN'S RIGHT TO VOTE]

[Ratified 18 August 1920]

The right of citizens of the United States to vote shall not be denied or abridged by the United States or by any State on account of sex.

Congress shall have power to enforce this article by appropriate legislation.

*Repealed by Section 1 of the Twenty-first Amendment.

AMENDMENT 20 [TERMS OF OFFICE, CONVENING OF CONGRESS AND SUCCESSION]

[Ratified 23 January 1933]

Section 1

The terms of the President and Vice-President shall end at noon on the 20th day of January, and the terms of Senators and Representatives at noon on the 3rd day of January, of the years in which such terms would have ended if this article had not been ratified; and the terms of their successors shall then begin.

Section 2

The Congress shall assemble at least once in every year, and such meeting shall begin at noon on the 3rd day of January, unless they shall by law appoint a different day.

Section 3

If, at the time fixed for the beginning of the term of the President, the President elect shall have died, the Vice-President elect shall become President. If a President shall not have been chosen before the time fixed for the beginning of his term, or if the President elect shall have failed to qualify, then the Vice-President elect shall act as President until a President shall have qualified; and the Congress may by law provide for the case wherein neither a President elect nor a Vice-President elect shall have qualified, declaring who shall then act as President, or the manner in which one who is to act shall be selected, and such person shall act accordingly until a President or Vice-President shall have qualified.

Section 4

The Congress may by law provide for the case of the death of any of the persons from whom the House of Representatives may choose a President whenever the right of choice shall have devolved upon them, and for the case of the death of any of the persons from whom the Senate may choose a Vice-President whenever the right of choice shall have devolved upon them.

Section 5

Sections 1 and 2 shall take effect on the 15th day of October following the ratification of this article.

Section 6

This article shall be inoperative unless it shall have been ratified as an amendment to the Constitution by the legislatures of three-fourths of the several States within seven years from the date of its submission.

AMENDMENT 21 [REPEAL OF PROHIBITION]

[Ratified 5 December 1933]

Section 1

The Eighteenth Article of Amendment to the Constitution of the United States is hereby repealed.

Section 2

The transportation or importation into any State, Territory, or possession of the United States for delivery or use therein of intoxicating liquors, in violation of the laws thereof, is hereby prohibited.

Section 3

This article shall be inoperative unless it shall have been ratified as an amendment to the Constitution by conventions in the several States, as provided in the Constitution, within seven years from the date of the submission hereof to the States by the Congress.

AMENDMENT 22 [LIMITATION OF PRESIDENTIAL TERMS]

[Ratified 27 February 1951]

Section 1

No person shall be elected to the office of the President more than twice, and no person who has held the office of President, or acted as President, for more than two years of a term to which some other person was elected President shall be elected to the office of the President more than once. But this Article shall not apply to any person holding the office of President when this Article was proposed by the Congress, and shall not prevent any person who may be holding the office of President, or acting as President, during the term within which this Article becomes operative from holding the office of President or acting as President during the remainder of such term.

Section 2

This article shall be inoperative unless it shall have been ratified as an amendment to the Constitution by the legislatures of three-fourths of the several States within seven years from the date of its submission to the States by the Congress.

AMENDMENT 23 [PRESIDENTIAL ELECTIONS FOR THE DISTRICT OF COLUMBIA]

[Ratified 29 March 1961]

Section 1

The District constituting the seat of Government of the United States shall appoint in such manner as the Congress may direct:

A number of electors of President and Vice-President equal to the whole number of Senators and Representatives in Congress to which the District would be entitled if it were a State, but in no event more than the least populous State; they shall be in addition to those appointed by the States, but they shall be considered, for the purposes of the election of President and Vice-President, to be electors appointed by a State; and they shall meet in the District and perform such duties as provided by the Twelfth Article of Amendment.

Section 2

The Congress shall have power to enforce this article by appropriate legislation.

AMENDMENT 24 [POLL TAX ABOLISHED]

[Ratified 23 January 1964]

Section 1

The right of citizens of the United States to vote in any primary or other election for President or Vice-President, for electors for President or Vice-President, or for Senator or Representative in Congress, shall not be denied or abridged by the United States or any State by reason of failure to pay any poll tax or other tax.

Section 2

The Congress shall have power to enforce this article by appropriate legislation.

AMENDMENT 25 [PRESIDENTIAL DISABILITY AND VICE-PRESIDENTIAL VACANCIES]

[Ratified 10 February 1967]

Section 1

In case of the removal of the President from office or of his death or resignation, the Vice-President shall become President.

Section 2

Whenever there is a vacancy in the office of the Vice-President, the President shall nominate a Vice-President who shall take office upon confirmation by a majority vote of both Houses of Congress.

Section 3

Whenever the President transmits to the President *pro tempore* of the Senate and the Speaker of the House of Representatives his written declaration that he is unable to discharge the powers and duties of his office, and until he transmits to them a written declaration to the contrary, such powers and duties shall be discharged by the Vice-President as Acting President.

Section 4

Whenever the Vice-President and a majority of either the principal officers of the executive departments or of such other body as Congress may by law provide, transmit to the President *pro tempore* of the Senate and the Speaker of the House of Representatives their written declaration that the President is unable to discharge the powers and duties of his office, the Vice-President shall immediately assume the powers and duties of the office as Acting President.

Thereafter, when the President transmits to the President *pro tempore* of the Senate and the Speaker of the House of Representatives his written declaration that no inability exists, he shall resume the powers and duties of his office unless the Vice-President and a majority of either the principal officers of the executive department or of such other body as Congress may by law provide, transmit within four days to the President *pro tempore* of the Senate and the Speaker of the House of Representatives their written declaration that the President is unable to discharge the powers and duties of his office. Thereupon Congress shall decide the issue, assembling within forty-eight hours for that purpose if not in session. If the Congress, within twenty-one days after receipt of the latter written declaration, or, if Congress is not in session, within twenty-one days after Congress is required to assemble, determines by two-thirds vote of both Houses that the President is unable to discharge the powers and duties of his office, the Vice-President shall continue to discharge the same as Acting President; otherwise, the President shall resume the powers and duties of his office.

AMENDMENT 26 [VOTE FOR 18-YEAR-OLDS]

[Ratified 1 July 1971]

Section 1

The right of citizens of the United States, who are eighteen years of age or older, to vote shall not be denied or abridged by the United States or by any State on account of age.

Section 2

The Congress shall have power to enforce this article by appropriate legislation.

AMENDMENT 27

[Ratified 18 May 1992]

No law varying the compensation for the services of the Senators and Representatives shall take effect, until an election of Representatives shall have intervened.

INDEX